FOUNDATIONS OF EDUCATION

FOUNDATIONS
OF
EDUCATION

[Useful for B.Ed./M.Ed. Students and Other Competition Aspirants]

By

P.K. Johri

ANMOL PUBLICATIONS PVT. LTD.
NEW DELHI - 110 002 (INDIA)

ANMOL PUBLICATIONS PVT. LTD.
4374/4B, Ansari Road, Daryaganj
New Delhi - 110 002
Ph.: 23261597, 23278000
Visit us at: www.anmolpublications.com

Foundations of Education

First Published, 2005

ISBN 81-261-2223-4

PRINTED IN INDIA

Published by J.L. Kumar for Anmol Publications Pvt. Ltd., New Delhi - 110 002 and Printed at Mehra Offset Press, Delhi.

Contents

PART-II
PSYCHOLOGICAL ASPECTS

Preface

In a broader sense the foundation of education inculcates the short and long-run objectives in a multifaceted and multi-dimensional environment. The genesis of a cultured society lies in its well-founded education system. The basic characteristics of the foundation, which include sociological, psychological, historical, political and cultural shades, cause the growth of posterity. The denial of any of these may lead to a gradual devastation in future. Since, most of the developing economies are at the threshold of becoming knowledge-economy and 'education to all' is now a universal concept.

Evolution of education has manifested the orthodox society, the world over, into a plural, secular, just and transparent one, leading to the concrete foundation of democracy, which alone can establish a liberal but sound system.

In fact, in the absence of value education, with cognitive approach, there would prevail anarchy and a sort of mayhem, which would ultimately hammer the very social fabric in our country.

Learning is a cumulative process, and its nourishment requires continuous practical and moral support from all quarters and at the same time, is certainly a major ingredient that helps building a pillar of sublime and superb intellect which, in turn, will greatly contribute to the development and growth of the nation.

Imparting education is a great task to be accomplished by the government in the context of social responsibility, it owes to its citizens. The role of the executive of the state becomes pivotal in relation to education, because the spirit of a democratic society lies in the awareness and consciousness of the masses.

Decentralisation of powers, regarding the implementation and execution of educational policies might have a wider and deeper impact on the whole society, if done in a scientific way with the spirit of our cultural ethos.

Strategic reforms become an important tool in order to cope with the incessantly emerging challenges for enriching the teaching methodology. In present scenario, a cursory look on the foundational aspects of education in India shows occasional failures. The method of teaching is most important, while grooming a new responsible generation. Keeping this in mind, book has been presented to quench the thirst of students, academicians and educationists with an eye on the social changes, taking place frequently and to match the global standards too.

Although much light has been shed by authors on the subject and many a book have already been authored by eminent people, yet there, remains, dearth for a comprehensive book.

A serious and sincere endeavour has been made to include all relevant matter in the present book. Hoping that this will meet the expectations of readers in every possible way, I wish to thank all my friends, colleagues and well wishers, who have contributed valuably.

Editor

Part-I

Perception and Theory

1

The Concept

A concept is defined as a class of stimuli having common characteristics or attributes. They are experiences coded in words or ideas or mental images. The experiences may consist of objects, events, things, persons, etc. It is a name given to these objects and happenings as experienced by a child or an adult; for example trees, men, animals, students, boys, girls, intelligentia, mentally ill person, leaders, teachers, school, church, and so on. All these concepts refer to classes or groupings or categories of stimuli. Particular stimuli such as persons or events or happenings can not be considered concepts; for example, Mohan, Dr. R.D. Singh, the school principal, Chandra Gupta (Jai Shankar Prasad's Novel), France, England, India are not concepts. This is so because a concept is not a particular stimulas, but it is a class of stimuli. Mohan is a particular person. It does not include any other individual. So, it is not a class, and hence not a concept. Concepts are variously described in the literature as abstractions, grouped experiences, assertions, constructs, ideas, decisions, identity (single instance), inferences, meanings, mental images, terms, units of thought, symbols, and so on. Kendler (1968) defines a concept as a set of connections between some response and certain attributes or cues in stimulus pattern. A person is said to have formed a concept when he is able to classify, generalize, discriminate, and apply it on a pre-determined criterion or criteria. They are constructs which mostly arise from incessent physical encounters with environment.

Concepts are formed on the basis of attributes (characteristics) of stimuli which enable a child or a person to put that into a class, group or category. An attribute is a specific, distinctive feature of a concept. Attributes are neither fixed in number, nor have fixed values. The attributes may vary in number from concept to concept. For example, cricket ball has two attributes, shape (round) and purpose for which used or made. Purpose makes it a different class from other kinds of balls. This attribute, thus, varies from one concept of balls to other concepts of balls. Similarly, the shape (round) is another attribute which differentiates it from other objects of different shapes such as squares, flat, hollow, triangular, etc. Thus, concepts are grouped or classified on' the basis of their attributes. Attributes may have different values for different concepts. For example, large schools, small schools according to attribute size or elementary schools, secondary schools, degree schools according to attribute level and similarly black pens, red pens, green pens, and so, on according to the attribute colour. Thus, depending on variations in attribute values of colour, size, form, shape, level, purpose, etc. the concepts may differ from one another for the same object, event or stimuli. Sometimes, it is more than one attribute that determines identification of a concept; for example, shape, size, colour and texture all taken together determine identification of the concept of orange. Such attributes have a wide range of values.

The number of attributes also varies from concept to concept. For example, the orange has several attributes such as shape, colour, texture, etc. Larger the number of attributes, more complex the concept becomes. For example, good teacher may have a large number of attributes which may vary from one class of good teachers (primary level) to another class (say college good teacher).

Dominance of the attribute is another characteristic of the concept. It refers to the most obvious or prominent feature of the attribute. Dominant attributes constitute dominant concepts. More dominant concepts are learnt more easily (James Archer, 1962). Lee Sechrest and Judith Kaas (1965) and John Wallace (1964) also reached the same conclusion on the basis of their experiments.

"Associating meanings with the objects and events and the names that embody them is the beginning of concept learning" according to Klausmeier and Goodwin (1966). Concpts range in inclusiveness from two units in a class to millions of units arranged in a hierarchy of classes as held by them, although they say that there is the identity concept represented in only one of a kind; for example there is only one person that is you.

The Properties

Klausmeier and Goodwin describe following properties that make something a concept :

Psychological Meaningfulness : An individual's concept of anything is the organized inferences, i.e., meaningful associations that an individual forms of objects or events. These inferences enable the individual to categorize objects as belonging to the same class. "A concept is not a word; however some words stand for concepts" according to Klausmeier and Goodwin. The common attributes or responses alone do not make a concept. Psychologically organized inferences or the meaningful association are essential ingredients of concept formation. Abstracting common elements of objects may also lead to concept learning in some cases.

Intrinsic, Functional and Formal Properties : Intrinsic properties are observable characteristics which allow certain objects to be put in one distinctive category; for example, 'birds' whose flying attribute distinguishes them from other kinds of living organisms. This is the intrinsic property of the concept of birds.

Objects can be classified and conceptualized on the basis of their use or function or purpose. For example, bread, butter, vegetables all can be put in the category food, although they have no common intrinsic properties. But, since they serve a common purpose of being used as food, they constitute a meaningful concept 'food'.

The concepts of numbers and alphabets are based on man-made formal properties. These are as usable as intrinsic properties in determining the class inclusion.

Abstractness, Inclusiveness and Generality : These are also attributes or properties of concepts. The concepts may be concrete or abstract, less abstract and highly abstract. Trip to a hilly station is a concrete concept having observable intrinsic properties, but the "pleasant trip" is a highly abstract concept. No one knows what makes a trip pleasant. Moreover, it may be pleasant to one person, but not to another person.

Concepts range in inclusiveness from one member to an unspecified large number of members or exemplars. The identity concept includes one exemplar only. Continents (few), nations (many), stars (infinite numbers) are concepts which have varying degrees of inclusiveness.

Concepts vary in generality also. Low generality concepts refer to only the members of the same lowest-order class, while the high generality concepts refer to unspecified number of members of the highest super-ordinate class; for example, men, animals, living beings. Men and animals have lower generality level while living beings have higher generality level.

Structure : Concepts have an attribute of structure or organization also. From structure point of view concepts are classified as (a) conjunctive, (b) disjunctive, and (c) relational.

Conjunctive Concepts : They are also called joining or connective concepts. In these concepts the appropriate values of several attributes are jointly present. For example, the concept of "sentence" is a conjunctive concept because a sentence has a subject and a predicate. If either of these is missing, the group of words is not a sentence. Similarly, the attributes of mammal are warm-blooded having mammary glands and bearing live offsprings. If any of these is not present in an animal, it is not an animal. Conjunctive concepts are easier to learn. Most of the concepts are of this type.

Disjunctive Concepts : Disjunctive means not joined or separated. These are concepts in which the attributes are not present in all the exemplars. Hence, disjunctive concepts can be defined in a number of different ways. For example, "two boys and two girls" is a disjunctive concept in which the attribute number remains the same while the attribute sex differs from one another. Another example is that of 'strike' in the game of baseball which occurs in a number of different ways. Yet, each is called a strike. "Teaching" is a disjunctive concept as it includes different kinds of teaching, different levels of teaching, teaching by different teachers, teaching for different purposes, and so on. At a more abstract level Hindus, Muslims and Christians are included in the concept of religious people, although they differ in many ways from one another.

Relational Concepts : These concepts are determined not by attributes only, but by the relationship between the attributes. For example, "distance" and "direction" are relational concepts as they are determined by the relationship, i.e., difference between two points in space and time respectively. They involve dependencies as is implicit in the words such as bigger, smaller, higher, equal, order, younger, wider, between, smaller, higher, equal, order, younger, wider, between, up, down, and so on. They also include 'if-then' statements. Geographic concepts such as south, north, east, west, warm, etc, are examples of relational concepts as we can not give their attributes without considering their opposites or parallels.

The Functions

Concept learning is extremely important because the concepts perform following functions as described by DeCecco and Crawford (1977).

They Reduce the Complexity of the Environment : Life would have been very miserable, if the individuals were to attend to, respond to and treat each object, event or experience of the environment afresh and a new every time. Grouping or classifying objects makes it possible to deal with thousands of objects by using one word or concept, for example books which may be millions of them. We need not enumerate all individual animals for the concept of "animal" does the job quite satisfactorily.

They Help Us to Identify the Object : In the absence of concepts we can not distinguish cats from dogs or any other object. Different objects in the world around us are known to us only through concept formation.

They Reduce the Need for Constant Learning: Once a concept it formed it becomes a part of our knowledge. For example, if the concept of a dog is formed and next time when the person comes across a dog he can immediately identify that. It is not to be learnt afresh. They save us from repeated learning.

They Provide Direction for Instrumental Activity: By using concepts one can know in advance what action he has to take in a situation. If one suffers from a disease and if he has a concept of doctor, he can plan to consult the doctor. They are very helpful in problem-solving, reasoning, planning, performing daily routine activities.

They Make Instruction Possible: Verbal instructions and communication involves the use of a large number of concepts. Teaching-learning is impossible in the absence of many previously formed concepts.

Besides these, concepts are indispensable for transmitting man's previous experiences, interpreting present situations, and projecting plans into the future. Interaction among people is possible only because of concepts developed by them.

Process of Formation

The initial stage of concept formation is experience, which in other words means child's encounter with the environment, his interaction with objects, incidents and people around. The first stage of contact with any new material at whatever age of maturity is, inevitably, of the trial and error sort. While playing with material or interacting with other age-mates and elderly persons including parents and family members the child learns many words which stand for objects, activities and processes distinct from one another on the basis of their specific characteristics. These meaningful words constitute his acquired concepts which help him in learning more concepts in future.

"Concept-formation involves essentially a way of putting unorganized information into some kind of mental-filing system by grouping together an array of dissimilar objects or events on the basis of some common property that they possess," (Hilda Taba). According to Hilda Taba concept formation is a cognitive task which involves grouping items according to some basis of similarity and the development of categories and labels for the groups. The process, according to her involves three phases : (i) enumeration, (ii) grouping, and (iii) developing categories. Enumeration calls for collecting data, which is analyzed in terms of identification of similarities and differences which, in turn, leads to making and labeling groups. Bruner, Goodnow and Austin (1956) describe concept attainment as a process by which learners discriminate the attributes of things, people, events and place them into categories. According to them concept attainment occurs by making decisions about what attributes belong in what category. It is, in other words, a process of determining criteria by which certain attributes are placed into certain category. She developed a complete model or strategy for developing concepts which is known as Inductive Strategic Model derived from analysis of mental process. Under these strategies the learner performs three overt activities: (1) enumeration and listing, (2) grouping, (3) labelling and categorizing. Each of these overt activities involves covert mental operations such as (i) differentiation, (ii) identifying common properties i.e., abstracting, (iii) and determining the hierarchical order of items; super and subordination respectively. Concepts are hierarchical in nature in the sense of representing different degrees of complexity, abstractness and generality, combining lower-order concepts into higher-order ones progressively and forming a developmental sequence.

Ausubel's Subsumption Theory of learning meaningful verbal material (1963) prescribes a process of concept learning in which a concept of more generalized nature and more inclusive (called advance organizer) is presented first followed by less general and less specific concepts (i.e. organizers). The continuum going from concrete to the specific is reversed prescribing going from more inclusive and general to less specific and less abstract. Thus, in this process one concept is included within another more general one and the organizational principle is that of progressive differentiation from regions of greater generality to lesser generality.

Kendler (1961) defined concept learning as "any situation that involves the acquisition or utilization or both of a common response to dissimilar stimuli". Hunt (1962) rewords this definition by adding "identifying" before response and holds that such acts as learning to call particular animals "dogs" will be classified as concept learning. Learning of the use of names is, to him, an example of concept learning. Concept-learning is certainly an example of pattern recognition which follows categorization of sensory input in which the use of a name learned is included under the rubric "concept-learning". In short, concept-learning is learning the use of names. Bruner, Goodnow and Austin (1956) consider concept-learning only as the process of concept-acquisition which they say is different from concept formation, in.which case the concept former discovers a new way of ordering objects into sets so that a meaningful classification rule can be found as it happens in case of the process of creativity. For Piaget (1957) a concept is just an explanatory rule or law by which a relation between two or more events may be described.

The behaviourists explain the process of concept formation in terms of S-R connections. When a picture or object or the real being as of "dog" is presented along with the sound "dog" and the process is repeated several times the child learns the meaning of the word which becomes a concept acquired by the child. Welch (1947) presented a concept-learning model based on the idea of direct conditioning of a response to a stimulus trace assuming that any stimulus object was represented inside the object, by a neural condition which was isomorphic with the stimulus.

Many concepts are such whose denotations are specified by symbols rather than by objects; for example "sin". Such concepts are learned via symbols at progressively more and more abstract levels. This is explained by the term "mediating response", an explanation which begins with the assumption that responses produce stimuli which may serve as cues for further responses. When a stimulus is presented its image in the organism is presumed to evoke certain previously learned responses. These provide stimuli which evoke another response, and so on. This chain of S-R may consist of overt and covert responses. In concept learning the chain is ended with the occurrence of an overt naming response.

2

Implications for Education

Human beings are not found anywhere in nature. There are only individuals. The individual differs from the human being because he is concrete event. He is the one who acts, loves, suffers, fights and dies. On the contrary, the human being is a platonic idea living in our minds and in our books. Thus, the individual is a particular being and the human being is a universal, a general being. It is, therefore, important to define and discover exactly the part of the human being and that of the individual. Educational Psychology is concerned with the individual. Indeed, individuality is fundamental in man. It permeates our entire being. It gives uniqueness to the self.

Individual Differences

Individuals can be easily distinguished from one another by their gestures, their ways of talking, acting and their appearance. And, these changes cause every man to be himself and any body else. Identical twins coming from the same single cell are two quite different persons. In the same way there are no individuals of identical mentality. The richer the personality the greater the individual differences.

Thus, it is an established fact that the individuals differ in mental abilities as well as in physical abilities and personality traits. The individuals not only differ from one another, but also each individual differs from one ability to another within his own self. Thus, there are variations not only amongst individuals, but there are variations within the same individual among his own abilities. The problem of individual differences, therefore, can be viewed from two sides :

(a) Differences in abilities from individual to individual.

(b) Differences in abilities within the same individual.

There is no definite measure of the extent of the Individual differences. It has been found that there is a continuous gradation from one extreme to the other. Freeman of Cornell University holds that the nature and extent of individual differences on a particular trait or complex of traits is represented by the unimodal curve which portrays the range of human potentialities for development in that trait under conditions as they now are. We can not, therefore, say that all persons fall naturally into two distinct types such as athletic or non-athletic, intelligent or unintelligent etc. The only thing that we can definitely discover is the average (mean) deviation. This can reveal to us the extent of differences.

Causes of Differences

Thorndike discusses the causes of individual differences under five main heads. These are :

1. Sex, 2. Race or remote ancestry, 3. Maturity, 4. Heredity, 5. Environment

Sex : As regards sex, it has been discovered that girls are superior to boys on tests of memory. Superiority of females over males has been found in linguistic ability. Small differences have been found in favour of males in reasoning, computation, arithmetical ability and number concepts. Males are found to be superior in manual performance and mechanical ability.

However, there are also found great overlappings between the sexes. According to these differences there have been found marked differences in interests, habits, preferences, educational and vocational preferences.

Race or Remote Ancestry : We generally enter into our common talk and make observations like-Do individuals differ because they belong to different racial, national or cultural groups?

"Russians are tall and stout," "Ceylonese are short and slim," "Germans have no sense of humour," "Yellow races are cruel and revengeful," "Americans are hearty and frank," "Indians are timid and peace-loving," as the myths of racial, national or cultural differences. Many studies have been conducted in the field of psychology, sociology and anthropology to see whether there are some significant inborn differences in mental abilities among the several racial or national groups. But, the investigations have not given any clear indication. There is no evidence of any national superiority in mental abilities. Similar studies have been made with white and non-white children. The fact should be subject to the general principle that the degree and form of mental development is the result of interaction between inherited abilities and the environmental influences. In fact, racial or national groups are compared by group averages and these cannot be more significant psychologically and educationally than are differences among individuals.

Maturity : As regards maturation, individual differences of mental growth are found in infancy. The rate of growth is not the same at all the stages. It differs from stage to stage. Not only the rate but the character of growth, differs from one age level to another as maturation marches on. Yet, the children tend to maintain their relative positions of mediocrity, superiority or inferiority.

Late in life, persons suffer from a decline in mental abilities. The decline proceeds gradually at first, then increases with age especially after sixty. But the relative position is maintained even now.

Heredity : The importance of heredity is now fairly accepted. An individual's height, size of his bones, the colour and texture of his hair, the colour of his eyes the shape of his face, nose, mouth. hands and feet, the nature of his entire physical structure, and in fact all that he is physically and mentally is determined largely by his inheritance. The general principle of heredity is that children resemble their parents and that "like tends to beget like." Children resemble both their parents but even within the same family children differ because they do not develop out of the same combination of genes. That is why even in large families complete correspondence of abilities is absent.

Further, children of bright parents tend to be less bright and the children of very inferior parents are often less inferior. Heredity is said to move towards the average. This is called regression as traits when passing from parents to children tend to move towards the average. The genius son of a genius father is a very rare thing. Again, there is a tendency among the off-spring to be higher in the traits in which their parents are low and lower in which their parents are high. They move towards the average, that is they regress.

The heredity of a child is not solely determined by his immediate parents. He inherits from all his forefathers and ancestors also or from the same stock their parents have inherited. It is said that one-half of inheritance is from the parents, one fourth from grand parents, one-eighth from great grandparents and one sixteenth and so on from gradually further removed ancestors.

Thus, heredity unquestionably has a considerable influence on individual differences.

Environment : The nature of the human being is shaped through the interaction which takes place between the human organism and the environment. Our environment is our habitation in the fullest sense. Not only our physical surroundings but also the people around us, social customs and traditions, culture, education and training, all constitute our environment. What we call our social heritage, ideas and ideals, is a part of our environment. A number of studies have been conducted to see the influence of the environment on the individuals. These are :

A study was conducted to compare the intellectual status of children coming "from different occupational and social groups. The occupational status of the father was treated as a general index of the mental abilities of the child. It was revealed by the study that (a) the I.Q.s, of the fathers correspond to their occupational status and that (b) the intelligence of the children would correspond to the occupations of the fathers.

In another study conducted on canal-born children and gypsy children it was found that their environment was very poor, they were isolated from the world, cut off from school and society, and lived and worked under the most humdrum conditions. The most striking fact revealed by this study was that with increase in age their I.Q. was depressed.

A detailed study was conducted to see the effect of environment on foster and adopted children. Their I.Q.'s., and progress in school behaviour were assessed. As the foster parents are not the true parents and the hereditary, relation does not exist, the influence of superior borne environment can be better evaluated. It was revealed that intelligence as well as development of the children was remarkably better in richer and more stimulating home environment.

A similar study was conducted on identical twins placed in different and similar environments. The study revealed that in later case there was high correlation between their physical traits, mental capacities, educational abilities, while in the former case in the same twins there was less difference; but other different environments did make a difference in educational achievement and I.Q.

On the basis of above studies, one can easily hold that environment unquestionably has a considerable influence on individual differences.

Kinds of Differences

Inter and Intra Individual Differences : Inter-individual differences are differences between two individuals. It may be possible that two persons differ in their intelligence, attitudes, and interests. No two individuals in this world are identical. Each one of them differs fiom one another.

On the other hand, intra-individual differences deal with the differences within an individual. These differences exist within the individual. A person may have variability in intelligence, interest, attitude, etc. It may be possible that he has high intelligence but other traits are lower than that.

Physical and Physiological Differences : Some individuals according to the structure of the body may be found differing in regard to height, weight, physique and colour, etc. But physiological differences indicate differences which refer to biological functioning like blood etc.

Differences in Ability : This has become an established fact that individuals differ widely as regards their I.Q.s. The distribution of intelligence quotients obtained by examining first grade children with the Standford Revision of the Binet Test has a range from 60 to 160 with 100 as its mean. Other tests of intelligence are used with groups at all levels and ages. The results so obtained go to assert that individuals vary greatly on the scale of mental ability. Heredity and environment are two great factors that cause individual differences in mental ability.

Differences in Aptitudes : When we speak of a person's aptitudes, we refer to his potentialities. They may be high or low, different in different fields. They vary from individual to individual. Aptitude of a person is one's ability to carry on a task to maximum success. It refers to one's special abilities. Scholastic aptitude pertains to potential learning ability. It is determined by one's intelligence. It is also called general aptitude.

But, as individuals differ from one another in the degree of intelligence, there are bound to appear differences in their general aptitudes. It is a common experience that all people cannot perform a particular activity with the same amount of ease and perfection.

Special aptitudes refer to the relative fitness of the individual for special types of work. But this "fitness" calls forth the requisite amount of various special abilities involved in the activity. But, as individuals differ from one another in the amount and degree of these abilities possessed by them, differences in their special aptitude too, appear.

Differences in Personality : Personality is not one single entity. It is a blend of a number of traits and abilities. But, these traits and abilities and their integration and the process of their blending differ greatly from one individual to another, Therefore, we find differences in individuals personalities. The individuals differ greatly as regards the physiological and biological conditions of their organs, their psychological development and mental functioning. All these individual differences find a clear manifestation in the total differences in the individual personalities. When there are differences in the component parts of patterns, there will be differences in the whole patterns too. Individual differences in intelligence, morality, sociability, temperament, etc., result into differences in individual personalities.

Thus, individuals differ from one another and they differ within themselves from ability to ability.

Emotional Difference : Some individuals are very sensitive while some others have normal level of emotionality. In the same way the ego of some persons is highly developed. As regards temperament of the individuals differences are found there also.

Actual Implications

Individual Differences in the children is a reality which is faced daily by the school teachers in their classrooms. It is never possible to lose sight of this reality and importance of individuality. Not surprisingly, they are less concerned about causes—than they are about the effects of individual differences on pupils learning ability and their adaptability to educational goals and procedures. Regardless of the cause of variability teachers of even the nursery age children must deal with these differences.

By the time children enter the first grade, differences in abilities are already marked and absolute variations become more pronounced as they progress. Whatever the reasons for these diversities, the fact is that the school should deal with them by means of differentiated curricula and individualized instruction as far as it is feasible.

A thorough knowledge of the individual differences is essential because they serve as the foundation upon which effective pupil guidance and good teaching can be built. They are often the source of one's most pronounced achievements, fullest self-realisation and greatest usefulness. They are evidences that distinguish individuals from one another.

Educationally, individual differences mean that a pupil's chronological age is an unreliable criterion upon which to base his educational programme. As the individuals differ from one another so their education too must essentially differ. Secondly, as the individual is not the same at all the stages of development and that he differs greatly with respect to his abilities at different stages and age-levels, so education should also differ accordingly at various age-levels. In other words, human variability should be given due regard in the content and methods of education. "Every person is a well-defined type and that in each type certain fixed trait-relationships exist," Education, therefore, must be adjusted to each type according to these trait-relationships. This has resulted into following specific trends in education.

Individualization : "Individualization" in the words of Courtis, "as a method of teaching or as a philosophy of education refers primarily to the attempt to adjust education to the nature of the individual." Individualization emphasizes the marked individual differences of human nature.

Homogeneous Grouping : Individual differences compel to think in terms of homogeneous grouping of classes according to the level of ability and not age. This is also known as "ability-grouping."

Adjustment to Special Interests : Individuals differ from one another as regards their interests. A great principle of learning is that education should take notice of the interests of the boys at all stages of development. This fact may be utilized in the adjustment of teaching to the speical interests of the boys of various stages of development.

Assignment : The teacher should modify the assignment in amount, quality, difficulty and sequence according to individual differences. The individual differences in personality traits, previous education, capacity and other factors must be taken into consideration to fit the work to the requirements of differing individuals.

The first Acharya Narendra Deo Committee of U.P. proposed a system of secondary education based on the varied needs of pupils and said that the schools should provide diversified curricula to suit the needs and aptitudes of our students. The recommendations are based upon the recognition of the "Importance of individuals differences in ability, intelligence and personality make-up of school pupils." The Acharya Narendra Deo Committee Report of 1953 says, "Aptitudes, intelligence testing and educational guidance are of prime importance in a widespread system of higher secondary education for a free and democratic country." The recognition of the fact of individual differences resulted into four types of courses-literary, scientific, counstructive and aesthetic, "Course-analysis," like job-analysis has been stressed by the committee. "Ability tests" and "scholastic aptitude tests" too have been recommended by it. All these are sound recommendations based upon the established fact of the individual differences. The same has been asserted by Mudaliar Commission Report of 1954 on Secondary Education.

Individual differences are of great significance for personal and vocational guidance purpose. On the one hand individuals differ from one another as regards their physical characteristics, general intelligence, aptitudes, personality traits, interests and likings, on the other hand there are differences in requirements of occupations. It is, therefore, essential that proper adjustment should take place between these differences so that the fittest man may go to a particular occupation and there may not be the wastage of national energy and genius.

Individual differences are of great importance for clinical and personal hygiene purpose. Students differ in personality traits and other abilities. Hence, there are differences in the adjustment that they make towards their environments. Deficiency of some traits in some of them may cause mal-adjustment which is to be avoided. The individual can be helped rightly only if we are able to know and measure the trait or ability that is responsible for this. Individual adjustments are to a very great extent determined by one's own abilities and traits. It is the duty of the schools, the home and the society to provide the individuals with an environment which suits their respective abilities and traits in order to avoid mental disorders. The psychology of individual differences gives an insight into adjustment problems of the individuals.

To sum up, Charles Skinner holds that, "A knowledge of the nature of individual differences is essential if the teacher is to improve the education that all children receive regardless of their ability."

Organizing Programmes

If the teacher recognizes and accepts the fact of individual differences his approach to pupils will be more positive. All that the teacher can do is to provide opportunities for learning and practice. By understanding individual differences the teacher will be able to devise such remedial programmes of instruction as will help slow learners to achieve better results. In attempting to meet the varying needs, interest and abilities of pupils and to enable each pupil to grow and develop at his own rate, several teaching procedures and types of pupil classification and promotion are being extensively used in progressive schools. Some of the earlier plans and procedures were directed primarily at helping the duller pupil and almost all of them neglected the brighter pupil. Some of the recent attempts however provide for all degrees of intelligence, both inferior and superior. They are :

Individual Instruction : Individualized instruction is considered as a ready solution of the problem of individual differences. The advantages of individualized instruction are obvious. It helps to concentrate attention on the work of individuals rather than on the average work of the class, and the teacher can acquire intimate knowledge of each pupil's interests and vocational tendencies. The slow pupil is allowed to work at his own rate and shows more satisfactory results. The bright, gifted pupil instead of marking time with the mediocre, average pupil has opportunities to go ahead and work on more advanced assignments according to his choice. The teacher gets an opportunity to develop diagnostic skills in discovering how different pupils respond to a task or a problem. Thus, individual instruction seeks to meet individual differences through a degree of variable instruction.

Group Instruction : Individual Instruction misses the social value of group work and therefore group instruction is advocated. It saves the teacher from duplicate preparation and explanation and simplifies the problem of class management. Providing for group work, co-operation, and competition young people are fired with a desire to win the good opinion of others and the class work acquires strong motivation. Group work provides for the social values of education. The slow pupil is stimulated to do better by the example of brighter pupils.

Winnetka Plan : The Winnetka plan was introduced by C.W. Washburne in the school of Winnetka. Its accent is on selection of subject matter, its organization for presentation and workable devices for checking the outcomes, keeping in mind the individual interests and abilities. The first part is known as the common essentials consisting of knowledge and skills which are needed by all pupils. This corresponds to the core curricula. The second part is known as group activities. The pupil's work on the common essentials is fully individualized. It is divided into units and accompanying each unit are prepared assignment sheets, work sheets and test sheets. Each pupil works at his own rate on each unit. When he has finished his work on one unit, he compares his results with the answer sheet. If he finds that he has passed, he proceeds to the next unit, otherwise he goes over his work to correct the defects. When he has completed a group of units he offers to be finally tested by the teacher before taking up the next-group of units. If he fails he does further work and is re-tested. The pupil has to secure cent percent score. Group activities like dramatics, excursions, entertainments etc., occupy nearly half the time and every day opportunities are given for creative work. The socializing influence of these activities are quite obvious.

Dalton Plan : Dalton plan was introduced by Miss Helen Parkhurst at Dalton. The main principles underlying the plan are freedom, co-operation and allocation of time. The pupils are free to continue without interruption in the work in which they are absorbed, unhindered by time-tables. The work is designated as a "job" and each pupil is given a written statement of the work to be done. He is free to do it in his own way and at his own rate. The year's work is divided into monthly assignments and each assignment is further divided into daily units of work. Each classroom becomes a "Laboratory" for a special subject and it is presided over by a specialist teacher. Each pupil may elect to work on any one subject throughout the month but he is not allowed to begin on the second month's assignment till he has completed that of the first. He is encouraged to spend more time on the subject in which he is weak. Group work is encouraged if a number of pupils are working at the same stage. General difficulties are explained in group lessons called "conferences". A pupil advances steadily job by job, through the curriculum. If in a school year of nine or ten months he only finishes eight jobs on account of balance or illness he begins the ninth job in the following year. The bright child may, on the contrary, accomplish in one year the work planned for eighteen months and the slow child working at his own rate may build a sound foundation.

Morrison Plan : Morrison plan devised by Prof. H.C. Morrison of Chicago University is based on direct guidance and stresses unit assignment. Directed guidance has five steps. The first is pre-test in which the background of the pupil in determined to see what approach the pupil will have for the new unit of work. The next step is presentation. Its purpose is to present the main points of the unit of work as effectively as possible to stimulate the pupil to work. It is followed by assignments growing out of presentation. The next step is organization in which each pupil presents his own outline of the matter learned, and the final step is recitation in which the assimilated material is orally presented by each pupil. The important task in this plan is to establish learning units. For Morrison a unit is "a comprehensive and significant aspect of the environment," of science, art or conduct whose learning affects personality.

Project Method: This method was devised by Kilpatrick. In this method few problems are given to students to solve on their own behalf such as cooking, tailoring, carpenting, playing drama, writing a letter, story telling, picture appreciation, to learn writing, solving problems like why population of Delhi is fast increasing? etc. A project has its own purpose and is activity -oriented. A pupil is free to select work of his own choice and capabilities. He works in his own way. From planning till execution of the project he is completely free to complete his work in accordance with his needs, interests and potentialities.

Decroley Plan : This plan was devised by Ovid Decroley, an educationist of Belgium. The underlying principle of this method is that for life a child receives his education from the life itself. The classification of the students to their classes is made such that with regard to their interests, intelligence, potentialities etc., they look alike. The child is given complete freedom at school to work. Attempts are made that the child should feel relaxed at school like his home. Students' interests are given proper importance. The teacher treats his pupils in a psychological manner with sympathy and pays proper attention to their needs and interests.

Contract Plan : Contract plan is the same as Dalton plan. In this plan too, the study subjects are prescribed to children, and like Winnetka plan the progress of child is tested through diagnostic tests. The teacher pays more attention to the subject in which the child is weak and is encouraged to spend more time on that particular subject. In other words we may say that Contract Plan is a combination of Dalton and Winnetka Plan.

Activity Programme : Activity programme lays stress on activity. The different subjects are taught with activity as centre of each subject. A child selects any activity according to his interests, aptitudes, potentialities etc. During the learning process the child does not sit quiet and passive but is equally active and interested like the teacher. It is thus, that whole learning process becomes child-centered instead of teacher-centred. The students plan, organize, evaluate and draw results of project independently with great success and effectiveness.

Programmed Instruction : Programmed instruction is a method in which a pupil learns according to his speed and capacity. A topic is divided into many sub-topics. There are various forms of programmed instruction, but that of Skinner's (programmed instruction) is most common in use. It is used for the purpose of self-study. Individual differences are paid proper attention in this programme. Keeping himself engaged in the learning process the child learns best according to his speed, need, interest and capacity. Simultaneously, his progress is also assessed through tests. Thus, in programmed instruction a pupil follows the entire instructions of the programme with keen zest and enthusiasm.

Grouping according to Ability : The general practice of grouping pupils for purposes of instruction is based on pupil ability. Attempts have been made to improve the system of classification by grouping pupils with greater homogeneity. The basis of classification may be age differences, mental age, I.Q., achievement, teachers rating, physical or social maturity etc. But, such grouping has been strongly criticized as harmful socially and psychologically. If bright pupils are placed in separate groups they acquire superiority complexes and if all pupils are separately grouped they may develop inferiority complexes; and all this is injurious to their social development.

In practice the same class is divided into three sections of bright, average and slow pupils. These three sections cover the same course of study but at different rates of speed. Or, these groups may be kept in the same class and given different tasks. The slow group covers less work and is given more drill. The work assigned to him is more concrete and practical. The bright group covers much more ground and the stress is on difficult problems and original work. Pupils with special abilities and handicaps have to be given special attention.

Diagnostic and Remedial Teaching : There are some children whose progress is rather, irregular owing to genetic or physical factors, habits, interests, purpose or environmental background. Ideally, then, it is the school's responsibility to find out not only each child's general intellectual level but also to discover his special abilities or weaknesses, if he has any. This may be achieved through careful observation by teachers and educational tests such as (Diagnostic, Achievement, Prognostic) or, through special clinical examinations. In brief, diagnostic tests point out individual's difficulties or weaknesses in a particular subject, while remedial teaching suggests remedy or educational provisions to overcome these difficulties. Hence, remedial teaching is a must after diagnostic tests point out individual's difficulties or weaknesses in a particular subject. Remedial teaching suggests remedy or educational provisions to overcome these difficulties. Hence, remedial teaching is unavoidable after diagnosis.

Acceleration : In India the system of promotions suffers from many defects. The system can be improved by making promotions more frequent and flexible. Here, brighter pupils are allowed to skip classes and double promotions are permitted to pupils who have done exceptionally well. Some schools have a system of trial promotions in which bright pupils are promoted to the next higher class on the condition that they make good, failing which they are sent back to their original class. Many schools hold classes for failed students during the summer vacation which follows the annual promotions and give them another chance to pass. This method of acceleration suits the junior classes but is not desirable for higher classes, as it may create some emotional problems for them.

Enrichment of Curriculum : Provision for individual differences does not end with differentiated curriculum. For, within the same course of study and within the same subjects, there may be appreciable differences in aptitudes. This is particularly true in the so called universals or constants that are prescribed practically for all pupils. Some of the pupils may be found creative in different fields. They may be requiring more of stimulation, high level assignments, wider reading and probably, experimentation with ideas. Guidance given to them may do wonders to some of them if not to all. Hence, fostering creativity in children and provision of co-curricular activities may do a great deal in this regard.

3

ADMINISTRATION OF EDUCATION

Educational effort in India is organised, administered and supervised by four types of agencies. Their functions and responsibilities, though different and distinct, quite often overlap, for none of them is singly and wholly responsible for policy-making, operation and finance. These four types of agencies are: (1) the Central Government. (2) the State Government, (3) Local Bodies, and (4) Private Enterprise.

Union Government

Historical Retrospect : During the British regime the alien government was not interested in educating the Indian masses, save some upper classes for the limited purpose of providing junior officials for its own administration and to keep its hold on India. Ripon, in 1883, placed primary education under the local bodies. Educational administration was highly centralised, the provinces were merely carrying out the policies of the Centre. The whole initiative, policy-making, organisation and administration, were dictated by the Centre as it suited their purpose. In 1901 was created the post of Director-General of education, and, in 1910, was established the Department of Education under the charge of a Member of the Viceroy's Executive Council. In the same year, a Secretary was appointed to look after the Department of Education, Health and Lands. In 1921, with the Montford Reforms, education was transferred to the Provinces. With this delegation of authority and responsibility to elected ministers the Centre became totally indifferent to education. The Hartog Committee deplored this apathy as unfortunate. This state of affairs continued till World War II, when the Centre again started taking some interest in education. In 1945, the Department of Education was separated from Health and Lands.

With Independence coming in 1947, full-fledged Ministry of Education and Scientific Research was established. The Centre's interest in education continued to grow. However, we find considerable overlapping in the efforts of the Centre and the States of the Union, specially in the matter of reorganisation of education. The Centre issued directive without sharing responsibility. The Slates looked at this with suspicion. They wanted to retain the power they had been enjoying for long. The result was that even after the Constitution of India came into force the Centre adopted an isolationist policy and gave no help to the States in the matter of education.

With the launching of the Five-Year-Plans the policy changed. The Centre allotted funds to the States; specially for the expansion and development of universal primary education and social education of the adults. With the control of these grants, the centre started supervising education in the States. The Centre's educational activities expanded and the Central Ministry of Education was reorganised from time to time. It discharged its responsibilities through the appointment of advisory councils for several purposes and continued to help the States with funds, technical advice, coordination and cooperation. At present, this is done by the Ministry of Education and Social Welfare through its various departments. Of these we are mainly concerned with the Department of Education and Culture.

The activities of the Central Ministry of Education of the Government of India are chiefly directed by the policy flowing from the clauses of the constitution of India.

Educational Policy

The following articles of the Indian Constitution form the bases of the Broad Educational Policy of India.

Art. 28 : (1) No religious instruction shall be provided in any educational institution wholly maintained out of state fund.

(2) Nothing in clause (1) shall apply to an educational institution which is administered by the state but has been established under any endowment or trust which requires that religious instruction shall be imparted in such institution.

(3) No person attending any educational institution recognised by the State or receiving aid out of the state funds shall be required to take part in any religious instruction that may be imparted in such institutions or to attend any religious worship that may be conducted in such institution or in any premises attached thereto unless such persons or, if such person is a minor, his guardian has given his consent thereto.

Art. 29 : (1) Any section of the citizens residing in the territory of India or any part thereof having a distinct language, script or culture of its own shall have the right to conserve the same.

(2) No citizen shall be denied admission into any educational institution maintained by the State or receiving aid out of State funds on grounds only of religion, race, caste, language or any of them.

Art. 30 : (1) All minorities, whether based on religion or language, shall have the right to establish and administer educational institutions of their choice.

(2) The state shall not. in granting aid to educational institutions, discriminate against any educational institution on the ground that it is under the management of a minority, whether based on religion or language. Part IV- Directive Principles of State Policy

Art. 41 : The State shall, within the limits of its economic development, make effective provision for securing the right to work, to education and to public assistance in case of unemployment, old age, sickness and disablement.

Art. 45 : The State shall endeavour to provide within a period of ten years from the commencement of this Constitution, for free and compulsory education for all children until they complete the age of fourteen years.

Art. 46 : The State shall promote, with special care: the

educational and economic interests of the weaker sections of the people, and. in particular of the Scheduled Castes and the Scheduled Tribes, and shall protect them from social injustice and all forms of exploitation.

Entry 63 : The institutions known at the commencement of this Constitution as the Banaras Hindi University, the Aligarh Muslim University and the Delhi University, and any other institution declared by the Parliament by law be institutions of national importance.

Entry 64 : Institutions for scientific or technical education financed by the Government of India wholly or in part and declared by Parliament by law to be institutions of national importance.

Entry 65 : Union agencies and institutions for:

(a) professional. vocational or technical training, including the training of police officers; or

(b) the provision of special studies or research; or

(c) scientific or technical assistance in the investigation or detection of crime.

Entry 66 : Coordination and determination of standards in institutions for higher education or research and scientific and technical institutions.

List II-State List

Entry 11 : Education including universities subject to the provisions of entries 63.64,65 and 66 of List I and entry 25 of List III.

List III-Concurrent List

Entry 25 : Vocational and technical training of labour.

Part XVII-Official Languages

Art. 344 : (1) The President shall, at the expiration of five years from the commencement of this Constitution and thereafter at the expiration of ten years from such commencement, by order, constitute a commission which will consist of a chairman and such other members representing the different languages specified in the eighth Schedule as the President may appoint and the order shall define the procedure to be followed by the commission.

(2) It shall be the duty of the commission to make recommendations to the President as to-

(a) the progressive use of the Hindi language for the official purposes of the Union.

(b) restrictions on the use of English language for all or any of the official purposes of the Union.

(c) the language to be used for all or any of the purposes mentioned in article 348.

(d) the form of numerals to be used for any one or more specified purposes of the Union.

(e) any other matter referred to the commission by the President as regards the official language of the Union and the language for communication between the Union and the State or between one State and another and their use.

(3) In making their recommendations under clause (2) the commission shall have due regard to the industrial, cultural and scientific advancement of India and the just claim and the interest of persons belonging to the Non-Hindi speaking areas in regard to the Public Services.

(4) There shall be constituted a committee consisting of thirty members of whom twenty shall be members of the House of the People (Lok Sabha) and ten shall be members of the council of States (Rajya Sabha) to be elected respectively by the members of the House of the People and the Members of the Council of States in accordance with the system of proportional representation by means of the single transferable vote.

(5) It shall be the duty of the committee to examine the recommendations of the commission constituted under clause (1) and to report to the President their opinion thereon.'

(6) Notwithstanding anything in article 343 the President may after consideration of the report referred to in clause (5) issue directions in accordance with the whole or any part of that report.

Art. 345 : Subject to the provisions of articles 346 and 347 the legislature of a state may by law adopt any one or more of the languages in use in the State or Hindi as the languages to be used for all or any of the official purposes of that State.

Provided that, until the legislature of that State otherwise provides by law. English language shall continue to be used for those official purposes within the State for which it was being used immediately before the commencement of this Constitution.

Art. 350 A : It should be the endeavour of every State and of every local authority within the State to provide adequate facilities for instruction in the mother-tongue at the primary stage of education to children belonging to linguistic minority groups; and the President may issue such directions to any State as he considers necessary or proper for securing the provision of such facilities.

Art. 351 : It shall be the duty of the Union to promote the spread of the Hindi language, to develop it so that it may serve as a medium of expression for all the elements of the composite culture of India and to secure its enrichment by assimilating without interfering with its genius, the forms, styles and expression used in Hindustani and other languages of India specified in the eighth Schedule, and by drawing, wherever necessary or desirable for its vocabulary primarily on Sanskrit and secondarily on other languages.

A Concurrent Subject

Art. 346 : The language for the time being authorised for use in the Union for official purposes shall be the official language for communication between one State and another State and between a State and the Union.

Provided that if two or more states agree that the Hindi language should be the official language for communication between such states that language may be used for such communication.

There had been large variations in the curriculum and structure of education, service conditions of teachers, examination systems, staffing patterns and standards of education over the various States of India right from the beginning of the modern system of education originating with the British rule in India. Uniformity in these matters could not be brought about as the education was on the State list and the States were free to make their own rules. It could be brought about only when the Central Government was made empowered to legislate on education. This was possible only when education was placed on either the Union list or on the Concurrent list. Efforts had been made several times, to place education on the Concurrent list, but success was not achieved. It was only in 1975 that education was voted to be on the Concurrent list. Since then, therefore, the Central Government has been empowered to. make legislations, on education also with the provision that if State act comes into conflict with the act passed by the Union Government, the latter act will prevail. This change has been very much welcome by the people of India, particularly the teachers. The present position in this regard after this change stands as follows:

(a) The State Governments even now can make their own legislations on education.

(b) The Central Government is also empowered to get any act about education passed through the Union legislative bodies.

(c) If the State act and the Union Government act happen to be in contradiction, the Union Government act will prevail.

Bringing education on the Union list has been considered a very progressive and useful step in the direction of educational development in India. It may be expected that this will ensure uniformity as well as adequate and desired diversity within the framework of this broad uniformity in the field of Indian Education. It may now be possible for the Central Government to pass a legislation in favour of 10+2+3 system, a uniform structure of education for all states. It may also pass legislations regarding a uniform structure of education for all States. It may also pass legislations regarding a uniform national policy on university admissions, vocationalization of education, teachers service conditions, uniform examinations system, etc. Another great advantage of putting education on concurrent list as put by Shukla (1983) is that this may lead to "Greater responsibility of the Central Government in educational matters. It may even have to find more funds from its own revenue to be spent on education, particularly in respect of those aspects of education which are covered by a Central legislation". He, therefore, considers this change to be in the larger interest of Indian Education.

Role of Centre

It is clear from the above that the Constitution restricts the role of the Central Government to the following activities:

1. The administration of institutions of national importance such as the National Library, the Indian Museums, etc.
2. The financing and supervision of the Central Universities of Banaras, Aligarh, Delhi, Visva-Bharati, JNU, etc.
3. The administration of institutions for scientific and technical education financed by the Government of India.
4. The coordination of facilities and determination of standards in respect of higher education, research, scientific and technical education.
5. Sharing responsibility with the State Governments and private bodies for free, universal and compulsory primary education of all children of the age group 6 to 14 years.
6. Coordination in regard to elementary and secondary education.
7. The administration of award of scholarships and fellowships.
8. Assistance for special provision for the education of the Scheduled Castes and Scheduled Tribes.
9. Co-operation with international organisations like the UNESCO.
10. Financing, directing and controlling of education in the Union Territories.

The role of the Central Government in education is limited to providing leadership, helping the State and Private bodies in expanding and improving education including higher education, maintaining standards of higher education, research, scientific and technical education, administering, expanding and improving education in the Union Territories and preservation of national culture.

The Ministry of Human Resource Development at present looks after about fifty subjects, of which the most important are the following:

(1) School Education, (2) Higher Education, (3) Technical and

Professional Education, (4) Social Education, (5) Physical Education, (6) Youth Welfare, (7) Book Promotion, (8) Educational Research, (9) Languages, (10) Cooperation with UNESCO, (11) Scholarships, (12) Exchange Programmes, (13) Cultural Affairs, (14) Archaeology, (15) Museums and Libraries.

The Central Government, discharges its functions and responsibilities through several advisory councils and statutory organisations. Of these the following are the more important:

1. Central Advisory Board of Education (CABE)
2. Central Board of Secondary Education
3. University Grants Commission (UGC)
4. National Council of Educational Research and Training (NCERT)
5. All-India Council for Women's Education
6. National Council for Women's Education
7. Central Schools Organisation
8. Language Centres

Central Administrative Machinery

The Central Ministry of Human Resource Development is run by the following administrative machinery as shown in the following table also:

The Minister of Education is a person elected to either House of Parliament. He is chosen by the Prime Minister and appointed by the President. He is responsible to the Parliament and is the executive head of the ministry. He may or may not be of the Cabinet rank. He is assisted by a Minister of State and two Deputy Ministers. With their help and that of the Education Secretary he frames policies and takes decisions on the advice given by the various advisory councils. He also disburses grants within the framework of the budget.

The Education Secretary is the administrative head of the ministry. He exercises general supervision and control over all the various activities and divisions of the ministry. All the submissions to the Minister have to be routed through him. He is assisted by two joint secretaries, three education advisers and three directors. The work of the various divisions of the ministry' is allocated to these administrative officers. The number varies from time to time.

The Educational Advisers hold charge of distinct divisions of the ministry. They are of the rank of joint secretaries. Besides coordinating the work of their divisions they are associated with the advisory councils, and as their designation implies, their duty is to tender advice on educational matters to the Minister through the Secretary. The advisers are assisted by a number of deputy, assistant and under-secretaries, holding charge of their respective subjects. In this category also fall the Deputy Education Advisers.

The Attached and Subordinate Officers: The HRD Ministry like other ministries, has a number of attached and subordinate offices under its control. Through these offices are conducted the policies, and activities of the ministry. These offices are responsible for implementation of policies and detailed execution of the decisions and programmes of the government.

Criticism :

(1) The Central HRD Ministry has been doing remarkable work. It has widely associated non-official experts and educationists in planning its policies and implementing its programmes. The association of State representatives ensures wide acceptance and cooperation. It makes the fullest use of available expertise and resources. It works in a democratic and constructive way of doing things.

(2) The tendency in the Central Secretariat is, however, developing towards uniformity and rigidity. Quite often, many good schemes are killed at the altar of bureaucracy and because of paucity of funds.

(3) Some of the advisory councils meet very rarely at long intervals, and work under the influence of officials. They have fallen into the nit of routine.

(4) The policy of matching grants is proving harmful for educational development. Poorer States and institutions, are unable to provide their share and remain backward. Consequently there is an increase in the inequality of educational opportunities.

Suggestions: The desirable improvement in the role of the Central Government in educational matters may be defined thus:

(1) The Education Minister must enjoy a Cabinet rank; this will give prestige and due importance and status to education. The recent reorganization making it a part of the Ministry of Human Resource Development has lowered its prestige and importance.

(2) The Centre should have a continuing and closer concern for education in the States. Re-introduction of the Indian Education Service (I.E.S.) will go a long way to achieve this.

(3) The Centre should provide adequate protection against the possible misuse of the education function. Democratic control should rest with the people and should be further strengthened. Education should not be allowed to propagate the ideology of any political party.

(4) The Centre should equalise educational opportunities all over the States and the whole country, which means giving more funds and encouragement to poorer areas.

(5) The Centre should collect and publish information on conditions and needs of different areas.

(6) The Centre should conduct co-operative research, coordinate and disseminate the findings and adopt means of implementing them.

(7) Some of the advisory bodies need to be raised to the statutory level. They should be made autonomous so that they become free from bureaucracy and red-tapism. They should include the teachers from the field and not only "big" people.

(8) Some more fields of education, such as pre-school education and teacher education, etc., should receive closer and more attention from the Centre and in general, it may be said that wherever the States are deficient the Centre must step in.

Some Advisory Bodies

***The Central Advisory Board of Education* (*CABE*) :** The CABE was first established in 1920. Its main function was to tender advice to the provincial governments. It was abolished in 1923 as a measure of economy. Later on, as a result of the recommendation of the Hartog Committee (1928), it was reviewed in 1935, and has been in existence ever since.

The resolution says "The Government of India feels that there was need for review and reform in the system of education, comprehensive examination of educational problems and the central government should play its part in educational reconstruction. The most valuable contribution towards the right development of education in India can come from a clearing house of ideas and information like the CABE.

The Functions of the CABE are:

(1) To advise on any educational question which may be referred to it by the Government of India or by any local government.

(2) To call for information and advice regarding educational development of special interest and value of India; to examine this information and evaluate it with recommendations to the Government of India and the local government.

These functions have been deliberately defined broadly so that the Board remains a live organisation endowed with incentive and growth. It should, however, be noted that the Board's recommendations are only advisory and not binding on the government.

Central Board of Secondary Education

The Central Board of Secondary Education was established to cater to the educational needs of those students who had to move from State to State due to their parent's transfer, etc. It has been making significant contribution towards raising the standard of education, specially secondary education, improvement of curricula, text-books, methods of teaching and evaluation.

In September 1971, it had 781 higher secondary schools, mostly Central Schools affiliated to it. The Board Conducts the All-India Higher Secondary Examination and the Higher Secondary Technical Examination. It also conducts the Matriculation and

Higher Secondary (Part I & II) Examinations for schools in Union Territories.

Besides conducting these examinations the other important activities of the Board are examination reform and orientation courses for teachers of affiliated schools. It has introduced physical education as an elective subject for the Higher Secondary Examination and job-oriented courses for its examinations. Work experience has also been introduced in its curriculum.

University Grants Commission (UGC) : As a result of the recommendation of the Sargent Report an advisors' committee was set up in 1945. Its function was to make recommendations for grants to be paid to the various universities. The Ministry of Education forwarded these recommendations to the Finance Ministry, which judged them for itself. Radhakrishnan University Commission (1949) recommended the establishment of a University Grants Commission with its own funds and this was done in 1953. The UGC was established "for the purpose of allocation and disbursement of grants to universities as well as for the purpose of coordination and maintenance of a statutory body by an Act of Parliament passed in 1956 (Act III of 1956).

Composition of the UGC : The UGC consists of nine members appointed by the Government of India. Of these, not more than three are from amongst the vice-chancellors of-universities, two are officers representing the Government of India and the remaining are from reputed educationists and persons of high academic distinctions. The Chairman is a non-official nominated by the Government.

Functions of the UGC : The functions of the UGC may be briefly stated as follows:

(1) Promoting and coordinating university education throughout the country.

(2) Determining and maintaining standards of teaching, examination and research in universities.

(3) Inquiring into the financial needs of the universities (and also colleges), to allocate and disburse grants out of its funds for the maintenance and development of the universities (and colleges) or for any other specific purposes, such as buildings, equipment, libraries, etc.

(4) Recommending to the universities (and colleges) measures for the improvement of standards and advise necessary action in that direction.

(5) Advising the Government of India or State Governments on the allocation of special grants out of their consolidated funds.

(6) Advising on the expansion of existing universities and establishment of new universities in the country.

Criticism : The UGC has been doing great service for the qualitative improvement of higher education. It has been able to introduce the three-year degree course, which is. a remarkable achievement. It has helped to bring, about improvement in university curricula, equipment of laboratories and libraries, pay and service conditions of university and college teachers. It has made efforts towards restrictive admission to universities and colleges, medium of instruction, examination reform and introduction of correspondence courses. It has encouraged research in the universities and colleges and by individuals serving and retired teachers.

The present activities of the UGC also include establishment of Centres of Advanced Study, running summer institutes and holding seminars and conferences, teachers' and students' services and welfare, scholarships and fellowships, book production, etc.

Among its recent achievements are raising the salaries of teachers, upgrading their basic qualifications for recruitment and experimentation on internal assessment and awarding grades instead of marks at the final examinations, establishing Academic staff colleges and National Education Testing service.

A very significant step in the direction of upgrading the quality of teacher of higher education has been introduction of the NET examination at the national level.

It is hoped that the Commission would be able to expand and improve its services as more and more funds are placed at its disposal.

National Council of Educational Research and Training (NCERT) : Historical Retrospect: Soon, after the publication of the

Report of the Secondary Education Commission (1953), the Government of India paid close attention to the improvement of school education. Education being a State subject, the Centre went about the task in cooperation with the States. The Central Institute of Education had already been established for the training of secondary teachers. From 1954 onwards a number of institutes were started, such as the Central Bureau of Text-Book Research (1954). Institute of Educational and Vocational Guidance (1954). All-India Council for Secondary Education, later converted into the Directorate of Extension Programmes for Secondary Education (1959). National Institute of Basic Education (1955). National Fundamental Education Centre (1956) and the National Institute of Audio-visual Education (1959).

In 1961, all these various institutes were brought together under an autonomous organisation, which enjoyed greater resources of personnel and expertise and larger freedom of operation. This organisation, established in September 1961 was named the National Council of Educational Research and Training (NCERT). The various institutes were put under one banner of the National Institute of Education (N.I.E.). In 1968-69 both the Council and the NIE were reorganised into their present form.

Composition of the NCERT : The council consists of the following members:

(1) President - The Minister of Education and Social Welfare.

(2) Chairman of the University Grants Commission (ex-officio).

(3) Secretary to the Ministry of Human Resource Development (ex-Officio).

(4) Four Vice-Chancellors of Universities, one from each zone, nominated by the Government of India.

(5) One representative of each State Government and Union Territory with a legislature, who shall be the Education Minister (or his representative), and in the case of Delhi, the Chief Executive Councillor (or his representative).

(6) All members of the Executive Committee not included in the above.

(7) Such other persons, not exceeding twelve, as the Government of India may, from time to time, nominate. Not less than four of these shall be school teachers.

There are one whole-time Director and a Joint-Director of the Council who look after the day-to-day administration.

There are two important Committees of the Council, viz., the Executive Committee and the Programme Advisory Committee.

Functions of the Council : The main functions of the NCERT are:

(1) To assist the Ministry of Human Resource Development in the formulation and implementation of its policies and programmes in the field of school education.

(2) To develop necessary research, experiments, pilot projects, advanced training and extension services.

(3) To maintain close liaison between the Central Ministry and the State Education Departments and Universities.

To discharge these functions the NCERT organises and undertakes educational studies, investigations and surveys, conducts pre-service and in-service training of an advanced level, organises extension services for institutions, disseminates improved educational techniques and practices, assists State Education Departments, universities and institutions, publishes books, periodicals and other educational literature and acts as a clearing house for ideas and information on all matters related to school education.

The activities and programmes of the council are carried out by the following Departments and Units of the National Institute of Education (NIE):

1. Department of Educational Psychology and Foundations of Education. (DEPFE)
2. Department of Pre-school and Elementary Education
3. Department of Education in Science and Mathematics (DESM)
4. Department of Education in Social Sciences and Humanities (DESSH)
5. Department of Teacher Education and Extension (DTEE)

6. Department of Educational Measurement and Evaluation (DEME)
7. Department of Computer Education and Technology Aids (DECTA)
8. Department of Educational Survey and Data Processing Unit (DESDP)
9. Division of Library Documentation and Information Services (DLD)
10. Publication Division (PD)
11. Department of Educational Research and Policy Perspectives (DERPP)
12. International Relations Division (IRD)
13. Department of Women's Studies (DWS)

Criticism : The NCERT has been doing commendable work in several areas of school education and has been successful in bringing about a lot of improvement. Among its outstanding achievements are in the fields of Science Education Curriculum and Textbooks. Teaching Aids and Examination Reforms. Some of the text-books produced by the Council are really very good, while others have not proved popular in the field. The Council should co-opt more-school teachers on the text-book and curriculum preparation boards to make its output more realistic and fruitful.

The Council is the most important national organisation for educational research and has done considerable and useful work. There is however need for greater stress on the development of basic tools for fundamental and functional research, an area in which India is very deficient. There is also need for coordinating the research being done in the country and to disseminate research findings. The Council has taken an important step in this direction by compiling and publishing the abstracts of degree and doctoral researches. It should also undertake training of advanced research workers.

The Council has launched integrated 4-year courses of teachers' training in its Regional Colleges. Recently a 2-year B.Ed, training programme has also been introduced. It may, however, be recommended that instead of diversification these colleges should concentrate on only a few intensive programmes.

The Council shows promise and much more will be achieved in coming years if it overcomes the limitations of finance and personnel. A possible solution is to associate more and more local persons in its programmes and activities.

State Government

Historical Retrospect : The State Government stated as units of educational administration with the appointment of Directors of Public Instruction and Inspectors to assist them. They mainly dealt with recognition and inspection of the schools and recommending grant-in-aid. However, the policy continued to be centralised. With Montford reforms education was transferred to the States in 1921. The I.E.S. was abolished. Education was put in charge of elected ministers responsible to the State legislatures.

Role of Government : After Independence the Indian Constitution made the States responsible for education at all stages with certain exceptions, such as the Central Universities at Banaras, Aligarh, Delhi and Shantiniketan. Institutions of scientific and technical education financed by the Central Government, institutions for professional and vocational education, higher institutions for scientific research and technology etc. Thus, education at all stages is a State responsibility, but the Constitution places the responsibility of coordination and maintenance of standards at higher levels on the Centre. Article 45 of the Constitution directs the States "to endeavour to provide, within a period of ten years from the commencement of this Constitution for free and compulsory education for all children until they complete the age of fourteen years."

In recent years there has been a rapidly growing trend of close cooperation between the Centre and the States. The Centre is in a position to give more and more financial help and so it secures their cooperation by appointment of a number of Central Councils and Committees, such as the Central Advisory Board, the All-India Council of Secondary Education (later converted into the Directorate of Extension Programmes for Secondary Education), the National Council of Educational Research and Training. On these bodies there are representatives of the States and the Centre and also some well-known educationists. Cooperation is also secured by exchanging views through seminars and conferences. However, in the present pattern the initiative for education and educational reform and reorganisation lies with the States.

State Administrative Machinery : The machinery for educational administration in the State is composed of the Department of Education headed by a Minister, who is responsible to the legislature and is appointed by the Chief Minister. In some States he is assisted by a State or a Deputy Minister. The Minister exercises his authority through the officers of the Department and other agencies like the universities, statutory boards, etc., and is assisted by the Education Secretary at the secretariat level and the Director of Education, who is the chief executive officer of the department. It may be known as follows:

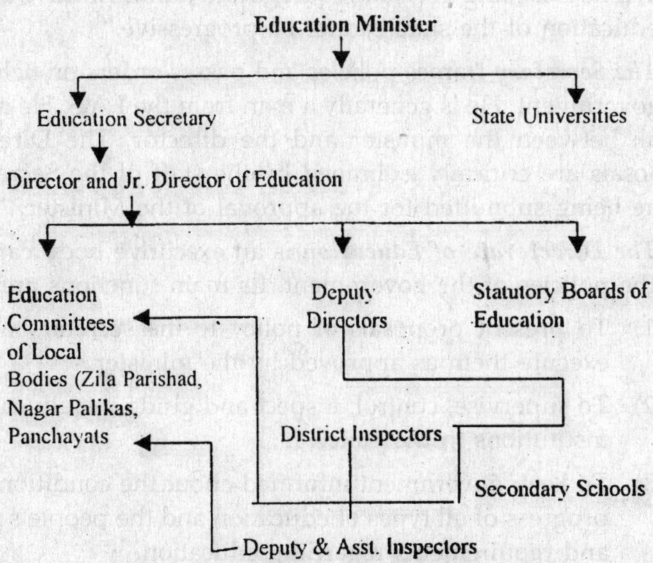

The functions of the Education Department are:

(1) Framing of policies, procedures, rules, regulations and determining standards.

(2) Inspection and evaluation to determine efficiency of operation.

(3) To run schools and colleges established by government and to control private institutions.

(4) To deal with matters regarding curricula and text-books.

(5) To coordinate educational programmes of the Stale in order to promote efficiency.

(6) To provide leadership-for planning and research.

(7) To provide consultative and information services.

The Minister is generally, a non-technical man with almost little experience of either education or administration. He has to lean heavily on the bureaucracy for guidance. He can make or mar the whole education system. "If he is a man of vision, courage and devotion to education, he can provide the leadership for the development of an educational programme in his state which will meet the needs of the individuals and of society..... On the other hand, if he is lacking in vision, courage and administrative ability, the education of the state cannot be progressive."

The Secretary frames policies and passes orders on behalf of the government. He is generally a man from the I.A.S. He acts as a link between the minister and the director. The Director's proposals are critically examined by the staff of the Secretariat before being submitted for the approval of the Minister.

The Directorate of Education is an executive body carrying out the policies of the government. Its main functions are:

(1) To present proposals of policy to the secretary and to execute them as approved by the minister.

(2) To supervise, control, inspect and guide the educational institutions in the State.

(3) To keep government informed about the conditions and progress of all types of education and the people's needs and requirements regarding education.

(4) To disburse funds as sanctioned by government.

(5) To provide expert advice both to the institutions and the secretariat.

The Director of Education is the highest officer of the directorate of education. Recently in some States a director has been appointed from the administrative services, but generally, he is a technical expert and chosen for his long teaching, inspecting and administrative experience in the department. As the highest executive he is responsible for the administration of education in the entire State. Assisted by a number of deputy and assistant directors he performs the following duties:

(1) To supervise the work of the government officials, inspectors, teachers of government institutions and to deal with their leave, transfer and discipline.

(2) To determine and disburse the grants-in-aid to the State Universities, Local Bodies, and the large number of Privately managed institutions.

(3) To supervise, control, inspect and guide the Private Institutions.

(4) To act as Chairman of the State Board of Secondary Education, an examining body, and to administer and exercise emergency powers in this respect. Some Boards of Secondary Education have a whole-time chairman who is not the Director.

(5) To act as a member of the syndicate/executive council of the State Universities.

(6) To frame policies and proposals and submit them to the secretary for the approval of the minister.

(7) To administer education throughout the State.

(8) To organise the training of primary and secondary teachers, where this is not done by the universities.

Inspectors: The function of inspection is carried on by the district inspectors (called District Education Officers in some States). They make a report to the director. The headmasters of schools are directly responsible to the inspector for administration and discipline. In government schools he supervises the work of headmasters. In non-government schools administration is carried on by their managing committees and the inspector merely assesses and recommends grants-in-aid. He has nothing to do with university education but in the field of primary education administered by district boards and municipal boards, he provides the inspecting staff, the deputy and sub-deputy inspectors whose work he supervises with leadership and guidance."

Criticism :

(1) The Central financial assistance is leading to the harmful tendency of "regimental uniformity". There is also "an increasing tendency towards centralisation in education in recent years..... the new plans of education in different states are based on the pattern suggested by the Centre." For example, we now have the 10+2 scheme on insistence of the central government.

(2) The minister is committed to the policies of the ailing political party. He is a non-technical man and therefore depends upon the secretariat, which is also manned by non-technical men. There is only a superficial efficiency. With the changes of ministers there is also a change of policy so that continuity is broken. The political ideology of the ruling party dominates educational policy. There is a lack of dispassionate treatment of educational matters on merit.

(3) The secretary is appointed from the administrative service. He lacks conceptual and technical skills, necessary insight, initiative and educational experience. He is with the department of education for a short period and may have to look after other departments of the government in addition to his educational duties. His staff is also non-technical and things are run by trial-and-error efforts.

(4) The Director's assignment of work is much too heavy. Though he is assisted by deputies, he is left with very little time for planning for progress and improvement. He is to work within the steel-frame of the budget. His proposal to the minister are routed through the secretariat, where they are pruned and cut-down beyond recognition. It has been often felt that the Director should have direct access to the minister. The Sargent Report says. "There can be no possible justification for interposing an officer without an expert knowledge of education between the director of public instruction and the minister of education to whom he should be directly responsible." The Secondary Education Commission too recommended, "where the Director himself is not the secretary of the department he

should have the status of a joint secretary and should have direct access to the minister."

(5) Like the Director of education, the inspector has to do much routine work, and even though he is a technical man he has little scope for initiating local plans. Secondary schools are in large number. Administration has to deal with managing committees. The government cannot have effective checks. Very often the plans and policies of the department are opposed by the managing committees. Under such conditions efficiency becomes a casualty.

(6) There is a growing tendency of political interference in educational matters. Local political pressure is rampant. There is also a lot of encroachment on the autonomy of the universities. Being dependent on government grants institutions are hardly free even in academic matters.

(7) More than half a century has elapsed since education was transferred to the States but they have failed to deliver the goods. "The States have also failed to show the educational leadership on which the development of the pupils depends."

Suggestions :

(1) There is need for a consistent educational policy, which is planned after careful thought, vigorously executed and critically evaluated. It should be applied continuously for a considerably long time before being altered.

(2) The policy should be free from the whims of political parties, including the ruling party. In fact, education should be free from governmental and political interference. "Education cannot depend upon the caprice of politicians."

(3) The Department of Education should be strengthened. To be capable of providing the right type of leadership, it should have an efficient and trained staff, adequate in quality and quantity. It should enjoy the confidence of the people and the educators, and freedom from political interference and bureaucracy. As recommended by the Secondary Education Commission the Director of education should have direct access to the minister.

(4) The Director of education and the inspector should be relieved of much of their routine work so that they can devote their attention to the real business of education-purposing, planning, organising, operating and evaluating.

(5) Most attention should be paid to and a large portion of the finances spent on the/improvement of teaching-learning in the schools.

(6) In general, we should agree with Moehlman (1951) that "The education responsibility of the State is to maintain and improve the education function, to remove education inequalities due to economic, social, moral, organisational and educational causes, to provide education leadership to improve the local operation of the education function by providing legal and financial means to assure an adequate education program."

Local Bodies

Historical Retrospect: In most countries of the world Local Bodies have been playing a very important role in providing educational facilities, specially in the field of primary education. It has been rightly said that democracy can be exercised best when self-government units are small. This was so in ancient India when every village was a republic. Later on the East India Company did not accept the responsibility of educating Indians. The events of 1857, however, changed the situation. The British planted in India educational practices prevailing in England and adopted the policy of non-intervention in education. Because of the awakening of political consciousness among educated Indians. Ripon was obliged to pass the Local Self-Government Act in 1883 and primary education was entrusted to Local Bodies- municipalities in urban and district boards in rural areas.

Due to the unsatisfactory state of affairs, gradually there developed a strong reaction against primary education being managed by local bodies. In 1929, the Hartog Committee opposed the practice, and even as late as 1944, the Sargent Report voiced its concern. However, arguments were advanced both in favour and against the practice. The delegation of authority leads to decentralisation and is, therefore, democratic, There is greater sense of participation and responsibility and prevention of wastage of funds. On the other hand, primary education is an important nation building activity, a source of wiping out mass illiteracy and ignorance, and so it should be handled by a strong governmental machinery. The local bodies have hardly enough resources and competence to bear the burden of universal primary education. Creation of powerful local bodies in the hands of uneducated and ill-equipped members fails to do justice to the important social activity of education.

Under the influence of strong opposition to delegation of powers to local bodies, a rethinking on the problem started and a Committee of the Central Advisory Board of Education recommended withdrawal of powers of inspection from the local bodies. The controversy was, however, set at rest when the Kher Committee of the CABE, in 1952, strongly recommended that "in the interest of mass education and in view of the Constitutional directive on universal, compulsory and free primary education, all types of local bodies should be made to shoulder responsibility for education." Thus, we find that after Independence the role of local bodies in primary education has become more and more active.

Role of the Bodies : The recommendations of the Kher Committee were not universally adopted by all the States. We find that there is no uniform pattern of administration. Even after the reorganisation of the States in 1956, in some parts of the country education is administered by the State Governments while in others responsibility for primary education has been entrusted to Local Bodies. Except Assam and Jammu and Kashmir, however, the major responsibility of primary education rests with the Local Bodies.

In most of the States, municipalities have the legal authority to administer primary education in their areas. In some States (Gujarat and Maharashtra) only the bigger municipalities are authorised to administer primary education and the smaller ones have to contribute their financial share without having any voice in the management. In some States (Uttar Pradesh) municipalities run secondary schools and colleges also.

In rural areas district boards (now called Zila Parishads are made responsible for administering primary education. Some of them run secondary schools also. In some States (Andhra Pradesh and Rajasthan) Panchayat Samities in Block areas and Zila Parishads in non-samiti areas administer primary education.

The educational functions of Local Bodies are:

(1) To organise and administer primary education in their areas.

(2) To implement the Five-year Plans for education.

(3) To provide and maintain accommodation, playgrounds and equipment for their schools.

(4) To enforce compulsory attendance under the prescribed rules and under the special directions of the State Government.

(5) To open new primary schools where needed.

(6) To conduct educational surveys and keep records.

(7) To carry on propaganda for the expansion of primary education.

(8) To recruit and exercise necessary powers over the staff of the schools.

Administrative Machinery : The municipalities and district boards have an Education Committee (or School Board) of elected members. These Committees are responsible for providing and looking after educational facilities in their areas. The budget is decided by the whole municipal or district board, but in a few cases the Education Committees act independently. Some Committees in larger area appoint administrative officers to look after administrative work. In smaller areas administrative work is entrusted to honorary non-officials.

Recruitment of staff is generally done through a selection committee on which the district education officer (inspector) also serves. The State Government is exclusively responsible for training of teachers, prescribing syllabi and preparing text-books and the Local Bodies have to follow them. The State Government gives grants-in-aid to Local Bodies. The district boards receive more generous grants than municipalities.

Inspection of primary schools, is the responsibility of the State and as carried out by the inspecting staff of the State Education Department. Some bigger municipalities (Greater Bombay, Uttar Pradesh, Delhi) appoint their own education officers and inspecting staff.

With the introduction of Panchayati Raj and the policy of democratic decentralisation, the Local Bodies have been playing an important part in the maintenance and improvement of primary education. They now have a three-tier system (two-tier in some States) of organisation (1) the village Panchayat at the village level. (2) Panchayat Samities at the Block level, and (3) Zila Parishads at the district level.

Criticism :

(1) The resources of local bodies for financing the programmes of primary education are very inadequate. The pay scales of teachers are poor and they are seldom paid regularly. This very much hampers progress.

(2) The administrative officers and staff are neither well-trained nor competent.

(3) The recruitment, transfer and discipline of teachers are unsatisfactory.

(4) There are pressure groups among the elected members, who, besides being uneducated or ill-educated, misuse the teachers' services for elections and other purposes. Due to this education of the children suffers.

Suggestions :

(1) Democratic decentralisation can be successful only when financial responsibility is centralised, that is, accepted by the State government and the Central government also shares the burden. Pay scales of teachers should be improved and their service conditions made attractive and satisfying.

(2) For better recruitment of teachers and administrative officers good selection committees of technical persons and experts should be set up and well-defined rules and practices established.

(3) The position of education officers of local bodies must be strengthened and members should be careful to see that discipline among teachers is not weakened.

(4) A uniform administrative pattern should be set up all over the country. Power should be delegated to a powerful local body exclusively set up for education and adequate finances should be placed at its disposal. Building and equipment should be improved. Administration of education should be brought closer to the people and their participation secured.

(5) Improvement of the programmes should include free textbooks, free transportation where necessary, uniforms and mid-day meals. Youth and community recreation centres and rural libraries should be established.

(6) Long-range planning for expansion and improvement of primary education should be undertaken and adhered to. Social education should also be entrusted to local bodies, while guidance, control, finance, and inspection should be the duty of the State.

Private Agencies

Historical Retrospect: Private, agencies have played a very important role, in education in India. In ancient and medieval times, educational institutions were wholly private. They received land and other grants from the rulers, but were free from their interference. The East India Company being a commercial organisation never accepted educational responsibility. The Christian missionaries, however, worked very diligently to spread educational activities in the country, though with the motive of conversion. Besides them, some British officials and non-officials established educational institutions, perhaps with the idea of encouraging private enterprise among Indians. A few Indians came forward to establish schools to impart English education. They had to face great odds, which they did with great moral courage. The growth of education continued to remain haphazard till the Wood's Despatch (1854) proposed to give government grants to schools and colleges if they satisfied certain conditions of the government.

The Indian Education Commission of 1882 surveyed the educational activities in the country and recommended that liberal grants should be paid to private agencies which were doing great service to the cause of education. During the period 1882 to 1902, hundreds of Indians created and satisfied public demand for more education and laid the foundation of national life in India. During the early part of twentieth century, education vastly expanded with improvement in both quality and quantity. But later on, during World War II (1939-45) private enterprise had to face great difficulties. The national movement gathered momentum and private enterprise fell from government favour.

After Independence the policy of grants-in-aid became more vigorous. The Government and private agencies have been working together in close cooperation. Private agencies have played a predominant role in all fields of education and at all stages from the primary to the university all over the country and have been specially active in the field of secondary education. There has been a very large expansion both in the number of schools and the students.

Administrative Machinery : Private agencies are registered bodies and have their own elected or otherwise appointed Managing Committees. They are required to fulfil certain minimum requirements for recognition by government to qualify to receive grants: They provide buildings- and equipment from their own resources and employ and control their staff in accordance with prescribed rules.

These private agencies are of several types. Schools and colleges are run by the Christian missionaries, well-established education societies and trusts like the Arya Samaj Ramakrishna Mission, Deccan Education Society, etc. There are smaller registered societies. Then there are the "public" schools providing good education without assistance from the government. Recently there has grown a large number of coaching institutions, which prepare private students to appear at various university and board examinations.

Criticism :

(1) It must be recognised that private enterprise has shown a lot of dynamism and vitality and has proved a valuable asset in the country's educational development. It has played a vital role, specially in rural areas.

(2) The financial condition of a large number of private agencies is not good. Their institutions have poor buildings and the teachers are underpaid.

(3) The majority of private schools lack originality and there is dull uniformity. "They submit to conditions that prevent independence and originality, and their proverbial paucity of funds has always prevented them to risk in such ventures of experimentation as would foster originality."

(4) There have crept many malpractices in some of these private institutions. Some of them charge high fees and capitation charges. There are also instances of irregular and underpayment to teachers with the result that standards are very unsatisfactory.

(5) The unrecognised private coaching institutes are doing great harm to the cause of education. They are generally one man shows with a predominantly profit-motive. Students and teachers alike are exploited to the maximum possible limit.

Suggestions :

(1) The government should come forward to regulate, control and more generously finance private enterprise so that it can make honest effort to share the educational burden of the state.

(2) Private enterprise should be encouraged to develop programmes that would suit the special requirements of their neighbourhood.

(3) It is high time that some measures are adopted to regulate the unrecognised coaching institutes. Their standards must be improved and malpractices curbed. The Delhi Administration was seriously considering to enact some law in this regard and it would not be too early.

(4) There should be a democratic control of education, which means that it should be administered by a partnership of parents, teachers and private organisations with the sole objective of fulfilling the educational functions and purposes.

In National Capital

Historical Retrospect : Originally Delhi was a district of Punjab. In 1912, it was declared a province and in 1952 it became a Part C State with a popular government. On 1st November 1956, It was given the status of a Union Territory. The Municipal Corporation was established on 7th April 1958. It was given the function of running pre-primary and basic education, medical, health, water supply, electricity, etc. Since then three local bodies, the Municipal Corporation, New Delhi, Municipal Committee and Delhi Cantonment Board have been working in Delhi.

The Education Department was established in 1916 under a Superintendent of Education. The post was upgraded and a Director of Education, was appointed in 1949, and he worked as ex-officio secretary of Education to the Union Territory of Delhi. The Director of Education is assisted by a number of Deputy and Assistant Directors and Inspectors of Schools.

Local Bodies: There are three local bodies in Delhi:

The Municipal Corporation has an Education Committee and a whole-time Education Officer. He is assisted by a deputy inspectors of schools also, and a number of assistant education officers. The entire area of Delhi is divided into zones for administrative purposes.

The New Delhi Municipal Committee has also an Education Committee and an Education Officer.

The Delhi Cantonment Board has a very small area. Its schools are administered by the Secretary of the Board.

The Director of Education is associated with all the three above mentioned local bodies.

Primary schools are mainly controlled and run by the corporation.

Private enterprize has been playing a prominent role in Delhi. There are a number of public schools which are recognized but not aided; and a few English Medium Schools prepare students for the Cambridge certificate examination also.

Criticism:

(1) The government is giving considerable grant. Its expenditure is steadily rising. More and more facilities are being provided, yet much remains to be done.

(2) Like all other parts of the country, many schools have no permanent buildings. Some are run in tents and temporary shelters, causing great hardships and frequent breaks during rains and winter. Many of them are poorly equipped. It is strange that private bodies are required to maintain certain minimum standards which the government and corporation do not hesitate to violate. As a consequence standards suffer.

(3) Government domination leads to uniformity and rigidity. There is little experimentations and less research and no application of research findings.

Suggestions:

(1) The improvement of buildings and equipment is an urgent necessity.

(2) There is also much need for improvement of instruction, teaching-learning programmes and techniques, supervision and inspection, experimentation and research.

(3) Teacher education for primary teachers needs a fresh look.

(4) Delhi serves as a model to the whole country. It has, therefore, special responsibility towards setting sound practices. The newly introduced 10+2 scheme requires careful and concerted action. If it is not accompanied by a new outlook and vigorous enthusiasm, it is likely to do more harm than good.

4

Basic Education

If one were to go to sleep in 1947 in India and wake up in 2001, he would not be able to recognize the educational scenario of India. At the time of independence the educational scene was very dismal. The British government designed the educational system in India only to produce clerks and middle level functionaries to support and sustain their own rule. India which gave scripts and literature to half of the world in ancient times remained a poor country with illiterate population. The percentage of literacy at that time was only 14.0 and the total expenditure on education was only 57 crores of rupees. In the age group 6-11 only one child out of every three was on the school register while in the age group 11-14 one child out of every eleven was enrolled in the school. Rural population was thoroughly neglected and girls' education was only in name. It was with this scenario that we in India began our independence with high level of illiteracy and poor standards of education.

During the past fifty years the educational system in India has expanded beyond recognition. Today, the number of primary schools in India is more than six lakhs as against one and a half lakh in 1947. About 14 per cent of children in the age group 6-11 are served by primary schools located within a radius of one killometre from the house of the child. Where the child is unable to go to school, the school goes to the child in the form of a non-formal education center. There are more than three lakh such centers in the country. Girls' education is free throughout the whole country upto class XII. The rate of literacy has gone up from 14 to 62.3 in 2001.

Yet, in spite of these achievements we are faced with a number of challenges and have miles to go before our targets are achieved. Eradication of illiteracy leading to total literacy is one of the most intricate problems which is alluding all our efforts. Universalization of elementary education to which we are constitutionally committed under article-45 and which was to have been achieved by I960 is still miles away from our reach. While most recent surveys indicate that nearly 70 per cent children in the age group 6-14 are attending schools, the painful fact is that while the net enrolment rate at the primary stage continues to be 70 per cent, it has dipped to a shockingly lower 40-50 per cent at the upper primary level. According to 1991 census the number of illiterates in the country was 48.22 crores out of which 27.47 were females.

Universalization of Education

This is an approach to achieve total literacy in India which emphasizes that all children in the age group 6-14 must be brought to schools. For achieving this objective there must be provision of schooling facilities for all children, i.e., there must be a school within an easy reach of every child This means universalization of schooling facilities which should be ensured by the government. Another aspect of this is universalization of enrolment. This requires enrolling every child of age 6+ in class -1. This also implies restricting admission of a child of higher age group to class-1. Again, the scheme of universalization of elementary education requires that every child who is admitted to class-1 should continue upto the last stage of primary education. This is the problem of retention and checking drop-outs in the middle and ensure permanent literacy. Thus, universalization of elementary education is a three-pronged strategy : (i) universal enrolment, (ii) universal retention, and (iii) universal provision for schooling. In fact the task of universal education begins when children are enrolled in class-I. It is completed only when they are successfully retained till they complete class VIII.

The Problems

It is a fact that universalization of elementary education which was to be achieved by 1960 is our cherished goal even in 2002. Only about 50 per cent of all children and 40 per cent of girls in the age group 6-14 attend schools. The rest either do not go to the schools at all or drop out before they reach class V. This is a serious problem and should be treated as a crucial area for national development. The most challenging problems of universalization are:

Wastage: Wastage in elementary education is generally understood to connote the premature withdrawal of a child from the school before completing the last grade of the stage, i.e., grade VII or VIII. Wastage is also known as 'retardation' or 'grade repetition'. It is also defined as the retention of a pupil in a grade for more than one year due to unsatisfactory progress. A ňumber of studies have been conducted to find out the incidence of wastage and stagnation. The figures vary from state to state, But the general picture reveals that wastage is very high at the lower primary stage- about 56 per cent for boys and 62 per cent in case of girls. At the higher primary stage it is much less about 24 per cent for boys and 34 per cent for girls. It is also reported that wastage is decreasing consistently although at a slow rate. Reduction of wastage and stagnation in class I is the most important element. There are a number of reasons of this stagnation and wastage. Stagnation means repetition of class by the student while wastage means drop-out, i.e., leaving the school before completing the primary courses.

The main problems of universalization of elementary education are (i) how to ensure cent per cent enrolment in grade-I, and (ii) how to check stagnation and wastage. The various factors that stand in the way of solving these problems are:

1. Uneven spread of education.
2. Low enrolment of girls.

3. Low enrolment of the scheduled caste, schedule tribes and backward sections of the society.
4. Apathy and poverty of the parents.
5. Lack of suitable reading and writing material for children.
6. Lack of qualified teachers.
7. Frequent transfer of teachers.
8. Lack of effective inspection and academic, guidance by the inspecting staff.
9. Failure to enforce compulsory attendance.
10. Lack of a suitable admission policy.
11. Conservative attitude of parents towards co-education.
12. Inadequate building facilities for schools.
13. Financial insufficiency.
14. Population explosion.

The Education Commission (1964-66) gave the following reasons of large stagnation and wastage in class I :

1. Heterogeneity of the age composition of students. It means that children of different ages varying from 5 to 12 + are admitted while their age in case of all admitted to class I should be 6+ only.
2. The practice in some states is of making fresh admissions throughout the year.
3. Irregularity of attendance.
4. Lack of educational equipment in the school.
5. Over-crowded classes
6. Unsuitable curricula
7. Inability of the teachers to use play-way techniques which can assist in initiating the children pleasantly to school life.
8. A wrong system of examinations.

The commission also suggested remedy for some of these defects as follows:

1. The examination at the end of class I should be abolished.
2. Adoption of play-way method of teaching in class I.

Causes of Stagnation

The Commission divided these causes into three categories-educational, economic and social. The Commission observed that 30 per cent of wastage was due to educational factors such as : existence of incomplete schools which do not teach the full courses, dull character of most of the schools and their poor capacity to attract students and retain them, absence of ancillary services like school meals and school health services and failure of the parent or the child to see the advantage of attendance of school. The social factors which operate mainly in the case of girls play a minor role. They include betrothal or marriage and opposition to sending grown up girls to school, especially to mixed school or school without a woman teacher.

The Commission observed that 65 per cent of the wastage is due to poverty. After the age of 9 or 10 the child becomes an economic asset because he can work at home. This is specially true in case of girls who have to assist the over-worked mother at home. The child is, then, withdrawn from the school and he becomes a "wastage" case. The solution to this problem lay in the general economic improvement. Another solution may be part-time education.

Problem of Enrolment

The Education Commission (1964-66) had estimated that after 1980-81 the enrolment at lower primary stage would decline due to anticipated effect of the fall in the birth rate and this decline was predicted to continue for a few more years. Then, it could be possible to concentrate resources to a greater extent on the development of higher primary stage. This did happen by 1985-86. But, the overall enrolment position could not be found to be satisfactory despite the apparent achievement in terms of gross enrolment as was observed in the Challenge of Education (p. 34).

Universalization of enrolment is still a big problem. For various reasons the number of non-enrolled children at the primary stage (Classes I to V) consists of children from the weaker sections of the society, such as scheduled castes, scheduled tribes, agricultural landless labourers and urban slum dwellers. Two-thirds of non-enrolled children are girls. Three-fourth of the non-enrolled children are in nine educationally backward states, namely. Andhra Pradesh, Assam, Bihar, Jammu and Kashmir, Madhya Pradesh, Orissa, Rajasthan, Uttar Pradesh and West Bengal. Even in advanced states low enrolments were found in respect of girls, scheduled castes and scheduled tribes. In certain states very low enrolments of girls had become a problem. The reasons of this state of affairs have already been discussed.

Steps Taken

Ministry of Education, government of India had taken special measures for checking wastage and stagnation and for increasing enrolments. These are:

Assistance for Non-formal Education: Run on 50-50 basis the entire administrative and academic expenditure is reimbursed by the center. The expenditure on non-formal centers is shared on 3: 5 ratio, i.e. for every three centers funded by the center, the cost of 5 centers is borne out of the state budget. Financial assistance is also given to voluntary agencies in the nine educationally backward states for running non-formal educational centers. Grant is also given to any academic organization/institution in any state/union territory run by the government or under private auspices for experimental and innovative projects with replicable potential.

Paper Assistance for Non-formal Education: Under Central Commodity Assistance the central government gives to all states including union territories paper for use in the production of textbooks and instructional materials for non-formal education for elementary age group children. The paper is purchased by the Government of India with the cash assistance given by the Swedish Government.

Early Childhood Education: By way of broad basing universalization of elementary education, a programme of early childhood education has also been started. These pre-school programmes aim at enabling out of school children to attend schools, thus minimizing the non-enrolment of children. The central government gives grant to voluntary organizations for running such centers.

Education of the Disabled: Programmes for the education of nine groups of handicapped children have also been introduced as these children constitute a substantial section of non-enrolled population of children.

Qualitative Improvement: Programmes of qualitative improvement of elementary education have been started in the states under the central government initiative. Under this scheme innovative projects have been in operation to improve the school curriculum. These programmes are being assisted by the UNICEF and are implemented in conjunction with the states and the Union Territories. These projects include various kinds of activities such as (i) nutrition, health education and environmental sanitation. (2) curriculum renewal. (3) Community education and participation. (4) comprehensive access to primary education, (5) early childhood education, (6) non-formal education programmes for women and girls.

Launched as a pilot project in 1976, the project on Nutrition, Health Education and Environment Sanitation was implemented till 1980. Curricular material on nutrition, health and sanitation habits for primary schools has been developed. It is intended to reach the community through teachers and children in regard to these aspects of elementary education.

Primary education curriculum renewal aims at a qualitative adjustment of the curriculum to the lifestyles of the children and to the socio-economic opportunities available in the areas of the project schools. Developmental Activities in Community Education Project launched along with Primary Education Curriculum Renewal aims at developing non-formal educational programmes for various target groups particularly for out of school children and adults so that the educational activities could meet the needs of those who are partly or totally deprived of any education. Comprehensive Access to Primary Education (CAPE) had been taken up for implementation in 29 states with a view to decentralizing the curriculum according to the needs and life situations, of out of school children. Under the project relevance based learning material was developed which may be used in the network of non-formal learning centers. Early childhood education project aims at developing new capacity for the training of pre-school educators, extension of research and developing activities and development of model pre-school centers. Non-formal Education Programmes for Women aims, among other activities, at introducing a substantial component of maternity and child care training in the programmes of adult education.

5

SOCIAL EDUCATION

In the late seventies, the Government at the Union level attempted major policy changes in some spheres of Public Policy except perhaps in foreign policy. In pursuance of its election manifesto, a radical re-alignment of priorities was attempted within the education. For the first time since independence, a National policy to educate illiterate adults was formulated to educate an estimated 100 million in the age group of 15-35 years. The target was fixed as 1983-84. The commitment of the government to adult education is reflected in Policy Statement on 'National Adult Education Programme' issued in 1978. It says "exclusion of a vast majority of the people from the process of education is a most disturbing aspect of educational and social planning. This has been uppermost in the consideration of the present government ever since it assumed office in March 1977".

Recognising the role of primary education in checking illiteracy, the policy statement says that "while determined efforts must be made to universalise elementary education up to the age of 14 years, educational facilities must be extended to adult population to remedy their educational deprivation and to enable them to develop their potentiality. Indeed, universalisation of elementary education and of adult literacy are mutually dependent".

Further, the policy statement says that "the government have resolved to wage a clearly conceived well planned and relentless struggle against illiteracy to enable masses to play an active role in social and cultural change".

Adult Education policy, thus, has been visualised as a major policy input to bring radical socio-economic and political changes. The report of the working group on adult education further confirms the government's intention on role of adult education as a 'change agent' when it says that : "Adult Education, looked upon as a method of human resource development, including literacy, functional development and creation of awareness among the poor regarding their inherent power to determine their destinies, should become the method in the new development process. It can contribute to the new development strategy in three significant ways : firstly, by making a substantial part of the work-force literate and better skilled ; secondly, by involvement of people in various developmental programmes which would make it possible to achieve optimum potential and minimize wastage ; and thirdly, by creation of awareness among the poor regarding the laws and policies of government, whereby, it would be possible to implement the strategy of re-distributive justice".

Touching on the various aspects of the problem of illiteracy, the policy statement clearly stated that "a massive programme should be launched to cover the vast segment of population in the 15-35 age group as early as possible". The planners of this programme dwelt at length on the organizational aspects of the National Adult Education Programme.

The role of non-governmental and semi-government agencies in the implementation of this programme was particularly recognised.

In fact, the policy document makes it very clear that "Adult Education must cease to be a concern only of the educational authority. It should be an indispensable input in all (major) sectors of development, particularly where participation of the beneficiaries is crucial to the fulfillment of development objectives".' Further it was stated that "A pre-requisite of an adult education movement is that all agencies; government, voluntary, private and public sector industry, institutes of formal education should lend strength to it". Thus, it can be seen that the policy planners rightly perceived the importance of non-governmental agencies (popularly known as NGO's) in the implementation of qualitative Public Policy like adult education.

A unique feature of the National Adult Education Programme is the special place given to voluntary agencies. The policy statement emphatically stated that "voluntary agencies have a special role to play and necessary steps shall have to be taken to secure their full involvement".

Thus the goal liquidating illiteracy in the country through a National Adult Education Programme is being planned and this programme was launched in 1978 throughout the country on Mahatma Gandhi's birth anniversary. It was planned to cover 100 million illiterates in the 15-35 age group within five years.

Apex Body

It may be recalled that the National Adult Education Programme was started as a result of the initiative taken by the then Union Government which was elected to power in late 70's. The preliminary work relating to the programme began with the establishment of a National Board of Adult Education in 1977. The Chairman of the Board was Shri Morarji Desai who was the Prime Minister then. The composition of the board includes some ministers of Central Government, a Minister dealing with adult education from each of the regions of the country, heads of organizations such as University Grants Commission, Central Social Welfare Board, Khadi and Village Industries Corporation, Federation of Indian Chambers of Commerce and Industry, Indian Adult Education Association and a host of other non-officials and field workers.

The National Board of Adult Education has set up five committees to attend to specific tasks relating to adult education programme. These were :

1. The Committee on Preparatory action.
2. The Committee on Motivation.
3. Committee on Voluntary Agencies.

4. Committee on Post-literacy and follow-up.

5. Committee on Evaluation.

It was stated in one of the publications of the Ministry of Education and Social Welfare that "all important decisions taken by various committees are generally endorsed by the National Board of Adult Education".

The overall responsibility for the administration of the national adult education grogramme rests with the Ministry of Education (now rechristened as Ministry of Human Resource Development). It provides secretariat to the National Board of Adult Education. The Ministry also deals with the various inter-ministerial matters and is charged with the responsibility of overseeing the implementation of National Adult Education Programmes in various states. The schemes of assistance to voluntary agencies and Shramik Vidyapeeths under the Ministry directly sanctions grants and is thus administered by the Central Ministry.

The organisational chart drawn here gives a picture of the administrative framework of the National Adult Education Programme.

As can be observed from the chart, the programme is being planned to be implemented through a variety of governmental, semi-governmental and non-governmental agencies.

The administrative structure for the programme extends from the central to the field level (i.e. Adult Education Centre). At the Central level, as has already been discussed, the Ministry of Education and the Central Directorate of Adult Education are the overall in-charge of the programme management. The Ministry and the Directorate have a special responsibility for involvement of various organizations like voluntary agencies universities and colleges. The specific functions of the Directorate include: (a) arrangement of training programmes; (b) production of teaching/learning material; and (c) evaluation. These two agencies are also charged with the responsibility of involving other developmental ministries like Agriculture Rural development and other autonomous agencies in the programme. In 1987, the programme has been re-designated as National Literacy Mission and target year had been put off to the year 2020.

At the state level, the State Board of Adult Education (S B A E) is regarded as an apex body for entire state. It is usually chaired by the State's Chief Minister or the Education Minister. The main functions of the Board are: (a) to provide policy guidelines; (b) creating a favourable environment; and (c) reviewing the progress of the programme.

A Steering Committee to aid and advise the state board of Adult Education is also created with such functions like working out implementation strategies like location of centres, target of coverage as well as co-ordination of the programme besides involving other developmental departments. Further, this agency is also expected to take steps to involve government, semi-governmental and voluntary agencies and the implementation. Monitoring of the progress of the programme is yet another task entrusted to the Steering Committee.

The government's determination to give a place of precedence to Voluntary Agencies was reflected in the terms of reference of the Working Group on Adult Education for Medium Term Plan (1978-83). One of the term of reference to this committee was "to apportion the areas of responsibility among the centre, states and voluntary agencies."

Thus, the policy makers envisaged almost a primary role to voluntary agencies after the State Government's in the implementation of National Adult Education Programme. Delineating on implementation agencies, the 'Outline on National Adult Education Programme' states that "the programme which gives importance to flexibility and diversity in organization as well as its content can be best implemented through voluntary agencies." Noting that the involvement of voluntary agencies is not much then, the policy planners of National Adult Education Programme recommended several steps for increasing their participation in National Adult Education Programme which include: (1) to involve all voluntary agencies working at present in the field of adult education or having the potentiality to do so; and (2) to create circumstances for emergence of new agencies, particularly in areas where such agencies are few. Further, the programme planners of N A E P visualised partnership role to voluntary agencies along with the State Governments and recommended the association of the voluntary agencies at all decision making levels particularly in matters which affect the work of these agencies, like the procedures for applying grants.

The report of working group on Adult Education appointed for medium term plan 1978-83 also identified the areas where voluntary agencies' participation was relevant and necessary. The report says that "these agencies should organise field adult education programmes, including post-literacy and follow-up programmes . . . resource development particularly training, production of teaching and learning materials and evaluation." The report further says that "the all India voluntary organizations should be encouraged to organize orientation programmes for other voluntary agencies." Commenting on the rigid procedures in government which may drive away the enthusiastic agencies from the programme, the working group recommended that "the government must also replace the mechanism which obstruct involvement of the voluntary agencies by enabling mechanisms." However, the group struck a note of caution regarding the selection of voluntary agencies in the implementation of N A E P and recommended that only those agencies should he selected for financial assistance which have potentiality to implement the programme.

The functional agency of the State Government for implementation of National Adult Education Programme is the Directorate of Adult Education, with specific tasks such as: (1) preparation of plans; (2) encouraging voluntary agencies to participate; (3) direction and overall supervision of government programmes; (4) overseeing and co-ordination of programmes taken up by various agencies other than the government; (5) selection and placement of personnel; and (6) monitoring and evaluation of the programme.

The next important agency in the Nation Adult Educational Programme is the State Resources Centre which is entrusted with such essential functions as: (1) preparation of teaching/ learning material; (2) organization of seminars; (3) development of methodological guidelines for curriculum preparation; and (4) training support to the programme, including postliteracy programmes, evaluation, research and publications.

Local Level

At the district level, the major responsibility for the implementation of National Adult Education Programme is vested with the District Collector. He/She occupies this position as the Chairman of District adult education board/committee. The government projects are expected to be supervised by the District Collector who would organize, co-ordinate and supervise the implementation of National Adult Education Programme through all agencies—governmental, voluntary and other agencies at the district level. The Collector is assisted by the District Adult Education Officer, now styled as Dy. Director of Adult Education in Andhra Pradesh. The District Adult Education Officer/Deputy Director of Adult Education acts as member secretary of the District Adult Education Committee/Board which first of all scrutinises the proposals for starting Adult Education Programme in the district. All the government project officers and some representatives of voluntary agencies, Universities, Nehru Yuvak Kendras are members of this committee. The committee is also charged with an important responsibility of processing the applications of voluntary agencies for financial assistance and also to assess progress of their work periodically. Besides, the district adult education committee also monitors and evaluates the work of all agencies in their jurisdiction.

Implementation of Scheme

A key unit for planning and implementation of national adult education programme is a project which usually consists of about 300 adult education centres. It is headed by a Project Officer. He/She is assisted by an Assistant Project Officer. In Andhra Pradesh, the geographical area of a project generally is co-terminus with that of a block. (Block has been further divided into Mandals recently). A project in National Adult Education Programme framework is visualised as an autonomous unit with Project Officer vested with powers to run administration, to manage finances, appointment and training of instructors and supervisors (which was since passed on to State Resources Centre:) taking steps to prepare the teaching/learning materials and finally organize post-literacy and other follow up activities.

For every 30 Adult Education Centres in a project, a supervisor is appointed who is expected to assist the Project Officer in resource development particularly in training instructors. Besides these functions, the supervisors discharge such varied functions like liaison with development functionaries, Mahila Mandals, ensuring regular supply of teaching/learning materials and payment of honorarium to instructor, and in organizing post literacy operations.

At the Centre

The critical unit of the administration in the organisational framework of National Adult Education Programme is the adult education centre under the charge of an instructor. The instructor's main functions, besides teaching, are: (a) Survey; (b) ensuring cooperation with village level developmental functionaries; (c) establishment of rapport with village elites and sending periodical reports about the progress of the programme.

Thus, it can be seen that a vast administrative machinery at various levels was created to Implement National Adult Education Programme. The National Board of Adult Education, The State Boards, Steering Committees, the Project Level Committees are expected to function as Co-ordinating bodies.

Role of Instructions

The policy planners of National Adult Education Programme have identified six categories of people as the, 'instructional cadre'. They include: (1) The School teachers; (2) Students; (3)Village youths; (4) Ex-serviceman and other retired personnel; (5) Field level grovernment and other functionaries and (6) Voluntary social workers.

School teachers in particular were regarded as the catchment area to take up the job of instruction in adult education centres. The students, as part of the National Service Scheme activities, were marked as another source.

The policy planners also gave a place to the village youth with some educational background in running the adult education centres. With an expectation that the retired people would be free and would accept a job which would yield a supplemental income to them, ex-servicemen and retired persons are identified as one of the sources for the teaching part of the programme. The village level workers and Gram Sevikas and voluntary social workers are yet another category who were identified for the job of instructors.

Development of Sources

The conceptual position spelt out in the policy statement implies creation and development of a resource base for National Adult Education Programme, the priority being given to diversified and need based learning material. The National Resource group consists of such agencies like the Central Directorate of Adult Education, various other agencies of Central Government and National level voluntary agencies.

The next important unit in resource development is the State Resources Centres (SRC's) which in co-operation with the National Resource Group and by continuous interaction with the field, are expected to attend to the task of resource development. Some of the important functions of the SRC's include: (a) development of competence in curriculum planning and development; (b) preparation of diversified teaching/ learning material to suit the learners' needs ; and (c) organization of training programmes to key level functionaries.

Fiscal Aspects

An amount of Rs. 200 crores had been allocated to this programme in the draft sixth five year plan (1978-83)21 by the then Janata Government. To cover 65 million adult illiterates, the cost was estimated at about Rs. 686 crores. The following table gives the details of the year wise expenditure outlay for N A E P from 1978-1983. Recently, the Union government announced that a 'National Literacy Mission' (NLM) to educate about 80 million adult illiterates would be implemented from 1987-88. The cost of the programme was stated to be Rs. 550 crores. It has been calculated then that the cost for 'educating' an adult illiterate would be Rs. 60 per year. Since the programme planners expected that one third of the participants would dropout the cost per learner was worked out as Rs. 90/-.

It was also expected that some funds would be available in the form of contributions and the final cost per learner was put at Rs. 80/-. This estimate, however, does not include expenditure on administrative structure and other activities connected with the programme.

The Structure

An impressive administrative structure seemed to have been provided at national, state and district levels to implement the N A E P. A number of state governments have created separate directorate of Adult Education. The State government send their proposals to the Ministry for starting projects. The Central Directorate is also associated in scrutinising such proposals. A set of guidelines were formulated which facilitate easy scrutiny of the proposals. Projects sponsored and entirely funded by the Central Government are known as Rural Functional Literacy Programme's (R F L P), projects funded by states are known as 'State Adult Eduction Programme's (S A E P's). The Central Ministry of Education directly sanctions the grants to voluntary agencies for running adult education programme. The State Governments are expected to be informed about the sanction of grants sanctioned to voluntary agencies by the Government of India and the state directorates are supposed to supervise the implementation by the voluntary agencies. However, like in any programme, we notice snags in the organisational design. In the earlier years of the programme some voluntary agencies got the financial sanction bypassing the State Governments, the Directorates of Adult Education and District Adult Education Committees using the political linkages they had with the power structure at the union level. Such situations gave rise to infiltration of undesirable elements into the programme. Monitoring of N A E P is stated as an important component of programme management. Elaborate procedures have been evolved to monitor the progress.

It was stated in one of the handouts, released by the Central Directorate of Adult Education, that qualitative reporting is desirable rather than reporting of mere quantitative data. One of the aspects of the reporting procedure is a column relating to the achievement of learners in terms of the main objectives of the programme viz., literacy, functionality and social awareness. However, except in the year 1979-80 we do not find it in the annual report brought out by either the Ministry of Education or the Central Directorate of Adult Education in the subsequent years.

The States are not coming forward to take up the programme on the scale expected. For the last five years, the Central Government's share" is very much higher compared with the other agencies.

Coming to the personnel policies, most of the staff of State Directorates are brought on deputation. The discussions with some officials revealed that the staff lacked the required commitment that is so necessary for the success of the programme. The visits by them to the 'Centres' either under the R F L P, or S A E P or by Voluntary Agencies is routine and their reactions to the problems is passive. Thus, the personnel policy with regard to the State Directorates warrants reconsideration.

While about twelve Deputy Directors at the rate of one for every two districts are required for effective supervision of the programme, there are about four or five Deputy Directors which indicates absence of commitment on the part of the State of Andhra Pradesh. The supervisory recruitment policy was marked by ad-hocism and short-sightedness. It is to be noticed that there is a lot of gap between what policy planners visualised and what is actually happening now in the States. The point is that since the over-all management of both centrally sponsored and other agencies programmes rests with the State Governments, the Education

Department of the State and the Directorate of Adult Education needs to be properly equipped in terms of staff and other requirements.

Coming to the District level administrative framework, the much burdened District Collector is further loaded with the Chairmanship of the District Adult Education Committee in which besides District Education Officer and Deputy Director of Adult Education the voluntary agencies participating in the programme, are also members. Most of the District level Education Committees are inactive for one reason or the other. Curiously enough, the Andhra Pradesh State Government made the District Education Officer the Convenor of the District Adult Education Committee, while the field representative of the Directorate of Adult Education is just a member. In this superior subordinate power relationship sometimes a junior District Educational Officer may act as a boss to the senior Deputy Director of Adult Education. The power conflict between them may have an adverse effect on the effectiveness of the programme.

As already pointed out, the National Board of Adult Education (N B A E) is not meeting regularly to give a higher and necessary policy direction. This has sometimes created vacuum in policy making. Even the meetings of State Boards of Adult Education and the State level Steering Committees are not held regularly as they are expected to. With the result, a clearly conceived policy on Adult Education is suffering from ad-hocism. The progress of the programme in terms of number of adult education centres opened from 1979-80 to 1983-84 for whole country can be gleaned from Table.

Data in Table presents the progress in terms of number of adult education centres opened and functioning in the country from 1979-80 to 1983-84. Reporting procedures seemed to have been modified since 1984-85. It was given to understand that the monitoring of the progress gradually became ineffective. The central directorate of adult education is not supplied information by its counterparts in the states. We only find number of projects (each project consists of 300 ABC's) sanctioned by the Union Government. That is the reason why data is not up to date.

Total Number of Adult Education Centres Opened

Sl. No.	*Name of Scheme*	*1979-80*	*1980-81*	*1981-82*	*1982-83*	*1983-84*
1.	Rural Functional	28,996	37,643	48,369	63,602	99,574
	Literacy Programme	(35.56)	(41.44)	(52.55)	(49.55)	(59.01)
2.	State Adult Education	19,644	38,178	37,352	59,840	59.015
	Programme	(24.1)	(41.72)	(40.58)	(46.62)	(34.97)
3.	Voluntary Agencies	19,029	11,293	339	822	5,873
		(23.34)	(12.34)	(36)	(64)	(3.48)
4.	Nehru Yuvak Kendras	7,129	1,514	4,884	1,519	527
		(8.74)	(1.65)	(5.31)	(1.1835)	(0.3)
5.	Universities & Colleges	3,684	2,340	585	899	644
		(3.91)	(2.56)	(.64)	(.69)	(0.381)
6.	Others	3,049	542	516	1,662	0837
		(3.74)	(.59)	(.50)	(1.3)	(1.83)
	Total	81,531	91,510	92,045	1,28,344	1,68,720

From the table, it will be clear that the majority of centres are run under centrally sponsored functional literacy projects followed by the States. Contrary to the popular expectations and policy statements, the role of voluntary agencies in the programme appears to be declining. This may be due to the mounting criticism against the participation of voluntary sector as it was alleged in Parliament and Press that some agencies are diverting funds earmarked for adult education to 'other' purposes. The Committee headed by Prof. D.S. Kothari appointed to review the National Adult Education Policy, however, gave a clean chit to voluntary agencies.

The role of Nehru Yuvak Kendras, Universities & Colleges and others also shows a decline. National Adult Education Policy appears to be almost under an eclipse for two years i.e., between 1980-81 and 81-82. The report of the review Committee on National Adult Education Policy had been withheld. The whole programme was in a state of suspended animation till 1982.

The New Education Policy—1986 mentions continuing priority to adult education. The document on 'Programme of Action' too delineates on various ways and means to stir activity on the adult education front. In 1987, the Union Government announced a

National Literacy Mission to educate about 80 million adult illiterates in the age group of 15-35 years by 1995. Thirty million are proposed to be brought under the programme by 1990. It should be remembered that this is the second time the Government changed the target year.

Changes in the institutional framework are on cards. The Union Directorate of Adult Education is proposed to be converted into a National Resource Centre. A high power board seems to be in the offing to give a new thrust to the programme.

The process of implementation of National Adult Education Programme is attempted in the next chapter starting with an analysis of the instructional cadre.

6

ROLE OF TEACHERS

The institutional framework of the National Adult Educational Programme as visualised by policy makers has already been described. The functions of each administrative unit of the programme are given i.e. at the central level, the National Board of Adult Education, the Central Ministry of Education, The Central Directorate of Adult Education; at the state level the State Board (s) of Adult Education, the State Steering Committees, the State Ministry of Education, the State Directorate of Adult Education; at the District level, the District Adult Education Committee National Service Schemes (NSS), (4) the Nehru Yuvak Kendras and finally (5) through the Integrated Child Development Schemes of the Women and Child Welfare Directorate of the State Governments. A variety of organizations, Governmental, semi-governmental and non-governmental thus, are associated for the first time in the implementation of National Adult Education Programme on a massive scale. The policy statement on National Adult Education Programme clearly spelt out the arrangements that have to be made to administer the progrrmme. Delineating on the organizational issues, the policy statement says that "from the organisational point of view it is of utmost importance that elaborate preparations are made before launching this massive programme. It is of greatest importance that implementation of adult education programme is decentralized". The policy of associating multiplicity of organization i.e. governmental, semi-governmental and non-governmental raises a number of administrative problems like co-ordination which is considered as one of the key problems.

Once the goals of the programme have been set, its plans and policies determined, money provided, organization tailored to the need, personnel assigned, directions given, delegations determined and supervision provided for, then the co-ordination is the means of bringing all those factors together in an inter-locking relationship. Coordination has further been viewed as a means by which a blend is secured.

There are a few, generalizations which are usually attributed to the principle of co-ordination.

1. The more the work of a bureaucracy is sub-divided, the more important it is that the components be assembled in a unified relationship, if the goal of the programme is to be achieved.
2. Co-ordination relies on the authority that accompanies hierarchy and position, it relies also on individual competence, understanding and voluntary co-operation.
3. The better the goals of the programme are understood and accepted by those who work for it the easier it is to secure voluntary co-operation.
4. Even when conditions evoke voluntary co-operation, co-ordination is difficult because people in a bureaucracy tend to have a natural desire to be left alone. Consequently, the application of the techinques of co-ordination is time consuming responsibility of the executive and becomes more so as he (The Executive) rises in the hierarchy.
5. Relatively more time is spent on external co-ordination than internal co-ordination.

Administration, therefore, is an attempt to bring diverse units into a working relationship so that, together, they result in achieving the goal. Co-ordination is viewed as placing the many aspects of an enterprise in proper position relative to each other and to the programme of which they are a part of the policy. In other words, it harmoniously combines 'agents' and 'functions' towards the achievement of a desired goal.

According to professor Mohit Bhattacharya, Co-ordination assumes importance in organization theory in the context of "intra-organizational interdependencies. Situations of interdependence have to be objectively identified within the organization". Discussing the various aspects of co-ordination, the author wrote that "co-ordination is a process of harmonisation of the activities of the different parts of an organization with a view to achieving the goals of an organization".

Keeping in view the above theoretical premise on the principle of co-ordination an attempt is made in this chapter to study how coordination is secured by the agencies which have run the programme. As the implementation of the programme forms chief concern of the investigator, it is proposed to analyse the problems involved in the following order.

1. The instructors, method of their recruitment, perceptions about the centres, curriculum and learners.
2. The views of the supervisory staff, those of the agencies on the one hand and of the governmental departments on the other about running of the centres (constraints and limitation), instructional material and instructors, mutual perceptions between the two branches of the supervisory cadres to highlight problems of coordination.
3. Structures and functions of the agencies, the opinions of the office bearers and other concerned about the programme and particularly their views on the government's role in organising the programme through the agencies, the problem of coordination in the governmental bodies connected in promoting voluntary agencies in he programme and the agencies themselves, will be highlighted.

Method of Recruitment

Instructors or organizers of Animaters of an adult education centre is virtually the king-pin in the entire administrative edifice of Adult Education Programme. The policy outline on National Adult Education Programme states that 'the governing consideration in assigning responsibility for instructional arrangements should be (a) the suitability of the persons concerned to organize programmes with a grasp of the conceptual standpoint and with a spirit of commitment'.

Further, the policy planners have identified school teachers, students, village/youth, ex-servicemen and others including retired personnel as the main reservoir from which the instructional cadre can be drawn.

The policy statement as well as the subsequent documents relating to the National Adult Education Programme, however, have not dealt much with the methods or procedures for recruitment to the posts of instructors and thus seems to have left enough autonomy to the agencies in selecting the instructors.

One hardly needs to emphasise the point that the selection procedures adopted by the implementing agencies to recruit instructors would go a long way in ensuring the success of the Adult Education Programme.

In this section, it is proposed to examine the methods of recruitment of instructors adopted by the agencies in the sample. The following table presents the methods followed by different agencies in the recruitment of instructors.

As can be seen from the table, the broad methods of selection of instructor adopted by the agencies in the sample are (1) Interview, (2) Personal contact, (3) Approach by the agency (4) village committees' recommendation.

Method of Selection

Sl. No.	*Agency*	*Inter-view*	*Per-sonal*	*Approach by contact*	*Village Agency*	*Total Committee recommended*
1.	Andhra Mahila Sabha (AMS)	—	8	2	—	10
2.	Bhagavathula Charitable Trust (BCT)	3	—	—	—	3
3.	Comprehensive Rural Operations Service Society, (CROSS)	—	—	1	2	3
4.	Durga Sangh Seva Samaj (DSS)	3	—	—	—	3
	Total	6	8	3	2	19 (100.00)

The method of selection of instructors through interview was followed by only two agencies in the sample. Each of these agencies has given wide publicity to the programme and this has attracted quite a few applicants for the posts of instructors. While the Bhagavathula Charitable Trus (BCT) did not specify preference in selection to the instructors posts, the Durga Sangh Seva Samaj (DSS) specified that it would give preference to the teachers, retired or in service. About 50 applications are said to have been received for 30 posts of instructors in the case of Bhagavathula Charitable Trust. The selection committee of this agency consisted of the project officer, Director of Adult Education, Andhra University (Visakhapatnam) and its own officials in charge of horticulture besides block level official in-charge of agriculture and education. All the three instructors in the sample reported that they were interviewed on such wideranging issues like problem of illiteracy, economic development, poverty etc.

The Durga Sangh Seva Samaj also received around 50 applications for the post of instructors out of which 30 were selected. As has already been mentioned, the agency gave preference to teachers, retired as well as those in service. The selection committee constituted by this agency included the Project Officer, the supervisor, block level official incharge of education. The candidates were examined on general topics.

Coming to other agencies, the Andhra Mahila Sabha did not seem to have followed formal methods of selection. A majority of the instructors in the sample (8 out of 10) reported that they were appointed by 'personal contact.' The supervisors visited the villages and ascertained the willingness of people, who in their view, would satisfy the requirements to work as instructors. However, in two centres, where the supervisor found it difficult to appoint instructors the project officer and the supervisor together approached a few candidates and after getting their willingness appointed them as instructors.

As far as CROSS is concerned, a different method of selection is adopted. This agency has established 'Village Sanghams' (associations) in a good number of villages in Bhongir Samithi which is its main area of operation. These 'Sanghams' were informed by the agency about National Adult Education

Programme and were asked to suggest the names of those interested for the post of instructors for undertaking teaching in the adult education centres. The candidates whose names were suggested by the Sanghams were selected by the agency and were appointed for two centres as instructors. In the case of the third centre in the sample, as the village Sangham could not arrive at a consensus about any candidate, the agency picked up a candidate who incidentally was also acceptable to the Sangham.

Thus, the methods of selection adopted by all agencies in the sample differed though not drastically. By and large, they have been guided by the exigencies of the situation. No doubt the investigator come across instances of nepotism and also role of subjective factors in the selection especially in the Sirsilla area where Andhra Mahila Sabha implemented the programme. As far as other agencies are concerned, the method of selection adopted by the Bhagavathula Charitable Trust has proved to be more rational compared to Durga Sangh Seva Samaj and Andhra Mahila Sabha. In the anxiety to entrust the job of teaching in the Adult Education Centre only to persons belonging to teaching profession the Durga Sangh Seva Samaj seems to have ignored other factors like age, interest, motivation, ability to teach and the capacity for running the Adult Education Centre. In the case of the Andhra Mahila Sabha also the investigator noticed such instances like selecting the instructors without taking into consideration their interest in the job. With this, we shall now turn to the socio-economic background of instructors.

Social Factors

In this section, an attempt would be made to know the general background of the instructors. The standard variables that are usually employed to determine the socio-economic status like Age, Caste, Sex, Occupation, Education, Income are taken into consideration besides the teaching experience.

It is evident from the table that half of the male instructors in the sample fall in the age group of 15-25 years. Further, about five male and three female instructors are aged between 26-36. The sample also consists of two instructors (12.50 per cent) who are above 48 years. It may be recalled that the Durga Sangh Seva

Samaj has given preference to teachers in appointments to instructor posts. There were two retired teachers who are above 65 years.

The Backdrop

Among nineteen instructors in the sample, 16 are male instructors and three (15.78 per cent) are female instructors. Regarding caste background, about 5 male instructors (31.25 per cent) and 1 female instructor (33.33 per cent) belong to scheduled caste, about 31.25 male instructors hail from backward classes. The representation of forward castes among instructors is about 37.50 per cent male and 66.27 per cent female.

Thus, scheduled castes and backward castes constitute about 62.50 per cent among male instructors and 33.33 per cent among female instructors which is in conformity with the policy objectives. The female instructors are lesser in number in whole sample. With great difficulty, the investigator could contact three instructors. The Government while admitting the agencies for grants stipulated that about fifty per cent of centres should be earmarked for women. None of the agencies in the sample could satisfy this requirement because of non-availability of women instructors and also learners.

Professional Background

An analysis of the occupational background of the instructors is considered necessary in order to understand which occupational group is showing interest towards the adult education programme. The policy makers, as has already been pointed out, identified school teachers, students, village youth and serviceman and retired personnel as the instructional cadre.

Of all the categories, educated unemployed constitute more than half of the instructors in the sample (56.25 per cent). About three instructors (18.75 per cent) of the sample belong to the small farmer category. There are three in-service teachers in the sample. Of them, one is male instructor and two others are female instructors. Retired male teacher constitute about 12.50 per cent. It will be interesting to not that there is one agricultural labour who has been given opportunity to teach the adults by one of the agencies.

Thus, an analysis of the occupational background reveals that majority of the instructors in the sample are educated unemployed followed by small farmers and retired teachers.

Fiscal Aspects

The data on income of the instructors is gathered in order to ascertain which strata of income group is showing interest towards the programme.

As can be gleaned from the table, an overwhelming majority of instructors in the sample fall in the income range of Rs. 101-500 per month. While out of 16 male instructors 14 (87.50 per cent) earned between Rs. 101-500, all the female instructors belong to this range. Only two instructors have comfortable economic position as they belong to a higher category of income (501-1000). Thus, the income level suggests that a majority of the instructors hail from very poor economic background.

Academic Status

A study of the educational background of the instructors reveal that they possess sufficient educational background to teach in Adult Education Centres. The following table gives the agency-wise details of the educational qualifications of 19 respondents in the sample.

Educational Status of Instructors

Sl. No.	*Agency*	*Qualifications*							
		S.S.C.		*Inter*		*College*		*Total*	
		Male	*Female*	*Male*	*Female*	*Male*	*Female*	*Male*	*Female*
1.	A.M.S.	2	3	4	1	—	—	6	4
2.	B.C.T.	2	—	1	—	—	—	3	—
3.	CROSS	2	—	1	—	—	—	3	—
4.	D.S.S.	3	—	—	—	—	—	3	—

A majority of the instructors (63.15 per cent) in the sample possess secondary qualifications i.e. either tenth class or matriculation. The remaining instructors have done up to intermediate. Thus, the sample consists of fairly educated instructors which is considered as a good catchment area for implementation of Adult Education Programmes.

Earlier Achievements

It is widely believed that it is relatively easy to shape a person with some experience and with some amount of educational background for adult education work rather than a notice. With this in view, the interview schedule convassed to the instructors carries a few questions relating to the previous experience in teaching.

The Justification

The instructors were asked to state the reasons for accepting the appointment as instructor. Eight out of ten instructors appointed by Andhra Mahila Sabha stated that they took up the job to supplement their income. Two instructors have cited that they were very much interested in teaching adults. The instructors appointed by B C T stated that they took up the job because it afforded some financial assistance, but also because it gave them an opportunity to take part in the developmental activities of B C T. They felt that besides providing some financial relief, the agency also gave them a chance to participate in its activities. It may be recalled here that the B C T has been a well-reputed organizations and a majority of the people in Yellamanchili area knew various activities of the agency. Similarly, all the three instructors in the Bhongir area which is the main operational area of CROSS stated that they were interested in taking any activity sponsored by the agency. Incidentally, this organization places high premium on education of masses as a liberator from exploitation. The researcher noticed commendable identity of the instructors in the sample with the main objectives of the agency. Coming to the instructors of Durga Sangh Seva Samaj which has implemented the programme in Gannavaram block, out of three instructors in the sample two stated that they took up the job only to supplement their income. The other respondent cited his keen interest in the programme.

Thus, nearly half of the respondents stated their interest in the programme the remaining half cited economic and other reasons.

Teacher Education

Training occupies an important place in the adult education programme as the National Adult Education Programme is stated as qualitatively and quantitatively superior to earlier Adult Education Programmes. The training of instructors is considered critical for the success of the programme as he/she is the key level or front-line worker. Further, the policy makers of the programme viewed training programme as an exercise in self knowledge or value clarification to the trainees. Besides, it has been observed in one of the documents released by the Directorate of Adult Education that the training programme "is fundamentally a process of . . . education and has to reflect the main characteristics of the methodology that the functionaries would have to follow while working with the learning groups at the block level".

All the instructors reported that they had undergone training after induction, although differences as to the length or duration and training among the agencies is noticed. While the B C T arranged a training programme for 27 days, the Andhra Mahila Sabha, the Comprehensive Rural Operations Service Society, and the Durga Sangh Seva Samaj arranged training programmes for 15, 14, 15 days respectively. All the agencies in the sample trained their instructional cadre in two phases. The venue for the training programme is their head quarters in case of two organizations. The B C T at Yellamanchili and the CROSS at Bhongir while Mahila Sabha and Durga Sangh Seva Samaj conducted training programmes closer to their areas of operation.

The content of the training programme for instructors did not vary much from among the sample agencies. All the agencies in the sample arranged lectures by experts from outside. However, B C T and CROSS have taken special care to make the training programmes 'discussion oriented' rather than lecture-oriented. The participants were encouraged to simulate the situations usually faced by illiterate adults in rural areas. The project officer and others clarified doubts raised by the instructors." The instructors in these two agencies (BCT & CROSS) seem to have been extremely satisfied that is the case with other instructors of other agencies in the sample. The respondents in the sample were asked by the investigator to comment on the utility of the training programmes.

About 9 out of 10 instructors in the centres run by Andhra Mahila Sabha and Durga Sangh Seva Samaj rated their programme as 'not adequate' while all the instructors of BCT and CROSS rated them as 'extremely useful'.

While the instructors of centres under A.M.S. and D.S.S. rated their training as 'inadequate' others confined its utility. Training as a critical input to achieve the policy objective appears to have been very well articulated by the organizers of the programme in BCT and CROSS.

The Distinction

In order to gauge the difference between NAEP and the earlier programmes to educate illiterate adults, the investigator asked a few questions about the objectives of NAEP. All the instructors of Andhra Mahila Sabha in the sample stated that literacy is the main objective. Only four out of ten could tell the other component the functional education and much less could tell (only two) the third component of the programme i.e., the awareness. In contrast, the instructors under B.C.T., CROSS, and D.S.S. listed out all the components of the programme. One major difference between the earlier programmes to educate illiterates and NAEP is that while the earlier one's focussed mainly on literacy (or 3 R's) the NAEP widened it and included functionality and social awareness also besides literacy. Absence of appreciation of the other two points out to the inadequate training programmes of some agencies.

The Value

Regarding weightage to each of the three components stated above, 7 out of 10 instructors under Andhra Mahila Sabha told that more weightage was given to literacy component and three reported that along with literacy, functional education also was given coverage. Only a couple of instructors at least felt the need to give equal weightage to all the components of the programme.

Coming to B.C.T. although preference seems to have been given to literacy, the other two components are not totally neglected. Since B.C.T. has been engaged in some productive programmes, which are found to be useful to the people in general in that area, it has succeeded to certain extent to motivate learners to attend

Adult Education Centres. The agency has announced through its instructors that preference in admission to carpentry training centres run by it would be given to those who continuously attend Adult Education Centres for ten months. Moreover, the Project Officer, Supervisors and others have taken interest in arranging lectures pertaining to social awareness. The learners were also taught some rudimentary techniques in carpentry, pottery and other such trades.

As far as CROSS is concerned, we notice relatively more emphasis on literacy and next to literacy, the awareness component seems to have been given preference. The instructors reported difficulties in implementing functional education component mainly owing to lack of study material as well as infrastructure.

The instruction by Durga Sangh Seva Samaj also gave importance to literacy component as attested by instructors. Two out of three instructors brought to the notice of the investigator the limitations in the implementation of functional education and social awareness components. Only one instructor stated that in his instruction all the three components were covered with only marginal success.

Thus, the perceptions of the respondents on the objectives of NAEP are not very satisfactory. By and large, the agencies have given preference to literacy component alone. Further, excepting B.C.T. and CROSS other agencies did not seem to have accorded priority to other components of the programme. This points to the inadequacies in publicity to the NAEP in general and non-appreciation of the value of functional education and social awareness to the cause of adult education. If policy components are not fully comprehended, there may arise a problem when they are being implemented.

Knowing the Students

A majority of the instructors (14 out of 19) adopted the method of identification of learners enrolled in adult education centres through personal contact. Some instructors reported that they orally enquired about the age, caste, interest and former educational background of adult illiterates in their villages. All the instructors belonging to B.C.T. were asked to conduct a survey of the entire village. CROSS, however, entrusted the task of selecting learners to its village sanghams with the help of instructors. All the ten instructors in the sample belonging to Andhra Mahila Sabha (AMS) relied on the personal identification method. In the case of the Gannavaram block where the Durga Sangh Seva Samaj (DSS) conducted the programme, two instructors told the researcher that they 'knew' all the adults who were illiterates and felt no necessity for a survey. However, one instructor in the sample told that he selected learners after enquiring about their background.

It appears that the 'survey' for identification of learners in AMS, DSS is not foolproof and reflects the agencies' casual way of treating the most important aspect of the programme.

Here, it must be pointed out that apart from their regular tasks of giving instruction in the curriculum, the agencies included some supplementary device; aimed at motivating the learners to go through and benefit from the programme. In this, the instructors are again to play a vital role. It is about this supplementary tasks towards motivation that we now deal with.

There are broadly two methods adopted by the agencies: (1) personal contact between learners and the instructors, (2) arranging frequent contacts between the officials of the agency and the learners. The instructors of AMS and DSS as has already been stated relied heavily on personal contacts in which the instructor was told continuously to highlight the benefits of adult education. Eight out of nineteen instructors reported using various methods like persuasion to attract and retain learners, while six instructors of the BCT and CROSS highlighted the role of their respective agencies in the development of the locality, and the people that is by projecting their agencies role as 'change agents'. By this method, they succeeded, to some extent, in controlling the dropout problem. This has been corroborated by learners also. Some of the instructors under BCT, CROSS reported that those who attended adult education centres for 10 months will be offered loans and various other inputs. Instructors of other agencies in the sample have not shown keen interest in motivating the learners except by occasional lectures. Thus, we notice prevalence and different methods of motivating.

The investigator sought suggestions for motivating learners. An interesting aspect to be noted here is that the instructors belonging to BCT and CROSS recommended for a preferential treatment to the learners in the distribution of loans and other benefits which these organisations arrange for, besides equalizing the 10 month course with 5th class in the formal system so as to enable the learners to get into such jobs like watchman, gateman etc. The instructors of other agencies suggested economic incentives to the learners. These suggestions reveal that there is not one single method of motivating adults either to attend or to continue in the programme. The trend confirms the popular view that incentives of some kind motivate villagers to take interest in any developmental programme.

Teaching Aids

The views of the instructional cadre on the material used are elicited with a view to improving them. All the instructors in the same reported the receipt of teaching material. However, they differed on the relevance of study/teaching material. A large number of instructors of the centres under Andhra Manila Sabha reported that the material supplied to them deals mainly with aspects relating to agriculture. The same appears to be the case with the teaching/learning material supplied by CROSS, which has incidentally prescribed the material produced by AMS. The BCT prescribed and supplied books prepared exclusively for N A E P by Adult Education Department of the Andhra University. Although the instructors were not unhappy about the contents, out of three responding to the queries, two complained about the small size of the print of the material. On examination of the material supplied to the learners by the Andhra Mahila Sabha, it was found that the books were prepared keeping in view a specific project i.e. Farmers Functional Literacy (FFL). Needless to say that the objective of FFL Programme and N A E P are different. Some of the instructors as well as supervisors who earlier worked in F F L programme corroborated this fact. When the investigator enquired about the material, the authorities concerned had not given a convincing answer. This would prove how organizations tend to perceive the policy objectives. Though one may argue that the material is not totally irrelevant, one gets an impression that the attitude of AMS is one of easy taking of the new policy to educate illiterate adults.

Broad Based Programme

One of the ideas of policy planners of NAEP is to make the programme as broad based as possible thereby putting an end to the tendency of treating adult education as the concern of education departments alone. The investigator attempted to ascertain the co-operation received from other departments especially the local leaders and other developmental functionaries of the government. Though the instructors reported good co-operation from their superiors within the organization, almost all were sore about the indifferent attitude of the government officials toward the programme (16 out of 19). A good majority of instructors rated as poor the co-operation given by local leaders (14 out of 19). They felt that their supervisors helped them in many ways in organizing and location of centres, in enlisting the support of local political functionaries as well as in keeping up the morale of the instructors. A few instructors (5/19) also reported the authoritarian attitude of the supervisors as well as project officers. It is interesting to note here that the instructors who were selected on the recommendations of their local leaders, received some support in running adult education centres." Some instructors faced a tough problem in locating an adult centre owing to the stiff opposition of local leaders. A few instructors narrated how the elite disliked the very idea of educating adults. Some brushed aside the idea of adult education, while others warned the consequences of imparting education to the illiterates in their areas. Their main fear as reported by the instructors was, that, if the masses are educated, it will not be possible for the vested interests to deal with them in the way they do when they are illiterates, uneducated and ignorant. That is why, according to some instructors the local leaders opposed establishment of centres in their villages. When the instructor refused to listen, he was harassed in many ways asking him to pay back all his dues, transferring him to a remote place, suggesting that the loan amount be paid from adult education funds, or from learners. Further, the learners were advised not to attend and when they flouted the writ they were asked to immediately repay their loans. In such hostile environment, the instructor, howsoever effective he is, fails to find a solution and prefers to close down the centre for sometime. Some learners held him responsible for bringing in a new set of problems for their already problem-ridden life. Such situation further demoralised the instructor. As for the co-operation of government officials, as stated earlier only three out of the nineteen respondents stated that the officials were extending the necessary co-operation. However, there are some saving features. For example, in the centres visited by the governmental functionaries, the instructors reported good reception to the lectures by them. Thus, a majority of instructors feel that more cooperation is needed from local leaders and government officials in running adult education centres effectively.

Difficulties Ahead

All the instructors are expected to approach their supervisor first and then the project officer in case they experience any difficulty in running adult education centres. This supports the view that, even in non-governmental agencies, the practice of respecting hierarchical norms and bureaucratisation is present.

The type of problems which occasioned the instructors seeking the guidance of their immediate supervisors related to matters like fall in the attendance of the learners and how to retrieve the situation. Non-cooperation of village elite/leaders in running adult education centres and also deliberate attempts to close down the centres in some instances, delays, and difficulties in the receipt of learning material and in matters relating to the availability of other material facilities like lighting and problems with the behaviour of learners in the class rooms instances of learners coming under the influence of drink and teasing of women participants in co-education classes did arise occasionally.

The response of the supervisors on the whole is reported to be encouraging. In many cases complaints about material necessities were personally solved by the supervisors themselves intervening either with the government officials or with the local elite. This was particularly visible in the case of supervisor, belonging to BCT and CROSS. The role of supervisors belonging to Durga Sangh Seva Samaj and AMS seems less encouraging. Where the village elite/leaders attempted to close down the centres, the supervisors and project officers visited them and attempted to persuade them. In some places it worked and in some others it led to further trouble.

Thus, co-ordination between the instructor and his immediate supervisors appears satisfactory. Further, there is evidence that good rapport existed between the instructors and the supervisiors in general. It is more or less a uniform opinion of the instructors in the sample that supervisors were sincere in exhorting the instructors to operate the programme in the proper spirit by constant reminding of the ideals of the programme. A general spirit of confidence was thus instilled in the instructor thanks to the positive interaction between the instructors and supervisors.

On the issue of the desirability of transfer of instructors from one centre to another for every three months nearly half of the respondents (8/19) did not agree with this, only one fourth (5/ 19) favoured it, others remained non-committal. One respondent, however, pointed out the practical difficulties of 'in service' teachers who cannot move around. The practice however, has been that the instructors were allotted to particular centres and no transfers were made. While the opinion of the instructors on transfers was largely negative, some instructors, however, agreed to the suggestion of the researcher that a periodical change of instructors would be better as it would expose them to different types of people. There is, thus, a clear difference in the views of the instructors on this issue. The learners too were divided on this issue. Whatever be the merits of `transfer', it would appear that, given the fact that some instructors are only part-time with a separate full-time job, transfers would prove to be extremely inconvenient to them. Apart from this practical difficulty, as the recommendation is that instructors should be drawn from the locality and community in which the centre is located, policy-wise too transfers are perhaps undesirable.

The Remarks : An overwhelming majority of the instructors (18/19) felt that at least 50 per cent of the learners acquired the skills of reading and writing and some amount of knowledge in arithmetic. An inter-agency comparison reveal that the instructors of BCT and CROSS are quite positive about the impact of literacy component on the learners. The instructors of DSS and AMS, however, felt that only 40-45 per cent of the learners enrolled in their respective adult education centres could improve their reading, writing and numerical abilities.

Almost all learners (17/19) pointed out the difficulties involved in imparting skills in functional education and in raising the awareness. The main reasons for their failure is lack of infrasctrutural facilities and proper learning materials. Some instructors regretted that instruction was confined to face-to-face teaching. Except black board no other teaching aid is made available. Perhaps audio-visual aids like radio, tape recorder, VCR and TV would go a long way in sustaining the interest of the learners. Thus the instruct rs were modest about their claims as far as achievement in the three components of the programme are concerned.

Views on job satisfaction as expressed by instructors show wide variance. A good majority of the respondents (12/19) reported that they were satisfied with their jobs. The remaining (5/19) were totally dissatisfied with their jobs for a host of reasons which include meagre remuneration, heavy work, apathy and politics played by the local leaders 18 and indifference of the government officials and authoritarian attitude of the supervisors and project officers. Two respondents have refused to react on this question.

The Guidelines : The suggestions given by the instructors touch several aspects of the programme administration. An overwhelming majority (87.8 per cent) wanted increase in the honorarium. Most of them said that an honorarium of Rs. 50/- per month was very meagre (it was enhanced to Rs. 100/- recently) and the requirements of the job demand lot of their attention and time. About 48.9 per cent suggested that unless some economic incentives were offered to the learners, it would be difficult to sustain the interest of an illiterate adult. A good percentage of instructors (46.9) also suggested the need for more diversified teaching and learning materials. Some suggested association of village level politicians with all aspects of programme management. The other suggestions include strong linkages with other development programmes (22.88), proper lighting facilities (52.33), increasing the involvement of government functionaries (70.3) and co-operation of village elite (57.33). Suggestions like less paper work, conducting regular tests, motivating the learners who show encouraging improvement by offering economic incentives are grouped under "other" suggestions which constitute about 43.81 per cent.

The instructors' reactions in the sample on various aspects of the programme thus suggest that there are clear gaps in the training programme, conducted by some agencies. However, it should be remembered that they were not totally disoriented towards the programme. It was given to understand that lectures as part of the training programme arranged by Andhra Mahila Sabha and Durga Sangh Seva Samaj are mostly stereotyped. And this had produced a negative effect on the trainees. As has aptly been commented by one of the trainees, "It appears silly if a resource person tells me how to look after my agricultural farm or how and when the paddy should be cut as a good number in the group hail from agricultural background". The agencies which organized training programmes have not even used audio-visual aids to sustain the interest of instructors. A couple of instructors were frustrated at the general attitude of the village elites. They felt that good programmes like adult education fail because of polluted political atmosphere. Thus, the training programmes appear to be not strong enough especially with regard to a couple of agencies in the sample. The Durga Sangh Seva Samaj in particular does not seem to be knowing that the NAEP is not a literacy programme alone but also contains two other components, functionality and awareness. The agency does not also seem to be aware of the fact that mere literacy drives will not succeed.

Coming specifically to the problem of co-ordination, we notice that purely in terms of the instructors on the one hand and the supervisors on the other, there has been adequate co-ordination. But co-ordination does not merely pertain to rapport and personal relationships. A greater effort on the part of the agencies to equip the centres would not only improve the programme but will contribute to increased morale in the instructors. In other words, a more intensive and constant interaction between the agency and the centre would generate a correspondingly greater degree of involvement as far as the instructors and other cadres are concerned.

Different Opinions

In the organizational framework of NAEP, the tasks of supervisors would be concerned with making instructors effective in the field. The supervisors are expected to guide and spport the work of a cluster of about 30 adult education centres as visualized in the administrative structure of a project. The main functions of the supervisor as conceived by the policy makers of NAEP include (1) to enlist community co-operation and support, (2) to help in the survey of the area and assess the learners' needs, (3) to help in the training programmes of instructors, (4) to help prepare flexible and need based curricula and materials, (5) to plan and organize the programme, (6) to keep open the channels of communication, (7) to evaluate and guide the work of the centres and (8) to take steps to give wide publicity to the programme.

The supervisors are expected to perform the above functions with the support and co-operation of project officer, development departments of the government, the instructors, resource persons from among the local people and above all with the help of the community.

In this section, an attempt is made first to analyse the socioeconomic status of the supervisors, their perception about the objectives of NAEP, their selection, recruitment and training methods of supervision, comments on resource material, steps initiated to secure co-ordination internally as well as externally, mechanisms to monitor the programme, job satisfaction and finally their impressions and suggestions.

Economic and Social Aspects

Thus, such standard variables like age, caste, and sex, education, economic, occupational status of the four supervisors in the sample will be briefly analysed in order to determine their socio-economic profile.

Age: Of the four supervisors two belong to the age group of 25-34 years and the other two fall between 35-44 age group. The supervisory staff' of all the agencies therefore satisfied the requirement prescribed by the policy planners that the supervisors should at least be of 21 years.

Sex and Caste: All the supervisors in the sample are male. Among them three are from forward castes and one belongs to backward caste.

Educational status: All the supervisors are fairly educated. Three out of 4 are graduates while the fourth one has studied up to twelfth class (or plus two equivalent). The supervisory cadre of the sample possess more than prescribed qualifications for the post which is in consonance with the policy objectives of AEP.

Occupation: Occupation wise, two supervisors are teachers and one a homeopathic doctor and the other an employee of the agency. Among the two teachers one is working as a full time employee of the agency on deputation from Zilla Parishad School. The other one is just attending to work on part-time basis.

Income: All the supervisors belong to middle income group.

Previous experience: On the experience in adult education work, two out of four have previous experience in adult education and the other two are new to the job.

Thus, the socio-economic background of the supervisors reveals that all of them are in the prescribed age group, and a majority are graduates. All of them belong to middle income group.

Aims and Goals

All the supervisors are aware of the three main objectives i.e. literacy, functional education and social awareness. However, they are divided in their opinion about the weightage to be given to each of the three components. The supervisor belonging to B C T drew the attention of the investigator to the impracticability of implementing functionality component as it involves large scale preparation. The supervisor of CROSS on the other hand is of the opinion that awareness is more important than functionality. Coming to the D S S though the supervisor is aware of the three components, he appears to be more interested in imparting three R's rather than the other two components. The case with the A M S is altogether different. The supervisor of this agency said that for imparting any thing, literacy is most important. In his opinion the material supplied by his agency to the learners is out of tune with the objectives of N A E P and hence questions on weightage does not arise at all.

Process of Selection

The criteria for selection and recruitment of supervisors as conceived by policy planners of the N A E P is as follows:

(1) As far as possible, the supervisors should be drawn from among the ranks of experienced and successful adult education teachers, extension workers, N S V S, N S S and Community Social Service Volunteers, social workers and also those who may have academic qualification in adult education.

(2) They should be familiar with the local language, and as far as possible be residents of the project or a similar area. They must be willing to live in the cluster area to which they are eventually allotted.

We also find reference to modern methods of recruitment in various policy documents. One of such method is to ask the interested candidates for the post of supervisors to submit in advance a full and honest account of their understanding of the N A E P, the tasks of the supervisor within this and the assessment of their suitability for the post.

Coming to the response from the supervisors about their selection, one supervisor (belonging to B C T) replied that he was just asked to look after the programme through an official memorandum. Further he said, he happens to be one of the co-ordinators of the agency put in charge of rural leadership programmes. The agency might have thought that he can look after the adult education programme as well. As has already been pointed out in the last section of the first chapter on profiles of the agencies, the Bhagavathula Charitable Trust is engaged in implementing a variety of programmes/projects in Yellamanchili block. That way this agency is placed in a better position vis-a-vis others in the sample. As part of the developmental programmes the agency sponsored and ran a few non-formal adult education centres too. The supervisor of N A E P of this agency looked after those centres and the same person was made Project Officer-cum-

Supervisor of the N A E P of this agency. Hence, no formal method of selection of supervisor was felt necessary by the agency.

The Durga Sangh Seva Samaj too did not follow any formal methods in the selection of supervisors. In fact the Honorary Project Officer in charge of the A E P appointed his own son as the supervisor. It is also noteworthy that the project officer himself is none other than Director of the agency. This instance brings to light the special problems or considerations that arise when a voluntary social service agency undertakes the adult education work as one of the items of its activities. In some cases, the head of the agency can himself become the head of the adult education programme. This has the advantage of solving the problems of co-ordination as the head of the agency himself is incharge of the A E P. On the other hand, this may mean that the programme may not receive the requisite attention given the project officer's busy engagements with other activities.

The supervisor of N A E P for this agency is full time teacher in a school in Vijayawada which is about 20 KMs from the area of operation. In spite of his best efforts, he could not strike a balance between his official responsibilities as a teacher in a school, and as supervisor of an adult education project. Some adult education centres are located as far away as 35 to 40 KMs. Distance naturally deterred the supervisor from undertaking frequent visits to adult education centres which are so necessary for ensuring their effective functioning. The Project Officer is quite an aged man and visits by him are totally ruled out. With the result, there is noticeable laxity in supervision. These things point out how voluntary agencies exhibit tendencies which may have negative effect on the objectives of a qualitative programme like adult education. It is not to say, that the agencies suffer from such an inadequacy.

The Comprehensive Rural Operations Service Society appointed the co-ordinator of its adult education programmes as the supervisor. The agency did not follow formal methods for selection of its supervisor taking into consideration the experience of the candidate.

With regard to Andhra Mahila Sabha, it has advertised the posts of supervisors and selected three candidates out of fifteen applied. The selection committee consisted of the Chairman and Secretary of the Literacy House (which looks after education programmes as the name itself indicates) and the Project Officer. However, it was given to understand that no expert in adult education seems to have been associated with the selection committee.

Thus, the method of selection of supervisors through advertisement was followed by only one agency. The other agencies in the sample selected and appointed the supervisors without official formalities. The reason could be that these agencies had more confidence in the personnel readily available in their organisations.

The training programmes to supervisors are intended to increase the understanding about the N A E P and the needs of the community and learners, impart the ability to prepare material work out, methods of organizing adult education centres, evolve techniques for gaining community support, increase their ability for planning the follow up programmes, develop skills arranging training programme for Instructors and finally enhance competence on various ways of achieving the co-ordination with other developmental programmes/departments. Besides these, the policy makers of N A E P recommended provision for practical experience in order to acquire skills necessary to perform their functions with confidence.

The organisers of the training programmes for supervisors are expected to arrange:

(1) Visits to villages for getting an acquaintance with the needs of learners and learning environment;

(2) Development of suitable programmes based on the field data collected through surveys;

(3) Preparation of need-based curriculum or adaptations of existing, available curriculum;

(4) Evaluation of the available teaching/learning material;

(5) Acquaintance with the procedures of monitoring (monthly, quarterly and annual reports);

(6) Preparation and use of simple visual aids.

The above are some of the functions that are supposed to be experimented by the supervisors in the course of the training programme.

The Central Directorate of Adult Education suggested that there be a two or three phased training programme, for supervisors starting with a three day initial orientation programme followed by two week pre-service training and further followed by a "process of recurrent training sessions through monthly meetings, refresher courses and correspondences".

Thus, training for the supervisors was visualised as a process of continuous learning.

Now, coming to the training part of the supervisors in the sample, it was found that all the supervisors did undergo training at the Sri Venkateswara University, Tirupati. The State Directorate of Adult Education, Government of Andhra Pradesh sponsored the training programme. The State Resources Centre, Tirupati conducted the programme. The duration of the programme is spread over a period of 10 days. The supervisors of B.C.T. and D.S.S. attend the training a few weeks before the inauguration of the adult education programme in their area. The supervisors of CROSS and AMS, however, could attend the programme after the starting of the adult-centres in their areas.

All the supervisors opined that the training programme attended by them was mainly lecture oriented. They were not given an opportunity by the organisers of the training programme to narrate individually or collectively to share their experiences for the benefit of the fellow supervisors in adult education work. In fact, a supervisor called the whole training a 'farce'. Coming to the utility of the lectures delivered in the training course, out of four supervisors, three felt that these were 'idealistic', miles away from realities in rural areas. Two supervisors felt that they did not understand some lectures owing to language problems. The regional language being Telugu, it is no wonder that the supervisors experienced some difficulty in following lectures in English. The investigator was further told that the supervisors in the training programmes were not encouraged to participate, be it in the form of discussions or other simulation exercises. The whole programme was a one-sided affair. A supervisor summed up the programme saying that the organisers of the training programme should first attend programme on how to organise training programmes to the key level functionaries of the N.A.E.P. Questioning the methods of training, yet another supervisor felt that the grasp of the organisers of training programme about rural areas in general and about the psychology of rural people in particular is so poor that he felt like withdrawing himself from the training programme half way through.

Regarding the material that they are supposed to receive, all the four supervisors said that they did not receive any. When a supervisor asked the organisers about the material, it seems he was told that he would get them by post. He waited for three months and got reconciled to the indifference of the organisers. On the utility of the lectures, two supervisors said that whatever little they could understand sounded 'upstartish', to them. A particular mention need to be made about "how to organise training programmes to the instructors". Two lectures, it seems, were given on the above theme. The supervisors were told that they should involve other developmental functionaries in the programme. A respondent in the sample remarked that the indifference of the developmental functionaries was experienced by the organisers of the training programme as out of five lectures arranged to such developmental personnel only two turned up. And, their performance was also poor. Thus, the supervisor told the investigator that "it is very easy to preach than to practice". Enquired about the field visits they were supposed to undertake during the training programme, all the supervisors in the sample said that they were not taken any where.

The above instances show the gap between the directives of the policy planner and the implementors. What is the main reason for the discontentment of the supervisors about their training ? The trainees say that it was because of the half-hearted efforts of the organisers. It surprised the investigator as to how the personnel of S R C could be so indifferent even to the medium of lectures. The fact that a good number reported their difficulties in following the lectures in English on the first day of the training programme itself and the consequent failure of the organisers to remedy the situation, clearly exhibit the formalistic/ritualistic response of the organisers of training programmes. Further, the failure to encourage participation in debates and discussions reveals the unchanged nature of the organisers towards training programmes. As aptly summed up by a participant, "the commitment of N A E P which they often exhorted us to cultivate, appears to be lacking in them".

Various Approaches

The effective supervisory methods seen to have been by almost all respondents in the sample. These include (a) regular visits (scheduled and surprise) to the A E C under their control; (b) checking the attendance, (c) guiding the instructors on methods of teaching, (d) getting the feedback on regularity of instructor; (e) method of teaching and (f) enquiring about the difficulties faced by learners.

Inter-agency comparison, however, proved that the two supervisors of B C T and CROSS are far more effective vis-a-vis their counterparts in Durga Sangh Seva Samaj and Andhra Mahila Sabha. In terms of number of visits to A E Cs the investigator noticed that the supervisors of the B C T and CROSS checked more number of centres in a day than the other two supervisors in the sample, which is of course made possible mainly due to the fact that the supervisors of BCT and CROSS are provided with vehicles. Because of this, on an average they could visit six centres per day. The supervisors of A M S and D S S could visit only one or two centres per day as they have to commute the long distances by other modes of transport. That is why, instructors of the B C T and CROSS reported a more number of surprise inspections by their supervisors. In case of instructors of A M S and D S S, this was not the case and they could not take up as many 'surprise' visits as was the case with the supervisors of B C T and CROSS. Moreover, as the two agencies (BCT & CROSS) are involved in a number of economic programmes and a readily available infrastructure running Adult Education programme posed no fresh infrastructural and other problem. Each agency as a matter of fact has got two to three motor vehicles besides jeeps etc. That is why, they could be able to maintain an effective supervision. So it must be understood that factors like conveyance also play an important role in ensuring effective supervision.

Visiting Teachers

We have mentioned earlier how the policy planners visualised A E P as the concern of the departments and should not be viewed as the job of educationists alone. Involvement of others like the Block Development Officer (BDO), managers of banks, project officials and small farmers development agency and other officials in-charge of agriculture, animal husbandry etc., is regarded as crucial for the success. The supervisors were asked about the role of other developmental functionaries. A number of reasons were cited by the supervisors for their inadequate role. The first is the indifference. Only one supervisor belonging to B C T could succeed to some extent, in persuading the officials in the block to visit some of the centres. But it was mainly because of the image of the agency in that part of the state. Right since its inception, it made sincere serious efforts to associate the block level officials in almost all its activities. The rapport it has established over a period of time was utilised by the supervisor at least to some extent which resulted in getting some cooperation from them.

But coming to the other two agencies, Durga Sanga Seva 'Samaj and Andhra Mahila Sabha, they do not have strong roots in the areas where they have implemented the programme. And naturally they had to encounter difficulty right from starting the project. These two agencies could not involve the block level functionaries in the programme to the extent they desired partly owing to 'unacquaintance' with the area and also partly due to indifference of the local level village elite. Further the investigator came to know that the agencies did not seek co-operation from either local leaders or officials.

With regard to CROSS, it could not involve block level developmental functionaries for a very significant reason. The very fact that CROSS's long standing work in the area seemed to have led to strained relations between block level officials and CROSS. This is because CROSS in pursuing the other aspects of its activities and as a matter of fact had on many occasions crossed swords with the block administration. For example, on issues like fertilizer distribution CROSS did not fight shy of taking up matters with the block officials wherever malpractices in distribution of fertilizers were identified. In any case, the block officials got the impression that there were instances of CROSS instigating some rural sections to vocally complain against block officials. This is an interesting instance of close contacts between a voluntary agency and a rural government resulting in estrangement rather than co-operation. To an extent, this should be assumed as a given factor. In such circumstances, problems of coordination in the implementation of a policy like Adult Education, arising out of the lack of rapport between the agency and the government becomes inevitable. The agency organized several processions against rise in prices of essential commodities, for establishment of fair price shops in villages, for distribution of fertilisers with subsidy to the needy etc. It brought to the notice of higher officials in the district about the rampant corruption at village and mandal levels and demanded stern action against corrupt administrators. Thus, CROSS has established itself as an agency of masses and earned the name of crusader for justice to the unorganised rural people. The activities of the agency to an extent antagonized the local bureaucracy. The landlords joined with police and taluq officials made several efforts to close down the agency by using all sorts of pressures and attacks but they could not succeed. This only shows how dedicated voluntary agencies are harassed with a view to continuing the status quo.

Thus, the methods of supervision adopted by the supervisors in the sample seem to be satisfactory. The checking of attendance registers and paying surprise visits did to an extent keep the instructors on alert. However, coming to the checking of the drop out rate is concerned, where the instructors failed, the supervisor also did not succeed much. Except the supervisors of the BCT and CROSS who tried and succeeded to some extent in helping the learners in their problems like securing a loan, settling disputes between two castes etc., the other supervisors in the sample could not do anything as they neither have access to other institutions which could do something to the learners nor could act in co-operation with officials concerned at the block/taluq level in finding a solution to some of the problems faced by the learners.

On the whole, one comes to the conclusion that the supervisory methods are satisfactory but there is a limit to what they can do as the problems of increasing the effectiveness of supervisors would depend on various other factors which are mostly beyond the control of the supervisor.

Learning Material

All the supervisors reported that they distributed teaching/ learning material for instruction to the instructors. Regarding the source of the material, the Andhra Mahila Sabha produced and supplied to the learner the material prepared by it. The Department of Adult Education, Andhra University prepared primers for learners in the centres run by it under N A E P University Adult Education Programme. The same material was ordered and used for its learners in Centres under the Bhagavathula Charitable Trust. The Comprehensive Rural Operations Service Society supplied to its learners the material prepared by Andhra Mahila Sabha. The Durga Sangh Seva Samaj acquired the material prepared by a private publisher. An attempt is also made to elicit the views of the supervisory personnel on utility and the relevance of the material in general. Of the four supervisors in sample, two supervisors felt that the material supplied is not totally irrelevant and felt that much needed to be done to revise or refashion the material in the light of the feedback from the learners. The other two supervisors opined that the material supplied meets the occasion.

All the supervisors reported the receipt of the material in adequate number. However, as has already been observed, the A M S in this respect is in a better position compared to others in the sample. The material which was prepared by it for another programme (Farmers Functional Literacy Programme) was reprinted at its own press in Hyderabad and it did not face any problem in its supply. It distributed a set consisting of six books to each learner. But the B C T and D S S distributed one book to each of the learners and CROSS distributed two books. The supervisors were by and large satisfied with the distribution part.

Cooperative Method

As has already been discussed, the success of programmes like N A E P depends to a large extent on how best the coordination is achieved or secured. The investigator examined the operation of the principle of co-ordination in the implementation of N A E P through voluntary agencies in the sample.

In this section, an examination of the mechanism created by each agency for achieving co-ordination is attempted. Broadly, there appears to be two bodies for securing co-ordination. One at the agency level for the purpose of the study called 'project level committee' and the other at the village level or adult education centre level, called 'village level committee'. It must be remembered that not all agencies have a two-tier co-oridinating bodies. Again, these bodies are referred to with different names.

Of the two bodies intended to secure coordination, discussion is more on project level committee, as the village level committees of almost all the agencies in the sample remained dysfunctional. The discussion that follows begins with the structure and functions of the Project Level Committees (P L C's).

It must be mentioned that the functions of the P L Cs are not precisely and exhaustively given in any documents relating to any of the agencies. It is possible to identify them both from what is contained in some other documents and from an informal study of their functioning.

The main functions of the P L C's include (i) to secure coordination between adult education programme and other programmes by the other development agencies; (ii) to ensure co-ordination between adult education programmes and other formal systems of education; (iii) to create necessary administrative infrastructure and supervision; (iv) to arrange lectures by resource persons and identifying the persons belonging to the developmental departments of the government for the same; (v) to make arrangements for the supply of reading material to the learners; (vi) to fix criteria for selection of supervisors, instructors and arranging for their training; (vii) to lay broad guidelines for managing day-to-day administration; (viii) to continuously monitor the progress by adhering to the proformae; and (ix) to take steps to associate local elite in the programme.

The membership of the P L Cs varied from one agency to the other. The Chairman of this body in BCT and CROSS was the Secretary and the head of the agency respectively. The

Chairmanship of the P L C of D S S was kept vacant. The Project Officer is made as the Convenor of the body. However, the A M S nominated the President of the Panchayat Samithi of the Sirsilla Block as the Chairman of its P L C. Regarding membership, the B C T had involved the supervisor and one third of its total number of instructors. For every three months, the representation of instructors changed and almost all instructors took part in the deliberations of the body at one time or the other. Local leaders and learners are also associated sometimes with the P L C meetings.

The Project Level Committee of the CROSS comprised the Chairman, Supervisor and three instructors besides other functionaries. It is given to understand that the learners are also invited sometimes to the meetings. But the criteria of learners/ instructors representation is not clear. As pointed out earlier, the Andhra Mahila Sabha made the President of the Sirsilla Panchayat Samithi as the Chairman of the Project Level Committee. The Project Officer, Supervisor, some officials of block level administration are the members. The P L C of the Durga Sangh Seva Samaj consists of Convenor, Supervisor and two women members and the Extension Officer incharge of Education of Panchayat Samithi.

There is, thus, a variation in the composition of the P L Cs constituted by the agencies in the sample. As for the Project Level Committee (PLC) meetings, again going by agencywise, the PLC of BCT met at the beginning of every month.

A cursory glance at the agenda of the monthly meetings of various agencies in the sample revealed that a number of problems were brought to the notice of the P L C for a decision. These include (a) dropout problem; (b) non-cooperation of village elite; (c) non receipt of grant from the Government; (d) trooping of children into adult education centres; (e) absence of instructors without intimation; (f) clash in timings of adult education centres and other developmental programmes of the agency; (g) criteria for consideration of applicants who also happen to be learners for loans; (h) non functioning of village level committees; (i) indifference or non-co-operation of the developmental functionaries to visit adult education centres for giving lectures etc.; (j) arrangements for inspections by the officials of the adult education directorate and other district officials; (k) arranging lectures by the functionaries in-charge of agriculture, animal husbandry etc., within the agency, and other problems.

The usual procedure for conducting the meetings of PLC is first to listen to the instructor followed by the supervisor on various aspects of the programme management. On several occasions, there was a difference of opinion and in such a situation the Chairman tried for a consensus. The methods of finding solution to the problem are through discussion, dialogue with the concerned and between the concerned.

As the Chairman of a P L C rightly summed up the "committee looked at each problem with an intention to solve it." Very often, the patience of the Chairman was put to test. Placed as he was in a difficult situation, conducting meetings with a widely stratified members is "a tight rope to walk on." On the whole, the P L C served the purpose for which it was created. An agency involved in diversified activities naturally confronts special problems of co-ordination which for that very reason may find solution easily. The organizers of the programme were once faced with the problem of finances. The second installment of the grant for running the programme was not released. The P L C of that agency took a decision to divert the funds from other sources. The agency could have closed down all centres after five months and could have shifted the blame on the government, but the organisers observed that it would have dampened the enthusiasm of learners. Moreover, it was feared that the other educational programmes of the agency may not succeed and secondly winding up a programme for lack of funds would impair the image of the agency. Thus, it can be seen that the P L C of one agency i.e., B C T was favourably situated to arrange co-ordination amongst its different activities. The village level committees of this agency however have not functioned to the extent the organisers desired.

Coming to CROSS as already stated, the P L C was not as broad in its composition as was the case with B C T. Problems similar to B C T were faced by this agency also, except in one area. The local leaders have not co-operated much with the agency, The wide network of village sanghams are a constant source of tension between the agency and local level bureaucracy on the one hand

and between the local leaders and the agency on the other. This agency too, sponsored several economic programmes like B C T. At the end of every month, the meetings of the P L C were held and problems of adult education centres were brought to the notice of the Chairman through the supervisor. Solutions were worked out to overcome problems and efforts were made to avoid clash with the adult education centres activities and other activities of the agency. Criteria for the processing of applications for loans to banks was framed and guidelines were formulated. Project Level Committee (P L C) prepared a list of resource persons for lectures in adult education centres. Methods of motivating and attracting illiterate adults were discussed and measures were suggested to the instructors to sustain the interest of learners. The members of the P L C visited some centres and recorded their satisfaction on the progress. Thus, the mechanism for achieving internal co-ordination is sound and produced the desired effect. But as far as external co-ordination is concerned, the agency found it difficult to secure. The environment around the agency is hostile. Local elite to a large extent suspect the agency. According to reliable source, the block level bureaucracy envies the agency for its initiative, boldness and result orientation. It was given to understand that some vested interests wrote letters to the Government urging it to stop the grants to CROSS for its anti-government activities. Pressures were brought on police to wind up even the agency. CROSS has some sort of a village level coordinating committees also and these are called village level - sanghams.

As regards the operation of P L C of A M S in Sirsilla, as pointed out elsewhere it was headed by a local leader as Chairman. It may be recalled that the Andhra Mahila Sabha is not new to organizing literacy programmes. The investigator hoped that with its vast experience, this agency would run the programme more easily and effectively. However, this very agency started facing problems right from the beginning. The PLC has not laid down a proper criteria for location of adult education centres keeping in view the local conditions. With the result, some centres had been shifted, closed down and re-opened. The policy guidelines on location of centres seemed to have been ignored.

The problems that arose in the implementation of the programme were not attended to. The PLC itself rarely met and naturally several problems of co-ordination emerged which called for higher policy direction. The Project officer tried several times to make the PLC to meet regularly. When it met, the Chairman was always in a hurry to leave. Hence, no proper discussion used to take place. The whole management of running 100 adult education centre fell on the Project Officer who, though had sufficient experience, was relatively young in age. In the absence of regular mechanism for co-ordinating the work, the programme could not be implemented effectively. The developmental functionaries have not shown any interest in the programme in spite of the fact that the President of Panchayat Samithi was associated with the programme. According to the Project Officer, the Chairman is so indifferent that on one occasion he suggested to the project officer to take his signature on all papers/cheques once in four months so that the work did not suffer. Thus, the PLC of the A M S largely remained on paper. As regards village level committees, A M S did not seem to have taken any initiative to organise them.

In the case of Durga Sangh Seva Samaj too, the investigator noticed the ineffectiveness of the PLC. The convenor of the committee is also the director of the agency. When enquired about the PLC, he observed that the matters relating to the PLC are confidential and will not be revealed. The investigator through other sources was informed that the PLC met only once at the beginning of the programme. The non-functioning of the PLC has adversely affected the functioning of the programme. The major casualty of non-functioning of PLC was internal as well as external co-ordination. Issues like the criteria for recruitment to the instructor's post, whether it is desirable to recruit the retired teachers, the quality of the teaching material, location of centres, lighting facilities, the problems involved in opening adequate number of women centres, the problems with regard to arranging lectures by resource persons etc., should have come up before the PLC as in the case of other agencies. In the absence of this vital co-ordinating body, the organizers were forced to look for ad-hoc measures to cope with exigencies which led to lot of dissatisfaction among learners as well as the instructional cadre. Thus, the agency failed to take the advantage of an important body like the PLC.

Inter-relationship

As regards co-ordination with other developmental departments of the Government, the supervisors cited several reasons. Giving benefit of doubt to the governmental servants, the supervisor of BCT and CROSS opined that the governmental functionaries did not have much time and the orders of the district collectors/director of adult education programme are not binding on them. The overburdened developmental bureaucracy hardly have any time to participate in adult education programme enthusiastically.

The supervisors of DSS and AMS stated that the block level functionaries wanted them to arrange conveyance to visit centres which they just could not do. The supervisor of AMS said that though his agency owned three imported two wheelers (gifted by Canadians) not even one was sent to the field in spite of several requests. When this question was put to the officials of the agency, they said that "the vehicles get spoiled if driven on dirty village roads" which left investigator to wonder as to the very purpose of keeping idle the vehicles at headquarters when the work is actually being executed in the field. The supervisor of the DSS said his agency did not have a vehicle.

The BCT, however, used its vehicles for bringing resource persons like block level officials. This enabled the officials to participate to some extent in the programme by giving occasional lectures and by answering several questions raised by learners. Presence of officials enthused learners to such an extent that they were feared to answer tough questions like the reasons for the administrative delay in processing their applications for loans etc. This trend in fact had produced a negative effect also on the involvement of officials as they felt that these centres had become a 'nuisance' to them and they stopped visiting on various excuses. This, however, does not mean that all officials felt shy to face learners.

With regard to co-ordination with other agencies implementing NAEP, none of the project officers in charge of adult education centres directly under the government cared to visit centres under the voluntary agencies. Adult education programmes sponsored by the Government of Andhra Pradesh are going on in places close by to those operated by agencies. When the investigator enquired about it, the Project Officers of the Government replied that to visit all the 300 adult education centres directly under their jurisdiction is proving to be an uphill task and, therefore, the question of visiting centres under 'others' according to them was unimaginable.

The same trend is noticed more or less in case of all the agencies like Universities & Colleges, NSS, ICDS Schemes etc. The involvement of developmental functionaries as envisaged in policy statement (and in other documents subsequently released by the Government of India) too had not materialised to the extent desired. The reasons for their partial involvement were already discussed. With this, let us move on to the systems of monitoring and evaluation.

Supervision and Measurement

One of the main functions of the supervisors is to ensure that they follow the reporting systems i.e. monthly and quarterly reports. All supervisors reported compliance with the instructions in this regard and all instructors sent the reports in time. It appeared that the formats for reporting too were lengthy. On this the supervisors felt that it should be smaller in size. Two out of four supervisors admitted that the instructors' reports did not exactly reflect the facts relating to daily attendance, dropouts etc. The position with regard to other two supervisors is interesting. They told the instructors that if they reported correct situation they would be rewarded and they would be punished for wrong figures. This seems to have led, at least to some extent, to correct reporting.

All the supervisors have stated that they are satisfied with their jobs. The supervisors of BCT and CROSS said that a little more co-operation from the government would have made them much more satisfied.

The supervisor of AMS felt that the officials of his agency should pay more interest towards programme by visiting some adult education centres. On the whole, all the supervisors observed that they derived a lot of satisfaction from their jobs.

Common Observation

All the supervisors opined that the success of the programme in terms of targets was commendable as they said that they could make at least 50-60 per cent of the enrolled literate. Most of them, however, are sceptical about success of other two components. Further, the supervisors of BCT felt that there were several limitations to put into operation functional and awareness components. To some extent, he viewed that the functional education component was attempted by admitting some learners in carpentry training centres but only after they completed ten month course. On awareness component, he said it would take some more time.

All the supervisors have unanimously endorsed the view that the NAEP would succeed if more voluntary agencies are associated. They further felt that the progress though not a spectacular success, it definitely resulted in creation of a favourable environment as anticipated by policy makers.

The supervisor of BCT suggested that the present policy of extending education 'free of cost' to adult illiterates calls for a thorough review. The value of education according to the respondents will be realised only when the learner pays from his pocket. The government may supply all resource material like books etc., but the honorarium must at least be met by the adults out of contributions or else it is difficult to check the casual attitude of the illiterates.

Furthermore, the supervisor suggested that government must take into confidence the voluntary agencies which were given permission to implement adult education programme. It should create 'demand' for education by equalizing the qualification acquired by adult illiterate to seventh or fifth class.

The supervisors from other agencies in the sample suggested effective involvement of developmental functionaries of government. This gained currency owing to reports that teaching by an instructor continuously may lead to monotony and the lectures by "others" might arouse interest. The other suggestions include change in pattern as well as emphasis on training, modification in resource material, relaxation of procedures for obtaining grants and other financial assistance for carrying follow-up or post-literacy programmes, delegation of powers from the PLC to the supervisors to select the instructor, supply of audio-visual equipment free of cost by the Taluq Public Relations Officer etc., provision for vehicles for effective supervision.

An analysis of the role and functioning of the supervisors reveals that they have a fairly good grasp and understanding of the NAEP all of them belong to the prescribed age group and the investigators noticed certain amount of commitment. Their dissatisfaction with the training programme has to be taken note of as it greatly helps them in appreciating their role as key level functionaries and directly contributes to increasing their effectiveness.

Sincere attempts by all the supervisors of all the agencies seemed to have been made to involve the developmental personnel at the block level but success in this regard varied. While the supervisor of the BCT, because of his good rapport with block level personnel, could involve at least some of them, the supervisor of DSS and AMS could not do much to involve them as the officials of their agencies themselves were not seemed to be aware of the benefits accruing from that. The limitations cited by the supervisors in imparting functional education and increasing awareness must be examined more deeply.

Inter-agency co-operation may yield better results in this regard. With regard to monitoring and, evaluation, the view of the supervisors that the instructor is overburdened with paper work merits serious consideration. The study also revealed as to how effective supervision depends on provision of conveyance facilities. Average number of visits by the supervisors belonging to two agencies in the sample to centres under their control are much higher than the case with other two. The fact that one agency got the vehicles and is not thinking of giving them to supervisors further reveals the agencies' belief in effective supervision. No doubt, there may be more number of supervisors than vehicles. But the solution does not lie in keeping the vehicles idle. Moreover, it appears that it is not a difficult problem to tackle.

As regards co-ordination, the project level committees attached to each agency need to be activated. Instead of meeting only once in 5 months as was the case with a couple of agencies in the sample, it should meet once in a month. Regular meetings of PLC's facilitate quick decision making pertaining to the project. The methods adopted by BCT for securing co-ordination appear to be more effective and hence deserve to be emulated by others in this regard.

After the discussion on the role, functions, problems of the instructors and supervisors of the adult education centres, we now turn to matters relating to the target group i.e., learners, dropouts and potential learners. In fact, any meaningful, measurement of the impact of policy can be evaluated only with the responses gathered from the 'target' group.

7

PROCESS OF LEARNING

In its biological nature it is the capacity to be found in plasticity of the nervous system which is due to the changes occurring in the formation of bonds and connections. Learning is the superstructure of our personality and characterised upon the basis of natural inherited organism by coming in contact with the world. Thus, learning is life and life is learning. Every experience is learning. Woodruff says that the process of learning is the vehicle by which the individual is changed from a bundle of potentiality to an active organism with ideas, habits, skills and other personality characteristics.

In the whole process of learning, the need arises, goal is set up, adjustment begins, changes in behaviour take place and stabilize. Further, learning involves problem-solving i.e., understanding and discovering relations between different contents in a situation. Here, one may argue that why should one learn? To answer it, it is sufficient to note that learning is an activity aroused by the personal and social demands. And, hence it is the demand of the individual himself; it is the demand of the society which makes him feel to learn. But, the individual may learn things both desirable and undesirable. The task of education, here, should be to enable the individual to learn the desirable and eliminate the undesirable. It is thus said that learning is a process of improvement.

Continuous Process

Learning at all stages is a continuous process involving progressive organization of human behaviour resulting from an interaction with the environment. A few defining characteristics of learning may be mentioned as under

All Living is Learning i.e., the individual is in active relation with his environment. He constantly is interacting with it and is constantly learning.

Learning Results in the Change in Behaviour : We note a change in the persons response to the light. It is a change of behaviour influenced by previous behaviour. It is the outcome of an activity that leaves a more or less permanent effect on later activity.

Learning is an Adjustment : Most learning in children consists in modifying, adapting and changing their original behaviour in order to adjust to life's situations. Thus, they acquire new forms of behaviour.

Learning Comes about as a Result of Practice : This characteristic eliminates sources of change such as illness and maturation. Potent effects of motivation on behaviour are worth considering here.

Learning is Universal : Every creature that lives learns. Man learns most. Human children have the longest period of immaturity and helplessness and hence the longer period for opportunity for learning. The human nervous system is very complex, so are human reactions and so are human acquisitions.

Learning is a Relatively Permanent Change : After a rat wakes up from his nap he still remembers the path to the food. Even if you have not been on a bicycle for years, in just a few minutes' practice you can be quite proficient again. This is due to change that was acquired and persisted.

Learning is Growth : It is never-ending growth. At each stage the learner acquires new ideas and skills which add to his growth. Each learning forms the basis of a fresh endeavour; and thus the constant urge of newer and higher ideals of work and achievement is progressively fulfilled.

Learning is not Directly Observable : The only way to study learning is through some observable behaviour. Actually, we cannot observe learning; the performance, and the consequences of performance.

Learning is not confined to human-beings only; animals also learn in a similar fashion. The jugler makes the monkey to learn so many tricks. Dogs are trained to catch thieves, elephants are taught to perform circus tricks, pigeons learn to play pingpong. Dolphin fish are noted playing net ball or passing through a ring. Hayes trained chimpanzees to perform acts as dusting, washing dishes, sharpening pencil, painting furniture etc. The only difference in animal learning and human learning is in the quality and extent of learning because all learning depends upon the physical and mental structure.

Various Theories

Various theories of learning have been advanced to explain the nature of learning process. And, all these can be broadly classified into two categories

(1) Connectionist or Behaviourist or Mechanicalistic or Associative or S-R theories.

(2) Cognitive or Gestalt or Purposive or Organismic or Field Theories.

S-R Theories : Generally, a student of psychology understands the paradigm S-R, which means that stimulus is connected with and leads to response. Stimulus is any change in external environment which excites nervous system and brings a response. Thus, response is the end product of S-R chain. Certain responses follow certain stimuli. Learning is a matter of connection between S and R. What we learn are habits and tendencies. The theory explains that the learner solves his problems by assembling his past experiences and responds to the new problem either according to elements common to the old and new situation or according to some aspects of the new situation which are similar to the old situation. If there is no similarity we indulge in trial and error behaviour. When these circumstances are studied and put together in some logical form, we have a theory. Within this broad category, the following three theories will be discussed in detail along with some others too.

(a) Pavlov's Classical Conditioning Theory.

(b) Thorndike's Trial and Error Theory.

(c) Skinner's Operant Conditioning Theory.

Cognitive Theories : This theory points out that even with the appropriate past experience, the organism may not solve the problem, if it is presented one way and he will solve it if it is presented in another way, because there is a spontaneous reactions to the contemporary structuring of the field which is not necessarily dependent upon the previous experiences. The supporters of this theory believe in 'intervening process' or 'intervening variable', as there is no such variable present in S-R theory according to the connectionist view point. As regards the nature of this 'intervening variable' the human being is believed to have a mind that controls behaviour to some extent. So we think, we know, we are conscious, we have purpose, we imagine, we believe, we will. Whereas, according to the connectionists, the human organism works only on S-R pattern like a highly complex machine; the will, the purpose, the intention, have no place here. The field theorist takes these processes into consideration and makes 'cognition' a significant aspect of his theory.

They look upon the learner as a dynamic energy system set into an environment, that is, in turn, a complex of other energy systems. Both the learner and the environment are dynamic and not passive. They both act and react in field. Within this broad category the following two theories will be discussed in detail along with some others too.

(a) Gestalt or Insight Learning Theory.

(b) Kurt-Lewin's Field Theory.

Classical Conditioning Theory

This is learning from the behaviouristic viewpoint. According to this viewpoint learning is "formation of conditioned reflexes" or "acquisition of involuntary anticipatory adjustment" or "a habit formation" so that behaviour may become automatic. By "anticipatory adjustment" he means "organic behaviour" which is "not complete" but "with a gap in the whole equilibrium pattern"; for example, hunger in which saliva gastric juice, function of the stomach etc., are the organic behaviours with a gap and so incomplete. It becomes complete when the object of hunger is obtained. Importance of anticipatory adjustment is very great for three reasons. Firstly, it is the foundation of all voluntary behaviour and secondly, it is the active desire that sets the goal and makes the organism strive. Thirdly, it determines "the mind-set" or "organic pattern of readiness." Unless this organic pattern takes place within, no real learning can appear. If we can control this anticipatory adjustment we can also control learning. This controlled learning is the conditioned learning. In this the thing to be learnt is termed as, the stimulus,' and this is then followed by a satisfying stimulus. This combination is repeated again and again and ultimately the learning of the 'cue-stimulus' is established. This is conditioned learning.

Conditioned learning is also accompanied by a generalization of the experience. For example, a child whose fear is conditioned to a white rat also begins to fear a rabbit, cotton wool, a white fur coat and other similar objects. When the same process is repeated again and again for a long time, after the conditioning has taken place, it produces adverse effects. The conditioned S-R becomes extinguished. For example, repeated exposure of the rat may gradually reduce the fear after it has been conditioned.

Conditioned learning actually means responding normally to a natural response and then to an unnatural situation or stimulus, even in the absence of the natural stimulus. We have watering of the mouth seeing a 'Gulab Jamun' or a child feels watering of the mouth when he sees or smells food and not by hearing a cell. But it is the common experience that the ringing of the recess bell leads to watering of the mouth. This teaming of watering of the Mouth on hearing the bell is conditioned learning. It is established when repeatedly the recess bell is followed by sonic refreshments, meals or lunch during recess and bell and food. are associated in quick succession. Much of the learning is by conditioning. Fear, anger and many such reactions are aroused by unnatural, irrelevant or unusual stimuli. The approaching peon of the boss, for example. aroused nervousness and fear though the peon is harmless and innocent. But that peon almost always brought an unpleasant message, letters or news from the boss's office and so the person is conditioned to the approaching of this peon which leads to rousing of fear and nervousness. Similarly, if two girls have been seen together a number of times; seeing one makes you think of the other. These are all illustrations of associative connections. This idea of association has been the basis of the conditioned response theory according to which learning consists in building up of new associative bonds between a stimulus and a response. According to Guilford "The most simple interpretation of this phenomenon is that when two stimuli are presented repeatedly together, the new one first, then the original, effective one the new one also becomes effective."

Experimental Evidences

The Russian Psychologist Ivan Pavlov experimented for long on dogs to study how the stimuli and responses are associated with different types of the stimuli of bell-different colours or lights and established conditioned response of salivation in the dog. In his experiment, he took a dog, kept him in a room and repeatedly gave the ringing of the bell as a stimulus soon followed by food (piece of meat) which led to salivation. Bell and food were presented in a sequence over a number of times (about seven days) and at every trial there was salivation, because there was food seen or smelt soon alter the ringing of the bell. A stage reached when ringing of the bell led to normal salivation even when there was no food supplied. Neurologically it could be explained that the stimulus bell followed by food led to the response of salivation in this planner.

This process is that by making the nerves carrying the stimulus of the food which leads to the response of salivation, come closer and closer with every trial to the nerves carrying the stimulus of the bell reaching a stage where there is an overlapping of the nerves carrying the stimulus of food with the nerves carrying the stimulus of the bell. In other words, a stage is reached when the bell meant food giving rise to the response of salivation. Such establishment of the nervous connections is the conditioned reflex. Here sight of food' was termed as UCS, 'the ringing of the bell' as CS and the 'salivation' in response to the ringing of the bell was termed as CR.

A schematic plan of the procedure is as under

Before Training (conditioning).

1. Bell (CS) -------------> (Head turning, cocking of ears)

Training

2. Bell (CS) and Meat Powder (UCS) ----------------> Salivation (UCR)

After Training

3. Bell (CS) ----------------> Salivation (CR)

In a similar manner. Watson, performed an experiment in which a rabbit was shown to a baby followed immediately by a loud bang which made the baby shriek with fear as the sudden and loud bang becomes fearful due to the bombardment of the sound waves on his delicate eardrum and auditory nerves. In the repeated presentation of the rabbit followed by the loud banging, a stage reached when the baby shrieked the moment the rabbit was shown even when there was no banging. This is learning by conditioning. The baby learnt to shriek at the sight of the rabbit which was quite harmless and quite incapable of instilling any fear. But with the association of banging, which is certainly shocking and arousing fear, the baby learned to react in the fearful manner at the sight of the innocent and harmless rabbit. Watson further experimented with the same baby when at last instead of being afraid, the child was made to be happy on seeing the rabbit.

It was reversing the conditioning or what was called reconditioning. It was done by giving a chocolate or a candy to the child when the rabbit was shown. After some trials when the rabbit was followed by candy, the rabbit and candy sequence established the connection between rabbit and the enjoyment of candy-as a pleasant experience. A stage reached when instead of being afraid, the baby began to play with the rabbit and was very happy to see it because the rabbit was the harbinger of the pleasant feelings of enjoying the candy. This situation of the natural response to an unnatural stimulus with the help of natural stimulus is the process of conditioning.

Similarly, a sleeping infant is frightened by the falling pillow but as it is dark when the pillow fell, the fear is conditioned to the dark and he learns to avoid dark places. The mother feeds the infant after placing him in a certain position on the bed but he starts feeling the pleasure of being fed as he sees her making the bed. All these illustrations throw light on the process of conditioning.

Principles : The success of the theory depends upon the following principles

1. Time Principle: It means that there should not be a wide gap of time between the cue stimulus and the satisfying stimulus. The longer the interval between the two, the less effective the association. Normally the CS (Bell) is presented before the UCS (food). When UCS is presented before the CS, some learning may take place, but it is not as effective as when the CS is presented before the UCS. It is for this reason that reward and punishment should be given immediately.
2. Principle of Intensity: It means that the satisfying stimulus should be of sufficient intensity, otherwise, it cannot produce the desirable organic behaviour.
3. Principle of Consistency: It means that the same process should be repeated in the same way without any change for several days.
4. The Situational Principle: It means that the situation or the surrounding in which learning is to take place should be such as there may not be in it chances of distraction.
5. Principle of Repetition: It means that repetition is necessary for reinforcement and fixation of learned response.
6. Principle of Inhibition: Inhibition should not be allowed i.e., there should not be allowed any factor or situation that inhibits learning. Pavolv's students often found that having set up a conditioned response in a dog they did not exhibit it to Pavlov because his presence in the room inhibited it. Likewise, we see student-teachers failing to deliver a very well planned and prepared lesson in the presence of the supervisor.

Educational Implications : Many things of the school-subjects are learnt more adequately through this process. Reading, writing, spelling or habits, etc., are learnt more effectively through the process of conditioning. Direct method of teaching English is just a process of conditioning. We learn many things in a better way through this process, and that is perhaps the reason why language is more efficiently learnt by living in the society in which it is spoken. Teaching through visual aids also implies the same principle.

Discipline may also be caused through conditioning. Good sentiments, good habits, virtues and ideals etc., which are the components of discipline are effectively learnt through the process of conditioning, and they are learnt surely in a society in which they are actually lived and manifested.

Class room procedures are often far removed from the natural procedures required for the process of conditioning. Languages are not taught as they ought to be in connection with many vivid and widely different experiences. If the regulations, commands and virtues are followed by the friendly behaviour and the most sympathetic attitude of the teacher, he can bring about a compliant emotional tone in the class that no amount of punishment can accomplish. But uniformity of procedure is essential. Voluntary action may be controlled through reasoning, punishment and reward but if its involuntary basis is neglected it will not endure. In conditioning, involuntary responses are controlled through the cue stimuli.

Many of our fears and phobias may be traced back to some kind of conditioning. When things and objects associate with an unpleasant experience and a sort of generalization is made, phobias appear. Such fears and phobias can be removed by de-conditioning. Dislike for a teacher or certain school subjects can also be helped to be overcome through reconditioning by associating pleasant stimuli with them.

Moreover, in experimental psychology the theory of conditioned reflex occupies an important place and it has revolutionised child learning. Before the advent of this theory the knowledge of learning process was vague. It is not a psychological truism that the child's learning consists in the establishment of conditioned reflexes leading to formation of permanent habits. The intelligent learner can establish conditioned reflexes with facility while the idiot cannot. Lastly, this theory brings learning under the teacher's control making desired learning conditioned by situations created or regulated by the experimenter himself.

"Different kinds of habits based on training, education and discipline are nothing but a long chain of conditioned reflex."

...Pavlov.

Criticism : In spite of the above merits, the conditioned reflex theory of learning is open to serious defects. It is in the first place, a mechanical theory overlooking the learner's interest, attention and other higher mental processes. For this reason this theory many a time does not work. Learning depends largely upon learner's will, interest and attention. Further, not all stimuli can be conditioned by unconditioned ones. For example, the child's natural love for the mother cannot, normally, be conditioned by the unconditioned stimulus of seeing somebody else, whom he naturally hates. Secondly, the theory of conditioning lays emphasis on repetition of stimulus and response to strengthen connection between them. But Dunlop demonstrated that the occurrence of a response is the probability that it will occur again when there is the same stimulus. Dunlop had the habit of typing 'the' as 'hte'. He was able to mend his habit by consciously typing 'the' as 'hte' thousands of times. Thus, the probability of occurrence of response (typing 'hte') was lessened when same stimulus (typing 'the') was provided. This law is opposed to theory that repetition strengthens connection. We can conclude from these two conflicting positions that it is not the occurrence of the response which determines the probability of its occurrence, but pleasant and unpleasant nature of the response. Thirdly, the theory is not put forward as an explanation of learning; it merely states the conditions of learning, the condition that must be present if learning is to occur A certain amount of frequency, or duration of time is required to permit the effective factors to operate. The space of time separating the two stimuli or responses to be connected must not be too great for the backward or forward spread of association. Finally, the theory has been considerably elaborated into ascending orders of conditioning to explain the higher thought and reasoning processes and even voluntary activity. At this point most psychologists demur. While conditioning gives a plausible account of the conditions of specific learnings, particularly those involving emotional reactions, its adequacy in the case of complex thought processes is widely questioned. To the educator, in particular, it is of no apparent value in describing higher learning.

Guthrie's Theory

E.R. Guthrie (1886-1959) of Washington University in line with the thinking of Skinner and Thorndike, though with some differences in approach particularly with regard to the purpose or motivation, developed his own theory of learning similar to J.B. Watson. But he rejected the law of frequency developed by Watson. Guthrie, as a matter of fact, elaborated Watson's views of behaviour in general and of learning in particular. He conducted a series of experiments on cats in puzzle boxes. He proved that for establishing connection between S-R only one trial was enough with the conditioned stimulus of full strength; but practice is useful because it helps to knit S-R bond together to form the larger units of behaviour that we call acts. Guthrie in his book '*Psychology of Learning*' says that learning can occur in the absence of reward only by sheer contiguity and the theory could be called the Contiguity Theory. For Guthrie, contiguity, which is temporal in nature is of situation or stimulus and the response. According to this theory temporal contiguity between a stimulus and a response is the basic condition of learning. When every time a response occurs in strict contiguity with the constellation of stimuli, it becomes associated completely in all or none fashion. If the stimulus pattern remains unchanged and a second response is caused, complete unlearning of the 1st S-R connection and complete learning of 2nd S-R connection occurs. The rat learns to trace the maze when one response becomes stimulus or reminds of the next step which in turn becomes the stimulus for the next move. To him learning is automatic with all or none response and frequency is not so necessary. Learning may be sudden and even a frequency of one is sufficient.

Guthrie considers that a child learns what he does. Whatever he perceives becomes a stimulus for the response that occurs at the same time. Whenever the stimulus reappears, he does what he did the last time. Guthrie developed no separate concept of motivation; for him stimuli are motives. Stimulation may be from within or without which arouses the learner and causes him to respond in many ways. The teacher should not teach when the students are absorbed in their own affairs or when the teacher is not able to attract the attention of the students. Guthrie stresses that the organism responds to various stimuli by contraction of muscles and secretion of glands. These specific responses are called movements. According to Guthrie, an act is a series of movements associated together by the law of contiguity. We can explain it with the help of walking which requires a number of movements of muscles and senses which combined together make an act. Guthrie rejected the theory of Thorndike saying that he was concerned with acts, not with movements.

In order to test the theory of Guthrie, two noteworthy experiments are described as below :

Experiment 1: Guthrie and Horton conducted the first experiment in 1946 on cats in a puzzle box to prove that learning is a process of association and of nothing else. The experiment was a simple one. A cat was kept in a box with a small pole in the midst of the box as a release mechanism. The touching of the pole from any side and in any manner opened the door. The cat could come out of the box and eat the food put outside the cage. The cat found the solution immediately and whenever put in the box, the cat repeated its previous behaviour. He concluded that what any animal would do at any moment was based on a record of what he did the first time in the past. In a similar fashion Guthrie noticed in teaching children to read printed word. The child looks at the symbol and while looking he speaks. When the child notices these symbols in future, he tends to say them correctly because of stimulus-response (S-R) connection. The principle of association by contiguity is important to analyse emotional responses of human beings in daily life. The emotional responses of school children are very significant in the teaching-learning process.

Experiment 2: Vocks conducted the second experiment in 1954 to prove the theoretical concept of Guthrie. He used a bell as a conditioned stimulus (CS) and eye blink as the conditioned response (CR). He found that the subjects acquirea conditioned response.

A typical subject might show no conditioning in the first six trials and then on the seventh trial showed the conditioned response in full strength. Here it is essential to mention that according to contiguity, forgetting is simply to do something else. We forget not by disuse but by other learning. It believes in interference theory of forgetting. Guthrie was quite hopeful of the possibilities of transfer knowledge from one situation to another by way of giving practice in that specific area of knowledge or by providing practice in wide variety of situations that are generally like the situation in which performance is expected in future. Also, Guthrie did not believe that, goal or purpose determines activity in any future sense.

"A stimulus pattern that is acting at the time of a response, if it recurs, tends to produce that response." ....Guthrie.

Principles : Guthrie developed several fundamental principles of learning.

The first and most important of them is the Principle of conditioning. He attempted to reduce all principles to this basic principle.

The second principle of learning is the inhibitory conditioning which means that responses are inhibited if any other response occurs in between the original stimulus-response.

The third principle, which deals with delayed conditioning in his opinion, is not conditioning at all.

The fourth principle is that improvement in performance is the result of practice. Guthrie believed that conditioning takes place after a single trial. The emphasis on practice to strengthen stimulus-response connection is for the purpose of enlistment of increasing numbers of stimuli as conditioners and not for strengthening of individual connections.

The fifth principle is a basic law of learning which is known as the contiguity principle. According to this principle a combination of stimulus which has accompanied a movement, will on its recurrence tend to be followed by that movement. In other words, we may say that when two psychological processes occur together in time or in immediate succession, the probability increases that an associative connection between them will develop.

Critical Appraisal : Guthrie was the most leading advocate of stimulus-response theory of association by contiguity. He rejected the law of frequency developed by Watson in favour of a principle of posterity which emphasized that only the last response in the series which was connected to the stimulus is important. Guthrie also rejected the theory of Thorndike saying that he was concerned with acts, not with movements. He explained his position on learning saying "our position is that what is associated is a stimulus and response. It would be perhaps more exact to say what is more associated is some stimulation of sense organs and a corresponding muscular contraction or glandular secretion.

By calling them associated we mean that the stimulation has become the occasion for the response because of a past association of the two. Thus, we see that Guthrie's system was the simplest one. He emphasized the importance. of the overt stimulus and overt response. There is no place for annoyers or satisfiers and reinforcement in his theory of learning. Guthrie's system, even being the simplest one, could not generate research. It was due to the reason that he had no research scholars who could carry on research on his proposed model. The other reason was that when his theory of learning was formulated, it stood outside the main stream of behaviour theory of that period.

In the meantime Tolman and Hull developed well-organized system introducing the concept of intervening variables. They attributed importance to the concept of motivation. But, Guthrie developed no separate concept of motivation. For him stimuli are motives; for example, when feeling of fear is generalized in the mind of the student about the various things and school situations including subject matter and teacher, the student will be compelled to repel from all these odd circumstances, and, if, on the other hand, a teacher makes the students feel good, then it means that he is making the students to like school and enjoy learning.

Guthrie's theory had an anachronistic quality when it first appeared in 1935. It was based on the principles of Pavlov and Watson. He explained behaviour in terms of stimulus-response connections excluding completely the concept of reinforcement. His analysis of extinction, punishment, habit breaking and other phenomenon had considerable impact on theory of education. His theory provided theoretical model for later workers. Behaviour therapists apply his methods of breaking habits in correcting deviant behaviour in children.

Briefly speaking, keeping all these points of view in mind we can say that though, no one point of view can explain fully the complex phenomenon of learning, and also, no point of view is also useless or wrong, yet, in fact, undoubtedly, the theory is a major contribution to the understanding of the various aspects of learning.

Trial and Error Theory

Edward Lee Thorndike (1874-1949) is generally considered to have been the foremost educational psychologist not only of the United States but of the world. He contributed profusely to research and theory in the field of learning and genetic psychology, testing and social psychology. Thorndike first stated the elements of his theory of learning in 1913 saying that connections are formed in the nervous system between stimuli and response. These connections formed are illustrated by the symbol S-R Another word used to describe these connections is the word bond' and hence, this theory is sometimes called a 'Bond Theory of Learning'. Thorndike has written. "Learning is connecting. The mind is man's connection system."

According to Thorndike learning takes place by trial and error. Some people call it "learning by selection of the successful variant". Accordingly when no readymade solution of a problem is available to the learner, he adopts the method of Trial and Error. He first, tries one solution. If it does not help him, he rejects it. "Then, he tries another, and so on. In this way he eliminates errors or irrelevant responses which do not serve the purpose and finally discovers the correct solution. Thus, in Trial and Error method, the learner makes random activities and finally reaches the goal accidentally. Here, one thing should be remembered that in Trial and Error also, there are often systematic and relevant responses. Activities are not wholly random. All these activities though apparently random, are suggested to him by the situation and the learner proceeds on accordingly. The stages through which the learner has to pass are Goal, Block (hindrances), Random Movements or Multiple Response, Chance-success, Selection and Fixation.

When and how the connection is accomplished was stated first in the following three laws :

Law of Readiness: First Primary law of learning, according to him is the 'Law of Readiness' or the 'Law of Action Tendency', which means that learning takes place when an action tendency is aroused through preparatory adjustment, set or attitude. Readiness means a preparation for action. If one is not prepared to learn, learning cannot be automatically instilled in him; for example, unless the typist in order to learn typing, prepares himself to start, he would not make much progress in a lethargic and unprepared manner.

Law of Exercise: The second law of learning is the 'Law of Exercise' which means that drill or practice helps in increasing efficiency and durability of learning and according to Thorndike's S-R Bond Theory, the connections are strengthened with trial or practice and the connections are weakened when trial or practice is discontinued. The law of exercise, therefore, is also understood as the 'law of use and dis-use' in which case connections or bonds made in the brain cortex are weakened or loosened. Many examples of this are found in case of human learning. Learning to drive a motor-car, typewriting, singing or memorizing a poem or a mathematical tables, and music etc., need exercise and repetition of various movements and actions many times.

Law of Effect: The third law is the 'Law of Effect' according to which the trial or steps leading to satisfaction stamps in the bond or connection. Satisfying states lead to consolidation and strengthening of the connection, whereas dis-satisfaction, annoyance or pain lead to the weakening or stamping out of the connections. In fact, the law of effect signifies that if the responses satisfy the subject, they are learnt and selected, while those which are not satisfying are eliminated. Teaching, therefore, must be pleasing. The educator must obey the Rings and interests of his pupils. In other words, greater the satisfaction, stronger will be the motive to learn. Thus, intensity is an important condition of the law of effect.

Besides these three basic laws, Thorndike also refers to five subordinate laws which further help to explain the learning process. These are :

Law of Multiple Response: According to it the organism varies or changes its responses till an appropriate behaviour is hit upon. Without varying the responses, the correct response for the solution might never be elicited. If the individual wants to solve a puzzle, he is to try in different ways rather than mechanically persisting in the same way. Thorndike's cat in the puzzle box moved about and tried many ways to come out, till finally it hit the latch with her paw which opened the door and it jumped out.

The Law of Set or Attitude: Learning is guided by a total set or attitude of the organism, which determines not only what the person will do but what will satisfy or annoy him. For instance, unless the cricketer sets himself to make a century, he will not be able to score more runs. A student, similarly, unless he sets to get first position and has the attitude of being at the top, would while away the time and would not learn much. Hence, learning is affected more in the individual if he is set to learn more or to excel.

Pre-potency of Elements: According to this law, the learner reacts selectively to the important or essential in the situation and neglects the other features or elements which may be irrelevant or non-essential. The ability to deal with the essential or the relevant part of the situation, makes analytical and insightful learning possible. In this law of pre-potency of elements, Thorndike is really anticipating insight in learning which was more emphasised by the Gestaltists.

Law of Response by Analogy: According to this law, the individual makes use of old experiences or acquisitions while learning a new situation. There is a tendency to utilise common elements in the new situation as existed in a similar past situation. The learning of driving a car, for instance, is facilitated by the earlier acquired skill of driving a motor cycle or even riding a bicycle, because the perspective of maintaining a balance and controlling the handle helps in stearing the car.

The Law of Associative Shifting: According to this law we may get any response of which a learner is capable, associated with any other situation to which he is sensitive. Thorndike illustrated this by the act of teaching a cat to stand up at a command. A fish was dangled before the cat while he said 'stand up'. After a number of trials by presenting the fish after uttering the command 'stand up', he later ousted the fish and the over all command of 'stand up' was found sufficient to evoke the response in the cat by standing up on her hind legs.

Experimental Evidence : Various experiments have been performed on men as well as animals to study this method. Thorndike made several experiments on rats and cats. Two important experiments are mentioned here.

Expt. 1 : Thorndike's most widely quoted experiment was with the cat placed in a puzzle box. The hungry cat was put in the puzzle box and a fish, as an incentive, was put outside the cage a little beyond its reach. The box was designed in such a way that the door of the cage could be released by some simple act like depressing a lever inside the cage. At first, the cat made a great deal of varied attempts to reach the food in a trial and error fashion such as jumping up and down, clawing at the bars, scratching the cage, walking around, trying to push the bars, pawing and shaking movable parts of the cage etc., but all attempts proved in vain. Ultimately by chance her paw fell on the loop of the rope and the door opened. The cat jumped out immediately and ate the fish. When next day, the cat was put in the box again, this time she took less time in coming out and in the subsequent trials the time decreased further so much so that the stage reached when the cat came out soon after being put inside by directly striking the latch with her paw without any random movement. This is how she learnt to reach its goal.

Expt. 2 : (Experiment with Human Subjects): Gopalaswamy demonstrated trial and error in human beings through Mirror-Drawing Experiment. This is a classical experiment in the psychology of learning. In this experiment the subject is asked to trace a star-shaped drawing, not looking at it directly, but as it is reflected in a mirror. The subject's hand movements are visible in the mirror only and not directly. The experimenter observes the movements of the hands and thus, records the time of tracing in successive trials and the number of errors committed in each trial. In first six trials the subject traces the star with the right hand and then in the next six trials he traces it by the left hand. Two graphs-the Time Curve and the Error Curve are then drawn, which show the general characteristics of trial and error learning. In the original experiment Gopalaswamy arranged his apparatus so that a record was automatically made of all the movements of the styles of the subject as it traced out the pattern. In this way the successive times of teachings and a record of errors were obtained.

Gopalaswamy analysed the errors into two groups-lower level errors and higher level errors. Those errors which did not involve any novel process on the part of the subject in tracing the star were lower-level errors and those which involved higher process of mind at the perceptual and conceptual level were higher-level errors. He discovered that improvement in the higher-level responses correlated highly with intelligence and that the improvement in the responses of the lower-level errors did not show much correlation with intelligence.

Educational Implications : Thorndike's theory of Trial and Error and his three basic laws of learning have direct educational implications. The law of readiness lays emphasis on motivation while the law of exercise compels us to accept a well known fact 'Practice maketh a man perfect' and the third one i.e., law of effect opens fairly a large scope to discuss the role of reward and punishment as an incentive in the child's learning.

The significant aspect of this theory is that to master a complex or elaborate task practice is essential. It is not possible to handle each difficult situation in a single trial, no matter what the degree of motivation or reward is. One cannot cram the entire constitution of India in one reading even if the reward is a crore of rupees or the threat is to be shot dead otherwise. Each task initially seems to be difficult and fatiguing but as practice continues, it becomes smoother and requires less effort. Finally, we say that habit or S-R is established. An expert driver, for instance, goes on driving, listening to the radio and talking to his friend sitting by. In the light of class room teaching blundering is a natural phenomenon associated with student learning. But, the teacher should not regard this as a symptom of inefficient teaching because this is the way the pupils learn. He should not be at all worried when blundering appears. Insights will emerge as the blundering progresses from simpler associations to higher units. There is no royal road to success.

Actually, we learn by doing. The teacher's duty should be, therefore, to arrange situations in which the student has a chance to discover for himself what is significant. The blundering must be directed and methods that are wholly futile must be eliminated. But at the same time the teacher must exercise constant restraint in his supervision. The child who can work mathematical problem-when the teacher's promptings keep him on the right path is still a long-way from learning anything about mathematics.

Finally, though the theory is not widely accepted for its educational significance, yet, there are certain subjects such as mathematics, tables of mathematics, memorising poetry, rules of grammar etc., in which learning by Trial and Error can not be avoided. All reasoning subjects afford the greatest opportunity for the application of the Trial and Error method.

Critical Appraisal : The theory has been criticised by various psychologists on the following grounds. Firstly, the theory is mechanical, for it leaves no room for an end or purpose in any sense whatsoever. On the contrary psychologist McDougall maintained that even the behaviour of the amoeba or the paramaecia consists in learning to face novel conditions to serve some unknown purpose. Even repeated trials are of no avail if the tendency to learn is not there. Again, if the tendency is there, even one trial may be fruitful. McDougall and Woodworth insist on readiness for reaching a goal in learning and Lloyd Morgan lays stress on persistence with varied efforts till the goal of learning is achieved. The hungry cat confined in the puzzle box with food in front of it goes on persistently trying various means until it gets out of it and has food. So its trials are not blind and mechanical. In fact, they are guided by perceptual attention and feelings of pleasure and pain. Yet, Thorndike pays no attention to these higher order mental processes. Secondly, in course of repeated trials the number of errors are not corrected of themselves or mechanically. The effects of Trial and Error depend to a great extent upon the psycho-physical state of animal making them. In the absence of any purpose in view the animal is so puzzled, rather than enlightened by the errors committed, that it goes on blindly repeating them without end. Thirdly, Thorndike assumes that learning consists only in the association of several separate movements. But learning is a whole process related to a whole situation. The hungry cat confined in a puzzle-box with food placed near it does not perceive the situation in a piece-meal fashion but as a whole. Finally, the laws of learning formulated by Thorndike appear to be unjustified. For instance, the law of effect seems to be inconsistent with his mechanical point of view. Satisfaction in or the sense of being rewarded by success and dissatisfaction in or the sense of being punished by failure seem to ascribe higher mental processes to animals like cats and rats than are psychologically ascribable to them. Or, it violates Lloyd Morgan's law. Similarly, the law of exercise has been severely criticised on the grounds that it does not regard other factors like motives, interests, special training etc. Mechanical repetition without motive, interest, significance or understanding does not make anyone learn anything and remember it. One rupee-currency note passes hundred times through the hands of a person, but hardly anyone is able to tell the size, the colour and other details of it. This shows that repetition without motive, interest or understanding is of no avail.

Hull's Reinforcement Theory

C.L. Hull an American was professor of psychology at Yale University. His theory is a stimulus-response theory; but he built a new system combining the law of effect with the concept of conditioning under the concept of reinforcement. His views have been applied to more complex learning by Miller, Dollard and Mowrer. His system of behaviour is studied under S-R reinforcement theories. His system is deductive, mathematical and testable. Hull's theory of teaming holds that association between S-R is not enough for learning. He is of the opinion that some kind of reward or other reinforcement is necessary in order to establish the stimulus as signal. Hull was highly impressed by Pavlov and his experiments. The way Hull explained the meaning of learning is known as systematic behaviour theory. It is also named as Refined theory or Precise theory as it elaborates beautifully the formula S-R.

Its Principle: Hull's theory is also named as Drive Reduction Theory which was explained by him in 1915 in his well known book, *'Principles of Behaviour'*. In the same book Hull explained this theory under the name of 'Reinforcement theory', which explains learning in terms of the change in behaviour which occurs under such conditions as of reward or effect as called by Thorndike. Complex learning, according to him, involves conditioning principles, although simple learning and complex learning do not seem to differ in the essential principles or laws. Animal learning and human learning both involve the same principles, though factors like language and meaning may complicate the study of learning in some ways. Hull as a mechanistic psychologist, avoiding recourse to consciousness and as a follower of Watson, worked for the fulfilment of the behaviouristic programme, as proposed by Watson. According to him behaviour or learning are more or less synonymous. The central concept in this theory is that habits are mostly formed by conditioning. Complex learning according to him, is derived step by step from simple learning and the law of effect or of reinforcement was at the roots of Hull's system.

Emphasizing the importance of drives in the theory Hull believed that these drives impel the individual to respond to certain cues which determine when he will respond, where he will respond and which response he will make. The cue value of a stimulus depends upon its distinctiveness and drive value on its strength. The responses made to cues in the presence of drives will be learnt if they are rewarded. The gradients of effect or reward are what Hull called the gradients of reinforcement and what Thorndike called the spread of effect. The cue-responses sequence is increased in the neighbourhood of the reward which means that nearer the reward the greater is the strengthening of bonds. This is the main difference between Guthrie's and Hull's theory. According to Guthrie association occurs when the cues and responses are together but according to Hull the association between cue and response is regulated by their relationship with drive and reward. In brief, according to Hull a stimulus (S), impinges on the organism. This results in a neural impulse which leads to a reaction (R). For this to occur, however, there has to be drive (D). Drive is a state of, tension resulting from a need. If the response or reactions (R) reduces the tension or drive (D), we have a condition of reinforcement. This reinforcement brings about an organization in the nervous system which is known as a habit or learning. In Hull's system, for understanding learning; the sequence is drive-cue-response-reward leading to further reinforcement making repetition easier and this leads to learning. Here we see that a factor of drive is also based on a need which is even more important than what was thought by Thorndike or Guthrie. Hull stated his theory in the form of sixteen postulates or general rules.

Basic Concepts : Some of the basic concepts involved in the theory are as under :

Stimulus: For Hull, responses are conditioned to the neural aftereffects of stimuli rather than to the stimuli themselves. The effective stimulus, in learning, is the trace in the nervous system caused by the environmental objects. According to Hull, the stimuli in the object would give rise to stimulus traces in the organism. The first we might designate S and the second s. Learning involves S and not the s.

Response: Hull was of the opinion that we may distinguish between tendency within the person to make a response and the actual response itself. If we designate the overt responses R we can refer to the pre-existing neural activities which initiate the response as r. These internal response tendencies are not observable but inferred from behaviour. Symbolically the learned association of S and R is represented as SHR where H represents habit. Changes in SHR constitute learning in Hull's system.

Need : It is the lack of something which is experienced by the organism. It then tries to perform that activity which culminates in the satisfaction of the need. Thus needs are associated with goals. In human beings, needs are relatively permanent tendencies which seek their satisfaction in achieving certain specific goals. When a need arises, the organism acts in order to reduce the need. Sometimes. Hull's theory of learning is called need reduction theory.

Drive: Word drive is usually used when there is a feeling of mental tension or restlessness on account of our bodily needs. A drive is a tendency of shifts in physiological balance tissue, tension-sensitivity to stimuli of a certain class and response in any of variety of ways that are related to the attainment of a certain goal. In other words, it is a general condition of deprivation in the organism. It is a common denominator of all primary motivations whether due to food, water, sex or any other cause.

Reinforcement: The term reinforcement means strengthening the tendency of a response to be repeated. When an organism responds to a stimulus and that response is reinforced, it is very probable that the same response will be repeated the next time if that stimulus occurs. Reinforcement according to Hull is like Thorndike's reward. In a way, it is a stimulus which has the ability to alter the probabilities of certain R following certain S. When a response is reinforced, this means that it has been followed by one of a certain class of stimuli. Hull postulated that reinforcing stimuli were those which reduced stimuli associated with the drives.

There are few concepts related to reinforcement which are discussed in brief as follows :

(a) *Primary Reinforcement:* A conditioned response is possible only if the child or animal has a need or a primary drive and the law of effect operates when that need or drive is satisfied or reduced. Psychologists agree that the reduction in the strength of primary drive or need is a reinforcing factor. The law of primary reinforcement may be stated in a simple form: a stimulus S is presented, it is followed by a response R and if this S-R bond helps in reducing the tension, there will be an increased tendency for that bond to be repeated. Activities which reduce tension are reinforcing.

(b) *Extinction :* When there is no primary reinforcement, with repetition the stimulus response connection will grow weaker till it finally disappears. This process is known as extinction. Occasionally the extinguished response will return spontaneously after a rest period. The ringing of the bell may lead the dog to salivate after some days during which it did not so respond to it, but the response is weak.

(c) *Gradient of Reinforcement :* Several experiments have been made with the time interval between the conditioned stimulus and the response, and they indicate that with the increase in time interval the response follows less frequently. If the interval is more than 30 seconds conditioning is negligible. This reduction in the frequency or strength of conditioning is called the gradient of reinforcement. In some experiments it was demonstrated that reinforcement did not work if it was delayed by 5 seconds and was maximum if it was delayed only by half a second. The dog would not salivate oil, the ringing of the bell if there was an interval of more than 30 seconds between the presentation of food and the ringing of the bell.

(d) *Secondary Reinforcement :* Hull puts forward the theory of secondary reinforcement to account for learning where there is a longer interval of time between the reinforced response and need reduction. All our needs are not primary. The need for food is primary but the need for money which can buy food is secondary. Secondary needs are acquired, and though they do not by themselves reduce any need, they are associated with things which help to reduce need. Money is a secondary reinforcer, its need-reduction power is remote but it is closely and consistently associated with need reduction. This is secondary reinforcement.

(e) *Stimulus Generalization :* If a child is bitten by a non-barking dog the sound of the word dog, its sight or smell will make the child shrink in fear though these stimuli did not function in the original situation. In a study described by Watson an eleven-month-old boy who was conditioned to fear a rat, later on showed fear in the presence of a rabbit, a dog, a fur coat, cotton and wool. The fear was aroused by the similarity of these stimuli- their woolliness or furriness. If a bell leads to salivation, any sound of higher or lower pitch resembling it will also lead to that. This Hull calls stimulus generalization, and it is responsible for many of the confusion and mistakes of children in both life and learning.

Operant Conditioning Theory

B.F. Skinner is a very staunch behaviourist. He was the professor of psychology at Harvard University. His theory of operant conditioning also known as instrumental conditioning is nothing but only an extension of S-R Bond theory of Thorndike, Watson and Pavlov. Skinner, considers man like a machine or an automation with no personality and no inner free will and is only a tool of the environment. His psychology is of engineering type and lays emphasis on application of psychological principles to actual life situations. Man is neutral and passive. His basic thesis is that an organism tends to do in future what it was doing at the time of reinforcement which meant that by reinforcing at each step, one could make the organism to do what one wishes it to do. In operant conditioning, the important stimulus is the one, immediately following the response and not the preceding one. Any response which leads to reinforcement is thereby strengthened. If the occurrence of an operant is followed by presentation of reinforcing stimulus, the strength increases. Hence, carefully stated, an operant is a class of responses of which a specific response is an instance or member. A rat presses a lever and gets food, so the rat will be more likely to press the lever again. What is changed is the future probability of the response made. The operant is a class of behaviour rather than the response at a particular instance. It is not correct to say that an operant reinforcement strengthened the response which preceded it. The response has already occurred and can not be changed. What has been changed is the probability of that class of responses that will occur in the future. Since each reinforcement builds up reserve of responses, a pigeon may continue to raise its head, or rat to press the lever several times even after food has ceased to appear.

The law of operant conditioning is that if the occurrence of an operant is followed by presentation of a reinforcing stimulus, its future probability of occurrence will increase.

In the words of Skinner

"Operant conditioning is the learning process whereby a response is made more probable or more frequent and operant is strengthened i.e., reinforced"

Classical and Operant Conditioning: There are some basic differences between classical and operant conditioning which are mentioned as below :

(1) C.C. was developed by Russian scientist, Pavlov and is called Pavlovian or type-1 learning while operant conditioning was developed by B.F. Skinner and is called Skinnerian or type-2 learning.

(2) In classical conditioning the CR and UR are the same while in operant conditioning they are different. For instance, in case of operant conditioning pressing the lever is different from eating the food.

(3) In classical conditioning there is pairing of UCS and CS, while in operant conditioning there is no pairing of UCS and CS.

(4) In classical conditioning there is definite bond between UCS and CS, while in operant conditioning the tendency to respond in a specific manner is developed.

(5) Classical conditioning is controlled by autonomic nervous system, while operant conditioning is controlled by central nervous system in the organism.

(6) Classical conditioning may be represented in the S-R form, while operant conditioning is R-S form.

(7) In C.C. the association between S-R is on the basis of law of contiguity, while in O.C. association between S-R is on the basis of law of effect.

(8) In C.C. reinforcement comes first, while in O.C. reinforcement is provided after the response is made by the organism.

(9) In C.C. stress is laid on time control, while in O.C. stress is laid on motivation and reward.

(10) In C.C. the essence of learning is stimulus substitution, while in O.C. the essence of learning is response modification.

(11) C.C. is stimulus oriented, while O.C. is response oriented.

(12) Classical conditioning is restricted to the animal learning only, while operant conditioning may be useful for animal and human learning both.

Experimental Evidence : Operant conditioning has come into considerablè prominence in recent years as a result of Skinner's success in training animals and more recently in shaping academic behaviour through programmed instruction. He performed many experiments on rats, cats, dogs, pigeons, etc. Below are mentioned few important ones.

Exp. 1 : In an experiment a hungry pigeon was kept in a Skinner box. The pigeon had to raise his head to a particular height and peck at a particular spot in order to get his food. In actual experiment, the pigeon was first rewarded with a food pellet when it approached a disc, then only when it nodded toward it and eventually only when it actually pecked it. By certain repetitions it learnt to do so quickly and automatically. Skinner called such behaviour of learning to peck or to press a lever or bar to get the reward as operant conditioning. Operant means effective or active and this term indicates that the organism is operating upon the environment. Here, the process of operant conditioning is the change in frequency with which the head is lifted to a given height. The reinforcer is food and the reinforcement is the process of food presentation, when the response is emitted (the head is raised to a particular height and a particular spot it pecked). The operant is the height to which the head must be raised. By judiciously rewarding the spontaneous action of birds, Skinner has shaped the behaviour of birds in many ways. Some pigeons have been taught, for example, to peck a bell back and forth across a table, to play ping-pong and to peck out tunes on a xylophone.

Exp. 2 : In a similar experiment Skinner put a hungry rat into his box. The box was equipped with a bar and food tray. The bar could be depressed. Occasionally, the rat would wander over and push the bar down. After a while Skinner would reinforce this action by permitting a food pellet to fall into the tray when the bar was depressed by the rat. Skinner, further modified his experiment. Food pellets would, now, be supplied under certain conditions when the bar was pushed down, for instance, when a tone was sounded but not under other conditions. The experiment involves all the basic principles of classical conditioning, as, the rat learned to press the bar more frequently, when the behaviour was reinforced by a food pellet. If it was not reinforced, extinction occurred. For a while the rat generalised and pushed the bar down at the same rate when the tone was sounded. Eventually after enough time it discriminated and pushed the bar only when the tone was sounded. Although the experiment seems similar to Pavlov's experiment as regards dog and the rat, Skinner's rats are more active as they operated on the bar. It is thus, that Skinner called this operant conditioning as instrumental since the behaviour of the organism is instrumental in accomplishing the purpose.

Exp. 3 : In 1950, a man of 70 who had lost his speech at the age of 50 years could not be cured by psychoanalysis and was later subjected to operant conditioning. Kessorla treated him. The subject was supplied food and Kessorla herself sat aside, watching the subject. The man looked and looked again at the food but could not speak. The woman did not pay any attention to him nor looked at in support. The man just moved his lips and did not perform any activity. The woman took away the food. Next day, when the food was supplied again, the subject made greater efforts with the speech apparatus. At this moment, the woman put some food before him. As a result of the experiment in about 25 days, 75% of his speech was restored. As the man, was 70 years old his 100% speech could not be restored. Operant conditioning technique (OCT) is often used to modify the behaviour in many cases in mental hospitals. Later on this techniques proved of great importance in the field of education also.

Its Principles : To repeat any desired activity or to make a desired behaviour permanent Skinner has suggested a schedule of reinforcement. On account of these schedules any desired behaviour can be made fixed or permanent. The behaviour which suits us is repeated again and again. The individual who performs desired behaviour in his first attempts is provided incentives so that he repeats the same behaviour again and again. Such incentives may be provided through schedules of reinforcement.

As regards schedules of reinforcement Skinner has suggested' the following schedules of reinforcement.

Fixed Ratio Schedule: Fixed Ratio Reinforcement is given when the frequency of reinforcement depends on the rate at which responses are given i.e., the pallet of food is delivered after each fourth, eighth, twelveth responses. Higher ratio should be approached gradually.

Variable Ratio Schedule: In a variable ratio schedule the reinforcer is presented after different number of responses on different occasions. Sometimes the difference amounts to one or sometimes two. Thus, the digit goes on changing as one, four, seven, nine etc.

Fixed Interval Schedule: On a fixed-interval schedule, a fixed interval of time has to elapse before the reinforcer can be presented i.e., every 2 minutes or 4 minutes. This is also known as periodic reinforcement. So, interval reinforcement depends simply on the passage of time. Shorter intervals yield more rapid response rates than the longer ones.

Variable Interval Schedule: When the interval between reinforcement is randomly varied it is known as a variable interval schedule. In this situation the subject is reinforced on a time interval basis but the interval of time is indefinite. Sometimes the subject is reinforced a couple of times very close together and sometimes a considerable amount of time is allowed to elapse.

Educational Implications : Skinner's operant conditioning theory is of great importance in teaching-learning situations. A few situations have been discussed in detail as under :

Conditioning Study Behaviour : For Professor Skinner, "Teaching is the arrangement of contingencies of reinforcement which expedite learning. He is convinced that operant conditioning, so effectual when applied to animal, promises equal success when used in schools." Further more, he thinks that the most effective control of human learning requires instrumental aid. He is appalled at the present inefficient practices in schools and recommends a procedure whereby they can be corrected. He thinks that, when teachers have taught successfully, they always have arranged effective contingencies of reinforcement, but they are more likely to do this if they understand what is it that they are doing. Hence, if the teachers want that students should learn something, they should reinforce such behaviours of students as coming well prepared in the class, sitting in the library and participating actively in school programmes through a variety of incentives such as prize, medal, praise, smile, affectionate petting on the back or even by giving higher marks in the examination.

Conditioning and Class Room Behaviour : In order to change the behaviour of the pupils in the class room and to bring about desired change in their behaviours, conditioning is of immense importance. If a child's experiences in a certain classroom, while studying a certain subject with a particular teacher are predominantly unpleasant, the unpleasantness becomes conditioned to the teacher, the subject and the classroom. If this is repeated, the child will develop a dislike for the subject as well as for the teacher. Hence, to check all these, suitable behavioural contingencies may be used. An atmosphere of recognition, acceptance, affection and esteem may help the child in approaching the teacher and the subject with good will. For instance, if a student is not serious in his studies, the teacher can control this behaviour by using negative reinforcement such as showing his negligence to other student or by criticising him in front of the whole class. On the other hand, a student who is serious in his studies should be provided positive incentives such as prize, medal, praise, smile etc.

Managing Problem Behaviour : Generally, students perform a variety of behaviours that seems undesired and problematic from social conduct point of view. Hence, to alter them success may be achieved through the process of operant conditioning. Operant conditioning has established as an important behaviour therapy technique in the recent years. In this regard Albert Bandura's views are of great significance. But, one has to admit here that instead of making use of negative contingencies such as punishment, a teacher must make use of positive contingencies such as praise, appropriate encouragement for better learning prospects.

Dealing with Anxieties : Students develop many fears, anxieties, prejudices, attitudes as well as perceptual discomforts through conditioning. When we see that a train or a car stops whenever there is a red light, we interpret the red light as a sign to stop. In war-time, when a siren is blown in a particular way, we interpret it as a signal for air raid. A child who has received a painful injection from a doctor, may develop an aversion to or fear of any doctor. Such are examples of conditioned anxiety in the human being. Anxiety is a generalized fear response. To break such habits or fears extinction process of conditioning may be helpful. For this, the subject should be kept repeatedly in the situation that causes fear in him and he may be treated by controlling fear producing response. The technique is known as desensitization. In this technique firstly we provide a very weak form of conditioned stimulus and then gradually the strength of stimulus is increased.

Conditioning and Cognitive Processes : Feedback or knowledge of progress is another fore of reinforcement. The concept may be utilized in controlling the cognitive behaviours of the students. Programmed instruction and Teaching Machines are based on this principle. As regards knowledge of progress much longer lapse of time between behaviour and its reinforcement should not be allowed. To make effective use of operant conditioning principle the technique of programmed instruction is best suited.

Shaping Complex Behaviour : To control complex behaviours which exist in the form of a chain of small behaviours, the extended form of conditioning, known as shaping technique may be employed. In this technique the smallest behaviour of an individual at the very initial stage is controlled. Then gradually the next order of chain of behaviour is controlled or conditioned on the basis of different contingencies. In schools the technique is widely accepted for its use to control students' behaviour. Skinner said that "Teaching spelling is mainly a process of shaping complex form of behaviour. In other subjects, for example, arithmetic responses must be brought under the control of appropriate stimuli."

Gestalt's Theory

Max Wertheimer is generally considered to be the founding father of Gestalt Psychology. The other pioneers in this field were Kohler, Koffka and Wolfgang. 'Gestalt' is a German word whose equivalent in English is 'form' or 'pattern' or 'configuration'. Max Wertheimer has explained the term 'Gestalt' saying that the whole is greater than the parts. For example a flower is just not a total of sepals, petals, calyx, corolla, colour, honey and fragrance but some thing more than that. The total of the parts is not equal to the whole. This is known as Gestalt view-point. According to this view "learning is the organisation and re-organisation of behaviour which arises from the interaction of a maturing organism with its environment. It is the bringing about, through this interaction, of new forms of perception, imagination, motor co-ordination and other organic behaviour." Sudden appearance of the solution is an essential characteristic of insightful learning. A sudden coherent pattern of solution appears at once. The individual does not perform random activities, but he perceives the situation as a whole, and intuitionally reaches the goal through awakened insight by continuous, definite and seemingly purposive reactions. Insight is the perception of a relationship between at least three factors, an agent, a goal and intervening conditions or obstacles. Insight is often called as the 'Aha' experience, the flash of understanding which comes to us all of a sudden. Insight when it occurs, is characteristically accompanied by an 'I have got it ! exclamation', the eyes light up, knit brows unravel and fingers snap.

The Gestaltians tend to place far more emphasis on the intrinsic organising capacity in the brain of the individual, and they emphasize the dynamic interactions of the elements in the entire perceptual field. Gestalt theory of learning essentially consists in problem-solving by understanding the relative position of the elements in entire perspective of situation. When a problem arises, it tends to disturb the equilibrium of the organism who seeks a balance. Actually, Gestalt psychology began with the work of German Psychologists who were studying the nature of perception. We are all now well aware that the 'moving picture' is not a moving picture at all but it is a series of still pictures. The reality of still pictures as flashed on the 'movie screen" becomes our perception of moving pictures. The focal point of this theory is the fact that when two optical stimuli are perceived by the human eye in quick succession the reaction is one of simultaneous patterning. Wertheimer called this the phi-phenomenon.

Principles : The Gestaltians have mentioned some laws involved in learning. The age at which memory begins is determined chiefly by development of a sufficient number of association fibres to bring about recall. There are different modes of connection or association among percepts and ideas. Suggestive forces work according to certain laws given as under :

(a) *Law of Similarity :* Makes the individual to grasp things which are similar. They are picked out as it were from the total context. Similar ideas and experiences get associated together. An object reminds another object which resembles it e.g.. seeing a man and remembering an intimate friend by some resemblance in his personal appearance, though never seen together in the past. A photo reminds us of the person it represents.

(b) *Law of Proximity:* Makes things proximate or near together to be picked up first and learned as to how near these are among the more distant things. In other words, percept groups are favoured according to the nearness respective parts. Items tend to form groups if they are spaced together. It states that objects which are close in time and space tend to form a gestalt.

(c) *Law of Closure:* It states that our perceptual patterns always tend to be simple, regular and complete with no loose ends. The gaps are closed by the perceiver.

(d) *Law of Continuity:* Makes the individual to grasp things which are joined together in a string or along the line which constituting a whole are grasped together than the disconnected. disjoined or scattered. In other words, experiences which occur together either simultaneously or in close succession tend towards reviving one another e.g. the perception of a ripe mango suggests the idea of its sweet taste and flavour because they are perceived together in the past or the idea of inkpot suggests the idea of pen.

(e) *Law of Contrast:* A perception or an idea tends to suggest its contrary opposite. For instance, adversity reminds a person of his days of prosperity. Similarly, the heat of summer suggests the cold of winter. In these laws of learning is brought out the Gestalt point of view that the organizational capacity of the brain makes to grasp the whole, in priority with the parts.

Educational Significance : Gestalt psychology's contribution to education lies in its concepts of the organization of stimuli and or insight. The world of the classroom in which the child is living, learning is not just a body of discrete stimuli nor are his responses to it those of trial and error adaptations. The world is organized; it has meaning. The child can react with understanding, he has insight. Arithmetic is not isolated fact but a system of numbers. History is not names and dates but the sweep of events through time, with one thing leading to or following another. Learning is meaningful. So say the educators and so says Gestalt psychology.

Gestalt psychologists suggest that the educators should conceive the problem of learning in more comprehensive terms. The teacher should organise the learning situations in such a way that significant relations emerge and understanding of the material results. The learning experiences should be so arranged that the learner discovers and generalises the relationship for himself. The subject matter should be organised into meaningful wholes. The concept of unit-planning is based on the same. The daily lesson plan is many a time fragmentary. It amounts to mere accumulation of facts, principles, concepts and skills. The student does not get a clear picture of the whole. A lesson of prose may be taught in four or five steps or periods. But, if the matter taught on the first day and the last day fails to establish relationship, students get confused. They do not see any, significance. It is thus said that whole is just not equal to its parts.

Briefly speaking this type of learning is very important in education because it discards memorizing type of learning. It does not consume much time and emphasizes meaningfulness, organization and interpretation of the lesson. Here, the individual is engaged in problem solving attitude. It encourages reasoning, develops thinking and trains imagination and creative activity of the child. Learning by insight can be cultivated. Thus, the teacher should emphasize it by encouraging. helping and guiding the child.

Critical Appraisal : As regards the criticism of the Insight Theory of Learning, it is worth mentioning that the theories of Trial and Error and of the Conditioned Reflex are not absolutely wrong. Insight, like a flash of lightning, as it occurs, does not totally discard trial and error behaviour. For instance, the chimpanzee who plucked banana joining two sticks altogether, does not do so instantaneously, but through trial and error by manipulating the two sticks repeatedly till Sultan reaches his goal. The only difference in the two theories is that the latter is governed from the initial stage by the perception of the situation as a whole. Further, insight is hindsight and foresight as well. It does not lie merely in perceiving the present situation but involves also what proceeds and what succeeds it. The controversy whether trial and error leads to insight or not is meaningless since the two concepts are of different nature. But, one has to admit here that Gestaltian view is subjective, less sophisticated and more useful in certain situations. It is wrong to say that every behaviour is the product of insight. For instance, many of our- day-to-day experiences are, the outcomes not of insight but of trial and error exercises. Again, the laws of perception, also known as laws of learning according to Gestaltians, are not very exhaustive and do not explain all types of learning.

Sign Theory

Edward C. Tolman (1886-1559) developed a theory of learning by combining the advantages of stimulus-response theories and cognitive field theories: and thus his system stands in-between S-R Theories and cognitive field theories. His system, no doubt, is rooted in behaviourism but he was strongly opposed to S-R associationism. He criticised stimulus-response theory and trial and error theory both by saying that all learning is not a hit-and-miss affair. Neither it is aimless nor random. According to him, learning is not mechanical: it is purposive. Striving towards a goal is the heart of the learning process for example, if a hungry rat is placed in a maze it wanders about in right and wrong paths until it finally reaches the food spot. If these trials are repeated, the number of errors grows less and the rat takes less and less time to reach the goal. According to the theories of connectionism and reinforcement the bond between the stimulus and- the response has been strengthened. Wrong response have been eliminated and correct responses learned. Tolman's explanation is that it is not a series of movements that is learned but signs. The learner perceives the nature of the situation, works on it, builds a cognitive structure or map of the environment. These perceptions are considered to have their correlations in the brain. The structure or the map provides guide or signs or stimuli with a meaning which decides what route the rat will take in the maze.

Tolman published his major work "Purposive Behaviour in Men and Animals" in 1932. His system is known as Purposive Behaviourism. He rejected molecular approach to behaviour developed by Watson and developed molar approach to behaviour which is goal-seeking and purposive. He was also influenced by Freud and McDougall in the development of principles of learning. Agreeing with Guthrie he thinks that there is temporal contiguity in terns of successive cognitions. For example, in maze learning the cognition that one event leads to another is accompanied by a second cognition concerning the behaviour. Behaviour route must be followed if this sequence is to occur. In learning tying the shoe laces, for example, pulling the two ends of the lace in two hands serve as a cue to put one end round the other which suggests to pull the two apart. It leads to making half the knot which further serves as a cue to slip the one string under the other and pull them again, thus making the knot complete. Here the movement serves as a cue for the other till the knot is completed. There is simple temporal contiguity. In maze learning also one movement serves as a cue for the other and that in turn for the next, and so on. In short, to Tolman goal is a name for a recognised need which the individual seeks to satisfy by action which enables him to reach it as the goal. This is a clear acceptance of the motivating forces or needs as the basis of learning. Here it is worth mentioning that even behaviourists depend upon some need to be at the base in conditioning. For example, satisfaction of hunger in the cat in the puzzle box or in the rat to learn to go through the maze or in the cat to stand on its hind legs is the basic need. If these animals were first fed and then made to do the work required they would not bother. The rat would sit silently or the cat would go to sleep instead of struggling to open the door. These needs are of course more physical in the case of animals and in case of human beings there are also psychological needs.

Tolman deals with patterns instead of reducing behaviour or activity into components. His concepts are similar to those of Gestalt but are more precise. His approach is holistic and concepts are larger and more comprehensive He agrees with Hull in stressing needs and their satisfaction but not through reinforcement or need reduction. He says that the response is learned in terms of the sign, and hence, the theory is named as Sign Gestalt.

Experimental Evidence : Several experiments have been conducted to test Tolman's theoretical system of behaviour.

Experiment 1 : In one of the experiments Macfarlane (1930) trained some rats to swim across a simple maze filled with water to reach the goal box. Assuming that the animals learned to reach the food, there remained the question of whether they had learned something cognitive about the maze or had learned a series of stimulus-response connections. To clarify this problem, he drained the water out of the maze. Rats were put into the maze so that they could run through, instead of swimming to reach the goal box. He found that the rats could reach the goal without committing any error. He, thus concluded that the animals learned the specific lay out of the maze acquiring a cognitive map of the maze.

Experiment 2 : The experiments known as 'place learning experiments' were conducted in 1940. These experiments proved that the learner does not reach its goal in a fixed or set sequence of movements but, instead, changes his behaviour according to the variations in conditions. In one such experiment rats trained to follow a right-angled path from starting point of goal were blocked on the original path and a number of paths going in all directions were provided. It was observed that mostly they chose the diagonal path to the goal. Tolman guessed that rats developed a generalized orientation and could trace alternative routes to reach the goal.

In the similar experiment with slight modification the rats were trained on simple experimental apparatus of 'T' type maze (A) to get the food and then were tested on the inverse maze (B). It was found that the rats could easily learn the place.

Experiment 3: A new type of experiments known as 'Latent learning experiments' were conducted by Tolman himself at Berkley. In one such experiment Tolman and Honzik (1930) conducted experiments on rats. A group of rats was allowed to run through the mazes without giving food. Later on the food, as a reward, was introduced. In the course of experimentation it was observed that the rats who had the chance to explore the maze, learned much faster than those of group B who had not explored the maze. Tolman concluded that some latent learning took place as a result of exploration of the maze.

Experiment 4: During this experiment Tolman found that those rats whose efforts were rewarded learned to reach the goal sooner than those whose efforts were not rewarded, and their errors in the maze were reduced. But the unrewarded rats also improved and showed less errors when they were rewarded. If goal directed rats are observed at certain selected points in the maze they look about seeming to hesitate and seeking a cognitive guide or sign. If they are given an electric shock, when they are reaching the food spot they will avoid it. Tolman argues on this basis that cognitive guides or signs are selected because they are significant aspects of the situation.

Critical Evaluation : Tolman was an electic theorist. He collected various ideas from here and there but could not shape them into a systematic theory. Also, he never adhered to a single explanation of behaviour. Even then Tolman and his associates made significant contributions to learning which may be explained as follows :

1. Tolman's main contribution is that behaviour is docile and purposeful. He always emphasized that what is learned is an expectancy or the value of signs rather than stimulus response connections.
2. Tolman developed a cognitive framework for interpreting learning. He stood outside the main stream of behaviouristic psychology, but was influenced to a great extent by the psychologists who were in the mainstream of behaviourism. He was against Watson's simple S-R connectionism and mechanistic philosophy of life. He attempted to combine the advantages of two families of learning theory and succeeded to a certain extent.
3. Preception and observation are two important factors in Tolman's theory of learning. Tolman is of the view that many retarded children who fumble in the classroom and indulge in blind trial-and-error show that there is something wrong with their capacity to learn and they are not able to organize their mental activity. Thus, self-activity accounts for higher forms of human learning. Tolman recognizes that in all learning some intelligence is at work, that the learner is an active participant in learning, who organizes his perceptions and observations and gives meaning to them.
4. Tolman recognizes that motives arouse, direct and determine the learning behaviour and that responses learned in one situation are generalized and apply to related situations also, but he goes further to emphasize that motivation or reinforcement improves performance only. Learning is not determined solely by an expectation of rewards. Though Tolman agrees with the importance of motivation but he warns also that strong motivation may interfere with progress in learning.
5. Educational procedures and practices attach great importance to purposes and meanings in class work and it appears that Tolman's views though not so well known, harmonize with them.

6. According to this theory cognitive process is the heart of learning. Therefore, a teacher should always bear in his mind that what he teaches to his students must be meaningful and related to real life situations.
7. According to this theory unsystematic and unplanned haphazard activities do not make any significant contribution to learning. Only intelligent behaviour seems to be responsible for learning. Therefore, the process of teaching and learning must not be a blind folded action.
8. According to this theory route is more important than the results. Therefore, a teacher must make use of proper and, effective methods in teaching. While solving numerical problems in science or mathematical problems it should be kept in mind that students choose a right approach rather than worrying about results. The same must be observed in practical work also.
9. In this theory special emphasis is laid upon goal or objective. Hence, before teaching something new to the students the teacher should announce well in advance the goal or objective related to content and also the means to achieve the same so that the students may take full interest in the teaching-learning process.
10. While imparting education to children due consideration should also be made regarding age and other experiences of the students.
11. If a student, while attempting a mathematical problem or learning some simple act, makes more irrelevant activities or trials and errors, then, according to this theory the teacher can conclude that the child is suffering from some sort of defects definitely. Either, he is a lazy fellow or a backward one.

In view of these points it is quite evident that the theory is of immense help as regards the elementary learning of the child, Briefly speaking, Tolman postulated a large number of laws of learning during his long career which vary with nature of learning situation and are concerned with conditioned reflex learning, trial and error and inventive learning.

8

Influencing Factors

One of the basic truths in education is that all discussions ultimately end in telling how learning can be made more efficient. Good teaching always focuses on effective teaching which means effective learning. Learning is not a unitary activity. It has at least three components: (i) acquisition of knowledge or information or understanding of principles, concepts, etc., (ii) retention of what is acquired, and (iii) recall or reproduction of what is acquired or understood. Hence, when we speak of learning, it refers to these three components put together as a single unit. In the same way when we discuss factors that influence learning we have to take into account all the factors that affect acquisition of material, retention of material and recall of material. Efficiency of learning, from this point of view means accuracy, speed and amount of material learned, retained and reproduced.

The factors that affect these variables of learning may be classified as those which pertain to :

1. The learner
2. The material to be learned
3. The method of teaching and learning

Each of these group of factors is discussed in detail as follows:

Pertaining to the Learner : The learner is the king-pin in the whole process of learning. It is he who has to make active efforts to learn. It is, therefore, the first requisite that he must have the capacity, abilities and entering behaviours needed for learning the proposed material. This factor is known as readiness on the part of the learner.

Readiness as a Factor of Learning: A person is ready to learn something when he has achieved sufficient physiological maturation and experiential background. For example, it is physiologically impossible for a child of 3-4 months to learn to walk or to learn to speak words, or to learn to read. Similarly, a non-science student can not be made to learn Einstein's theory of relativity. A youth of 10 years normally is not ready to study subjects such as calculus, Sankhya philosophy, romanticism in literature, etc. Learning and understanding of these tasks requires suitable experiential background which a child of ten is not expected to have. Exceptions may be there, but on an average certain level of physiological maturation and experiential background are essentially required for learning corresponding tasks.

If a child is incapable of learning to read at six and a half when children, normally, begin to read, he may face a year or two of failure and eventually may develop a mind-set against reading which will make it difficult for him to learn to read at any age.

Readiness for learning includes not only the physiological maturation, mental growth, but also such factors as interest and motivation. It is said that a child may achieve necessary coordination to perform a particular physical task at the age of 12, but if he begins trying at an earlier age he may significantly accelerate the development of the necessary coordination with the result that he may be able to perform the task at the age of ten. But, there is a limitation of this earlier training and this varies from individual to individual. Studies, however, indicate that not much can be gained by starting youngsters on a particular learning task earlier than readiness normally permits. If started at the proper level of maturation, children learn more speedily and quickly and catch up with those who started earlier.

De Cecco and William Crawford (1977) say that the student can not acquire new performance learning of which depends on other performance which he has not learned. To quote them "learning builds on learning in the way success builds on success", (p. 48). This they call entering behaviours, "behaviours the student must have acquired before he can acquire particular new terminal behaviour".

Thus, readiness is the most important factor that influences learning. Ausubel (1959) defines readiness as "the adequacy of the student's existing capacity in relation to some instructional objective." Robert Gagne and his associates (1962) talk of "learning sets" which means more or less the same as readiness. They define learning sets as the capabilities the student possesses at any given stage in the learning of a given task. In slightly a different language Jenson (1965) also emphasized the importance of readiness principle when he said, that a students performance on any given task will be a product of the levels of his learning abilities and the degree to which the task involves these abilities.

Motivation: Child's level of motivation is another important factor that influences learning. Learning is a kind of behaviour; and behaviour does not just occur. It is caused by some need and is oriented toward a goal. In other words behaviour is purposive. If the child sees purpose in his act of learning he will willingly strive to achieve this. The importance of this factor has been comprehensively discussed in the literature of psychology and has been widely accepted by teachers too.

Learning Set: This factor of learning emphasizes that there should be a "proper set for learning". It means several things; for example, learner's good study habits, his mental preparedness and cognitive awareness of the task to be learned. De Cecco and Crawford (1977) describe two kinds of learning sets - (a) learning to learn and (b) learning set and structures By learning to learn they mean progressive improvement in performance as a result of previously learned mode of working through learning of related tasks. It may be considered as the "general mode of attack" available to the student for learning various tasks. Learning set and structure as defined by Gagne means the most basic and general capabilities that the student requires for learning. Clausmeier and Goodwin (1966, p.456) hold that giving short instructions to students before starting to teach may generate a kind of learning set. Instructions including information about purpose of learning, abilities required, relationship with other relevant knowledge already acquired, outcomes of learning, etc., may comprise a learning set, a predisposition to learn. Presenting advance organizers to the students may also contribute to establishing a learning set.

The Material

The kind of material to be learned also influences students' learning. Ausubel (1963) has emphasized that meaningful material can be learned and retained better. If the material to be learned is organized in a systematic logical sequence it would be more easily learned. Ausubel's Advanced Organizers Theory comprehensively describes' the sequence. It proceeds from the most generalized idea to, less and less generalized one. If information and knowledge to be learned are organized in such a way that they consist, largely, of the mastery of simple concepts followed by the organization of these into larger systems of concepts and generalization or principles about facts and concepts, this becomes more meaningful to the students and is learned more efficiently.

Meaningfulness of the material has two aspects: the relatedness of the parts of the material and the ability of the individual to incorporate new material into his cognitive structure. Meaningful material is recalled better. Advance organizers have on learning a facilitating effect. Well structured material is easily learned.

The Methods

Quite a number of factors that affect efficiency of learning pertain to methods of learning and teaching. These are described as follows :

Practice as a Factor of Learning: This is the same as Thorndike's Law of Exercise which said that learning is merely repeating an act a number of times, and, thus, improving the performance. But, this is true only when the learner is motivated to learn. "Practice makes a man perfect" is only a half truth. Practice is a necessary condition for learning, but it is not a sufficient condition. Practice in the absence of learner's intention and will is of little avail. Yet, it is a fact that improvement in performance can not take place in the absence of practice. It is, therefore, necessary to encourage practice in order to promote a greater degree of understanding, retention and transfer. However, certain considerations should be kept in mind in this connection as follows :

(a) Practice should take place in meaningful setting. Most effective type of practice is that in which the learner uses his previous learning in dealing with more advanced work, such as mathematics.

(b) Practice should not be of monotonous type. If it is meaningless, uninteresting and disliked by the learner, it may lead to development of negative attitudes toward the subject or the task as the case be.

Distributed Practice vs. Massed Practice: Distribution of practice periods is another factor that affects efficiency of learning. This can not be a general rule that distributed practice, i.e., broken into a series of relatively short periods is always the better approach to learning. It depends on the nature of the learner and the nature of the material to be learned whether distributed practice or massed practice will be more effective. Research (Kingslay and Garry, 1957) has shown some advantage in the spaced practice periods in case of long term retention. But, in case of immediate recall not much difference is found between the two methods. In general, short practice periods over a certain length of time produce maximum efficiency in learning (Starch, 1927). In case of distributed practice of short periods learner's motivation is high, concentration is better and fatigue, is also absent. There is, however, no conclusive evidence as to the optimal distribution of lessons. The teacher must decide for himself how long a period is more productive of learning for a group of learners.

Part Versus Whole Method of Learning: Whether a unit of the material should be learned as a whole or in parts is also an important consideration in learning. Earlier the whole method was considered superior. But, recent studies have not supported this view. Research in this area has not been conclusive. Hence, the principle should be that whatever the learner can grasp clearly and meaningfully whether it is a chapter, a paragraph or a sentence that must be the best for him, the optimum unit of learning for him is to learn at one time. He should study it as a whole provided he perceives that as meaningful and useful from his point of view. But, in case of nonsense material the part method is found to be as effective as the whole method. Even in this case the learner will be more benefited if he gets an overview of the material and structures the field by relating the parts to one another and also to the whole field.

Over Learning

Over-learning (i.e., additional practice) means learning something over and over again for an indefinite time. A person can learn something well enough to make a perfect score immediately after learning; he then has continuous practice for a long time on the same material. This is over-learning the material which results into more stable and permanent retention of the material learned. It has been found that over-learning does contribute to better retention. Hence, it is considered a factor of more efficient learning. Over-learning is measured in terms of the percentage of additional practice spent after initial mastery. Krueger

(1929) showed that practice carried on after the material is learnt and mastery is achieved first time is of great value in learning as, in that case, retention is more durable. Over-learning is a kind of massed practice. It is learning beyond mastery.

Over-learning is, generally, used and is more effective in case of learning meaningless material. When the material is sufficiently meaningful it is unnecessary. It is, particularly, more fruitful in case of learning tables, vocabulary, spellings, etc., i.e. the content which is of discrete nature, and can not be structured. Over-learning reaches a point of diminishing return when it goes much beyond the first mastery level. At this point additional practice increases retention only slightly and the effort surpasses the gain (Krueger, 1929).

The Review

It means giving some time for revision, recall or test after having learned the material. It may take several forms. It may be in the form of a test to just check how much and what has been learnt. It may be in the form of just making a hurried revision or restudying the material. It may be in the form of mentally summarising the whole material. It may be any form, but the fact is that it helps retention. Each form, however has its special advantage. It is more useful to have a recall test immediately after learning the material. It may be the form of a test or just in the form of a point-wise summary - at this stage rereading or restudy of the material is less valuable in comparison to recall test. Restudying is, however, more useful when sufficient time (say 2-3 weeks) has passed after having learned the material, as held by Sones and Stroud (1940).

Meaning and Structure

Of all the factors that affect learning, particularly memory and retention, meaningful structure is perhaps the most important to be kept in mind. There is much less forgetting when the material is sufficiently meaningful and well-structured. If it is not well structured but is quite meaningful, even then it may be remembered, but only in proportion to its meaning (McGeoch and Iron, 1952). As a general rule meaningful material is remembered for longer period of time. Much of the factual material is forgotten after a year or so, but very little is forgotten in case of conceptual material.

Meaningfulness consists of relations between facts, generalizations, rules, principles, etc., for which the learner sees some use. Solitary facts, too, are meaningless. McDougall (1959) said that mere learning of any kind of organizing principle, in itself, contributes to retention of learned material.

Stephens (1956) says that in case of meaningful material there may be no forgetting whatever, nonsense material is headed for extinction before the last syllable is uttered.

9

HIERACHICAL THEORY

Learning, undoubtedly, is the consequence of an interaction between the two groups of forces-internal (i.e., the individual's capacities) and the external, i.e., the environmental conditions. External conditions necessary for learning exist outside the learner in the environment. An individual's success in learning is, largely, the result of the effective interaction of these internal-external conditions. There are different theories that explain how these factors interacting with each other determine what and how much will be learned by an individual. This chapter discusses how Gagne explains learning and the learning events. The learning event comprises the learner, the stimulus situation and the learner's response.

Learning as an Event

Gagne (1970) considers human learning as an activity which involves simultaneous operation of three components the learner, the stimulus (i.e., the learning situation) and the response. The learner represents internal conditions in the form of his previous learning or entering behaviour. The environment or the learning situation presents the stimulus or stimuli which interact with the learner's previous knowledge or his entering behaviours. The consequence of the interaction of these two internal external conditions of learning results into response which is a part of human behaviour. For example, "seeing the snake an individual runs away" is the event in which "running away" is the response resulting from the interaction between the stimulus, snake and individual's previous knowledge of the snake and of the fact that if the snake bites the man dies. Gagne has developed a whole theory of learning to explain the learning event. He explains how learning taken place, particularly, how an individual learns principles and generalizations. His theory is known as Hierarchy of Learning. Gagne's name is associated with the attainment of general principles in the same way as Ausubel's name is associated with meaningful learning. Ausubel emphasizes meaningfulness of the material to be learnt, the structure and organization of the material; Gagne emphasizes the process of learning, the sequence and chaining of responses involved in the process of learning.

Hierarchy of Learning

Gagne's theory is most comprehensively described in his The Conditions of Learning (1970). He describes eight types of learning which, actually, are the stages, in the sequence of learning complex behaviour. According to Gagne learning of simple to complex behaviours is sequential activity. A higher level learning can not occur unless the learning at lower levels in the sequence has taken place. In fact, these learnings of Gagne's are types or classes of behaviour. Learning of one class or type of behaviour is contingent upon learning of the behaviour corresponding to the lower level. These eight types of learning, or conditions of learning or classes of behaviour from simple to complex are hierarchically linked to each other. He calls them conditions of learning for the reason that each one of these is necessary for learning the next higher level behaviour. For example, mastery of a certain number of principles is a prerequisite for problem-solving. To master a Principle, it is essential, that the learner must have acquired related concepts. To have developed concepts, he must have learned multiple discriminations. And this, in turn, implies that ability to link words to things and words to each other, i.e., acquisition of verbal associations which themselves are based on combinations or chains of simpler S-R associations following conditioned responses or signal learning

Thus, the eight conditions of learning as described by Gagne are (from lowest to the highest)

Signal Learning: This is the most elementary behaviour learning, a kind of classical conditioning as referred to by Gagne. All learning begins with this elementary S-R unit of learning, the brick with which the wall is constructed. This kind of learning is involuntary, diffuse and emotional; for example, withdrawal of the hand from fire. Pavlov studied such learning in great detail. Stopping the vehicle immediately seeing the red light at the cross, salivation of the dog seeing the food, running away of the child seeing the dog, etc., are examples of sign learning. In these examples red light, food and dog are the stimuli or the signals in the language of Gagne. The conditioned responses are stopping the vehicle, salivation of the dog and running of the child.

Stimulus-Response Learning: This is learning of precise response to specific stimuli. The responses in signal learning are diffuse and emotional. But, in S-R learning they are fairly precise and are called, often, operants. This is used more profusely in acquiring verbal skills, as well as behavioural skills. For example, the child learns to say 'dog' when shown a picture of dog and asked to say 'dog' and is rewarded on correctly speaking 'dog'. Words of foreign language are learnt by adults mostly in this way.

Chaining: This is the stage where the person combines previously learned S-R associations together, thus, acquiring a new structure. Learning of this kind of response consists of a series of events which are, generally, not noticed. For example, a child who learns to say 'dog', then, learns to say 'dogs eat', 'dogs are in the street', and so on. In chain learning, each learned response gets linked to another response relating to the same object, thing or situation. According to Gagne' verbal learning is like skill learning in that it involves a chain of at least two links. The first link is the presentation of the object (S) and the observing of the object (R). In the second link the observing response results in certain internal stimuli which give rise to the verbal response - the utterance "dog", etc. At the most basic level according to Gagne verbal learning is just labelling behaviour, i.e., naming. Gagne' diagrams the simple act of naming as follows :

Ss -------------------> ~ s -----------------> R
(object) (response) (dog)
observing

The small 's' refers to internal stimulus.

The observing response enables the child to distinguish 'dog' from other objects and is acquired through operant conditioning. The second link connecting the internal stimulus to the actual utterance of the word 'dog' is also acquired through operant conditioning. Both these links are considered necessary entering behaviours for naming or labelling. More complex form of verbal learning consists of longer chains and verbal hierarchies.

Verbal Associations: This kind of learning is just the chaining of verbal units. In its simplest form it is verbal association in the activity of naming an object, which involves the chain of the links, as is explained in the previous section on chain learning. The observing response enables the child to identify the object that he sees and the internal stimulus (s) enables him to name the object. But, when he associates this object with some other quality or characteristic, this becomes association of three links. For example, when the child has learned to name the object 'dog' and, then, also learns to say 'black dog', he has learned a verbal association of three links.

Gagne' talks of one more kind of a common verbal association, the translation responses or verbal mediation, an internal link which helps the person associate, for example, an English word for Hindi word.

Discrimination Learning: This is the kind of learning in which the learner must learn to discriminate between different responses to different stimuli. For example, he must learn to distinguish between the new stimulus "pet dog" and the verbal chain he has already acquired. He must learn that "pet dog" is different from "dog", similarly, he must learn to distinguish between "street dog" and the "pet dog". When he is associating the word with the correct type of dog, what he is doing is discrimination. When there are several objects and names, linking the name with the same correct object and no other object illustrates discrimination learning.

Concept Learning: In concept learning the student's behaviour is not under the control of particular physical stimuli but of the abstract properties of each stimulus. In this kind of learning the individual responds to stimuli in terms of abstract characteristics like height, size, shape, colour, movement, position, number, etc., as opposed to concrete physical properties. For example, if given a series of numbers, he is able to select those which are odd as opposed to those which are even.

Rule Learning: This involves combining two or more concepts to explain an event, fact or a situation. A rule is the chain of the concepts. This takes the form "If x, then y" or "If it rains, I will be drenched". "If the dog is hungry, it will salivate if food is brought before him." It is said that knowledge is, largely, a hierarchy of rules; a system of rule within rules.

Problem-solving: In this kind of learning rules are used to achieve some goal. According to Gagne' problem-solving is learning of higher order rules in which case two or more lower order rules are combined and used for understanding the situation. It involves internal events such as thinking. Without the knowledge of rules which are necessary for solving the problem, success is not possible. For example, a student planning to qualify the competitive examination having been unsuccessful on the first occasion is solving a problem.

There are eight types of learning Gagne has described.

The Application

Gagne explains how his theory can explain various kinds of learning.

Learning of Skills: According to Gagne a skilled performance involves a chain of motor responses. A skill has three important characteristics- (a) a chain of motor responses, (b) coordination of eye-hand movements, and (c) organization of chains into complex response patterns. Motor responses are muscular movements, movements of the fingers, arms, legs, toes, etc. Each motor movement is an individual S-R association. A number of such chains of movements coming together constitute a skill. They are to operate in series. Gagne (1970, p. 124) gives an example as follows of a novice driver's starting a car engine.

S (Start the engine)	R (looking forward and to the rear)
S (Sight of rear road)	R (testing for gear in neutral)
S (gear in neutral)	R (turning the key to activate starter)
S (Sound of motor catching)	R (release of key)
S (key released)	R (depressing the accelerator)

In the above R = motor responses or muscular movements. They are and must be performed in a sequence. In the same way S =internal muscular tension (kinesthetic stimulation), the feel of the matter. Gagne's work (1970) calls for the careful development of lower-order skills before these are called into play in more complex activities.

Transfer of Learning: Transfer of learning occurs when whatever is learned in one situation is used in a new or different situation. Gagne (1970) talks of two kinds of transfer - lateral and vertical. In lateral transfer the individual is able to perform a novel task of about the same level of complexity as that which he has learned. For example, a child having learned the meaning of some words in his class reads and understands then when he finds them in the advertisement on the T.V. screen: This is lateral transfer and is based on the acquisition of S-R associations. But, when a person is able to learn more advanced or more complex outcomes, this is vertical transfer which is based on previously learned verbal associations, rule learning and problem-solving. For example, having learned to add, subtract and multiply lays the foundation for performing long divisions. Any hierarchical organisation of knowledge follows a similar pattern. Subordinate concepts lay the basis for the subsequent learning of superordinate concepts. For example, possessing the concept of subject and predicate is essential to learning the concept of sentence. Similarly, ability to read at one level permits learning to read at the next higher level. Gagne (1962) also said that verbalizing the method one is using while solving a problem also facilitates transfer by high school students.

Problem-solving: Gagne calls problem-solving, sometimes, as rule- learning also (1964, 1970). This is so as it combines two or more principles previously learned into a higher-order principle. To Gagne problem-solving represents acquisition of substantive knowledge. Gagne (1964) holds that problem-solving is different from other kinds of learning in that problem-solving has high generalizability or transferability. In problem-solving the single solution to a single problem is not important. Students' solving a type of problem (may include solving a number of problems instead of a single problem) should be encouraged.

Importance of Gagne's Hierarchy: The hierarchy has following implications which are important from the point of view of teaching: (1) While teaching a complex principle, the teacher should concentrate on the subordinate skills and should ensure that they have been mastered by the students. These subordinate or lower-level skills or learning constitute learner's entering behaviour necessary for learning new material. Ensuring these entering behaviour contributes to effective learning. Eustace (1969) found it helpful to begin with a noun as a specific name, and then to work up to the use of a noun as an abstract general concept, before teaching the role that noun plays in the sentence. This approach is most important in the teaching of a complex task in which there is considerable risk of failure.

10

MODERN THEORIES

Education is said to be preparation for life. Whatever we learn in schools and colleges is useful only when we can apply the same in day-today life. All education is based upon the assumption that the knowledge, the skills and the methods of learning which are used in relation to definite school tasks will not only be available in the future but will be applied in some measure; at least to the solution of new problems as they arise in the life to come. Learning is the most fundamental problem of education. But, nothing is learnt for its own sake. Learning is a dynamic process and so what is learnt in one situation must be capable of being applied in future life's situations. It means what is learnt in one situation must have some transfer value. If we learn any given thing, does it necessarily follow that what was learned will automatically be applied when the need arises? Is the fact, that certain subject matter has the effect of exercising the student's intellect, of such prime importance as to justify the teaching of that subject more than other subjects? Does the manner in which information is acquired have anything to do with whether or not it will be used in new situations? These and other questions of educational and practical significance are such as must be considered in dealing with the general problem of transfer of training. In brief, the problem of transfer of training raises the following questions. Can the forgetting tendency be minimized? Do abilities acquired in one situation help in another?

Does the study of science develop scientific attitude in the student? Does study of one subject improve our mental process in general? Does participation in games develop a sense of fair play and good sportsmanship? Can we improve imagination, perception etc., by training one aspect only? Does the child who completes his assignment neatly also keep his room neat at home? Can we improve character and personality more broadly by practising one specific trait or virtue, such as honesty and originality? Does a student observe honesty in examination too, who is honest at his home? Does the study of English help a student to learn French or Russian? All such questions may not be answered in a very definite manner either in 'Yes' or 'No'. But, whatever the answers be, they all depend upon the operation of the psychological process known as transfer of training or transfer of learning.

The psychologists differ in responding to these questions. Previously the philosophers and scientists believed that there were several faculties independent of each other which resided in the mind of each individual such as memory, imagination, attention and reasoning, etc. The oldest psychologist R.M. Hutchins believed that each subject trains a particular faculty of the mind e.g., the teacher of algebra assumed that his pupils would apply their knowledge of algebra to the solution of problems in physics and chemistry, the teachers of social sciences assumed that their students would gain the ability to interpret the social problems more intelligently than others. A professor of mathematics would always say "mathematics and language are the meat and potatoes of the educational diet." But, on the other hand, the modern psychologists say that there are no faculties of the mind, but we do make use of the experience gained in one situation in another situation. Thus, transfer is possible, though it is not same for all individuals. Individuals differ in the capacity to make use of the past experience.

Briefly speaking, the process of carrying over knowledge, skills, understanding, attitudes and habits of thinking from one learning situation to another is called the transfer of training or transfer of learning. The fact that transfer of training does occur is rather self-evident. The fact is that learning through practice has a cumulative effect. Having learned to walk, the child transfers his skill in maintaining balance and in locomotion to the closely related task of running. When learning or the development of skill is sequential, it is obvious that transfer takes place. If this were not true formal schooling would be utterly impossible. Future learning depends upon past learning. The whole concept of readiness is based on this premise. We do not learn independently of what we have experienced in the past. In learning anything new we bring to bear on the task as much of what we have previously learned as possible. In memorizing a poem, for example, we use coordinated eye movements and the ability to read that we have previously acquired. We also apply what we have learned about learning to the new poem to be memorized. The attitudes about poetry, and memorization that we have formed through learning are transferred to this new situation with either positive, neutral or deleterious effects.

Transfer is an all-important matter for those concerned with curriculum construction and for those concerned with aims and methods of instruction. Education for the future necessarily must be concerned with the applicability of the learning in the school to life situations beyond the formal classroom situation.

Transfer of training has been defined by various educationists and psychologists as under :

According to Bigee, "Transfer of learning occurs when a person's learning in one situation influences his learning and performance in other situation."

According to Lovell, "Transfer of learning means the effect which some particular course of training has on learning or execution of a second performance. Such an effect may be of a helpful nature, or it may hinder."

Sorenson defines transfer as, "recognition, use and application to a given situation of knowledge, skills and habits that were learned in another situation.

According to Crow and Crow, "the carry-over of habits of thinking, feeling or working of knowledge or of skills from one learning area to another usually is referred to as transfer of training."

Transfer of Learning

Modern researchers lead only to believe that there is the "possibility of general training in the sense of training for adaptability." This is only a little more than the new version of the old formal discipline theory. This is referred to as transfer of training.

Through recent researches on transfer of training, it has been discovered that "carry-over from one situation to another," is definite. Thus, transfer of training is concerned with the question whether or not the learning of a material A, aids, hinders or has no effect in the learning of another material B. Transfer of training assumes nothing about the faculties. It is concerned with how the organism meets the situation B, C, D, and so forth, after having had an experience in the situation A. Educationally, it is concerned with finding out how the organism can benefit to the largest degree from its experience in one situation, when it finds itself face to face with other situations. Thus, transfer of training means transfer of experience in one situation of learning to another situation of learning. When, that which is acquired in one situation, appears in another; we speak of transfer of training.

Experimental Evidences : Experimental investigation began with Wiliam Jame's experiment on memory training (1890). Between 1890 and 1940 about 211 experiments were performed. Out of these; in 53 experiments 25% transfer took place (considerable); in 95 experiments 45% transfer took place (appreciable); in 16 about 8% (varying with conditions of learning), in 20 about 9%. (very little); in 9 only 4% (no transfer) and in 18 again 9%.

Thus, there can be little question about whether or not there is transfer. The problem of education is how to achieve the greatest amount of favourable gain in one situation as a consequence of experience in another.

Transfer problem studied with reference to school subjects is important from teaching point of view. Prof. Bridges took two groups of seventh grade pupils, equal in intelligence. One studied grammar and the other language and composition. The grammar group improved in the ability to see likeness and differences. He proved the positive transfer. Many other studies have been made. H.O. Rugg found that a course in descriptive geometry transfers 32% to another geometrical material, but only 7% to non-geometrical material. Hewins, a teacher showed that 34% transfer takes place between two kinds of botanical material, but only 5.4% between botanical and non-botanical. Thorndike and Rugger showed that study of Latin improved knowledge of English language. The degree of positive transfer was found to have varied from a very slight amount to 93%.

Theories of Transfer

The revolt against the doctrine of formal discipline was now well under way, and the problem of transfer of training had become a legitimate topic for research. To explain how and why transfer takes place, psychologists have propounded various theories. These theories also describe what transfers from one situation to another. The theories are :

1. Theory of Formal Discipline
2. Theory of Identical Elements
3. Theory of Generalization
4. Theory of Ideals-of-Procedures
5. Configuration Theory

Theory of Formal Discipline : This theory is based on the theory of mental faculties. It is an old important theory of education that mental faculties can be developed uniformly as a whole by providing training in one subject. The word 'formal' means that it is form of the activity that is important in education and not the subject-matter itself or its content. If one wants to improve the reasoning one has merely to practise the forms of reasoning. Similarly, if one engages in activities of memorization, memory would be improved no matter what is memorised.

Formal discipline should not be confused with transfer of training. The modern psychologists do not accept the original theory of formal discipline. They believe in the transfer of training. Yet, the influence of formal discipline has not died even uptil now. Formal discipline seems to have been an outgrowth of the belief in the faculty theory of the mind. Two faculty theories of the mind are distinguished- general-faculty-theory and, organismic-unity-theory. In the 'general-faculty-theory' mind was considered to be composed of various powers or faculties, each working independently. Formal discipline theory meant that one study sharpens this or that faculty and the result transfers to another study. 'Organismic-unity-faculty-theory' is found to be stated in Greek literature. To the Greeks mind was unitary whole which expressed itself in the activities of judging, reasoning, remembering, etc. These powers or faculties were not considered as isolated from one another but were viewed only as distinct modes of activity of the same mind.

Modern psychology with its stress on neuro-physiology to explain mental processes has discarded these faculties of the mind.

Thus, formal discipline simply means that the powers or the faculties of the mind may be trained or influenced by the study of special subject matter. In the middle of the 19th century Huxley and Spencer advocated the inclusion of natural sciences in the curriculum on the same ground.

Theory of Identical Elements : This theory propounded by Thorndike, suggests that transfer takes place to the extent to which there are identical elements in the old and new tasks. These identical elements may be in the form of content or technique. To quote the words of Thorndike himself, "Transfer occurs from one situation to another because the situations have identical components. The components may be in the form of skills, generalizations, information, procedures, principles or attitudes." Thorndike explains transfer by this theory. He says that transfer takes place when there are the same neural bonds in the two situations which happen because of identity of element. This is perceptual in nature, that is, the common elements must be perceived by the subject. In other words transfer depends on the common element and perception of the same by the learner.

Theory of Identical elements holds that because in two situations certain elements are common and they require the functioning of the same mental abilities, therefore, transfer takes place. The study of Sanskrit improves mastery over Hindi because of identical elements. Similarly, Anurag is a good player of cricket and Abhishek is a good player of hockey. Both make an effort to learn football. Abhishek will be at advantage because hockey is more similar to football than cricket. In case of rote memory, Identical elements theory is helpful. Some may like to extend it to embrace identities of substance or content or procedure, mood or attitude.

When it has been established that the amount of transfer depends upon the presence of common components, it is obviously essential to make the classroom teaching and other school activities similar to real life situations. Then and only then the transfer of knowledge, habits, accuracy and techniques of learning and problem-solving to the real life conditions will be large. This notion will help in removing the unreal and fantastic problems and impractical information.

The idea of identical elements as the sole means of securing transfer was not fully accepted when applied to education or when contrasted to the theory of mental discipline. Experiments conducted revealed small amount of transfer that actually took place and yielded information as to the positive or negative effect of transfer. These experiments also provided evidence for or against the theory of 'Identical components' and from that other theories were derived.

Ruger (1910), in his study of puzzle solving in adults found that training in a particular portion of a puzzle very often did not help in the solution of the puzzle as a whole. He felt that the mere presence of identical elements as such did not ensure transfer. His experiments yielded information, too, on problem of the possible negative effect of transfer. He found that when the principle of solution is the same but the details of the puzzle are different, the transfer effect may be negative and actually a detriment to the solution of the new puzzle.

A large number of experiments performed on transfer revealed that the amount of transfer in most situations was discouragingly small and that such transfer had in some cases an inhibitory rather than facilitative effect. Moreover, these findings served as bases for further theorizing.

Theory of Generalization : The theory of generalization was propounded by Charles Judd (1908). Generalization means process of attending to common features, principles or relationships in a variety of specific situations. According to this theory transfer takes place due to certain generalizations of experience in one situation, and it takes place to the extent to which one generalizes his experiences. Judd said, "When a pupil fully grasps a scientific generalization or when he gains a view of a wide range of relations, he acquires independence and breadth of intellectual power, and becomes capable of transferring training to situations that are different from those in which he was first trained. Transfer by generalization is transfer of principles.

Judd performed an experiment in which he tested the ability of students to hit a target with a dart placed under water. Some of the students had studied the principle of refraction of light, how the rays of light shift direction when passing from one medium to another and how this makes objects appear to be where they are not. The remaining students (controlled group) had not been given any such instruction. It was discovered that when the target was one foot below the surface of the water, there was no significant difference in the abilities of the two groups (controlled and experimental) but that when the target was raised to 4 inches instead of one foot of the water's surface, the students who had been taught refraction were able to adjust better than the others.

In another experiment M.C. Barlow tried to study the transfer of a technique through generalization (1937). Children were asked to interpret Aesop's Fables. One fable was the tale of a widow who doubled the amount of food she fed her hen, expecting two eggs a day. The best interpretation was that 'figures are not always facts.' Then the experimental group was given training through lessons in reasoning by induction, reasoning by analogy and reasoning by analysis, but the other group was given no such training. The trained group was found to have done sixty percent better than the other group.

In this theory, method of teaching or study is the most important factor. The content or the subject matter is of little significance. The function of training is to discipline, to develop a scientific attitude, training in observation, discrimination and reasoning which may transfer to real situations of life. This sounds well and seems to be possible if viewed from the standpoint of this theory.

Theory of Ideals: Ideals-of-Procedure is another theory formulated by W.C. Bagley. It is a special form of the generalization theory. It is generalization plus appreciation. Bagley holds that generalization itself will not tell the whole story. To be effective the generalization must be made emotionally toned so as to take the form of and rise to the level of an ideal. He conducted an experiment in which children were taught to be neat and tidy in a particular subject. But, this neatness and tidiness did not transfer itself to other tasks or subjects. Such specific training does not go beyond the immediate field in which training is imparted. But, as Bagley suggests, if neatness is stressed in a general way as an ideal to be pursued, it may be transferred to the whole of life and learning. Ideals facilitate transfer. It is obvious that ideals involve generalization and are effective when learning situations have identical components.

In education, ideals have always been emphasized. One may feel that they have been overdone. We should not stress impossible or unrealistic ideals such as absolute obedience, preferring duty to death, self-sacrifice at all costs. Instead, if we emphasize ideals that are well within the reach of young people like love of learning, toleration, eagerness to minimize difference of opinion, putting one's best foot forward etc., one would have a better chance of transfer or realization from one situation to another.

The teacher can do well in this regard to emphasize transfer of an ideal to be achieved through his programmes of instruction. If some of the practicable ideals are ever kept in view, teaching methods will secure greater transfer.

Configuration Theory: This theory put forth by Gestalt Psychologists is a hypothesis of the Gestalt Psychology. It is a negation of the Theory of Identical Elements. According to this, it is the 'insight' gained in one situation that transfers. So, unless a task is carried out with insight, training cannot be transferred. It emphasizes that the more meaningful an experience, the richer its conceptualization and deeper its understanding are, the greater will be transfer possibilities.

Configuration theory is also known as Transposition Theory. Transposition means that it is not the specific skills or facts or principles which are the basis of transfer but the understanding of the relationships between facts, processes and principles. Gestalt psychology emphasizes the total pattern of behaviour, wholeness or unity of response. Parts do not function in isolation and transfer is dependent upon the whole part relations, between the old and the new situation as well as upon the learner's perception of these relations.

In an experiment chicks were trained to peck at corn from a six inch circle and not from a four-inch circle where corn was glued. Later on, they were presented with four-inch and three-inch circles and they chose the previously ignored four-inch circle, showing preference for the bigger circle. They had responded to the relation rather than to parts. A song learned in a certain key, may be recognized even in a different key, even though the components of the song are different. Some studies have demonstrated that transposition does not occur with very young child and occurs increasingly with older children.

Educational Implications

Education is essentially a social process. It begins with the psychological nature of the child, but ends with the needs of the society. The new education is progressive and aims at preparing the individual for the community life. It aims at enabling the individual to take his place as a worthy citizen in his complex social order, particularly in a democratic community. For this aim in view, the new education seeks to develop desirable social attitudes, moral sentiments and good habits in the children. In order to achieve this, the content of education, method of teaching, school environment and the whole of situation in which the child is educated should be such as the greatest amount of transfer of desirable attitudes, habits, emotional patterns and ideals may take place. Education should be so planned as the way of life cultivated in the school may continue in the community life outside the school. Thus, transfer-problem becomes fundamental to all education. The teachers can bank upon the following suggestions :

Transfer depends upon the content of education, methods of teaching, subjective conditions of the pupils, mental ability of the pupils and the environment in which learning takes place.

Transfer value of the subjects of the curriculum is very great. This is essential for the intellectual development of the pupils. Transfer occurs from Sanskrit to Hindi and Persian to Urdu. In each of the field the languages, the social sciences and the natural sciences, there are interrelationships that should be emphasised by the teachers. Facts in various fields, should be brought together. The thrilling relationship of knowledge makes it educationally unwise to try to approach a problem in too commercialized a way. Related facts should be brought into connections regardless of the fields from which they are taken. Much better education will be produced by bringing to bear on a subject the pertinent facts from many fields. Teaching should be planned for this purpose. History should not be taught as a mere narration of dates, facts, wars, battles and events. It should be taught as a story of the past describing and explaining the forces and factors that cause people to behave as they do. True History of this type will help to understand people, interpret their behaviour and predict what they will do under certain circumstances. Thus, history should be made the foundation of the present.

The problem of new education centres largely around the actual social life. Education is life and not a preparation for life. So, for maximum transfer, the teacher should instead of relying upon the subject of the curriculum and formal teaching should choose those occupational activities which are most typical of life, which offer the greatest opportunities for enrichment of experience and the practice of the social virtues. The habits, thus formed, may transfer to life to be actually lived in the larger community. In this way, education may contribute to the reconstruction of the social life.

Two movements have got spurred in education. The one is

that education should have some utility for the child. Transfer of training may be made a good basis for social-utility-movement. Many valuable social dispositions transfer to the actual situations of life, if the subject matter and activities of the classroom are similar to those encountered in the community life. Methods of knowledge and insight, technique of learning and problem solving, interest, poise, habits and ideals of caution, honesty, accuracy, thoroughness and initiative are a few things that may transfer. All these are of great social utility. But, success in this depends upon the conditions of the environment, the methods of teaching and approach by the teacher.

Second movement in education is a logical outgrowth of the Theory of Identical Elements. It assumes that methods of teaching must be suited to real life. It must be problem-solving, as people are largely engaged in solving practical problems. Initiative is required everywhere in every walk of life. So, methods of teaching must foster it in the boys. In other words, problems and activities of the school ought to be life-like. The most life-like the problems are, the greater the transfer will be to the out-of-school life. It signifies that education be more closely related to significant personal and social activities, and that it should be less academic, artificial and isolated. The school must teach the pupil how to participate fully and effectively in all phases of modern life. The same is the ideal that lies behind the 'Community School' and 'Project method' of Dewey. It emphasizes that education should be real. Only then maximum and useful transfer can take place.

A life-situation in the school and real problems of life alone are not enough. Subjective conditions of the pupils are also important factors in the determination of what and how much will transfer. W.C. Bagley opines that generalizations must be raised to the level of ideals to ensure transfer. A sort of emotional generaliaztion around the ideals, attitudes and dispositions is essential part of community life.

Transfer may fail if the pupils are not able to find out the common identical elements. So, the teacher should pay attention to it. He should train pupils to 'dig-into' situations as a whole and find out their more subtle features. He should himself point out the critical or essential facts of relationships which a pupil otherwise will miss. This he may achieve through thought provoking questions and arousing curiosity at right time. Insight as a whole will transfer in this way.

The amount of transfer also depends upon the mental ability of the pupils. The teacher should keep this fact in mind. Bright children profit more from a situation than average children and average children profit more than dull children. Thus, transfer value of subjects and situations vary according to the mental ability of the pupils. The teacher should adjust his planning, therefore, accordingly :

1. The teacher must decide what he wants to transfer to the child.
2. He should help the students to apply their old experiences to the new situations.
3. He must learn by experience and experiment as how he should adjust or organize his teaching to allow maximum transfer.
4. He should stress the general aspect of all that is learned.
5. He must take into consideration the subjective conditions and abilities of the pupils.
6. He should take pains to integrate different items of the curriculum so as to bring out their affinity.
7. Students should be encouraged to detect similarity between two situations.
8. The teacher must have the long-run view rather than merely for the sake of its immediate utility.
9. Students must be made conscious of as many widely useful relations as possible.
10. The teacher must avoid spoon-feeding his pupils and supplying them all sorts of information himself. He should

rather provoke independent thinking in them, create in them a desire to explore and devise the solution of given situations themselves.

11. Theory of identical components must be taken into consideration while teaching similar subjects viz., History, Geography and Civics can be well correlated.
12. Insight may be promoted by Heuristic method or Project method.
13. The teacher must devise appropriate methods of teaching, create proper school environment and adopt himself a favourable attitude and desirable disposition. Thus, the teacher can best fulfill his responsibility towards society.

11

CURRICULUM DEVELOPMENT

According to its Latin origin a curriculum is a "runway", a course which one runs to reach a goal as in a race. In education it is, sometimes, called a curriculum and sometimes a course of study.

Curriculum has been defined as "all the experiences of the learner that are under control of the school" (King, 1950, p.9). It is a regular course of study organized in the school. It includes all those activities which the school considers sufficiently educational to warrant credit towards a degree or the certificate. It may include even those activities for which credit is not given; for example, NSS, scouting, sports, cultural activities, etc. Walton (1971) said that those aspects of any culture that are selected and organized for transmission constitute the curriculum of the school. The school exists in order to provide the child with experience that is deemed to be desirable. The kind of knowledge or experience that school provides to the child constitutes its curriculum. But, this decision can not be and has not been left entirely to the school. There are several considerations which enter into the decision regarding the selection and organization of the knowledge and experience to be provided to the school students. The question 'what principles ought to govern the choice of school studies and how the content of the curriculum should be determined' has been answered differently by different philosophies of education.

Philosophical Viewpoint

Though the various philosophies of education significantly differ in their views about curriculum, they, instead of being contradictory, only supplement the views of each other. An extreme view in this regard was presented, by naturalism which said that the child's present experiences, activities .and interests unhampered and unhindered by adult interference and direction should be the only curriculum of the school. Fostering the growth of a free, active, happy, well-adjusted human being the only goal, emphasis on imparting knowledge was disregarded. Pragmatism did not contradict this view; but it supplemented it by putting forward the idea of utility-based curriculum which was undoubtedly, more practical. The pragmatists said that the curriculum must include the knowledge and skills that the child requires not only for his present life as a child but also for his future life as an adult. The children should be taught those useful things which are really necessary. While emphasizing the utility criterion of curriculum, the pragmatists do not disregard present interests, activities, and experience of the naturalists' child. They while agreeing with the naturalists only go a little beyond their narrow views as reflected in Dewey's expression who said that learning is an active process rather than a passive acceptance of facts. He emphasized that promotion of child's natural interests in conversation or communication, in inquiry or finding out things, in making things or construction and in artistic expression is important in view of child's active growth. Child's skills in reading, writing and counting must follow out these natural interests and must be mastered by the child not as ends in themselves, but as tools, Thus, for John Dewey the curriculum was concerned with the realities of child nature and of life. Child's real life needs and his natural interests were considered, by him, important determinants of school curriculum. Idealism, however, approached the problem of curriculum from the domain of ideas rather than from the child and his present or future life. Plato, the supreme among the educational idealists declared that training" which leads you always to hate what you ought to hate, and love what you ought to love" is rightly called education. Idealists concentrate not so much on the present experience of the child as on the experience of the human race as a whole, whole of human knowledge stressing that the curriculum should reflect the civilization itself. Nunn developed the idea of intellectual discipline and said that the curriculum should contribute to consolidating nation's spiritual strength, maintaining its historic continuity, securing its past achievement and guaranteeing its future. The curriculum must reflect those human activities that are of greatest and most permanent significance such as care of health, bodily grace, manners, social organization, morals, religion, literature, some form of art, handicraft, science. The curriculum was thought of in terms of activity and experience rather than of knowledge to be acquired and facts to be stored. It was emphasized that subjects should be taught as ways of thinking and doing as ways of dealing with the world. Dewey and Nunn both asserted that the work in school must consist of activities. But, Dewey said that activities should be selected for inclusion in the curriculum keeping the child in the mind, while Nunn made civilization as a whole the determining factor for this purpose. Ross (1947, p. 203) said that there was no fundamental divergence between the two approaches to the problem.

Curriculum Choice

This section discusses the criteria or approaches that have been and are employed for introducing, retaining and modifying the various subjects within the curriculum. In other words, it means to discuss on what basis the content of the curriculum is chosen.

Social Needs as a Criterion: These include those various kinds of knowledge and skills that society needs to maintain its enterprizes. This included apart from the technical side of vocations a quest for a common language and a common set of values that would enable individuals within society to agree on common goals and to communicate with one another. In fact, the social needs criterion is a form of a more general doctrine of social efficiency. To put it in the words of Franklin Bobbit (1924, p.7) it means preparing men and women for the activities of every kind which makes up or which ought to make up well-rounded adult life. Nothing should be included as held by him, in the curriculum which does not serve this purpose. It should aim at educating the young to become efficient and productive members of the society.

Social Problems and Solution as a Criterion: This criterion looks to society rather than to the academic community or to the individual for its warranty. It is concerned with social reform. This criterion urges that the curriculum should be organized around the problems encountered by the society. The society faces many problems resulting from cultural, scientific, industrial and technological changes. The curriculum of the school is required, therefore, to impart knowledge and skills to students which enable them to help in solving these social problems. First, the content of the curriculum should enable the students to understand these problems and, then, develop in them insight into the ways and means of solving these problems. Problems may be economic, political, artistic, scientific, and pertaining to social reconstruction. The curricular content should provide abundant opportunity for direct critical study of the whole range of problems embracing human values including such controversial issues as religion, culture, politics, sex, etc. The school, in view of this criterion is seen as an agent of social reform.

Academic Disciplines as a Criterion: Academic disciplines constitute another source of criterion for curricular choices. The traditional pattern of curriculum has been a set of subjects, each subject sampling a whole body of knowledge. The fundamental aim of this approach to curriculum is to impart knowledge under each subject to the students. It is also hoped that certain habits and skills (intervening processes) would develop as the students mastered the information contained in the subject matter-such habits as observing accurately, thinking clearly, and logically, being prompt, neat and hard-working.

The list of subjects to be put in the curriculum is not fixed and rigid. When knowledge grows and becomes complex it is broken into branches and, thus, new subjects emerge and are included in the curriculum at the same time certain subjects lose their significance and are eliminated. Thus, change in the discipline-based subject becomes an ongoing necessity. In United States of America far reaching changes were made in the 1960s as a sequel of Russia's launching of the first satellite Sputnik in 1957. America felt left behind of Russia in the quality of her education, particularly education in science and mathematics. It is said that Sputnik (1957) put subject matter back into the curriculum (Goodlad-Stoephasius-Klein, 1966, p. 11). One of the characteristics of this reform was that it was discipline-centered rather than the child or society centered. The emphasis was laid on updating and reorganizing those academic disciplines that were considered basic in the pre- collegiate curriculum. The ends and means of schooling were derived from organized bodies of knowledge. The word "structure" replaced "the whole child in the curriculum jargon". Knowledge in each discipline was organized around the primary structural elements such as concepts, key ideas, principles and modes of enquiry. The whole movement of curriculum reform was marked by an updating of content, a reorganization of subject matter and some fresh approaches to methodology.

Founded on the foregoing principles several curricula were developed in mathematics, physics, biology, chemistry, social science and language in United Sates of America. School Mathematics Study Group (SMSG), emphasizing teaching of concepts and their relationships (i.e., the structure of mathematics), the Greater Cleveland Mathematics Programme (1959) with "guided discovery" as an essential ingredient, PSSC (Physical Sciences Study Committee) a first physics course for high school students, BSCS (Biological Science Curriculum Study), CBA (Chemical Bond Approach) based on conceptual schemes, Science A Process Approach. Social Studies Curriculum Program emphasizing inductive method of teaching as influenced by Bruner's, The Process of Education, etc., are some of the examples of discipline-based approaches to curriculum construction. These are described in detail in The Changing School Curriculum (1966).

Specific Patterns

The subject-centered curriculum has undergone several modifications. Several patterns have appeared within the framework of the subject curriculum. At least five of these can be identified.

Correlation Pattern: Under this pattern efforts are made to organize subjects, maintaining their separateness from one another, in such a way that they can be taught by correlating one with the other. Gandhiji's basic education curriculum is one such example. The subjects in this kind of curriculum organization remain separate but show some interrelation between them. For example, while spinning-weaving remains the main subject, arithmetic, Hindi language and social studies may be taught by correlating each of them with the craft spinning-weaving.

Fusion Pattern: It is an attempt to merge two or three subjects by combining the content of these subjects into one. For example, instead of having history, civics, geography as separate subjects in the curriculum, just one subject as "social studies" may be put as a fusion of all these three subjects. Similarly, instead of having physics, chemistry and mathematics as separate subjects, there may be a fusion of these three in physical science. Another fusion may be biological science. Fusion of the content of these subjects may center around the common principles, processes and generalizations. It is claimed that this may lead to better understanding of the learning process.

Broad Fields Pattern: This is just an expanded form of the idea of fusion. This approach, too, is based upon the concept of subject-centered curriculum. But, it is not keeping subjects as independent fields of knowledge. In this case, it is not two or three subjects only which are brought together into one unified course, several subjects are recombined into one broad course. This is an enlarged pattern of subject content grouping. For example, content of physics, chemistry, geology, astronomy and physical geography may be brought together and put under the unified course called Natural Sciences course. Another may be life sciences course including contents of Zoology, Botany, Biology, and physiology. Social science may be still another such course.

Problem-centered Curriculum: Smith, Stanley and Shores (1957) discuss two major types of curriculum organization in addition to the subject matter type: (i) the activity-centered and (ii) the core curriculum. The activity-centered curriculum is basically the same as the problem-centered curriculum. In case of this curriculum the pupils, under the guidance of the teacher, deal with a problem in much the same way as does a scientist, i.e., defining the problem, seeking the data relevant to it, using his previous knowledge proposing tentative solutions or hypotheses, and finally testing the solutions. Thus, the pupils learn by thinking. This approach to curriculum grew out of John Dewey's Experimentalist philosophy and was developed by J.L. Meriam, Ellsworth Collings, William H. Kilpatrick and others. Instead of standard subjects, the purposes and interests of pupils furnish the guide to this activity or problem-centered curriculum. One great advantage of this curriculum is that the pupils find the learning situation highly stimulating.

The argument that goes in favour of this approach to curriculum is that if the child solves these problems intelligently along with other children in the class, he will, when he grows older, find himself embroiled more and more in the problems of the adult community and thus, becoming a more effective citizen. Under teaching-learning according to this curriculum the school is a community in the process of growing up. There are no lessons. Only real tasks are there. Play and work both become one. There are no subjects. Only funded knowledge is there as resources to be used as needed. Skills of reading, writing, spellings and computation are not the basic objectives, They are developed only as means to achieve solutions of the problems as needed to attack genuine problems.

Core Curriculum: The core curriculum is an attempt to correct the shortcomings of the subject matter curriculum. It involves two concepts- (a) Correlation (hence the name "Core") and (b) the Central i.e., essentially required courses in the curriculum. Alberty (1953) defined it as "all or part of the total curriculum which is required of all students at a given level", Douglass (1947) an authority on curriculum studies defined core curriculum as "the instructional programme for the common needs or at least a major part of it taught in close relationship as a whole." One of the distinguishing features of core curriculum is that knowledge under this is organized on the basis of correlation between various discrete subject matters.

Core curriculum may not be based on the correlation of various subject matters. It may be an attempt on elimination of fragmentation and compartmentalization of knowledge of the subject-centered curriculum. Or it may be an attempt on giving imperative social needs the central place in the curriculum. It was this viewpoint which formed the basis of recommending core curriculum in the National Policy on Education (1906). The policy recommended (p. 4, para 3.4) that "The national system of education will be based on a national curriculum framework which contains a common core alongwith other components that are flexible. The common core will include the history of India's freedom movement, the constitutional obligations and other content essential to nurture national identity. These elements will çut across subject areas and will be designed to promote values such as........". Thus, clarification and development of common values and common social perspectives was the focus of this core curriculum.

A major development that took place in America in the 1940s in the area of curriculum development was a growing emphasis on general education which was considered to be that part of educational program which is designed to meet the needs of all pupils in contradistinction to the education provided to meet each pupils special needs. But, there had been a wide divergence of judgement as to what the nature and pattern of this general education should be.

Many and varied are the ways in which the curriculum and especially the core curriculum can be designed. But within recent years in the U.S.A. a completely different conception of the curriculum has come into general acceptance by educational leaders. Instead of thinking about the curriculum as consisting of the subjects taught in the school educational leaders, now, conceive of the curriculum as Composed of the learning experiences which children have in the school. One of the most generally accepted definitions of the experience curriculum is that "it consists of all the experiences the learner has under the direction of the school".

The concept of core curriculum is the revised version of this concept of general education and is defined in different ways by different people. In fact, all over the world there had been two basic and opposed curriculum types, each with different assumptions and characteristics. Krug (1957) clarifies this point of view saying that the courses of study may be organized primarily either in terms of the logical patterns of human knowledge or in terms of some conception of the needs and problems of children and youth and of society. The organization of the course of study must choose one basic underlying principle or the other. It is not possible to have an either-or pre-positions. Today, the term core is understood to mean that part of the curriculum which is concerned with those types of experiences thought necessary for all learners in order to develop certain behaviour competencies considered necessary for effective living in a society. Coswell (1946) in Virginia defined core curriculum as a "continuous, carefully planned series of experiences which are based on significant personal and social problems and which involve learnings of common concern to all youths. Pierce (1942) defined core curriculum as the program that consists of the activities of living necessary for all as worthy members of our social order. Leonard (1953) said that the term core program refers to that part of the curriculum which takes as its major job the development of personal and social responsibility and competency needed by all youths to serve the needs of a democratic society. Anderson's definition specifies four characteristics of core curriculum: (1) important common learnings, (ii) using problem-solving approach, (iii) having personal and social problems significant to the youth as its content, (iv) and development of the behaviours needed in a particular society as its purpose.

Development in India

Prior to independence, the curriculum of schools and colleges was designed to cater to the needs of the foreign rule in India. The need for educating the village people who constituted most of India was never considered important. But, the leaders of India who were fighting for India's independence were conscious of the fact that the problem of India's liberation in the true sense was essentially linked with the education of the masses. Mahatma Gandhi, then suggested that primary education of children should be comprehensively reorganized. The first serious attempt in India on reorganizing the curriculum at the grass root level was made in 1937 when Gandhiji's ideas about primary education known later on as basic education were discussed at Wardha and a complete plan was formulated. This plan of basic education was finally approved by the Central Advisory Board with a few modifications. This is also, sometimes called Wardha Education Plan. Its curriculum was craft-centered, child-centered and activity-centered. It was against the traditional subject-centered curriculum. All subjects were to be taught through correlation with some craft. It was emphasized that whole of the knowledge is a single unified unit, the fragmentation of which, into watertight compartments is unnatural and undesirable. Mahatma Gandhi (1937) said, "By education I mean an all round drawing out of the best in child........ literacy itself is no education. I, therefore, would begin the child education by teaching it a useful handicraft and enabling it to produce from the moment it begins its training. Thus, early school can be made self-supporting, the condition being that the State take over the manufacture of these schools." The Central Advisory Board, however, accepted the craft only as a means of teaching-learning. The production and self-supporting aspect of it was not accepted.

Radhakrishnan Commission (1949) made suggestions about changes in the curriculum of higher education. It recommended incorporation of a component of general education in the curriculum for colleges and universities so that students of science may acquire knowledge of fundamental facts and concept of arts and students of arts may learn basic knowledge of science. Thus, an integration of science and arts, general and specialized courses was suggested. The Secondary Education Commission (1952-53) examined critically the prevailing curriculum and suggested farreaching changes in the curriculum for middle and higher secondary stage. The commission recommended multipurpose scheme of courses according to which students could opt for one of the diversified courses in humanities, science, technical, commerce, aesthetics and home science. In some states these courses were introduced (for example in Uttar Pradesh), but by and large the recommendations remained only on paper. After this the Education Commission (1964-66) made a detailed survey of the curriculum followed in the country. It came to the conclusion that the curriculum was inadequate, outmoded and not properly designed to suit the needs of society. The commission noted that due to the tremendous explosion of knowledge the prevailing school curriculum had gone out of joint with the reality; and hence, there was a widespread dissatisfaction with the curriculum in the people. Therefore, the commission said, there was an urgent need to raise, upgrade and improve the school curriculum.

The Education Commission (1964-66) recommended that :

(i) For the first seven years of schooling there will be an undifferentiated course of general education; and this will remain as such for all those who continue their general education upto class X, thus rendering the school curriculum as a single curricular stream from class I to class X ending with the first external or public examination.

(ii) The prevailing scheme of multipurpose courses was discarded and recommended that upto class X in all non-vocational schools a common curriculum of general education should be provided in the first ten years of school education and that diversification of course and specialization should begin only at the higher secondary stage.

(iii) The Commission also recommended broad areas of curricular studies for different stages and sub-stages with a discussion of special features of the curriculum for each stage as follows:

Lower Primary Stage (Class I-IV): The curriculum for this stage was to have one language (mother tongue or regional language), mathematics, study of environment (covering science and social studies in class III and IV), creative activities, work experience and health education.

Higher Primary Stage (Class V-VIII): For this stage the curriculum had to include two languages (mother tongue or regional language and other Hindi or English), mathematics, science, social studies, art, work experience, physical education, education in moral and spiritual values.

Lower Secondary Stage (Class VIII-X): Curriculum for this stage as recommended, should include three languages, mathematics, science, history-geography-civics, art, work-experience and social service, physical education, education in moral and spiritual values.

Higher Secondary Stage (Class XI-XII): Only 50 percent, as recommended, should go up for general education and the rest of 50 percent should take up part-time vocational courses. Diversification and specialization of courses should be introduced at this stage, but in the schools providing for general education only arts and science subject should be taught. Technical, commercial, agricultural and also fine arts and home science should be taught in special vocational schools. The commission provided for greater freedom and elasticity in the grouping of subjects within the limited range in the classes XI and XII. The commission also recommended in addition to three electives two languages to be studied by all the students. Also, it was recommended that work experience and social service, physical education, arts and crafts, education in moral and spiritual values should also be taught.

The commission recommended that about one half of the total time should be devoted to the three electives, one fourth to the study of the two language and one fourth to the complementary activities or other subjects.

The Education Commission (1964-66) recognised the merit of basic education, the movement launched by Mahatma Gandhi in the 1930s which proposed manual and productive work to be the centre around which elementary education should be organized. Its essential elements were (i) productive activity in education, (ii) correlation of the curriculum with the productive activity and physical and social environment and (iii) intimate contact between the school and the local community. Similar to these essential elements, the commission proposed work experience equivalent in spirit to productive activity, integration of work experience with the content of the curriculum and correlation of teaching subjects with the environment at secondary level and interdisciplinary studies at the level of higher education. With regard to third essential element namely, the school community relationship it was emphasized that at all levels the schools and educational institutions should establish close contact with the community outside. The commission further emphasized that there should be "a more unified approach in framing the entire school curriculum" (pp. 208-209).

The NCERT has been functioning as a nodal agency for the development of curriculum for the past several decades. The council (NCERT) published in 1975 the *Curriculum for the Ten Year School-A Framework* which provided an impetus to the teaching of environmental studies, science and mathematics as part of the general education curriculum from the primary level.

In 1988 the Council (NCERT) brought out The National Curriculum for Elementary and Secondary Education which was, largely, an effort on meeting the needs as emphasized by the National Policy on Education (1986) and Programme of Action (1986). This curriculum incorporated socio-cultural, political, economic and pedagogical concerns, such as equality of educational opportunities, preservation of cultural heritage, constitutional obligations, fostering national identity and unity, value education, global perspective, protection of environment and conservation of natural resources, observance of small family and future-oriented education, education for all round development, child-centered approach to education, facilitating learning to learn, facilitating creative expression, inculcation of scientific temper, interface between education and the world of work, continuous and comprehensive evaluation, utilization of media and educational technology. The Curriculum Framework (1988) assumed that "the dynamics of education and its role in social transformation and national development makes it essential that the content and processes of education are continuously renewed in order to make them in tune with the changing needs, aspirations and demands of the society". The NCERT in view of the National Curriculum (1988) developed guidelines for developing syllabi. Detailed syllabi were also developed for different stages of school education. But, much could not be achieved. Out of eleven areas only a few could be implemented, that too in a limited manner.

The NCERT, again, in 1999 brought out a National Curriculum Framework for School Education: A Discussion Document which said (1999, p.6) "Curriculum renewal and development is an ongoing process. It must meet the learners' needs, societal expectations, community aspirations and international comparisons". A large number of curricular concerns have been stated in this document. Some of these are: education for cohesive society emphasizing equality of educational opportunities and removing disparities and imbalances, education of children with special needs and children from disadvantaged groups, education of the girl child, strengthening national identity and preserving cultural heritage, integrating indigenous knowledge and India's contribution to mankind, responding to the impact of globalization, meeting the challenge of information and communication technology, linking education with life-skills, education for value development, non-formal and alternative schooling, integrating diverse curricular concerns, relating education to world of work, reducing the curriculum load, child as a constructor of his knowledge, recognizing interface between cognition and emotion, using culture-specific pedagogies, education and development of aesthetic sensibilities, continuous and comprehensive evaluation, education as a life-long process, and toward a curriculum of the unknown. This last item includes latest developments in communication system, space technology, biotechnology, genetic engineering, recent health issues, energy and environment, world geography, multinationals and archaeological findings, etc. This has to be only 10 percent of the total curriculum to be added to the curriculum every 2 or 3 years after deleting 10 percent of the deadwood from the curriculum.

The Curriculum Framework (1999) contained a detailed syllabus for stages from elementary to higher secondary stage. The emphasis was laid on common core components designed to instill a "nationally shared perception and values and creation of an ethos and value system in which a common identity could be strengthened."

The Curriculum (1999) listed a number of general and stagewise objectives of education along with a detailed stagewise scheme of studies. It also made valuable suggestions about examination reforms, implementation and management of the system. It is a very comprehensive document on what the schools of the nation should teach and how they should teach. It is a valuable document to depend on in case organization of future education is undertaken at any time.

Systems Approach

Before discussing systems approach to curriculum development it seems necessary to define and describe what a system and a systems approach means. A system is defined by Flagle (1960, p. 58) as an "integrated assembly of integrating elements designed to carry out cooperatively a determined function. Several authors have offered a classification of systems. Boulding (1956) classified them into static, clockworks (simple dynamic systems), thermostat (control system), cell (open and self-maintaining), plant, animals, human being, social systems. Miller (1965) wrote of conceptual, concrete and abstract systems. Systems can be either closed or open, living or non-living. The living systems are open systems. Ludwig von Bertalanffy, (1952) is said to be the father of general systems theory who said, "The principle of wholeness, of organization, and of the dynamic conception of reality becomes apparent in all fields of science." The largest system is the universe itself and the smallest system is the atom. The concept of system emphasizes the process of organization; i.e., combining various elements into a whole which serves a particular purpose. A system is thus, a whole composed of a certain number of parts, each part having a specific function and interacting with other parts in a specific way as designed. The chief characteristics of a system are:

1. As a whole, it is to perform a particular task; it has a well-defined purpose for which it is designed.
2. It consists of more than a single element. Larger the number of elements, more complex is the system.
3. Each part or element has to perform a specific function.
4. Each part has to interact with other parts in a specific way as designed.
5. Each part or element interacting with other parts contributes to the purpose for which the system is designed. If something goes wrong with one part, it affects the functioning of the system adversely.

Any person who approaches his job from a systems point of view must think in conceptual as opposed to concrete terms, must focus on the whole and the parts both, must recognize the dynamic interrelationships among various aspects of a situation, must keep his eyes all the time focussed on the goal or the objective. Conceptual thinking means the examination of general propositions to determine their relevance for the specific purpose. It is a process which is analytic and holistic both.

Systems Approach to Curriculum Development : When applied to curriculum development, the approach emphasizes that the curriculum should be conceptualized as a system having well defined educational goals to be achieved through its various components and also in interaction with other systems. These other systems are the community, the teacher, the training programes for teachers, professional support system, communication and technology system, evaluation system, etc. The National Curriculum Framework (1999) has described these systems in detail (chapter-V). The various components that constitute the whole curriculum are: (1) goals of education, (2) the detailed stagewise scheme of studies, i.e., the syllabus, (iii) the package of instructional material and suggested teaching strategies, (iv) the teacher' competencies and preparation, (v) suggested evaluation system. Having identified the specific components they have to be designed meticulously keeping in mind their specific interrelationship and specific contributions to the overall goals which are predetermined. Each of the components must synchronize with other components as predetermined and designed. If any component fails to do so, the implementation of the curriculum will not be successful. The National Curriculum Framework (1999) has emphasized this aspect repeatedly. It has described in detail what will be the objectives to be achieved, what kind of instructional material will have to be prepared and how, how teachers will be prepared to handle the courses, how evaluation will have to be done. It is an integrated whole designed to achieve well-defined objectives determined by local and national concerns.

Every system is an input-output system. It processes the input and turns it into the desired output. Looking from this point of view the curriculum construction is a three-stage process-input, process and output. A few experts have conceived curriculum development in this frame of reference. For example, Saran (1976) developed a curriculum using systems approach. The input component implied (1) identifying needs, sources and experts views about curriculum and its various aspects, (2) identifying objectives of teaching-learning and selecting the content, (3) development of the draft syllabus. The process part consisted of identifying the relevant instructional procedures, methodology, techniques, instructional material, teacher preparation, etc., i.e. taking decisions about all aspects of ways and means through which curriculum has to be implemented. The output refers to the finished form of the curriculum which emerges after having been evaluated, researched, modified, and validated. It is the result of a comprehensive try-out and evaluation.

There are various models of curriculum. They all have more or less the same procedure underlying their development with little differences here and there. The National Curriculum Framework (1999) satisfies the most modern criteria and concerns when viewed in Indian context.

Curriculum Evaluation

The curriculum is a multi-component system. Its major components are objectives, content, methods and the evaluation. The characteristics of these components are, largely, determined by the needs and characteristics of the pupils, the community and the changing society. Curriculum development is a cyclic process which involves processes such as planning, developing, implementing and evaluating the curriculum and the instructional materials with a view to modify it and make suitable changes. Having analysed all these and keeping in mind their characteristics when a curriculum has been prepared, it becomes imperative to evaluate it or try-out on a small scale to see how it works, whether it conforms to the needs and objectives for the achievement of which it was prepared. Generally, when a curriculum has been prepared, it is taken for granted that it would serve the purpose for which it was prepared. Rarely it is ever evaluated and put to the try-out process before it is fully implemented. The Curriculum in Transaction (1978), an NCERT publication presents case studies of curriculum changes and curriculum renewal from different states of India. In no state such a procedure of evaluation and validation prior to implementation of the curriculum was adopted. In the case study of Tripura state only it was mentioned that "Before a curriculum innovation is incorporated into the curriculum such as new mathematics and new instructional strategy in science teaching, try-outs are, generally conducted on a micro-basis to test its efficiency and effectiveness. Limited trials are followed by more extensive trials before an innovation is considered for statewide implementation. But, this is not always the case as it should have been (p. 109). In the State of Tripura before the implementation of curricular innovation or change an orientation programme was organized which includes (1) exposure of the curriculum to the teachers and supervisors, (ii) compulsory study of the curriculum in the inservice teachers' training courses, (iii) revision of the teachers' training course where necessary, (iv) preparation of teachers' guide and source-books, and (v) short orientation training. This procedure also, to some extent, serves the purpose of evaluation of the curriculum. It may reveal shortcomings of the proposed curriculum and provide an opportunity for correction and modification.

Need for Evaluation : The need for curriculum evaluation arises from the fact that however perfect or good the formulated curricular change may be, chances are high that there may be some mismatch somewhere among its components. The evaluation prior to implementation may bring this out and, thus, efforts may be made to rectify that. At the stage of formulation of the curriculum the experts only theorize, conceptualize and mentally visualize what the situation may be with regard to the setting, teachers' and students' characteristics, environmental conditions and people's perceptions. But, their perceptions may not be errorless. What the constraints on implementation are is revealed only when the proposed curriculum is put to trial on a micro-basis. This kind of evaluation of the curriculum may also reveal the extent to which it is accepted by various sections of the society such as parents, teachers, political and social leaders. The try-out may reveal the reactions of these groups which, sometimes, become a great hindrance in the implementation of the curriculum. Many a time sociopolitical, economic and ecological constraints are not revealed at the stage of formulation of the curriculum. Micro-level try-out of the curriculum may reveal them and. then, proper action may be taken to counter them or handle them rationally.

The purpose of this kind of evaluation is to find out how it works. It answers several questions such as (i) under the circumstances prevailing are the objectives relevant and attainable, (ii) does it correspond with students' entering behaviours? (iii) will the teachers willingly accept the proposed changes? (iv) are the economic resources sufficient to carry out implementation of the curriculum? (v) do the teachers have sufficient skills and competence to handle the proposed curriculum? (vi) is the sociopolitical environment congenial to implementation of the curriculum, and so on. Evaluation, thus, is functional part of curriculum construction.

From the standpoint of the teacher, aspects of curriculum evaluation may be pin-pointed as follows:

1. Its relevance to the needs of the child and the group;
2. Achievability of objectives in terms of the child as a learner, a person, worker and citizen:
3. Built-in flexibility.
4. Difficulty level of the content
5. Appropriateness of time factor so as to complete the syllabus
6. Linking the previous and present levels of achievement of pupils.
7. Learning experiences provided.
8. The environment around the child.

***Strategies of Curriculum Evaluation*:** There are three strategies of evaluating the curriculum as follows:

1. Pre-implementation evaluation or micro-level evaluation
2. Formative evaluation
3. Summative evaluation.

Pre-implementation evaluation has already been discussed in the foregoing section. It is, in fact, a kind of analysis of the proposed curriculum to test the workability of the formulated curriculum.

Its purpose is to examine its suitability from different points of view before it is implemented. This analysis is done at micro level; may be in a few schools of a district.

Formative Evaluation: This is evaluation done during the process of the curriculum function. This is done after the formulated curriculum has been implemented and it is functioning. It is a continuous process. After the curriculum has been implemented, periodically at fixed intervals during the school year views of teachers, students and other concerned persons are collected through well-prepared questionnaires, observation schedules and other tools and techniques developed for this purpose. To measure students' progress in different directions standardized tests may also be used. These data are, then, discussed analyzed and interpreted in the context of the objectives. Discussion may be in the form of meetings, seminars or workshop in which teachers, curriculum experts and even students and parents participate. Through these discussions lines of action for further modification, if necessary, are evolved. If found necessary changes in the scheme of studies, instructional material, time allocation, examination system, etc., are, then, made. Whenever the deficiencies are discovered the curriculum has to be renewed. These deficiencies may be due to the defect in the curriculum itself, or they may be lack of teachers' competencies or administrative functioning. The purpose of formative evaluation is to identify deficiencies, constraints and inadequacies of the curriculum of whatever type they may be so as to bring about suitable changes and make the curriculum meaningful and worthwhile.

The evaluation done simultaneously when it is being used or when it is in action is called formative because it, then, contributes to the progressive shaping of the curriculum. The teacher may also do this kind of evaluation when he is using the textbooks, instructional material, etc., in his day-to-day work. The purpose of formative evaluation is to see that the curriculum is functioning properly. It helps in the improvement of teaching-learning process. When the teacher puts pinpointed questions during the formative stage so as to improve the teaching-learning situation, done at individual level in his classroom situation, it is known as micro-level evaluation. But asking very broad questions after completing all the stages amounts to macro-level evaluation. This kind of evaluation can be taken up by larger institutions having adequate men and material resources.

Formative evaluation is basically comprehensive, continuous and takes the form of internal assessment. It is diagnostic and oriented towards remedial teaching and qualitative improvement of teaching-learning. The main aim of this kind of evaluation is to ascertain as to how well or poorly a student has performed with reference to his own growth and the standard set by the curriculum designer (such as the minimum level of learning, MLL). Formative evaluation has to be regularly done by employing a multiplicity of techniques covering all aspects of all round development of the learner. It has to be a regular feature of classroom teaching-learning for which even informal ways of evaluation are also adopted. The National Curriculum Framework (1999) and National Curriculum Framework (1988) both have strongly recommended the introduction and practice of formative evaluation.

The Summative Evaluation: The summative evaluation is done at the end when the task is over. This is evaluation of the end result of some performance. Unlike formative evaluation which is within-performance evaluation, summative evaluation is done when the whole task has been completed. It may, therefore, be termed as post-task or post-performance evaluation. Examples of this kind of evaluation are the annual examinations, mid-term examinations and Boards external examinations. This is, by and large, traditional promotion-based examination. It is concerned with the ultimate product of teaching-learning. The National Curriculum Framework (1988, p.38) says, "Examinations as in vogue have been primarily used more for grading the students than for ascertaining the pupils' progress in terms of the stated objectives with a view to guiding them or evaluating the effectiveness of teaching-learning process for necessary modifications, if required." The Framework was of the opinion that the evaluation was quite restricted in scope, purpose and utility. The ultimate objective of evaluation is to bring about qualitative improvement in education and, hence, it should be considered as a powerful tool for improving teaching-learning. Instead of using it mainly for grading it should be used more as an effective feedback mechanism for the benefit of the learners, teachers and parents. The purpose of evaluation should be diagnostic and remedial. These views were reiterated by the National Curriculum Framework also (1999, p. 87). All these criticisms apply to summative evaluation which is done only once at the end of a certain duration without caring what happened to the pupils during the period. In the language of the National Curriculum Framework (1999) this kind of evaluation is "lopsided, impersonalized, non-transparent and incapable of reinforcing proper teaching learning in schools and providing help and guidance for further learning leading to self and self-directed learning" (p. 87).

Tools and Techniques : Evaluation to be diagnostic, comprehensive and continuous needs new techniques to be evolved and used for assessing effectiveness and suitability of the curriculum. Following is the tentative list of tools and techniques which may help the teachers and administrators for achieving these purposes:

1. Surveys of local human and physical resources, local economic growth capacity, local natural assets, local needs, local occupations and job availability, local consumption capacity, local availability of raw materials.
2. Interviews with parents, children and community workers.
3. Personal records of children and records of children's family background
4. Observations
5. Teacher-made tests for measuring children's achievements
6. Standardized Psychological Tests
7. Rating Scales for measuring various personality traits
8. Personality tests including interest inventories, attitude scales and adjustment inventories
9. Questionnaires and Checklists for various people of the community and children regarding different aspects of curriculum expectations and aspirations
10. Anecdotal records for children
11. Academic Attainment Tools

The National Curriculum Framework (1999) recommended that the existing system of written tests and examinations needs thorough change on the following counts:

1. It should be competency based
2. It should help evaluate all aspects of learner's growth (cognitive and non-cognitive).
3. It should give least importance to memorization and more and more emphasis on understanding, skills, application and creative aspects.

Interpretation of Results

In this connection it would be worthwhile to reproduce what the National Curriculum Framework (1999) said regarding maintenance of records and reporting results of evaluation. It said. "Practice of positive reporting should be encouraged so that the youngsters do not feel condemned. However, suggestions should be made for their improvement on the basis of proper diagnosis of the weaknesses of learners. Records should be maintained for both cognitive and non-cognitive growth and development of learners. The best way would be through preparing the profiles. The results should be communicated to the parents on regular intervals of time and each time the progress of the learner should be reviewed with a view to deriving corrective measures for further improvement (p.92)."

Interpretation of evaluation results depends on how the assessed or measured traits are expressed. In India the whole system of assessment and evaluation is geared towards assigning of marks on 101 point scale it provides numerical description about achievement of learner on particular attributes. This does not tell specifically where the weakness of the learner lies and what kind of guidance or help he needs. The interpretation of the point score (say 65/100 or 65 percent) may mean nothing. It may mean just average level of growth and development or even below that. It may also mean very high level too. To avoid these difficulties the National Curriculum Framework (1999) has recommended use of grading system.

Interpretation of evaluation results to be functional and realistic should be diagnostic, analytical and oriented to remedial teaching. It must reveal the areas and extent of weak and strong points of child's growth and development. It has to be therefore, descriptive and child-centered instead of being quantitative and class or group centered. Instead of being norm referenced, it has to be criterion referenced. On all areas of growth and development, cognitive as well as non-cognitive judged against some well defined criterion such as MLL the grade assigned to the child may be placed on a profile. If it needs indicator for guidance and remedial teaching 'or advice for parents to be mentioned, it may also be done. It must be comprehensive. The profile may be a detailed account of child's continuous progress. Qualitative description of grades may be given at the end of the profile chart. If suggestions are to be made for the curriculum designers with regard to the difficulty level of the teaching material or use of instructional material, this may be shown separately.

The Administration

Curriculum construction and curriculum administration are two sides of the school's task of teaching-learning. If development of a more suitable curriculum is important, its effective administration and implementation is equally important. The instructional program of the schools consists of curricular opportunities offered to the pupils. Once the educational goals of the organization are known it becomes easier to develop a suitable curriculum and its administration. The administrators in India are involved at both the stages, the development as well as administration of the curriculum. In foreign countries like the U.S.A. decision making about the school curriculum is frequently surcharged with conflicting philosophies of education. Hence, construction and administration of curriculum become the focus of conflict. The traditionalists emphasize the three R's and the traditional college preparatory subjects, while the modernists do not care so much for specific body of knowledge to be taught, Similarly, in the area of theory of learning as the basis for teaching methodology also there are found disagreements. Thus, these sorts of conceptual problems make it difficult for the administrators there to make value choices.

But, in India such problems are only occasionally experienced. Curriculum development in India is, largely, the responsibility of school boards and apex academic bodies like the N.C.E.R.T. The school principals and the teachers who have to implement the curriculum have to accept what is given to them. The process of curriculum development is highly centralized. Theoretically, goals are the basis for all responsible administrative activity. Little can be accomplished in the classroom unless teachers focus upon tasks related to clearly understood and personally appreciated goals. This is essential that all administrative activity must be consistent with the goal-task focus. The goals of the school should be attainable. They should be socially relevant, individually challenging and consistent with the needs of the culture. Again, the goals must be meaningful to the teachers who are directly concerned with program development and progress implementation. Translating goals into specific programs is extremely important because this is where teachers can determine whether they know what they want and need.

Broad goals of education for all levels of education have been stated in the Reports of various commissions and educational policies. But, they have not been specifically made clear and meaningful to the teachers who have to teach the courses and organize various other co-curricular programmes. By and large, they are not in the focus of classroom teaching. To be meaningful the statement of goals must the thoroughly legitimized and internalized intellectually by school administrators, teachers, students and their parents. Moreover, they must be spelt out in detailed form. This is possible only when there are processes and procedures which encourage as many persons as possible to participate in the development of the school mission.

The successful implementation of the curriculum depends on a number of factors such as its suitability to a wide variety of cross cultural setting where it has to be given a concrete shape in the form of syllabi, teaching learning material, evaluation and above all these on the strong politico-administrative will and insight that would facilitate its effective implementation along with a comprehensive understanding of the curriculum and its implications by the teachers who, ultimately, have to translate that into actual practice. For this, various programmes and activities by way of implementation strategy have to be organized. For example, an effective strategy for preparing teachers who can effectively transact the curriculum must be developed, technical support system must be strengthened, some procedure for continuous monitoring of the implementation of curriculum transaction should be established. The Curriculum Framework (1999) visualized and described following essential activities in this context:

1. Professional support for curriculum development
2. Professional support for Teacher Education system
3. Integration of Information and Communication technologies into schooling
4. Implementation of evaluation strategies
5. Institutional and Organizational reforms and instruments of intervention

For organizing all these activities strong governmental and political backing and national acceptance are imperative.

PART-II

PSYCHOLOGICAL ASPECTS

12

DEVELOPING INTELLECT

Intellectual Development is very much the same as the development of intelligence which by most psychologists, is regarded as a system of thought and awareness dealing with child's subjective experience. It is also considered as a sort of cognitive systèm consisting of various parts or structures such as concepts, beliefs, abilities or perceptual styles. Piaget (1964), a Swiss scholar developed and presented this view of the intellect as a cognitive system. Bruner (1964) building upon Piaget's theory described child's cognitive development in terms of three stages of his acting upon his environment, these stages being the enactive, iconic and symbolic.

The Characteristics

A few aspects which clarify the meaning and nature of intellectual development are as follows:

1. It means an increase in the ability to deal with the abstract and with symbols in manipulating one's environment. Child's ability to use language is the most important indicator of his intellectual development. This development is most rapid in early years. There is corresponding increase in the clarity of his concepts and in the length and complexity of the sentences with which he expresses his ideas.

2. It involves a widening of child's mental horizon. In the beginning the child is confined to stimuli immediately impinging upon him. But, gradually, he learns to respond to more remote objects and things in time and space. He, then, gradually becomes more capable of thinking in terms of stimuli which are not physically present before him.
3. It involves an increase in child's span of concentration on things, objects and happenings. Progressively, the child becomes capable of concentrating for longer periods of time.
4. It involves a decline in daydreams and make-believe and a progressive increase in the ability to deal with reality.
5. It means an increase in child's memory.
6. It means an increase in child's ability to think and reason out. It can be inferred from child's ways of manipulating his environment.

According to Piaget "Cognitive behaviour evolves from doing to doing knowingly and, finally, to conceptualization. An object is, first, known for its use, then for its permanency, its representative symbol, its place in space, its properties (weight, etc.) and finally for its relativity in space, time and utility" (Maier, p. 156). Around the ages 14 and 15 the individual's basic pattern of thinking and reasoning has been established. The individual has reached intellectual maturity, as held by Piaget.

Piaget's Theory

Piaget described the process of intellectual development as the process of acquiring various cognitive structure such as concepts, beliefs, abilities and perceptual styles with proper sequence. He considered acquisition of these the result of continuous interaction between maturation and experience. This was regarded by him the key to child's intellectual development. This process, according to him, involved the sub-processes of equiliberation, assimilation and accommodation. Assimilation is the process of taking in and incorporating what one perceives in terms of what he knows and understands. He processes the data in terms of his conceptual systems. It means ignoring the differences and treating the new experiences and things as if they were not different from what the child had already met and experienced. For example, having seen a horse earlier and, then, seeing its picture for the first time creates no problem for the child. This wards off a possibility of disequilibrium. Piaget calls this a process of treating things invariants. But, the process of assimilation is not always easy and possible. So when it fails it is the process of accommodation that comes to help. Then, a new equilibrium is established, a new or modified structure emerges. Accommodation is the process of reshaping and reorganizing conceptual structures until they fit and account for perceived events. So long as the existing structure is enough adequate the child experiences some sort of harmony or equilibrium with the world around. When a very different experience comes along, the child faces a problem. But, while maintaining or failing to establish an equilibrium, some new equilibrium is acquired. This process of maintaining or regaining an equilibrium is called, by Piaget, the process of Equiliberation.

Attainment of invariances is important as it helps the child treat many objects, things and experiences similar. This enables him to subdue the confusing flux of experience and deal with the confusion effectively. For example, 'crow' is child's existing cognitive structure and he, for the first time, comes across a parrot. He sees it flying and says it is a bird. It is no more worrying for him. As the child grows older the invariances he achieves become more and more inclusive. They, then, take care of larger areas of potential disequilibrium. They also become organized around more dependent criteria. In the beginning they are quite unconscious and consist of mechanical conditioned reflexes. Later especially with the advent of language they may become quite conscious and sophisticated.

Stagewise Development

According to Piaget's theory child's developmental life has been divided into four stages separated by transition periods. Within each of these stages there are found a vast number of sub-stages, These stages are: (1) 0-2 yrs (ii) 2-7 yrs. (iii) 7-11 yrs and (iv) 11 Years onward. The stage 2-7 years has been further broken into 2-4 and 4-7 years.

Stage-1 (0-2 years): Sensorimotor Stage : This is the sensorimotor phase which is dominated by child's coordination of his actions or motor activities and use of reflexes such as crying, sucking, and variations in the rhythm of breathing. Reactions are closely related to stimuli. Experience is closely tied to the environment. Language is almost non-existent during the period. The child uses only sensory-motor linkages to impose some order on his experience. Piaget refers to these linkages as "sensory-motor schemata". The term "schema" means anything that links or organizes or ties together. It is an organizational pattern by which two or three factors are organized into a relationship pattern. For example, swallowing, sucking, crying are all schemas. During the first two years these develop and become internalized. They, then, become cognitive structures which the child uses even in the absence of the stimuli that originally brought them into being. Piaget holds that these sensorimotor schemas serve as the fast symbols available to the child. A few most important developments are: (1) the child reacts to distant objects, (2) the beginning of differentiation between cause and effect, (3) various and distinct reactions and response patterns are unified into a single unified action sequence., (4) separate experiences are coordinated into schemas leading to an awareness of surrounding environment, (5) notion of time is not quite clear in the mind of the child. He has little awareness of 'before and after'. Synthesis of all these indicate child's actual intellectual development. Sensorimotor patterns are slowly replaced by semi-mental functions. The child perceives simple causality by perception alone. Without resorting to trial-error he can initiate alternatives to most simple forms of behaviours.

Stage-2 (2-7 Years): Preoperational Stage : Piaget deals with this phase in two parts: (1) 2-4 years which he calls pre-conceptual phase and (2) 4-7 years which he describes as the phase of intuitive thought. These are discussed as follows :

Pre-conceptual Phase (2-4 Years) : This is the period of continuous investigation. Everyday the child discovers new symbols and possibility of his actions. The child is egocentric in his approach. Language involves much speech with self. The child begins to think in terms of relationships and establishes his own view of cause and effect. He attributes life and consciousness to inanimate objects. The child is not able to take the viewpoint of another person. Another characteristic of this period is that of centeration, i.e., tendency to center attention upon the most striking features of an object or occurrence. Child's thinking is largely preconceptual in content. Thought and reason in the 2 years old are entirely egocentric with a predominance of self-reference.

Phase of Intuitive Thought (4-7 Years) : This is the period of widening social interest for the child. Egocentricity is reduced and social participation is increased. The child begins to use words in his thought. He increasingly acts in a consistent pattern of reasoning. He exhibits the first real beginning of cognition. He employs speech to express his thinking. Yet, his thinking is largely egocentric. The child increasingly acts in a consistent pattern of reasoning. He can think only of idea at a time. But, at this point the child is still incapable of thinking in terms of the whole and is mostly preoccupied with the parts. He attempts logical reasoning, though not deliberately. This reasoning proceeds from particular to particular.

Part of this period is spent on learning more precise names and concepts made possible by language. The process of classification of objects becomes more refined. He learns to place rectangular wooden pieces into one pile and circular wooden pieces in another pile. He can distinguish between 'cats' and 'birds'. But, still he is not capable of forming genuine concept of class or class as an intellectual structure. The realizaiton that all birds are not of the same kind has not, yet, emerged in his mind. Classification of objects according to attributes is not possible for him. He finds it difficult to deal with two systems of classification at the same time, e.g., small and big and red and white pencils. He can separately identify them, but can not identify "small and red ones". as one single category. Similarly, conservation of other attributes (number for instance) gives much trouble to him. He finds it difficult to separate them from objects. If a cluster of articles is scattered, the child will say that they are more in quantity while the number of articles remain the same. The child at this stage of development fails to conserve substances (small lump of clay seems to him containing more material when spread out), fails to conserve volume (the same quantity of milk poured into a tall glass appears more in quantity), fails to conserve attributes (fails to see the number as an attribute. Conservation means things remaining invariant in spite of differences in their appearance.

Stage-3: Concrete Operational Stage (7-11 Years) : The child at this stage incorporates the notion of reversibility into his intellectual structure, i.e., he is, now, in a position to classify and reclassify objects relating them to a total system of interrelated parts. For example, he can classify birds as separate from mammals on the basis of criterion (sucking the young) and, then, into one class on the basis of another criterion (warm blood). During this period the child achieves a new level of thought, namely the operational thought, i.e., the mental capacity to order and relate experiences to as organized whole. Child's mastery of classification ability has increased markedly.

During this period the child is able to deal with *conservations* and *classes.* He attains conservation of substances and weights (at about the age of 9). Weight may become invariant for him for a number of things and objects, i.e., an attribute of many things. He can see that the same quantity of milk poured into any kind of glass or cup means the same thing.

Basically, the child at this stage shifts from inductive to deductive mode of thinking. Leaving aside the mythology he reaches nearer and nearer to science and reality. The child has learned to generalize and to deduce from simple experiences. The preoperational child is mainly concerned with the immediate and the real, not with things that are theoretical, geographically remote or in the future.

Stage-4: The Period of Formal Operation (11-15 Ys. and on) : This is the last phase in Piaget's scheme of child's intellectual development. This occurs between the ages 11 to 15 years when childhood ends maturationally and youth begins. The nature of thought undergoes a change which Piaget links to maturation of cerebral structures. Assimilation and accommodation receive little concern in this phase. The child is capable of thinking in abstract terms. He can think in terms of a variety of possible solutions to a problem and can adopt logical procedures for that purpose, This is the stage where this child can develop and use formal rules and logical procedures. Intellectual operations are, then, controlled by these rules, by general operations that are independent of particular objects to which they are applied. For example, "treeness" (in Plato's language) is independent of the tree, the actual object. Thus, it is the "form" not the actual object "tree" which is part of child's intellectual structure. This is final cognitive structure according to Piaget, final stage of equiliberation and invariances, a stage of truly adult cognitive structure. The individual at this stage can deal with things that are eternal and that apply invariably to all items in the concerned field.

Bruner's Conception

According to Bruner (1964) the growing human being has three means of acting upon his environment. These are through (1) direct action, (2) imagery, and (3) language. These are represented in the central nervous system as their counterparts in the form of sensorimotor acts, percepts and thoughts. Bruner named these internal representational schemes as enactive, iconic and symbolic means or phases of intellectual development. According to him the development of the child follows this sequence from early childhood to adulthood. The child first acts upon concrete things and objects. He plays with them and manipulates them. This is the enactive phase. Then, he develops a mental image of these which is iconic phase. And lastly he associates names with the objects and things. This is the symbolic phase.

The enactive and iconic phases of development are concerned with the immediate environment. Objects and events in the immediate environment are represented in the cognitive structure. Afterwards as the child grows up he develops language ability and can translate these experiences into words. This makes possible for him thinking, reasoning and problem solving.

Intellect Vis-a-vis Intelligence

In certain sections of psychologists the story of intellectual development runs parallel to the development of intelligence. By them intelligence is regarded as a system of thought and awareness. In England and in United States discussions of intelligence have been organized around the tests used, i.e., intelligence as measured by psychological tests. Mental development is, then, measured in terms of mental age or MA which is the average of a group of individuals of a certain age. For example, MA of 6 years would mean average mental age or mental development of 6 years old children. The mental age is obtained from the performance of the individual on a test of intelligence. The Stanford-Binet Scale of Intelligence gives mental age scores of children from 2 years of age to adulthood. The California Test of Mental Maturity yields scores which can be converted into mental age scores by means of a scale or the table of norms. On the basis of these mental age scores it may be known whether the child has average level of mental development, is bright or dull. For example, if a child of 10 years has mental age of 9 or 8 or below then he will be considered below average, if 11 or 12 then above average, and so on. A person is not bright or dull by himself. In fact, he is brighter or duller than the members of the group that serves the basis of comparison. Thus, intelligence is a relative term. A child's MA is considered in terms of his chronological age (C.A). This relationship or ratio between his MA and CA is known as his I.Q. (Intelligence Quotient). The formula is written as :

$$I.Q. = \frac{MA}{CA} \times 100$$

The I.Q. is an index of one's relative mental development, brightness or dullness. On the basis of I.Q. distribution of American children Terman gave the following classification (Kumaria, 1950)

1.	Near genius or genius	above 140
2.	Very superior intelligence	120 - 140
3.	Superior intelligence	110 - 120
4.	Normal or average intelligence	90 - 110
5.	Dull	80 - 90
6.	Borderline Cases	70 - 80
7.	Definitely feebleminded	below 70.

The feeble minded were further classified as under

1.	Morons	50 - 70
2.	Imbeciles	25 - 50
3.	Idiots	Below 25

A person with on I.Q. below 50 can not fend for himself and needs institutional care. In 1929 Dr. C.H. Rice gave the following classification for Indian children

1.	Genius	165 and above
2.	Very superior	140 - 165
3.	Superior	120 - 140
4.	Average	85 - 120
5.	Dull	70 - 85
6.	Borderline Cases	55 - 70
7.	Feeble-minded	Below 55

Mental Growth

This should be noted that mental growth does not continue throughout the entire period of one's life. In fact, it begins to slow down sharply in rate during the early teens and reaches its peak somewhere in the middle twenties. According to general consensus one's mental development starts to taper off around age thirteen. During 13-16 year mental development increases only by two years mental age instead of three. At age 16 a person is said to have mental age of 15, not 16. Hence, in order to compute I.Q. of persons aged beyond 16 it is only 15 which is used as the devisor for chronological age. The age at which mental growth ceases is, however, open to debate. Yet, the current practice of using 15 as the maximum divisor is reasonably acceptable. The gains in test performance occuring after age fifteen are relatively small. It is believed that between 20 to 40 a person's mental level remains fairly constant. After 40 a gradually accelerating decline sets in. It is also found that this loss is not appreciable for the average person till the age sixty and the mental level of gifted people probably never goes below the maximum level of people of average intelligence.

Constancy of the I.Q. **:** There is considerable evidence to indicate that constancy of I.Q. is not absolute. Yet, this is a fact that the dull child becomes the dull adult and the gifted child the gifted adult. Serveral researches (Bayley, 1945; Honzig, 1938) found the I.Q. to be far from being constant. Fluctuations can be expected to occur for a number of reasons including the unreliability of tests used, administrative factors, practice effects, growth factors, test to test variations, experience of the testees, etc.

The problem of the constancy of I.Q. is related to the relative influence of heredity and environment. The influence of heredity and environment upon intelligence has been the subject of very comprehensive investigation over the past several decades.

Role of Heredity : Research evidence in this regard may be divided into following categories -

Family Studies: These are based on the assumption that "like begets like". Woods (1908) showed that intelligence tended to run in certain lines of the royal families of Europe. In England the study of the Jukes by Dugdale (1910) and Estabrook (1916) revealed a heavy concentration of thieves, feebleminded or insane individuals among the descendents of an early New England settler. The studies of Kallikaks by Goddard (1912) and of Edwards family by Winships (1900) also revealed similar evidence. Galton (1925) showed that for every 100 Fellows of the Royal Society there were 28 notable fathers, 36 notable brothers, 20 notable grandfathers and 40 notable uncles. Terman found that for every 15 gifted children there was, at least, one relative in the Hall of Fame.

Studies of Twins : Provide most conclusive evidence of the role of heredity in the area of intelligence. All studies comparing the I.Q. differences among twins and siblings are agreed that the closer the blood relation between two persons the smaller the difference between their I.Q.s. Wingfield (1928) found the following correlations between intelligence of various twins

Identical twins	.90
Like-Sex twins	.82
Fraternal twins	.70
Unlike-Sex twins	.59
Siblings	.50
Cousins	.27

It may be seen that as the degree of blood relationship decreases the I.Q. similarity also decreases. This proves that intelligence is, perhaps, largely hereditary.

Burks (1938) concluded that some 75 percent of the I.Q. differences among individuals were accounted for by heredity.

Role of Environment : The influence of environment on intelligence was demonstrated by the studies of foster children. A study made by Freeman et. al. (1928) revealed that low I.Q. adopted children made an average gain of 7.5 I.Q. points when tested after a few years, while children adopted at an early age made twice the gain as compared to the group adopted later. The Iowa studies (Skeels, 1940; Wellman, 1945) pointed to great improvement in I.Q. as a result of environmental change. In a study made by Schmidt (1945) gains of 30 or more I.Q. points were registered during a period of six years by more than half of the 195 subnormal children involved.

These studies are, however criticized on several grounds as has been already mentioned. The problem. is still the subject of controversy. The general consensus is that heredity is likely to be more important than environment in determining their intellectual level. Most of the researchers (Loevinger, 1943; Shuttleworth, 1940; and Shuttleworth, 1935) hold that heredity accounts for upto three-quarters of the individual differences in intelligence while environment accounts for upto one-fifth only. The general - consensus is very well stated by Boynton (1941) who said that there seems to be a significant tendency on the part of individuals to maintain relatively the same I.Q. ranks over a long period of years. Ordinary changes in environment are not likely to produce much variation in the I.Q. A similar view is presented by Goodenough (1954) who says that research does not seem to support the view that the intellectual development of children can not be easily modified by experience.

An analysis of all the researches and the views leads to the conclusion that rigid support of either of these extreme positions is not desirable in view of the inconclusiveness of evidence.

Nature and Theories

Previously intelligence was regarded to be a faculty of the mind. But, in the 18th and 19th century different theories were evolved to explain the nature of intelligence Most important of them were Monarchic (unifocal), Oligarchic (multifocal) and Anarchic (nonfocal).

Monarchic doctrine believed in one great power of the mind dominating over others. Prof Spearman defined this to be an "all pervading mental power" or to put it in the version of Ross "conscious adaptation to new situations" or "inborn all-round mental efficiency".

Oligarchic or multifocal doctrine did not believe in this. This said that mental capacity consisted of not only one great power but of a few great powers. Binet, a French psychologist believed in three great powers of the mind. But this doctrine, too, could not find support. Psychologists then went further and held that energies of the mind are dominated neither by one great power nor a few great powers; there is only anarchy in the kingdom of the mind and that the average of all these energies is intelligence. This theory also remained unsatisfactory because it was difficult to find out the average of energies. By the same time when theories were spinning in this way Prof. Spearman came with Two-Factor-Theory of Intelligence.

Two-Factor Theory of Intelligence (Eclectic Theory) : According to this theory, intelligence is that ability of the mind which is a combination of two factors 'g' and 's'. The 'g' is the general factor and 's' is the specific factor. The 'g' remains the same in all the activities and never increases or decreases from activity to activity. It remains constant wherever the individual moves. Yet it varies from individual to individual as well as from activity to activity in the same individual; for example, in music 'g' and 's' both are combined together. Here 'g' is innate and fixed amount of mental energy, while 's' is that factor of mental energy which is specifically required by the activity of music. In the same way in the profession of Law legal activity implies the presence of two factors 'g' and 's'. Here 's' is the specific ability required by the legal activity. Thus, factor 's' refers to specific ability required by the specific activity and 'g' is general ability which according to Burt is "innate, central, permanent and constant" and with which an individual is born in this world. The 'g' factor is gifted and cannot be increased even with one's all the best efforts. If this conception of intelligence is accepted the success of a person's achievement in a particular activity depends upon the play of these two factors 'g' and 's'. This may be represented by the following equation

$$A \text{ (achievement)} = \text{'g'} + \text{'s'}$$

Thus, following are the characteristics of the factors 'g' and 's' :

Characteristics of the 'g' Factor

1. It is gifted and constant.
2. It runs through all activities in whatsoever quantity it be
3. It varies from one individual to another.
4. Presence of a high 'g' guarantees a good quality and quantity of success.

Characteristics of the 's' Factor

1. It varies from individual to individual.
2. It varies from activity to activity.
3. Presence of high 's' guarantees a high success its that very activity; but without a high 'g' one cannot succeed to that very level.

Prof. Spearman calls this "Eclectic Theory" because it includes the truth of all the three theories already described. If we regard the 'b' factor as one big factor or the sole factor, monarchic doctrine is satisfied. If we regard the 'g' factor not the sole one and take into consideration so many 's' factors, oligarchic is satisfied. If every 's' is broken into a number of parts (constituents) there will be anarchy in the kingdom of the mind.

Factor 'g': Its Nature : The question arises what is the nature of the factor 'g'. Really speaking 'g' does not represent intelligence in the same sense in which an ordinary man understands it. Prof Spearman did not identify 'g' with intelligence. To him it is highly technical and simply a mathematical quantity which plays a very high role in all mental operations. Spearman tends to view it as mental energy, "an ultimate hypothesis". In his own words 'g' is "some force capable of being transferred from one mental operation to another different one", that is "mental energy derived from the whole cortex ....switched off from one operation to another."

Thus 'g' seems to be a perceiving capacity of the mind. It may be understood as mind's capacity for analysis and synthesis i.e., the capacity to observe certain things or situations when certain relations are involved. The individual who possesses this capacity is a person more intelligent than others who do not have the same to that extent.

Spearman announced his two-factor-theory in 1904. Later he

modified it and added to it certain group-factors, less general, widely spread and homogenous than 'g' and 's', e.g., intelligence in composition, according to this modified version, consisted of 'g' + 'v' (consisting of several sub-factors such as capacity of writing, thinking, imagination, expression.)

Several criticisms were levelled against Spearman's theory. They said, it is too mathematical. Hamilton once remarked, "thinking over intelligence much in terms of factors we shall get further and further away from the psychological realities".

Though, surprising variety of opinion is found regarding the nature of intelligence, it is quite possible to group the various opinions under three heads: those who think of intelligence as "a single ability common to all intellectual processes"; those who regard it as "a group of two or three abilities of varying degree of generality" and those who regard it as "representing all specific abilities". Stern, Woodrow and Spearman hold the first theory. Stern defines intelligence as "general adaptability to the problems and conditions of life." Woodrow calls it "a capacity to acquire capacity". Spearman regards it as "general ability". Binet, Terman and Maxwell Garnett hold the second theory, the group theory. Binet regards intelligence as involving at least three factors. Terman summarises these factors as "tendency to take and maintain a definite direction, the capacity to make adaptations for the purpose of attaining a desired end, and the power of auto-criticism." Maxwell Garnett holds that the general factor 'g' is compounded with one or perhaps more than one group factors to constitute intelligence. The third theory of the independence of the several traits is advocated by Thorndike, though not with full confidence. G.H. Thomson's Sampling Theory of Ability also comes under the same head. He assumes that "each man's mind is a sample group of qualities".

Dr. Johnson holds that "every individual has certain abilities and the most important of these goes by the name of intelligence." He defines it as "the ability to solve the general run of human problems, to adjust to new situations and in short the ability to think."

According to Prof Woodworth "Intelligence is a characteristic of behaviour". Terman holds it to be "an ability to think in abstract terms."

Behaviourists give a mechanistic definition and say "Intelligence is a physiological mechanism integrating stimuli and producing adequate and uniform response."

Munn identifies it with "flexibility of the mind to meet new situations." To Woodworth "Intelligence is innate capacity to solve the problems easily in the light of the past experiences and knowledge". In short, it is an ability to perceive the right thing at the right moment in the right way. In the words of Wyatt it is an ability of the mind to "apprehend relevant relations." It is the discovery of relations and education of correlates.

Physiological Account

Thorndike in the United States opposed these 'g', 's' and group-factors. He said this is over-simplification of intelligence. In Britain, Spearman's most active critic had been Thomson. Prof. Keley also criticised it and proved with his improved techniques that 'g' itself is a combination of group factors which his method can thrash out. To him mental life operates "in a network of canals." Thorndike said that intellectual tasks are carried out by a complex nervous system operating in many different patterns, patterns too difficult to be described fully. He regards mind as a multitude of functions. He asserts the independence of the several traits that go to make up the mind. He defines intelligence in terms of physiology as a "capacity for mere association or connection forming". His theory is also known as the Multi-factor Theory of Intelligence.

This is also known as the theory of specific intelligence. Thorndike (1927) said that intelligence is the summation of all the abilities involved in mental work. Each of these abilities, according to him is separate and independent of the others. He defined intelligence as a multitude of specific and independent neural connections, a totality of thousands of different abilities or habits or stimulus-response connections.

Thurstone's Theory

Thurstone (1938, 1955) using factor analysis approach was able to demonstrate that intelligence was neither a unitary thing, nor a vast number of things, rather, it was made up of fewer than a dozen separate factors or components. Each of these factors could be considered as a unitary thing representing an ability quite distinct from others. Thurstone found that on these factors there existed visible inter-individual and intra-individual differences. He also said that tasks, generally, involve combinations of these abilities. A person may be high or low on any of these abilities. He identified seven primary mental abilities and developed tests also for measuring these abilities. These primary mental abilities were: (1) Verbal, (2) Numerical, (3) Spatial, (4) Word-fluency, (5) Inductive Reasoning, (6) Deductive Reasoning, and (7) Memory. These were measured by his Chicago Primary Mental Abilities Test (PMA Test). But, his later test known as SRA Primary Mental Abilities Test measures only five of these abilities. He abandoned the distinction between inductive and deductive reasoning and measured them as a single ability of reasoning.

Three Dimensional Model

Guilford (1956, 1959, 1967) presented a single three-dimensional model of intelligence which included all the factors mentioned by Thurstone and many more in addition to these. He integrated these into a single system. These three dimensions as mentioned by him were: (1) Contents, (ii) Operations and (iii) Products. Each of these was further divided into smaller units as follows :

Operations: This included cognition, memory, divergent production, convergent production, and evaluation. These are mental functions which are involved in all kinds of intellectual functioning such as perceiving, reasoning, remembering etc.

Products: This is further broken into units, classes, relations, systems, transformations and implications.

Contents: This is broken into figural, symbolic, semantic and behavioural.

Thus, five factors of operations dimension, six factors of products and four factors of contents taken together measure 120 abilities which constitute intelligence according to Guilford. These three dimensions of Guilford's structure of intellect represent the important attributes of any task that any one is engaged in. Whatever be the task the individual has to deal with a certain kind of material (content), which is manipulated by him in a certain way (operation) to produce something or achieve some outcome (Product). For example, if a child is asked to add 3+2 and gives the answer 5, he is using the ability having three dimensions as convergent production + unit + symbolic. Different operations may be involved in dealing with a kind of content. For example, a child may recall a single number 5 (unit) or a class of number (odd number), or a relation between two or more numbers (25 as the square of 5) or a system of numbers (5,25,125 ad so on) or a modification or transformation of a number (such as I/5 or 0.2) or and implication of the nature of a given number (any number having 5 at the unit place will be divisible by 5). Thus, while dealing with different contents a person makes use of different products. Similarly, while just seeing the book the person is at a point of applying operation of cognition to the figural content as a unit of product. But, if he is considering the book as a book on psychology he is dealing with the product class; and if a good book, he is using product relation between this book and other books on psychology; if considering a book dealing with different theories of learning, he is using systems product; if he thinks that the book is very useful and should be published as cheap student edition, he is dealing with product transformation; if he comes to the conclusion that the book should be read by all teachers, he is applying cognition operation to the area of figural content and implication product.

On the basis of contents dimension Guilford named three types of intelligence concrete, abstract and social intelligence. Concrete intelligence, according to him, involves abilities connected with figural content. Mechanics, operators of machines, and musicians, etc., depend heavily on these abilities. Abstract intelligence pertains to abilities concerned with symbolic and semantic content. Learning to recognize words to spell and use numbers involves abilities with symbolic content. Understanding of verbal concepts and ideas. of all types call for abilities with semantic content. Social intelligence is concerned with behavioural content, with behaviour of other people and his own behaviour.

Crystallized Intelligence

Spearman's two-factor theory of intelligence was criticized by Cattell (1963) saying that Spearman's "g" factor can not be a single unitary factor. It is made up of at least two factors. These two factors were named by him as fluid intelligence and crystallized intelligence. He defined fluid intelligence as that function of the human mind which enables a person to turn his attention to almost any area. It may be language or mathematics, poetry or science. According to Cattell this is that ability which is most closely linked with the general notion of brightness. It is fully developed by the age of sixteen or so. On the other hand, crystallized intelligence is closely linked to the culture to which one is exposed. It represents achievement in the tasks of that culture. Unlike fluid intelligence it is not free-floating energy that can be directed to any task. This is specific to the task. It is specific and particular emerging from the application of fluid intelligence to a particular task of an area; for example, learning parts of speech in Hindi grammar. These achievements once acquired remain with us and, at any given time, these remaining specific items constitute our crystalized intelligence. This intelligence can keep on growing well into maturity as the individual learns many things and acquires knowledge and information and has a great transfer value.

Conceptual Tempo

Kagan (1965) identified two specific functions of human mind, rather two specific ways in which human mind operates upon his environment. These he calls impulsive dimension and reflective dimension. The impulsive dimension is represented by the state of mind when a person blasts out the first idea that comes to his mind. On the other hand, if a person spends a good deal of his time in thinking about each possible idea before taking any overt action, he is said to be reflective.

Most people fall somewhere between these two extremes. A child with impulsive tempo, for example, may also be more adventurous and more fidgety. On the other hand, the highly reflective child has a longer attention span and is less subject to distraction. He is more persistent when facing a difficult task.

Tempo and general intelligence have not been found to be closely related. Two children might be quite bright, but one may be impulsive while the other reflective. With some material the impulsive child may be more successful; for example in learning to pronounce foreign words the child who takes a second look at the first experience will get along better in many kinds of school work.

Measuring Intelligence

By the close of the 18th century Gall discovered a science of the study of the head to measure one's mind. This science was known as phrenology.

Lavater published an essay on physiognomy and said that face was the index of mind. Graphology discovered that mind is revealed by handwriting. But these methods were all untrustworthy.

At the end of the 19th century Lombroso said that the abnormalities in the shape and size of the skull, forehead and nose, etc., could give an idea of one's intelligence.

In 1906 Karl Pearson by the method of correlation disproved that intelligence could be guessed from face or the head.

Scientific Testing : The crucial point from which a definite scientific wave of measuring intelligence emerged was in 1879, when Prof. Wundt established a laboratory at Leipzig in Germany.

About the same time in England Galton began his discoveries. But he could not develop his intelligence test. In 1890 in America J.N. Cattell published a work on "Mental Tests and Measurement" and described single tests of separate factors of abilities such as sensation, reaction time, speed of movement, and so forth. But the real work appeared in the hands of Binet of France. In 1905 he published a test, but he was not satisfied with this. So he began to rework and in 1908 a revised version of the 1905-test was published which was meant for the pupils from the age of 3 to 11 years.

With this test, Binet introduced the concept of mental age. He revised problems and exercises to test comprehension, memory, power of comparison, ability to draw conclusions, reasoning and other mental powers.

But again with the help of Prof. Simon another version of the same test was published in 1911 called as Binet-Simon-Test. This last revision included more tests and it could test pupils from age 3 to the age of adulthood.

This Binet-Simon test was introduced in America by Goddard. In America this test was modified and revised again by Terman and Merrill in 1916. This revision is known as Standford Revision of Binet-Simon-Test.

Terman chose six tests for each year from 3 to 10 inclusive and also for ages 12, 14, 16 and 18. He assigned 2 month's mental-age-credit for each test passed. Many of Binet's items were included, though some were shifted to higher or lower age-levels, and several new test-items were added. It had in all including alternate items 90 tests instead of 54 of Binet's scale of 1911. Binet had introduced an idea of mental age. A German psychologist Wilhelm Stern suggested in 1912 to replace mental age by "I.Q." found out by dividing the mental age by chronological age and multiplying by 100.

The revision of Binet-Simon scale of 1916 was again modified in 1937 by Terman and Merrill. It was a considerable improvement upon that of 1916. The 1937's revision had two forms L & M, while 1916's test had only one, so that when a person was retested he could be tested with a different form thus avoiding its practice-effects. It was lengthened to extend from the year second up through the superior adult e.g., the maximum mental age that could be tested was 22 years. Meanwhile revisions of the form L for British children had been prepared by Burt and by Kennedy Fraser.

Thus, following revisions of Binet-Simon scale were made :

1. Standford-Binet-Simon-Test by Terman and Merrill in 1916 and then in 1937 and again revised third time in 1960 and fourth time in 1986.
2. London Revision by Prof. Burt in 1960.

In India it was adapted in Hindi in 1960 by Dr. S.K. Kulshrestha at Allahabad Bureau of Psychology.

Characteristics of Binet-Simon test of 1911

1. It consisted of 54 tests.
2. It extended from 3 to 16 years excluding 11, 13, 14.
3. It had 5 tests for each age but 4 for four years old children.
4. It included questions on sex, name, number and picture, etc.

Characteristics of Burt's Revision

1. It had 65 tests instead of 54.
2. It covered a period from 3 to 16 years.
3. Number of tests was not the same for each age.
4. Nature of the test was almost the same e.g., it had questions such as: For the 8 years old children.
    1. What will you do if you miss the train? For the 11 years old children ?
    2. Why should you judge a person by what he does and not by what he says ?

Questions based on differentiation between abstract terms such as happiness and pleasure are put.

Characteristics of Standford-Binet-Simon-Test of 1937

1. Nature of tests varies from the lowest age level to the superior adult. At the lowest age level the verbal nature of the test is minimised by using concrete objects.
2. It covers the age from 2 to 22.
3. At the lowest level the child is asked to identify a toy, a cup, a spoon, chair, fork etc.
4. At the upper age levels the intelligence is measured by verbal and abstract terms.
5. There are pictures in which missing parts are to be filled according to a definite pattern.
6. Tests of word-meaning appear at a number of age levels.
7. Memory is tested by reading a section of a story and writing how much the subject can recall. Both auditory and visual memory are tested.
8. It has two forms L and M.
9. It gives us I.Q., derived from mental age.

This in brief is the history of intelligence tests.

Classification of Tests

Intelligence test are of two kinds-Verbal and Non-Verbal or Linguistic and Non-linguistic. The Verbal test requires the use of language. In the Non-verbal tests language is not used. The subject is required to do something. He does not use language. Non-verbal tests thus require only the manipulation of muscles.

Non-Verbal Tests, too, are of two types :

(a) Paper and Pencil Tests and (b) Performance Tests.

Paper and Pencil tests are also of two types :

(a) Pictorial, and (b) Perceptual.

Binet test required normal functioning of vision, hearing and language ability. It could not be applied to the blind, the deaf or the illiterate. So performance tests were devised to meet these special conditions.

About 1950, a French physician Seguin constructed a test for the feeble-minded children. Later Dr. Healy made a completion test. Then Pinter and Paterson two psychologists of the University of Ohio State combining together the Seguin, Healy and other similar tests prepared the first performance scale in 1917. In this scale all the tests call for a motor response. Some of the most famous performance tests are :

1. Pass Along Test.
2. Knox's Wooden Cube Test.
3. Pintner Paterson Test.
4. Portius Maze Test.
5. Kelley's Test of Building the Best Thing.
6. Gooddard Form Board Tests.

From another point of view tests are of two types, Individual and Group Tests. In the Individual Tests subjects are tested individually one by one.

Group Test is a test that can be administered to a group of people at the same time. The stimulus came from World War First in 1914. The problem was to test the intelligence of a number of people to be employed for various war-services. The result was that Army Alpha for literate and Army Beta for illiterates, two tests came into existence. When the war was over more accurate group tests were constructed.

Construction of Verbal Group-tests : Following eight types of problems saturated with intelligence are contained by these tests :

1. Number series e.g., 3, 6, 12, 24, 96.
   The subject is asked to complete this.

2. Alternatives or Multiple Choice Tests— e.g., The mango is to a fruit as potato is to ....
3. To designate superfluous part or Classification Tests. The subject has to underline the odd word, mango, table, chair, tool, bench.
4. To arrange in order the mixed sentences.
5. Matching Tests. The subject has to select two objects matching one another as "the grass is green as the sky is .... cloudy, far away, rough, blue".
6. Analogies e.g., Sun is to dry as rain is to .... cloud, shower, wet, pool.
7. Sentence Completion: The subject has to complete the sentence e.g., Man is perhaps the only animal that has the .... reason.
8. Synonyms and Antonyms-type tests.

Advantages of Group-tests

1. They save time testing hundreds and thousands of the subjects simultaneously.
2. No expert is needed in administering them.

Disadvantages

1. They are not as accurate as Individual Tests. Validity and reliability of Group Tests are less than those of the Individual tests.
2. Language difficulties may influence the achievement of the candidates.

Advantages of Intelligence Tests : Intelligence tests are very useful :

1. For educational guidance and for providing checks at different stages of the courses of study.
2. To detect the superior and the dull and adjust teaching accordingly. This implies that method of teaching must be different for children of different ability.
3. They can be used to supplement traditional examination.
4. In awarding scholarship etc., we may have intelligence test examination:

5. They can be used in vocational guidance.
6. They may also be used in the recruitment for various services.

Criteria of Good Test : Following are the criteria of a good intelligence test :

1. Objectivity It must be objective. It should eliminate the effect of the whims and pre-occupations of the examiner with the scores.
2. A high degree of validity: It should be able to test the same thing which is desirable.
3. Reliability: It is the degree of correctness to which it measures the thing required to be tested. A good test must have a high degree of reliability.
4. Accuracy in administration: It must be accurate and simple in administering.
5. Scoring should be simple and quick.
6. Economical: It should not be expensive.

While administering the test the following precautions should be taken :

1. A good acquaintance with the process should be acquired.
2. Prescribed conditions should be secured and maintained.
3. Temperament of the subject should be noted.
4. Temptation for copying should be minimised.
5. Proper arrangement for calculation should be made.

Besides intelligence tests there are tests and devices to measure so many other capacities and achievement of the individual.

Types of Test : Following are the kinds of other tests :

1. Achievement Tests or Attainment Tests or Accomplishment Tests.
2. Aptitude Tests or Special Abilities Tests or Prognostic Tests.
3. Personality Tests and Character Tests.

13

Projective Methods

The various methods of assessing or finding out the traits, by asking some people who know the individual, by asking the individual himself some questions (as in interview sessions), making him to mark some written questionnaire and observing him in the natural setting or under controlled conditions, as in a laboratory, do tell us quite a lot about the individual, his qualities, attributes, traits or aspects of his personality. But still there are many factors such as hidden drives, complexes, anxieties, unfulfilled wishes, hatred, hostility, prejudices and frustrations of various sorts, of which the individual himself may not be quite aware but which determine his pattern of behaviour and problems of his adjustment. Such unconscious or subconscious elements have also to be known, as far as possible, to not only supplement the data gleaned by other methods and means but to have a clearer picture cf contents of ones personality or the traits which determine his unique structure and mode of behaviour. These unconscious or subconscious mental contents are revealed in the way one projects himself by reacting in any manner to the presentation of material or ideas in all forms. His reactions reveal his perceptions of the material; and what one perceives, if fully known, becomes the full expression of himself. The material can be pictures depicting life situations, vague patches of ink or colour, words conveying some ideas or concepts, some vague or incomplete drawings, and so on. The reactions can be verbal expressions of the perceptions, bodily movements, facial gestures, manual manipulation in the form of drawings, designs or other creations. This whole field of catching the individual unaware, as it were, to make him reveal himself in all way by perceiving any material contents or other sensory presentations is called the use of projective techniques as one perceives things and meanings in them as are determined by his inner mental contents which he himself may not be aware of, but which seem to break the barriers of his conscious mind or will come out unwillingly or unwarrantedly and involuntarily. This means that the individual is projecting himself thus giving vent to his inner self.

The term projection was first used by Freud to describe how an individual unable to accept certain thoughts, wishes or characteristics in himself, attributes them to certain environmental objects or persons. This was, according to Freud, one of the defense mechanisms unconsciously used by the individual to solve his own mental conflicts. It was Freud who first made inquiry into hidden motives. His interpretation of behaviour, both verbal and motor, in terms of their symbolic rather than their obvious meaning and his distinction between latent and manifest contents had profound influence on the significance of projective productions. A child, for example, wishing to hit his rather cruel father, may hit a male rubber doll, kick it or break its neck or the neck of a toy elephant by calling it a devil. Here the toys symbolized the cruel father and the child expressed his anger against him. The projective methods for the study of inner contents of personality, therefore, involve the presentation of stimulus situations which are designed or chosen not because they will mean to the individual what the designer has arbitrarily decided they should mean, but rather whatever they must mean to the person who gives it meaning according to his own private idiosyncrasies or mental make-up. These methods are systematic attempts for exploring and comparing the inner personality structures of individuals.

There are a number of these projective methods in use and no, one method can possibly reveal the whole personality. These methods supplement one another in a sense and yet personality contents cannot all be taken as exhausted or completely understood with the use of even all the methods combined. But the material revealed with the use of these methods gives us an insight as to how the individual perceives, feels and looks at the world and persons in his social group. The projective methods, therefore, are all those methods in which the individual has been given an opportunity to live empathetically, that is, by involving himself in contents of the presentations and giving meanings to them which have his own personal stamp. Projective methods came to be designated as such after 1939 when L.K. Frank (1943) used it in an article.

The various projective methods or techniques in use are the following which will be dealt with here briefly.

1. The Rorschach test
2. The T. A. T
3. CAT and Picture Frustration Test of Saul Rosenzweig
4. Role playing as in psycho-drama
5. Play including doll playing and clay modelling
6. Free Association and Controlled Association
7. Picture Completion
8. Sentence Completion
9. Story Making
10. Drawing, Painting and Sculpture
11. Poetry, dramatics or writing novels
12. Autobiography or Biography of an Unknown Person

Rorschach Ink-blot Test

The ink-blots, were used earlier also before Rorschach used them for evolving his series as a systematic diagnostic test known by his name. Rorschach was not the first investigator who used the ink-blots but he was the first to develop a workable method what was called as a shorthand method by Beck (1944) later for understanding the responses of an individual. Hermann Rorschach was born in Zurich in Nov. 1884. He was the son of an art teacher. He studied medicine till 1910. After this he pursued the study of ink-blots for 10 years starting in 1911 and using hundreds of them in 1921 he published his studies called *Psychodiagnostik* (1921) before his premature and early death on April 2, 1922. The Rorschach Test is very widely used for clinical diagnosis and had been introduced in the armed forces for diagnostic and research purposes and applied to various people for the study of psychopathology, developmental psychology, vocational guidance and other problems of personality study. There is no other single test or technique on which so much work is done for research and diagnosis of individual cases. The Rorschach Institute was founded in 1939 with Klopfer as its guiding spirit. In 1937 Beck's (of Michael Rees Hospital, Chicago) famous book *"Introduction to The Rorschach Method"* was published. It was the first systematic guide to administration, scoring and interpretation of Rorschach Test. In 1942, two books appeared almost simultaneously, one by Klopfer and Kelley and the other by Ruth Bockner and Florence Halpern which popularised the test still further. There is hardly any topic in psychology concerning which there has been so much for and against feelings expressed than the Rorschach test, but in spite of this, the test has grown in use and reputation over all these years and is still so much in use.

In the Rorschach test there are 10 cards on each of which one of the final set of Ten ink-blots is printed. The last 5 cards are coloured here and there. The cards are given to the subject one by one and he is asked to tell whatever he sees in the card by marking the portion in the blank (giving bare outlines of the portion of each card drawn on another paper) which he has taken in view for the response. He could turn the cards upside down, on the left or on the right. He is asked to see attentively and to tell all that he could make out. The time is noted for each card and all the responses for each card are put serially and scored in accordance with the four categories of location, contents, popularity or originality and the determinants.

Location means the portion of the card seen that is the whole of it, major part of it, or some small details in it. Contents mean whether the response pertains to human beings or to parts of the human body, animals or some part of the animal body, and so on. Popularity or originality stands for the response being popular or being very unusual or original. Determinants means whether it was human movement, animal movement or inanimate movement, three dimensional vista or loose expanse like clouds or smoke, and so on, as given in the chart. Every response is judged in terms of these four categories and the symbols for them are given to each response. Then all the responses are arranged to find out the percentage of each category and the protocol is made about each person and interpretation is given in accordance with the meaning attached to all the categories and their importance in terms of their percentages of occurrence in all the cards. To illustrate the scoring procedure and the interpretation one case out of so many studied by the author while at Bureau of Psychology, Allahabad is given here.

Categories in Rorschach Test

Location :

W Whole card seen which means interest in abstract thinking and capacity to synthesize elements into meaningful wholes.

W Failure stands for inaptitude to see problems as a whole.

D Major detail means generally strong common sense.

d Small details indicate involving in petty

ddd Issues or attention paid to less important matters.

S White space seen indicates fantasy life and escape from reality with stubbornness and opposition to authority it is more a trend to rebellion and selfwilled activities.

Contents:

H Human figures as a whole indicative of human interest.

HA Human details of parts of the body mean the same.

A Animals as whole

Ad Part of some animals body. Show juvenile tendency and need for development of animal instincts to mature human level.

Aobj. Animal objects like fur, skin, skulls etc. goes with A and Ad.

At Anatomical parts of inside of the body.

Obj. Some object in concrete form indicate organizational capability.

N Natural scenery or landscape, river, etc., show artistic mind.

Geo. Geographical map, gulf or geographical details.

Popularity-originality :

O Original or rare responses characterised by the individuals themselves.

P Popular responses as given by people at large.

Determinants :

M Human movements, indicate depth of feelings, creative thought and rich human experience and maturity.

FM Animal movements mean pent up urges wishing to unload themselves.

m Inanimate movements, like washing, fluttering in wind, show hostile forces or deep buried unconscious powers with no outlets.

K Diffused expansion like water, smoke, clouds, indicative of darkness, dreariness which is threatening.

Kk 3 dimensional shading on 2 dimensional plane indicative of some control and rational way of dealing with forces.

FK shading in a 3 dimensional expanse as in vista or perspective indicative of superior mental qualities and artistic bent of mind.

F Form shows critical controlling power of mind and reason which prefers solid facts & it shows good intelligence.

Fc Shading as surface appearance or texture. It indicates lack of handling others with very little sensuality.

FC Coloured object when form is more important as a tomato.

CF A coloured object where colour is more important as a red shirt.

C Colour responses, indicate emotional instability and extensive disposition.

C Achromatic colours as grey which is indicative of liveliness of movements and agility and many sided life.

This is rather a very brief and sketchy presentation of the various symbols standing for the different categories and sub-categories and what they stand for or were indicative of the personality factors which were more underneath or hidden. The administration of the test and particularly the interpretation needs experience, training and insight for using the Test. Everybody can not just give the test and score it, as if to find out the mean or percentages and quickly reach the conclusions. One has to undergo training in the use of the test and to closely study from books particularly from Beck and Klopfer & Kelley or Klopfer and Klopfer.

Thematic Apperception Test

Another important test, in the family of projective techniques, which made its appearance in 1935 was the Thematic Apperception Test first described in a paper by Morgan and Murray in which the technique of using phantasy to understand deeper mental contents was explained. The test consisted of pictures which the subject was asked to use to create his own plot of the story as to what the picture could mean. Historically, the beginning of the major trends for the final publication of T.A.T. was the five year investigation of children's phantasy published in England in 1935 by Griffith. This study which utilized imagery tests, drawings and dreams of fifty normal children came to the conclusion that phantasy was one of the ways children use for facing their problems. This finding became the basis for diagnosis and therapy and the corner stone of the T.A.T. (Thematic Apperception Test). This test is called thematic apperception test as according to Murray each individual perceives things or drawings in the light of his earlier experiences or as he apperceive them, and he apperceives them thematically which means that there are emotional reactions or themes built up in the mind (themes being a combination of need arising from the individual and the press or force arising from the environment (or a thema = need x press) of the individual and so he apperceives the drawings in the light of those emotional reactions or themas and that is why the test is called Thematic Apperception Test. Murray said that this test was a method of revealing to the trained interpreter some of the dominant drives, emotions, sentiments, complexes and conflicts of personality. This test has special value because it has the power to expose the underlying or repressed or inhibited desires and tendencies, anxiety, guilt or inferiority which the subject has.

The test consists of 20 pictures (there are, of course, about 30 pictures, some are for females and some for males and some for both and there is a blank card also) including a blank card to be shown to each individual. The pictures depict common human situations of tussels between children and parents, love affairs, parental relations, frustrations in achieving or securing things of interest, jealousy or rivalry, aggression and hostility as in Oedipus and Electra situations, and so on. The çards on which the pictures are printed are given to the subject one by one and he is asked to see the picture carefully and think of the contents as to what these could mean and give a coherent account of the meaning of the contents in the form of a story involving his imagination or phantasy. The stories could be of 300 words each for adults and of 150 words for children, though there is no such strict limit and there is no time control. (The test is adapted for use in India by Uma Chaudhary and Bureau of Psychology, Allahabad).

Any and everybody cannot and, of course, should not use this test, as the handling of such projective techniques is more of an art. Their effective use demands lengthy clinical experience, broad understanding of humanity, empathy, psychological mindedness and insight. Adequate projective testing as for T.A.T., rests on understanding of personality dynamics which can be gained only from intimate or first hand association with diagnostic and therapeutic work.

After the test has been given and the 20 stories or description material is recorded with other particulars of the subject like age, sex, parents (dead, alive or separated) sex and age of siblings, vocation and marital status, etc., the next task is the analysis of stories with a view to understand the most prevalent themas (need-press combinations). as the question is what issues, conflicts or dilemmas are of the greatest concern to the author of the stories.

The analysis of the stories is done along the following aspects of the story.

The Hero: It stands for the character in the story who is the chief figure. The hero may be showing superiority, submissiveness, cruelty or criminality, solitariness, leadership, quarrelsomeness or some mental abnormality. Generally the subject identifies with the hero. The identification may shift and may be there in a sequence of heroes, as for example, the hero may now be a criminal and in latter part of the story as the law enforcing agent. There may be partial heroes, as in a group of people who may function equally in a situation and the hero is one of them.

Needs, Motives, Trends and Feelings of the Hero: The needs or motives are expressed in activities initiated by the hero with regard to objects, situations or other people and also in reactions of the hero in the activities initiated by others. What each of the 20 or more heroes feels, thinks and does, even anything unusual or unique, may give evidence for extraversion, introversion, masculinity, feminity, ascendance or submission. The needs or motives as come out in these 20 stories are judged with regard to their strength on a five point scale and the criteria of strength are that of intensity, duration, frequency and importance of the motive in the plot. After the 20 stories have been scored in this way, the total for each variable is compared with the standard score for subjects of the given age and sex and the variables which are either well above or well below the standard are listed and scrutinised in relation to each other. Murrary gave a list of 20 basic needs and 8 other latent needs of psychological nature.

Forces of the Hero's Environments: These also stand for the presses which emanate from the people which the hero deals with. There may be affiliation, dominance, rejection, aggression or even physical danger from others to the hero.

Outcome of the Story or the conclusion or ending of the story is also important. This, in fact, is the result of the interaction of the comparative strength of the forces emanating from the hero and the presses or forces emanating from other persons or other circumstances in the environment. Viewing each event, each interaction of press and need from the point of view of the hero, the interpreter estimates the amount of hardship and frustration experienced, the relative degree of success and failure and also the ratio between happy and unhappy endings.

Interests and Sentiments or cathexes expressed by the hero are also studied. These stand for the objects, activities, people or ideas which attract or repel the hero, which are said to be positive and negative cathexes. For example, the boy saw the violin in the window and wished to buy it or that the sight of the gun made him cringe. He had to turn away because he could stand it no longer.

Inner States of joy, elation, happiness, excitement, suspicion, dejection, pessimism, sorrow, grief etc., expressed by the subject while looking at the cards, are also noted.

The Manner : The manner in which the behaviour is expressed is also noted. He may pause, may be restless, may scratch his head or rub his hands or back, his gestures may change, he may be sweating, may start smoking, may be hesitating and he may exhibit other ties and twitches. His reaction towards the examiner is also noted. He may stare at him, show his teeth and may frown or express himself in other verbal forms.

Reaction : The subject's reaction to the testing situation as a whole and to each of the cards is taken note of.

The Objective Characteristics of the Picture, as noted or pointed out by the subject as omissions or additions done by him or distortions pointed out and also the attention to particular details paid by him, are all taken note of.

Characteristic : The language used by the subject in describing the pictures and use of any symbolism in all is also noted for proper understanding of the personality syndrome.

Reliability of such a test (which really is a technique rather than a test) cannot be high, nor is there any need to talk about reliability of such techniques. When moods are fleeting and the situations also change, one cannot expect too high reliability, even though the bulk of the content objectifies tendencies and traits that are relatively constant. The data on this point of reliability is lacking and, perhaps in such projective techniques applied to individuals to study more deeply each individual, the question of reliability is not quite relevant, as these techniques are not for quantification and for application to large numbers as other tests are given for generalizations.

Children's Apperception Test

Children's Apperception Test (C.A.T.) is the projective test on the lines of T.A.T. developed by Leopold Bellak of the School of Education, New York University. It consists of 10 pictures, printed on cards depicting animals in various life situations. The test is devised for children from 3 to 10 (of both sexes) years to elicit responses to problems presented by children such as feeding fads, sibling rivalry, parental attitude, reactions towards parents, Oedipus situation, primal scene, child's fantasies around aggression, acceptance by adult world, fear of being rejected and being lonely, toilet behaviour, etc. More animals are shown since children are more interested in animals and the test is said to be culture-free, meant for children of all groups- white, coloured and other groups except for those groups which might not be familiar with things like bicycle, for instance. In such cases some items, animals and situations are changed. For example, in an Indian adaptation (by Uma Chaudhary) fox is substituted for Kangaroo, European type of toilet seat in bathroom is changed into Indian type of toilet seat. The chicken are shown eating without spoons. The 10 pictures are (a) Mother hen at the breakfast table watching chicken (as children) eating from plates, (b) Mother fox going shopping, with the little young one of the fox following her on a cycle, (c) Bears pulling at a tug-of-war and the little cub siding with one parent (d) two monkeys sitting on a bench are seen conspiring, as it were (e) Dog mother is beating the pup for going to the pot (f) Two bears as mother and father sleeping in a double bed and the younger ones are seen talking (g) A little rabbit is shut in a room alone (h) A lion sitting with a pipe in mouth and a stick by his side (i) Two bears are shown together and a cub sitting in the corner.

To study the reproductions or stories of children after seeing these pictures one by one and to interpret them, 10 variables are kept in view.

1. The main theme

2. The main hero with whom the child identified himself as the interests, wishes, deficiencies, gifts and abilities with which the hero is invested are those which the subject possesses, wants to possess or fears that he might not have them.
3. Attitudes towards parental figures. The attitudes may be like compliant, respectful, devoted, grateful, dependent, resourceful, competitive, resistant, aggressive, fearful, demanding etc.
4. Family members' role or how the hero identifies with the father, mother and siblings and how is the father seen? How is the mother seen and how are brothers or sisters seen?
5. The figure or objects or new external circumstances introduced are as punishers, pursuers, benefactors or what?
6. Nature of anxieties: Whether these are about physical harm or punishment, about disapproval of behaviour, about denial or loss of love and affection or of being deserted or rejected.
7. Significant conflicts as between autonomy and compliance, between achievement and pleasure, between super-ego and aggression or between acquisition and sexual desires.
8. Nature of punishment for the crime or something done wrongly, whether the punishment is just, too severe, lenient, immediate or delayed.
9. Outcome of the story, whether it is happy or unhappy, realistic or unrealistic or wishful.
10. The objects or figures which are committed or not taken note of are also noted.

The application of this test and the interpretation of it cannot be done as in the case of ordinary tests and requires special experience, study of human nature and insight as in the case of T.A.T. In the hands of an experienced and trained interpreter, the test is found to be very revealing about the problems which children present and this diagnostic information is found very handy to deal with those problem children or the problems presented by some children.

Picture Frustration Test

Picture Frustration Test of Saul Rosenzweig is devised for assessing the degree of frustration, guilt feelings and punishment for something going wrong by presenting to children certain frustrating situations through pictures like a child trying to find something nice in a cupboard by getting on a stool and not finding anything, missing the bus just on reaching, breaking something, etc. In a study of the test applied to 1002 Indian children from 4 to 13 years of age, it was found that smaller children upto 8 years of age had a tendency to expect a solution from others but on becoming a bit older they were more independent and wanted to contribute to the solution of the problems. With increase in age, increase in the tendency for self-criticism and guilt feelings are more pronounced. These results, about some unconscious mental contents, were said to be useful for planning educational and mental hygiene programmes for children.

Play: a Therapeutic Method

Through play, as in a child guidance clinic, the play therapist not only finds the clue for the mental problems of the child but helps him to have some catharsis for his pent up feelings, guilt, hostility for anxiety. Play is for diagnosis and for therapy for children as psycho-analysis is for adults. Doll playing is also a form of play where instead of having a free choice of toys, the child plays with dolls and gives free vent to his phantasies which reveal his unconscious mind. These dolls may represent the father or mother or elders with whom he is living and also siblings, friends, classmates, ghosts, devils or other frightening objects. The various emotional crosscurrents of an inhibited, repressed and unconscious nature flowing in the child's mind pertaining to people in his social environment, find easy outlet. In a similar manner clay modelling like playing with mud in the child guidance play room enables the child to have a free expression to his phantasies, hidden desires and other troubling thoughts.

Role Playing

Role playing as in psycho-dramatic sessions, popularised by J.L. Moreno (1944) provides an opportunity to live through an experience which the patient wishes to live through. He may play the role of a tyrant, wielding his sword and hitting a dummy with full force, as if he were cutting the throat of the winner in a race or competition where the patient lost some years ago and the patient may have harboured the grudge and may have felt agitated looking for a chance to wreak his revenge. This failure to find an opportunity may have upset his balance of mind and in the psycho-dramatic session he finds relief in thus having played the role to hit his adversary. Psychodrama is one of the very effective projective methods both for diagnostic and therapeutic ends.

Free Association Method

Free Association and controlled association techniques are two kinds of this method. Interest in the association of ideas began with the associationistic school before the advent of experimental psychology, as the speculations of John Locke. Galton's work in 1879, Wundt's in 1880 and the introduction of association experiments into American laboratories by Cattell, Jastrow, Munsterberg and others in those days, marked the beginning of scientific studies in the use of association of ideas with the help of given words and the interpretation of the responses to find out underlying bases for those responses.

Galton began his more systematic study in 1885. He noted that the responses to the words were not random in character but gave ample evidence that thought travelled through significant "ruts" of the mind or already set channels, as it were. He found that about 40 per cent of these associations dated back to boyhood, 45 per cent to manhood and 15 per cent or so to the recent events and that the recent associations were the least stable. Freud used free association when the patient was required to freely associate his ideas and go on speaking about himself freely by lying in a couch in a relaxed mood. This was Freud's technique, in addition to dream interpretation for psycho-analysis both for diagnosis and treatment of mental patients. With the publication of Jung's *"Studies in Word Association"* in 1904 and the extensive experiments of Kent and Roseroff in 1910, the significance of association of ideas for personality study became more impressive. Stressing the importance of studying psychic functions through word association Jung wrote. "We must bear in mind that the association experiment cannot deal with a separated psychic function, for any psychic occurrence is never a thing in itself but is always the resultant of the entire psychological past". Then again Bleuler in his chapter in Eder's translation of *Studies in Word Association* writes "In the activity of association there is mirrored the whole psychical essence of the past and of the present with all their experiences and desires. It thus becomes an index of all the psychical processes which we have to decipher in order to understand the complete man". Eder points out in his own introduction to Jung's studies that the departure in Jung's application of the association method was to reveal the unconscious mental processes and to bring out his theory of unconscious complexes. His method was to study the deeper strata of personality by an experimental technique. Jung utilised word association technique to investigate the unconscious. He assumed that the deviant behaviour in the responses occurred because the stimulus word had touched off a deep conflict or complex. He used the controlled association technique in which the list of words. for the patients' responses to each of them, included words that were specially meant for calling up personal experiences. As an evidence of the emotional nature of the responses which had touched of some sore point in the patients' unconscious, Jung found accompanying changes in the psycho-galvanic reflexes, muscular movements and respiration. A large number of such emotional reactions touching some complex or conflict, was found in disordered people more than in normal persons. He also found that schizophrenics tended to give a large proportion of subjective responses dealing with inner feelings and thoughts, whereas manic-depressive patients tended to give more objective responses dealing with outer objects. This tendency to respond with subjective or objective responses later led to the formulation of his theory of introversion and extroversion which was considered an important contribution of Jung.

A more systematic study of free association by using long lists of ordinary words with a view to find out the various laws of association was made by Kent and Rosenoff. They found that the response words on hearing the stimulus words were either similar or contiguous, opposite or in contrast, in comparison with the stimulus words. So they established the laws of similarity, contiguity, opposition and contrast. But these investigators, by using ordinary or common words like, table, dark, music, sickness, man, deep, soft, eating, mountain, house, black, etc., and not those which aroused personal emotional associations or personal experiences, compared the responses of normal people from 8 to 80 years of age with those of individuals showing various mental disorders. The differences of the responses, of the normal and mentally ill persons in terms of the proportion of common or popular words were found in the two groups, and it was shown that normal people gave more common reactions as compared with the mental patients who gave a much larger proportion of highly individual responses.

Picture Completion Method

Picture completion is another method to study the unconscious mental contents. If certain bare outlines or incomplete pictures are given and the subject is asked to fill in the gaps and complete the picture, he will imagine the lines to mean something and this imagination will be his own phantasy and he will project himself on those outlines of incomplete picture to complete it. This procedure was long time ago studied by Bartlett for serial reproduction of certain outlines of vague pictures by presenting the reproduction of one person to the next and his to another, and so on, through many hands. He showed that every individual added something of his own and did not reproduce only what he saw. The bare and vague outline of something like a fish, for example, when passed through serial reproductions of a number of children became a clear picture of a bird eating from a cup. This process also explained how rumours spread. But as a projective method the reproductive attempt to complete the picture gives some data about one's mental make up.

Sentence Completion Method

In a similar manner sentence completion is used to find out the hidden desires, interests or feelings. For example, incomplete sentences like these :

I wish I ....

When I am alone I ....

When somebody weeps I ....

and the material used to complete them and many more like these can make an individual to reveal himself in many ways.

Story Making Method

Story making or story writing by seeing pictures is used as a projective device, as was used by Symonds to have a peep into the mental working of the individual. This method is elaborately made use of in T.A.T. described above. The central idea is the same, that is, the subject projects itself on the pictures or persons shown therein by identifying himself with anyone of them and so interpreting the scene in the picture in terms of his own hidden desires, repressed feelings or unconscious motives, hostility, jealousy or anxiety.

Drawing and Paintings

Drawings, paintings, sculptor and such art media, when freely used by the artist are used to paint his own mental contents as a poet uses his pen to express himself and a painter uses his brush. The frustrated desires burst open in songs or in strokes on the canvas. An artist, frustrated in love, paints the picture of his beloved and feels as if he is in union with her while painting her arms, breasts or cheeks. Art creation in many cases is the story of the artists own personality makeup, as no one can jump out of himself. What he makes is his own; it has his own personal stamp. Great masters wept out their own heart through brush, colours and chisel and thus projected themselves through these media. Drawings of children have been extensively used in guidance clinics both for diagnostic and therapeutic purposes.

Poetry, dramatics, story and novel writing reveal the personality both through the language used as well as the theme or contents of the writing. An individuals' choice of language for self-expression reveals one aspect of his personality. According to Piaget the manner in which the child uses the language forms, as in egocentric expressions, reflect the inner or emotional level of the speaker. Language is said to be the vehicle of thought, but not only the form of the medium as semantics is important but the thought expressed, is perhaps, more important. What the writer of poems or novels or stories writes, expresses the inner life of the writer. Many novels of Sarat Chander like *Shrikant* are, in a way, the autobiograp: ical portions of his complex life. In the psycho-analytical sense Meera's poems and Bhajans are the expressions of her frustrated love. After all every writer writes what he is and he cannot be other than himself; he cannot jump out of himself to be something entirely different. Shakespeares' *Hamlet* is, in some respect, Shakespeare himself minus the Prince of Denmark. The literary critics analyse the personality of the writer from his creations.

In the same way autobiographies provide ample material which give insight into the working of the mind of the biographer, as in the heat of the moment while writing on certain events, episodes or experiences, the writer forgets himself and digs up his unconscious and pours out his heart about his failures, frustration and ambitions. The biographer of an "*Unknown Indian*" e.g. writes all about himself and like a patient in free association sessions in the room of the psycho-analyst, the writer as a patient is revealing his unconscious. While writing, the biographer projects himself on paper with pen and ink.

A unique device introduced by Skinner and adopted by Shakow and Grings is the so called Tautophone or verbal Summator. This instrument produces low vowel sounds which resemble speech. Subjects hear it and are asked to tell what the voice is saying and they thus project their own preoccupations and meanings into an auditory medium.

Reliability and Validity of Projective Methods : The projective techniques, sometimes, called tests also, are not like other tests and the problems of standardization and quantification of the data often raised by some strict experimentalists do not quite apply to these methods. The complex personality cannot be expressed by a psychograph of traits. The application of standard methods of estimating reliability and validity further complicate the problem of quantification. In psychometrics, the usual checks on reliability have been the split-half technique and correlation either between repetitions of the same test (as test-retest method) or between alternate forms. None of these methods are wholly satisfactory for projective test. For example, split-half correlation of Rorschach factors mean little because the ten cards are quite uneven in the type and number of responses they produce and the responses of the same individual do not remain the same due to dynamic nature of personality. Hertz (1942) does not recommend the finding of reliability for Rorschach. About T.A.T. the repetition is found to be dubious as each time new elements appear. Tomkin showed that to bring out all the significant Themas in a group of subjects, he had to give the test to them daily in 20 sessions. So test-retest for reliability is meaningless in projective techniques because each time new elements are revealed.

The frequently used methods for establishing validity are (a) correspondence with other criteria (b) Internal consistency and (c) Predictive success. In handling the projective test material the correlation technique cannot be applicable since it is impossible to reduce a complicated personality to a single variable for plotting a chart or finding correlations as the variables are so many and differently expressed each time.

In projective techniques internal consistency applies to agreement found between results of assorted projective tests administered to the same subjects. But the soundest way to find validity of projective techniques was predictive capacity of the tests and this can be done by studying the behaviour, performance or degree of adjustment of the person as indicated by the psychogram of the traits found in the use of projective techniques.

On the whole, projective methods furnish the most promising hopes for a science of diagnosis and treatment of mental aberrations and clinicians are unwilling and unable to rely solely on objective criteria. Murray remarked that psychology has the choice of two alternatives, to study important problems with inadequate instruments or to study with adequate instruments unimportant problems. The interest in projective procedures is evidence of an attempt to use them more and more; and there is a growing recognition that we must not be limited by narrow conception, of what constitutes the scientific method but instead must be on the watch for new approaches which conform to the broad aim of science rather than to its dogmas. After all, science arose in response to the need for knowing and dealing with the natural world and projective methods reveal the inner world of man.

14

Non-projective Methods

No doubt man has had some judgement of man from time immemorial. But some earlier methods of judging personality traits or characteristics were too subjective with hardly any scientific basis. On the whole, there are three types of methods for assessing personality qualities or traits (a) subjective (b) objective and (c) projective. These three main categories further, have some methods grouped under each and need some detailed description of them for better information for the student of personality study. Among the subjective or pseudo-scientific methods are (i) Phrenology (ii) Physiognomy (iii) Graphology (iv) Palmistry, and (v) Astrology, which are no more in use now and, hence, are not discussed. In any case, the strictly scientific procedure would regard the methods such as phrenology, physiognomy, graphology or palmistry and astrology as museum pieces in the realm of personality appraisal. These methods of judging character traits or attributes of personality based on physical constitution, facial expressions, cranial measurements, morphological indices or chemical analysis are subjective and unscientific. We now rather observe people under natural and controlled conditions, carry on field studies, question people who know the individuals to be assessed, or ask the candidates themselves certain questions in interview sessions or through valid and standardized tests or questionnaires. Some of the techniques have been worked out to assess areas of personality qualities such as intelligence or intelligent behaviour, ethical character traits, attitudes, personal and social adjustment, neurotic trends, special abilities and other character traits or aspects and components of personality. The techniques evolved are chiefly the following :

(A) Rating scales or objective assessment of the traits, to be known, by impartial judges who know the individual very well.

(B) Questionnaires to be answered by the individual. These are in the form of paper-pencil tests of inventories carefully developed to bring out the traits.

(C) Observation of behaviour by impartial observers under natural conditions, such as children at play.

(D) Observation of behaviour under controlled conditions or under experimental situations.

(E) Interviews when the individual answers questions by an impartial investigator in personal interview sessions.

Some details need to be given about these methods one by one.

Rating Scale

Rating scale is one of the objective methods of assessing personality traits. It consists in asking certain persons, who know the candidates to be assessed on certain traits, to put the candidates at any position in the scale ranging from 1 to 5 or 7 or as it is required, in accordance with their objective judgement about the presence of the trait. The idea behind this procedure is that people who have known a candidate for some time while living or working with them can certainly form an opinion about him and can estimate his particular quality or trait asked for more objectively. But, human beings as they are, the judges can have their own subjective judgements and may differ from other judges. For example, in an experiment reported by Walter Dill Scott when 6 sales managers were required to rank 36 applicants for jobs under them, it was found that the candidate who was 3rd best according to Judge A was put 13th by judge B and applicant 18 who was thought to be the best in the group by manager E was ranked for 32nd position by manager D. One way to iron out these differences is to pool the ranks given to each candidate by the judges and then to make the order of merit. This method was evolved, particularly during world war I when due to the exigencies of the war some objective and quick method was required to select officers in the army for filling higher posts. Walter Dill Scott reports that for such promotions judges (higher officers) were required to do the rating of the junior officers for promotion on five characteristics, that is, physical qualities or stamina, intelligence, quality of leadership, personal qualities, general value or suitability for the service required. The officers could be ranked for these attributes on a five point scale ranging from highest to lowest with 3 positions of high, middle and low in between or with marks 5,4,3,2 and 1. The following difficulties are found in this method which could be met by pooling the ranks awarded as mentioned above :

(i) The personality traits to be assessed are fluctuating in the individuals and are not of a unified nature all through and the earlier impressions of the judges may not be the same, as at the time of assessment.

(ii) Even if the judges are very careful, honest and objective with an impartial and scientific attitude, errors of judgement due to sheer subjectivity of the judges cannot be ruled out, as every body has his own power and capacity to judge, observe and report.

(iii) There is such a thing as 'generosity error' in human evaluation. Howsoever, objective one may try to be, there are certain factors not quite under the control of the judge which may make one more generous towards one candidate as compared to others.

(iv) Halo error' is also found in such assessment, as the standing of a candidate on the rating scale about one trait can carry its halo in the mind of the judge regarding another trait. A great sportsman e.g. may be ranked high in intelligence or leadership due to the halo effect of his high position as a sportsman.

In schools records for children entries based on the class teachers' estimate, recommendations of other teachers, the reports and ratings done by heads regarding various other traits or qualities like working qualities, ability to organize work, cooperation, morals and general standard of conduct may also be recorded. Such entries are really no personality rating but only behaviour description done by individual teachers as observers and its value depends upon the accuracy and reliability of the observations. Even if the observations are reasonably made in an organised manner, the final interpretation should be made by trained, experienced and qualified persons.

Questionnaire Method

Questionnaire method of assessing personality traits consists in questioning the individual himself by drawing up a list of questions pertaining to the particular trait and asking the candidate to record his answers by reading the questions printed on a paper which is given to him during the testing session. Many questionnaires or inventories are made by so many people to assess so many traits or personality variables, such as temperamental trends as introversion-extroversion, ascendance-submission, neurotic tendency, self-sufficiency, various attitudes towards movies, racial problems and social questions. Personality tests (as they are called) are devised for assessing fear, anger, humour or incidence of inferiority, likes, interests, beliefs, preferences etc. The psychological questionnaires require one to answer questions which touch on what he has done in the past, how he feels about certain matters concerning his adjustment now and how he thinks he might act with respect to given situations in future. In some inventories direct questions are asked; in others the purpose of the enquiry is disguised. Lists of words or situations are given and the candidate is asked to underline every word or situation he dislikes for any reason; other lists are given to record his likes. From these reactions and answers certain conclusions are drawn regarding characteristics or traits of the person examined. By these psychological tests or inventories, efficiency drive, motivation, ambitions, use of aptitudes, philosophy of life and desire to achieve cannot be assessed. But every test score has diagnostic value in relation to the case data and so scores have to be interpreted with the knowledge of the case record as a doctor uses his thermometer in his clinical procedure. Each test is for a specific purpose to tap the attribute or traits it is made for and the untrained guidance workers may assume that the test can give a complete picture of the personality. There are hundreds of such personality tests some of which are good, others ineffective; each one measuring some or a few aspects of personality. Some of the more popularly used inventories may be briefly mentioned here.

Personality Schedule: Prepared by L.L. Thurstone and T.G. Thurstone at the University of Chicago. It has 223 items for finding out the neurotic trends in the individual. Items are to be answered by drawing a circle round Yes, No, written in front of each question. Questions are as under :

As a child did you like to play alone? Yes, No., Do you get stage freight? Yes, No, Do you love your father more than your mother? and so on. In some of them 'Yes' will bring out the neurotic trend and in some others 'No' answer shows the neurotic trend. The scoring is done by counting the answers which brings out the neurotic trends. The inventory was standardised on 380 men and 302 women students (682) of Chicago University. The personality scores were grouped to indicate the extent of neuroticism as under

Group	Personality	Description Scores
A	0 - 14	Extremely well adjusted
B	15 - 29	Well adjusted
C	30 - 59	Average
D	60 - 79	Emotionally maladjusted
E	80 and above	Should seek psychiatric advice.

The reliability of the whole schedule of 223 questions by comparing the parallel halves of the schedule was found to be .95 and validity was quite high. It was found in this study that the university students with more neurotic trends were, on the average, better students scoring more mean grade points in their studies than their well-adjusted classmates. This finding looked reasonable because neurotic students had fewer social distractions and so concentrated more on scholastic attainments.

R.S. Woodworth's: *The Personality Data Sheet* and L.L. Thurstone's *A Neurotic Inventory* (1930): are for the same purpose to find Neurotic tendencies. The former has 116 items and the latter 200 questions to bring out troubles like nervousness, inferiority, worry or anxiety, shyness, lack of self-confidence, insecurity, stage fright, etc.

Personality Inventory by RG. Bernreuter (1933) and J.C. Flanagan was prepared in 1935. In this inventory there are 125 questions with "Yes", "No" or do not know responses. These questions pertain to the six characteristics, 4 developed by Bernreuter (B,-N, BZ-S, B3-I and B4-D) and 2 by Flanagan (1935) (F,-C and F2-S) as described below and 6 scoring keys were used for scoring the 6 traits separately. Weights from +7 to -7 were assigned to each response in accordance with the diagnostic values for each of the 6 traits brought out by the response to each question. The total score for a trait is the algebraic sum of the weights which correspond to the response made by the individual, as given on the key for that particular trait.

The total scores are converted into percentile scores in order that the scores may be intelligible to the layman. A profile can be made with the percentile scores, of the particular individual studied on the 6 traits and his standing on the 6 traits can be judged by comparison.

The 6 scales for 6 traits (4 by Bernreuter and 2 by Flanagan) have been prepared. The scales are for the traits :

1. B_1-N for neurotic tendency. The person scoring high was emotionally unstable and if any one was found above the 98 percentile he was required to seek psychiatric advice. One scoring low was well-adjusted.
2. B_2-S for self-sufficiency. One scoring high on this trait preferred to be alone, seldom asking for advice, sympathy or encouragement and even ignored the advice or opinion tendered by others. One scoring low disliked solitude and often would seek advice and encouragement from others.
3. B_3-I for Introversion- Extroversion. One scoring high was introverted. He was imaginative and confined to himself. One scoring above 98 percentile needed psychiatric help.

One scoring low was extroverted that is to say, he was rarely worried and was emotionally well adjusted.

4. B_4-D for Dominance submission. One scoring high was dominant and one scoring low was submissive.
5. F_2-C for a measure of confidence in one's own self. One scoring high was self-conscious and had inferiority. One scoring low was self-confident and well adjusted to his environment.
6. F_2-S for a measure of sociability. One scoring high tended to be unsocial, solitary or independent. One scoring low tended to be social and gregarious.

Reliability of this Inventory by split-half method was found to be very, high ranging from .89 to .92 for the different traits.

Validity of the Inventory was established by correlating the scores with the scores on other similar Inventories such as Thurstone Neurotic Inventory, Laird Introversion Test and the Allport (1928) Ascendance Submission Reaction Study and ranged from. 81 to 94, which was very high.

Minnesota Multiphasic Personalitv Inventory **:** It is a psychometric instrument with scores on all the more important phases of personality.

There are 566 statements covering 26 phases of personality ranging from the physical conditions to the morale and the social attitudes, each phase being tapped by items ranging from 5 to 72 under each heading as given below :

The subject is asked to sort out the statements into 3 categories. True, false and cannot say. Time varies from 90 to 30 minutes depending upon the individual (but no time limit given). Scores are obtained on 9 clinical scales which are for hypochondrias, depression, hysteria, psychopathic personality, masculinity, feminity, paranoia, psychasthenia, schizophrenia and hypomania.

The phases are: (1) General health (9 Items), (2) General Neurologics (19 items), (3) Cranial nerves (11 items), (4) Mobility and Coordination (6 items), (5) Sensibility (5 items), (6) Vasomotor, trophic, speech, secretary (10 items), (7) Cardiorespiratory system (5 items), (8) Gastrointestinal systems (11 items), (9) Genitourinary system (5 items), (10) Habits (19 items), (11) Family and marital (26 items), (12) Occupational (18 items), (13) Educational (12 items), (14) Sexual attitude (16 items). (15) Religious attitudes (19 items), (16) Political attitudes, law and order (46 items), (17) Social attitudes (72 items). (18) Affect, depressive (32 items); (19) Affect, manic (24 items). (20) Obsessive and compulsive states (15 items), (21) Delusions, Hallucinations, illusions, ideas of reference (31 items). (22) Phobias (29 items), (23) Sadistic, masochistic trend (7 items). (24) Morale' (33 items), (25) Masculinity-feminity (55 items); (26) Limelight behaviour or submission (15 items).

The 9 scales, though symptomatic of abnormal manifestations, have meaning within the normal range. In the presentation of the results the usual procedure is to translate the raw score of the measured trait into a standard score (the T score) and plot it on a profile chart.

The basic assumption is that among the 550 items there are some items, that, when grouped together. form numerous potential scales. The original normative data were derived from a sample of about 700 individuals representing a cross section of the Minnesota population as obtained from visitors to the University Hospital for ages from 16 to 55 of both sexes. In addition to these data on normal individuals, data were available on 250 pre-college and college students. Data on several special groups such as workers, epileptic and tuberculosis patients, were also available.

Scales were developed by contrasting the normal groups with carefully studied clinical cases of which over 800 were available from the neuropsycluatric division of the University Hospitals..

For validity a high score on a scale has been found to predict positively the corresponding final clinical diagnosis or estimate in more than 60 per cent of new psychiatric admissions. Reliability by test-retest method ranged from .57 to .82 for the various scales.

The Adjustment Inventory Bell; Hugh, M. The adult form of this inventory provides 5 separate measures of personal and social adjustment. There are 5 areas of adjustment tested :

1. *Home adjustment.* Individuals scoring high tend to be unsatisfactorily adjusted to their home surroundings.

2. *Health adjustment.* High scores indicate unsatisfactory adjustment.
3. *Social adjustment.* High scores indicate submission.
4. *Emotional adjustment.* High scores show unstable emotionally
5. *Occupational adjustment.* High scores show dissatisfaction with the present occupation.

There are 6 items each marked A. B. C. D or E corresponding to the five measures of adjustment so that the counsellor cart easily discover to which measure the particular question relates. The questions asked were like these :

(a) Do you feel your friends have happier home environments than you
(b) Do you frequently experience vomiting or diarrhoea ?
(c) Do you feel your employer is paying you a good salary?
(d) Does it frighten you to be alone in the dark?
(e) Are your feelings easily hurt ?
(f) Do you make friends easily?

There is a scoring stencil which is placed on the columns of page 2, 3 or 4 of the blank. If scores for Home are to be obtained all the 3 pages are scored by noting the ends marked falling under the vertical lines of the blank. In the same way scores for health, social, emotional and occupational adjustment are obtained and the scores are interpreted in terms of the 5 classes as :

Excellent	
Good	
Average	for all the 5 Categories
Unsatisfactory	
Very unsatisfactory	

Reliability: The coefficients of reliability for each of the five sections of the inventory and for its total score by Split-Half method are found to be as :

Home adjustment + 91. Health adjustment + 81.

Social adjustment + 88 Emotional adjustment + 91

Occupational adjustment + 85 Total score + 94.

Validity: The items for each of the sections in the Inventory were selected in terms of the degree to which they differentiated between the upper and lower fifteen per cent of the individuals in a distribution of adult scores. Only those items which clearly differentiated between these groups were included.

The "very poor" and "very well" groups as determined by specialists were differentiated by the inventory.

V. A Study of values by G.W. Allport, P.E. Vernon and Gardner Lindzey (1960). This study is confined to the following 6 values :

1. Theoretical, 2. Economic, 3. Aesthetic, 4. Social, 5. Political, 6. Religious.

Part-I : There are 30 situations presented with controversial statements with 2 alternatives which are to be judged. For each question there are 3 points which may be distributed in any of the following combinations :

1. If one agrees with alternative (a) and disagrees with (b) 3 is written in the place specked for (a) and for (b).
2. If he agrees with (b) alternative and disagrees with (a) alternative 3 is put for (b) and 0 for (a).
3. If he has a slight preference for (a) over (b) 2 is given for (a) and 1 for (b).
4. If he has a slight preference for (b) over (a) 2 is written for (b) and 1 for (a).

Totals are found for all the positions in terms of points.

Part II : In part II there are 15 situations with 4 alternatives and for each situation 4 places are provided to put 4,3,2,1 as the case may be.

4 is put in the place if the statement appeals the most.

3 is put in the place if the statement appeals second best.

2 is put in the place if the statement appeals third best.

1 is put in the place if the statement represents the interest or preference least of all.

Scores are found for the 6 columns along with the places as arranged in view of the values tapped by the statements and the necessary weight to be given to it.

A score on one of the values may be considered definitely high or low if it falls outside the following limits

Theoretical	34-46
Economic	34-46
Aesthetic	34-46
Social	35-45
Political	35-45
Religious	33-47

VI. The A-S (Ascendance-Submission) Reaction study by G.W. Allport (1928) and Floyd H. Allport. There are 2 forms, one for men with 33 items and another for women with 34 items. The items are like these :

1. Do you stand up for your right on all occasions?
2. Do you insist on good service from the tradesmen?
3. Do you like to manage things and assume responsibility?
4. Do you enjoy being host at a party? .

The situations are presented to gauge ascendance or submission. In the revised blank, 8 more items are added for men and 9 for women.

The responses vary from simple 'yes' and 'no' on a two point scale, or on a 3 point scale as in 'no', 'somewhat', 'very much' or along 4 point as (1) more than six times, (2) less than six but more than once, (3) only once, (4) never. Different weights are assigned in view of the intensity of the ascendance or submission involved in the various responses. The weights for all the statements and the responses required for them are already decided upon. They may vary from +7 to -7. Plus scores indicate ascendance and minus scores denote submissive reactions. A few responses have no diagnostic value either way. These are given a value of Zero. There are separate tables for score-values for the items for men and for women. Omissions or items in which more than one choice is marked count (O). The final score is the algeberaic sum of the scores for the separate items. There is no time limit. This inventory scores can be used for vocational selection and placement. The median scores are as under :

General Managers	+21
Store Managers	+18
Assistant Managers	+ 3
Floorman	+ 3
All Executives	+10

Reliability for split-half method was found to be .85 for men and .9 for women. Using ratings, correlations for validity were from .29 to .79.

Science Research Associates or SRA Youth Inventory prepared by H.H. Remmers at Purdue University. It was standardized on 15000 teenagers of 100 High Schools. This is an inventory to check 298 questions, concerning the common matters that bother teenagers and include items regarding :

1. School and Studies (1-33)
2. After High School What to do (34-70)
3. About ones' own self and personal problems (71-114)
4. Getting along with others (115-154)
5. Home and family (155-207)
6. Meeting friends of opposite sex seeking a mate (208-239).
7. Health - (240-264).
8. General problems of social, political and religious nature (265-298).

It is a tool to help teachers, counsellors and school administrators to identify quickly the problems that young people say worry them most.

Norms are given in terms of the percentages for all the 298 items.

But there is a separate scoring key for the basic difficulties.

There are 101 basic difficulties marked and there are separate norms in terms of percentiles. The raw scores are converted into the percentiles both for boys and girls separately.

Reliabilities are given for all the 8 areas and range from .75 to .94 found by Kuder-Richardson method which involves the correlation between each item and the total score in any particular area.

The measure of validity becomes, in a sense, the reliability coefficient, for no test can be any more valid than it is reliable and here the figure varies from .30 to .95 for different areas.

Observation Method

Observation under natural conditions is the method, when the investigator himself observes and makes the assessment of the traits expressed by the individual or individuals in their overt behaviour in certain situations. The investigator is the impartial spectator and his observation is not to be influenced by his own desires, wishes or hopes to fit in the data for his own pet theory. In the study of personality traits, it is specially found of use when we study children's behaviour in the class, on the play field and in other social occasions. The keen eye of the teacher can see, if a child comes to school in time, does his home task regularly, sits in the last seat or on the last bench, never asks a question in the class, does not speak much with other children and is hardly seen participating in games, dramatics or other extra-curricular activities. Such a child can be spotted as a very shy or withdrawn child. Direct observation is also done in the play room in a child guidance clinic, where it may be observed (through one way screen) that a child picks up many toys from the shelf, throws some on the ground, kicks some and breaks the legs of some male toys or the neck of an elephant. He splashes water from the bucket all over and even at the play-therapist engaging him in play for clinical purposes. Such a child is very aggressive as evident from his overt behaviour pattern in the play room. He may later be found to be suffering from deprivation of love and his case history may reveal that his real mother died some years ago and that he was looked after by his step-mother who naturally could not give him the love of the real mother and so the child was destructive and aggressive taking his revenge on everything, person or toys he comes in contact with. For close observation of behaviour traits, the observer is to be well motivated and keenly interested to look for the traits. Errors of observation by personal factors can not all be avoided by the observer but he should be trained to be keen, impartial and an interested person who should record his views and impressions soon after the session and not to postpone the recording, as lapses of memory may distort the data.

Controlled Observations

Experimentation or observation under controlled conditions is also used to study psychological phenomena as discussed elsewhere but mention of it may be made as it is used by some investigators to study specific personality traits such as honesty or cheating, deceit or lying, self control, cooperation, social service, self-denial, charity persistence, etc. Hartshorne and May report some experimental procedure adopted to study some personality traits. For example, a dictation from some difficult text was given to children in a class. The scripts were collected and the spelling mistakes committed by each child were recorded without making any mark or remark on the scripts. These evaluated scripts were handed over back to the children after sometime and they were asked to check their spelling mistakes themselves by comparing the script with the text. Naturally some children had the temptation to correct an 'e' here or 'O' there and counted the mistakes according to their own marking. The difference in the number of mistakes recorded by the investigator, and by the child himself gave an indication of the degree of dishonesty shown by some children, though some were found honest and some less honest than some others. In a similar manner cheating as a trait could be studied by asking a group of children to write down the names of all the books they had seen, consulted or read during the last year. The lists drawn up by each child were to be checked by putting questions to each child to test if he ever knew the book. The degree of cheating could be known from- the number of titles put in the list by each child without knowing anything about them. Cooperation could also be tested by asking children to contribute as much money as they could from their own pocket money to the relief fund of flood affected people and children, in particular. In a room a tray or box was put for the money to be deposited by individual children going into the room one by one. There was also a device installed (without the knowledge of children) in the room by which any child putting the money in the tray could be seen as reflected by a mirror in the ceiling. The amount donated by each child could be thus known. Some may not have donated at all. The amount of the money thus donated by each child could be taken as the basis of the measure of the children's sense of cooperation to help in such a cause. This could also reveal their sense of social service or even compassion for suffering children. Some such experimental situations can be created to bring out the character traits and to assess them in different children or others.

Interview Method

Interview is another method to assess some personality traits of the individual by asking him some questions and his answers noted (or recorded) as revealing the traits. In selections for various jobs the selection committees or even public service commissions interview some candidates with a view to find out the more suited candidates for the jobs. The suitability for the job implies certain qualities, attributes or traits which should be present in the candidates. This requires job analysis to pin down the traits to be looked for in the more suitable candidates. For tote selection of teachers for secondary schools, for example, the selection committees, could look for traits like sense of personal cleanliness or smartness, good audible voice and power of expression, depth of knowledge of the subject to be taught, interest in children, sincerity for the job or the teaching professions, objective and impartial attitude, honesty, and so on. The candidates have to be asked pointed questions to bring out these traits, though appearance and voice or power of expression could be judged otherwise. The task of putting questions to the candidate can be divided among members of the selection committee who are supposed to come prepared for putting the relevant questions. Thus, interviews require planning and adequate preparation before hand by even having recording sheets to enter marks against each of the traits to be judged and strictly limiting the interview to relevant question, though interviews are often very arbitrary and many irrelevant or even silly questions are put by the selection committee members, who unfortunately are sometime not well informed themselves. In a selection committee for the post of an ecologist, for example, one member of the selection committee asked a candidate, "what is the frequency or meter band at which Delhi-A of All India radio broadcasts"? In another case for the selection of a Lecturer in Economics, a candidate who had done his Ph.D. from the London School of Economics was cornered, as it were, by a member of the selection committee by saying, "How could you do your Ph.D. from a school"?. Such cases may be rare but it is well known that interviews at various levels to judge the suitability of candidates for different jobs requiring the presence of certain traits are not conducted in the manner these should be done.

15

Development and Growth

The child is born with a sufficiently integrated physical apparatus. After his birth he begins to grow and become mature year by year. He displays definite signs of physical, intellectual and social behaviour. The changes that occur in these areas in course of time characterise his growth and development which continue till he reaches the stage of adulthood. This whole process of his growth and development involves an interaction between his organism and the environment in which he is placed.

The Meaning

In the beginning development would mean only the physical and biological growth of human organism. It would mean observable changes in the size, height, weight, structure of the organism over a period of time. With the development of behavioural sciences the term 'development' came to be understood as "progressive changes in adaptive functioning emphasizing socio-psychological development, while physiological and biological changes were indicated by the term 'maturation' or organic growth. Today, development is understood as "an integration of constitutional and learned changes which make up an individual's ever-developing personality." It is considered a continuous process which follows certain well-defined socio-psychological principles.

Later development is separately influenced by the growth and development of the earlier stage.

Generally, the terms 'growth' and 'development' are understood to have different implications. They are considered two different processes, but integrated and inseparably bound together. Development can not be possible in the absence of growth. The term 'growth' particularly refers to increase in size of the body structure involving changes in the height, weight, shape and various body-structures such as nervous system, skeletal system, muscular system, etc. This happens as a result of increase in the size and number of cells in the bodily parts.

Development, particularly, refers to changes taking place in the functions of the body-parts which depend on integration and coordination of functions of various units of the physical structure of the human being. Truly speaking development means functional development of the human being as distinguished from physical development. The Basic mechanism of development lies in the increasing interconnections of neural cells. A person may be physically mature. Yet he may not be able to perform various functions which require eye-hand coordination. Ensuring integration, coordination and interrelationship of various bodily units of the human being are the key characteristics of the process of development. This is a life-long and continuous process while the growth process is confined to a certain age-level only. Development is qualitative in the sense that it determines the efficiency, accuracy and effectiveness of human functioning, while growth is, largely quantitative as it involves change in the size, number and shape of the parts of human body.

The Characteristics

Following are some specific characteristics of growth :

1. Growth has its beginning in single cell which grows into an individual of its own species as ensured by the enlargement of the bodily cells.
2. Growth is not co-extensive with life. It stops after the individual attains maturity. It is not uniform also throughout the period of growth. Rate of growth varies

from one stage to another. It is a gradual rather than a salutatory process.

3. It is most rapid in the early years of life.
4. Acceleration in growth begins earlier in girls, but lasts longer in boys. There is rapid growth at puberty both in boys as well as in girls. This is preceded and followed by a period of slow growth in both the boys and the girls. Again, in both the boys as well as girls rapid growth in height precedes rapid growth in weight.
5. Growth is measured in terms of growth-coefficient which is calculated by dividing the weight by height. Greater coefficient means greater maturity.

Principles of Development

These principles pertain to child's behavioural development, the functional aspects of human organism. Only a few major principles are discussed as follows :

1. The development of behaviour proceeds from generalized mass activity to responses which are more differentiated, but localized and specific.
2. Although discussed stagewise by some psychologists, development is a continuous and gradual process. Distinct stages or levels of development can not be identified.
3. The rate of development varies from child to child; but the sequence remains the same. This seems to be true in case of the average child, not in case of the individual child. The Harward growth studies (Dearborn and Rothney, 1941) for instance found some children with a fairly constant rate of development while a few others were found to be highly variable. A short child remaining short throughout his whole life is an exception.

   The uniformity of sequence is demonstrated by the fact that the child crawls before he walks, and walks before he runs.
4. Development proceeds in a *Cephalo-Caudal* and *Proximo-Distal* direction. Cephalo-Caudal means from the head toward the feet and proximo-distal means from the spinal

column toward the extremities. This is true about both the physical growth and motor development.

5. No phase of development is independent. All aspects of development are highly interrelated and interdependent. Hence, proper understanding of any phase of development is possible only in its relationship with other aspects and phases. Adequate development in one area depends on corresponding development in other area or areas. For example, physical growth is necessary for promoting mental development. Similarly, emotional development is closely related to intellectual development which in turn affects emotional control and social development. Hence, emphasis on any one kind of development is undesirable. This fact is more important in case of young children than adults. The theory of correlation among various kinds of development is supported by research evidence also. Terman (1925) showed that gifted children were superior not only in intelligence; they were superior to other children of their age in physical size and strength, in social and emotional maturity, etc., although this correlation was not found to be high. This was supported by Harward growth studies also.
6. The principle of differentiation is well recognized. Diffused patterns of responses of the life's beginning are gradually replaced by more specific movements that are more limited in extent. This kind of differentiation may be found in case of emotional responses also.
7. The process of differentiation and of regular sequences are often linked with the phenomena of Critical Periods of development. In literature references made to "golden period", "tides in the affairs of men" to the need of "striking while the iron is hot" are indicators of the recognition of these critical periods.
8. During the first year and a half of life a more extended critical period is found during which the child is found engaged in hectic activities of responding to various kinds of stimulation . The child has vigorous need of stimulation. He is stimulas hungry seeking out sources of stimulation.

General Principles

The general principle of growth and development is the principle of maturation and learning, which says that an individual level of development at any given stage of life is the result of both the maturation of the innate potentialities and their modifications resulting from environmental influences. It is the interaction between the hereditary and environmental forces which determines the level of an individual's development. This is known as Nature-Nurture principle of growth and development.

The terms Nature, Heredity and Maturation are used interchangeably. They all refer to that phase of development which relates to the unfolding of the characteristics inherent in the genes transmitted to the individual from his ancestors. On the other hand, there are terms Nurture and Learning which mean the same thing, i.e., environmental influences giving rise to changes in earlier-stage growth and development.

Growth and development, thus, means the results of the interaction of maturation and learning which characterize what an individual is at a particular stage of his life. These two factors, maturation and learning work together and can never be separated as factors of growth and development, although their relative effect on one's present level of development has been the subject of considerable speculation and disagreement.

Various Stages

It was assumed by early thinkers, as held by Fleming (1948), that children were basically different from adults and that there were distinct stages in individual development; and discussion of development carried echoes of spectacular initiation ceremonies marking the transition from childhood to adolescence. The basic idea here was that the child, on reaching puberty, experienced a new birth, as it were, with sudden and dramatic changes in various aspects of his development. Later, Juan Luis Vives (1492-1540), re-echoing the idea of growth in stages assumed that development in the early period of childhood was by learning through the senses alone. He said that the senses were our first teachers in whose home the mind is enclosed. The next stage of development, according to him, was through imagination, and, from that, there was a progression to the mind, of which learning was the life and nature.

A century later, John Amos Comenius (1592-1670), in *The Great Didactic,* clearly demarcated stages of growth. He divided schooling into four six-yearly periods of infancy, childhood, boyhood and youth. Corresponding to these periods he advocated the establishment of four institutions: a mother school, a vernacular school, a gymnasium and a university for cultivating the senses, imagination and memory, understanding and the judgement, and finally the harmonizing will, as if these mental functions developed systematically and one after the other during the four six-yearly periods of life.

This classification of the periods of growth was further elaborated by Rousseau, who made a plea for each stage of life having a perfection and maturity of its own (Boyd, 1921). To Rousseau there was a correspondence between the growth of a person and the development of the race. The first period of life from birth to the age of two was that of infancy where the child "to all intents and purposes was like an animal in a state of undifferentiated feeling and scarcely more conscious of himself than in the prenatal life" Boyd, (1921). This was followed by the period of childhood from two to twelve years of age where the child was said to be like a savage with his mind dominated by the senses and with no proper reasoning or moral considerations. The third period was that of pre-adolescence from twelve to fifteen where the child (now a boy) was able to live a self-sufficient life like Robinson Crusoe with new physical strength and mental vigour making its appearance but conscience still remaining undeveloped. 'In the fourth period of adolescence proper, from fifteen to twenty-five, the youth in the eyes of Rousseau has a new birth as it were and with sexual functions emerging true social life begins. "Soul is now added to intellect and sense of beauty, goodness and truth acquires a personal value. Conscience rules life and virtue becomes possible (Boyd 1921 p. 298).

Rousseau influenced later writers like Pestalozzi; and the work of Froebel and Stanley G. Hall inherited all this theorizing which passed into current educational discussions. Stanley Hall as the pioneer of the Child Study Movement of America, stood half way between the philosophic fiction of past centuries and the controlled observations and experiment of the present (Fleming, 1948, P. 35). Studying children's minds and attitudes through questionnaires and reporting his results in terms of averages and percentages, Hall derived various discrete stages of child life and development.

To the stages of transition from babyhood to childhood, to maturity through adolescence, Hall assigned specific characteristics. The years from about eight to twelve, for example, constituted a unique period of human life when perception was acute but reason, morality, religion, love, sympathy and aesthetic enjoyment were hardly developed. This was nothing but echoing Rousseau's idea that the pre-pubescent years till twelve were dominated by senses. The child was said to revel in savagery since insight, understanding, interest, sentiment were for the most part only nascent (Boyd, 1921, p. 393).

The next stage of adolescence, to Hall, was a marvellous birth when the higher 'and more completely human traits were born, when selfishness and egoism of childhood changed into altruism. Hall wrote, "Life", after puberty. "is no longer ego-centric but altra-centric" and so "are the alterations between goodness and bad conduct generally. Perhaps at no time of life can goodness be so exotically pure and true, virtue so spotless, and good works spring from such a depth of goodwill, which since Kant, is often made the source of all real morality. In adolescence curiosity and interest were said to be the first outcrop of intellectual ability and the youth was considered greedy for knowledge.

Another advocate of the theory of mental development through stages is Piaget to whom the mental structure of children is different from that of adults. The mind of the child, to Piaget, gives an impression of appalling chaos. Studying particularly the thinking and reasoning processes in children. Piaget distinguished sharply between the animistic (meaning thereby that the child endows all things with consciousness) and egocentric thinking of the child- and the truly logical and more abstract thinking of adults. According to him the child's curiosity is satisfied by an answer which could amount almost to the characteristics of imbecility in Billet's terminology. Thought in the child, according to Piaget, is intermediate between autistic thinking and the logical thought processes of the adult. The child's thinking is egocentric (Piaget, 1926, p. 177) in so far as it goes straight from premises to conclusion, and it is syncretistic in that children take things in by means of a comprehensive act of perception instead of by the detection of details; and thus they try to connect everything with everything else. In thinking the child is ignorant of logical justification. He juxtaposes propositions instead of connecting them; but he is able to give a reason for everything to justify every phenomenon and every coincidence.

The child, according to Piaget, thinks for himself without troubling to make himself understood, nor does he place himself at the other person's point of view. The child is not really aware of arranging his sentences in a logical order and before the age of seven (Piaget, 1928) there seems to be no pronounced desire for logical justification. Upto seven years there is no introspection in thinking, and from seven or eight years until eleven or twelve there is a consistent effort on the part of thought to become more and more conscious of itself. It is only after eleven or twelve that, according to Piaget, formal thought and logical harmony develop (Piaget, 1928, p. 31).

These theories though differing a good deal from one another in point of detail seem to believe, on the whole, that the mental growth of a child passes through distinct stages which are characterised by the development of first the senses, then the power of perception, then the imagination and the memory, then reasoning and cognition, until maturity of judgement and harmonizing will were attained in the late teens or early twenties.

The transition from one stage to another is thought to take place with something of the suddenness of a new birth-culminating in adolescence in the emergence of a new creature, who is less given to fantasy but who has greater artistic and religious sensitivity, who is less effective as a memoriser but is more competent in all forms of abstract thinking.

Continuous Process

The idea of stages of growth is an old one, but these theories of development through various stages with recognisable patterns, exercised a strong influence upon educational thinking. Their echoes are still to be heard in some educational schemes designed to meet the needs of so-called different stages of growth. In the light of modern findings. However, these theories of growth in discrete stages with entirely distinct characteristics of their own, are of the type "which can fairly be described as more akin to philosophic fiction than to observation based upon actual experiment or research. (Fleming, p. 34). Many believe that one stage or level of development shades gradually into the next, although each period has its own specific problems (Cole and Hall, 1970). Development is simultaneous in all aspects and not in a successive way stage by stage.

The contention that children do not reason as adults do had been challenged earlier by Susan Isaacs (1930) in her *Intellectual Growth in Young Children.* The thought forms in children, according to her, are not different from those in-adults. She considers that Piaget's conclusion as to discreteness of mental stages is not borne out by her data (Isaacs p. 73-79). Her records show that many disparate types of behaviour coexist in the same child ranging freely between Piaget's categories (animistic, egoistic or syncretistic thinking) to clear logical statements and reasonable action. Burt (1919) in his *Graded Reasoning Tests* and also in his *Mental and Scholastic Tests,* has upheld the same view that children reason in the same way as adults, and that the reasoning of children is comparable with that of adults. Tests of reasoning for children involving syllogisms and 'analogies' were of the same structure as the forms of reasoning described in logic, and as used by adults.

Harter (1932) using non-verbal tests, reported that performance of adults was similar to that of children who succeeded on the tests; and that there were no differences in kind of thinking as between children and adults.

Hazlitt (1930) tested children and adults on their ability to make exceptions and reported that no real differences between thought processes of children and of non-scientific adults were found. Johnson (1938) also did not agree with Piaget that children, before the age of nine or ten, do not engage in conceptual thinking or that syllogistic thinking is typical of adults only. Jersild (1947) discussing this problem stated: "There is no essential difference between the reasoning of children and the reasoning of adults. The reasoning of both really involves the same processes. That the child's conclusions are sometimes bizarre and absurd, that he seems irrational and unable to make correct inference at times. does not mean that the adult is a rational animal while the child is not."

Abel (1932) is of the opinion that the type of thinking seems dependent more on the type of the individual (child or adult)- the extent of development of his psychological functions, his past experience, his organic set up at the time of being observed and his cultural heritage, than on his being simply a child or an adult in terms of age.

Oakes in a study of the answers given by four groups of school children and one group of adults to direct questions regarding various natural phenomena, reported that each subject regardless of age, mental ability or grade level, gave explanations of a wide variety of types. All types of answers were given by all age groups. No evidence was found in support of Piaget's claim that there is a definite stage in the child's thinking which is characteristic of a given age. This study supports the view of Hazlitt (1932) who, on reviewing Piaget's book *"The Child's Conception* of *Physical Causality"* points out the fallacy of Piaget's assumptions and conclusions, and maintains that there are no differences in kind between the thinking of children and the thinking of adults. Oake's findings corroborate the views of the other investigators cited above that whatever differences there are between the explanations of children and those of adults, they are largely, if not entirely, of degree rather than of kind.

Certain investigators have made studies of animism and the idea of magic in children. Mead (1933) for example, studying children in a primitive culture (Manus-tribe, Admiraly Islands) used observations, drawings, interpretations of ink-blots and direct questioning to find out the extent of animistic responses. She was unable to discover any such tendencies in those children. 1n fact, she found preference for cause and effect explanations and the rejection of animistic terms. She concluded that animistic notions were not characteristics of intellectual immaturity in children only but were the results of social tradition.

With regard to the use of language in pre-school children, McCarthy as quoted by Oakes reports five per cent or less of the child's language as being egocentric as against fifty per cent reported by Piaget. One of her chief criticisms was that Piaget used a child's language to study his thought and logic and this she considered to be very difficult even with adults.

Matheson (1931) said that pre-school children are found to employ immediate insight, exploration and elimination in solving problems, just as adults use these methods. Albert quoted by Oakes classifies the responses of pre-school children to problem situations as (a) primitive. (b) random (c) exploration and elimination. (d) immediate solution; and types of solution as with (a) immediate insight, (b) gradual insight, (c) sudden insight, as we find in the case of adults.

Jersild (1933) and his associates, on making extensive studies of children's fears. Wishes, likes, dislikes, day-dreams, dreams, pleasant and unpleasant memories, found much overlapping of types between children of different ages: differences were quantitative rather than qualitative.

In addition to these, and other studies of children's abilities and attitudes, mention may be made of certain specific studies of childhood imagination. In the opinion of Griffiths (1935) egocentricism in imagination is not peculiar to the child, as many of the phenomena described under this concept belong not to the child's thinking as such but to difficulties he meets in expressing his thoughts in adult language. She said "There is no real inability to understand relations as such, but there is difficulty in using the formal terms that apply to logical relations."

Audemars (1936) held that children at the early age of four are found to show intense appreciation of colour and form, and have a passion for what is beautiful. Little children are noted to compare dresses, toys and things bought for them and say, "Mine is beautiful, yours is not. Yours is ugly and bad." Creativeness and appreciation of beautiful things stem from a child's fresh perception of life and experience and from the uniqueness of his own fantasy when he is free to share it as found by Murphy (1947).

Selfishness is not characteristic of a child alone as was thought by Hall. Suttie, (1935) said that a child is both egoistic and altruistic since the need to give and to receive, are fundamental human needs. The child feels happy in sharing his toys or sweets with others. The need for insight, understanding and the "passion for knowledge" are as basic in the child as in the adolescent or the adult. From the age of four or five onwards, the metaphysical questionings of the little child are directly in line with the religious and philosophic thinking of the adolescent and the adult (Fleming, p. 46) as in asking the cause of rain or other natural phenomena.

In the experience of Moreno (1934) also with children's societies consisting of many hundreds of members it was found that children—boys and girls - who had reached the eight years of age level or were near to it were able to run a society of their own without the aid of older individuals.

Morality, love or sympathy do not develop only at the adolescents stage, as was thought by Hall. Concrete examples of responses of children in situations involving co-operation, generosity, honesty, persistence, self-control, truthfulness, feelings of guilt and the like have been collected. If, for example, an incident seen by a child is wrongly reported later at home by the parent who was with the child at the moment of the occurrence, the child will protest and will correct the parent saying, "No, Papa it was not like that, you are telling a lie, the other man was at fault", and so on. In a test of honesty, Hartshorne and May (1929) found almost a normal curve of distribution of this trait; and in helpfulness. also the findings in the case of children were similar to those got from groups of adults. No doubt, every individual acquires his character in conformity with the laws of conditioning and socialization, but the potentialities for such acquisition are there in the child. (Vernon Jones; 1946).

Basically, the child is a 'whole' from the beginning with potentialities peculiar to human beings. There is no doubt that certain functions gain in strength and maturity as the child grows, but to say that at one stage he is a complete savage devoid of reasoning or social life, or that appreciation of beauty, goodness and truth appear only in the youth, is an imaginative rather than a scientific statement. All aspects of the child's personality—physical, emotional, intellectual and moral—develop gradually but continuously at different rates at differing periods in life. Dimock (1937) said that the fully fashioned social and moral being is the result of this continuous growth which does not appear to be salutatory in nature; and it may, with confidence, be stated that changes that take place in the development of the adolescent are probably not so numerous, so radical, so farreaching or so abrupt as to justify the concept of various stages of growth assumed by earlier psychologists. Fleming, (p. 203) also said that the development is more comparable to a journey through a border land whose boundaries are unmarked than it is to the crossing of a rubicon or the experiencing of a new birth. Growth in itself is not a new experience to persons; it is an accompaniment of living from the beginning in an imperceptible manner. If there are no clear-cut stages or development from infancy to adulthood it does not mean that infancy, childhood and adolescence do not have certain characteristics of their own in general. In infancy from birth upto three or four years, bodily functions are weak and there is hardly any self-control on these functions. The infant is more pleasure seeking, lusty and grabbing, when he is more concerned with milk and mother. The muscles are growing and there is less sphincter control. He is shy in new environments and hides his face in his mother's garments. He is suggestible and credulous. Ego strength and super-ego formation is nebulous. In childhood there is still physical immaturity. The child is more interested in play and seeks the company of like sex partners and not of opposite sex. He is linguistically, emotionally and intellectually more grown up and so in his ego-strength. He is curious about outside things and is interested in acquiring more knowledge and skill as in games and sports. He is interested in film stars, cricket and hockey, marbles, kite flying, etc. Adolescence is characterised by feelings of awkwardness due to rapid physical growth and secondary sex characters. He seems to be losing his bearings and finds himself in a world where he is neither a child nor a grown-up adult. He is self-conscious and lives in a world of fantasy. He is moody and critical of traditional values, and has now a growing independence of judgement and is often un-conforming or revolting and thus feeling ill-adjusted; he experiences stress and strain.

The Discussion

It is difficult to ignore the concept of stages while discussing the growth and development of human being. Most psychologists like Piaget, Sears, Erikson, etc., have confined themselves to the stage theory while discussing development of human personality. The stage theory implies (1) that one stage is necessary forerunner of the next as during this foregoing stage the organism develops structures that are needed for a later stage, (2) unless the child has reached a proper particular stage, the child can not be benefited by any special training in the related area, (3) during certain stages there are critical periods during which needed stimulus must be provided to the child in the absence of which child's development may suffer.

During the past few decades there has been a great controversy about the existence of stages in the development. Many people in the field feel that stages are not a universal feature of development. On the other hand, many psychologists hold that stage-wise consideration of human development is necessary for getting the true picture of physical, intellectual, social and moral development. Also there are some psychologists who oppose this view and say that there is little evidence supporting the stage theory and we do more harm than good by splitting the continuity of human development into sections like stages. Bijou (1968) and Kessen (1963) and several others hold that human development is continuous and gradual without showing marks of discontinuity of significant differences at any point. Stopping at any one stage and abruptly moving from one stage to another is not a fact of human development. More true is the fact, according to them, that changes in height, weight, use of language and words, feeling of security, etc., occur quite gradually: This continuity theorists argue against stage theory as follows :

1. They say that the stages in human development instead of being a reality are an artifact of the way the child is treated. Instead of being a built-in process, it is to them an environment-generated phenomenon, artificially produced phenomenon. This argument does not seem to have much weight in it as qualitative changes in several

aspects of development at certain age levels are obviously observed by most people, even the psychologists.

2. They challenge stage-theorists claim of regularity of certain developmental sequences, the claim that one stage prepares the way for the next. The continuity theorist say that it is not necessary; experience in crawling may not be necessary or helpful in child's learning to walk. These arguments of the continuity theorists are rejected by the stage theorists by saying that it has been observed that deficiency experienced at one stage leads to unforeseen effects later on. For example, in monkeys playful tussling and fumbling which is normal to adolescence is necessary experience for sexual competence in the adult. In the second place they also say that till it is proved that the experience of one stage is not vital to some later development, it would be wise to accept the stage-concept of development. The proponents of stage theory advance some positive claims for their theory as follows :

    (a) The concept of stages helps in explaining and understanding the qualitative changes that occur at different age levels. It helps in describing the characteristics of the child of a particular age.

    (b) To describe the whole long process of human development is too unwieldy to describe. It is more convenient to segment it into areas, phases or periods more homogenous but comparatively more different from one another.

Most psychologists, today, hold in this regard that continuity may be the more basic rule as we may find constant forces or principles at work moving the organism through one stage on to the next. From the viewpoint of scientific truth this emphasis on continuous forces seems preferable. But, for convenience sake and guidance, the concept of stages may be considered more useful.

Heredity or Inheritance

It is outside the scope of this chapter to go into the details of the much debated and intricate problem of disentangling nature from nurture, but a brief mention of it seems absolutely essential. Just as a plant's capacity for growth lies in the seed as the contribution of heredity and as the oak or the elm have their distinct characteristics growing out of their own seeds, so does the human organism, growing out of its seed, comes to have a distinct nature of its own. But the original seed is now considered to contain thousands of minute particles called the genes. The development of an organism is said to begin with the interaction of these particles, and different individuals start life with diverse combinations of these genes. The way a given individual develops, what characteristics he has and what he becomes, depend, other things being equal, on what set of these elements or genes he starts with. The altering of a single one or several of these genes gives different results, leading to deformed, normal or superior individuals.

In recent years revolutionary discoveries in genetics have been made. Even artificial or synthetic genes have been produced under laboratory conditions and there are possibilities of changing the genetic constitution one is born with. After the "test-tube baby" (which survived for 29 days in the test tube), produced by Dr. Daniele Pertrucci in Bologna in Italy in 1959 which may be a forerunner of controlled procreation or production of 'babies' according to advance specifications, there is phenomenal advancement in genetic surgery which even surpasses research, in recent years, in astronomy, nuclear physics, electronics and space explorations.

The task of controlling production of future human beings involves the control of two genetic chemicals— DNA (Deoxyribonucleic acid which is the throbbing centre of life) and the RNA. DNA molecule governs our past, our present and our future and controls all aspects of body formation. It is like a computer containing in its arrangement of atoms, the key to heredity, ageing, disease, mind and memory. DNA's genetic messages are written out in a four letter code, each letter being a specific chemical compound or base unit of the DNA chain. Using its code of four chemicals adenine, thymine, guanine and cytosine, DNA transmits its genetic instructions via RNA, a nucleic acid structurally similar to DNA.

Any control of the genetic material in DNA will involve the synthesis in the laboratory of artificial DNA with the atoms arranged in a specific order to produce a particular type of individual, "The new man". Dr. Hargobind Khurana the Indian born Nobel Laureate has synthesised two RNA (Transfer Type) molecules and the current new discoveries have proved that genetic constitution may be changed as desired with the possibility of producing the type of human beings desired.

The genes are said to exist in the egg cell, and grouping together they form structures called the chromosomes. In the case of human beings, the fertilized ovum called the "zygote" contains 23 such pairs of chromosomes, and they are said to be the carriers of heredity to partly determine physique, temperament, mentality and the personality. There is antecedent life in both the ovum and the sperm before fertilization which is called ontogenic (depending on the individual) and phylogenic (racial) by Gesell and there is the dictum that "Life begins with the past or earlier life", which is due to character of the genes coming from the parents, some of which may be recessive or weak and some may be dominant as proved by Mendel. The inheritance in the genes may be due to mutation when acquired characteristics are passed on to progeny as held by Lamarck. There may also be sudden variations of the genes due to what Morgan called "Emergence", as nature was said to evolve not by creeping only but by "Leaping" to new changes also.

At conception the new organism "the fertilized ovum" receives 46 chromosomes (except in some rare deviations as Mongoloids have 47) in which 44 are antosomes and 2 sex chromosomes XX (in female) or XY (in males). Every ovum contains X but some sperms contain X and some contain Y. So X bearing sperm will lead to XX or female and Y bearing sperm will lead to XY or male. The substance of the genes is a chemical (DNA) which contains nucleotides of 4 bases, which in numberless varieties of combinations, appear to be capable of encoding all the characteristics that an organism transmits from one generation to the next. Genes do not act alone; one characteristic may be emerging from the action of many genes, e.g., height, pigmentation, longevity, degree of resistance to disease, intelligence, etc., and the same gene may contribute to many characteristics such as mental impairment or disturbances in the pigmentation of hair.

The expression of a gene may be influenced in various ways, with the result that it is changed, suppressed or modified. Some genes are changed by mutation and their expressions may be modified by environments, as for example, the height of Japanese children is affected when reared in U.S.A. instead of in Japan.

But since for the growth of the plant, the seed has to be posited somewhere in the environment, so there is inseparable relationship between the seed and the environment. For the growth of the plant, not only are the chromosomes essential but the supply of water, air, soil, etc., also. In the same way it is natural to think, that the human organism starting life with the fertilized ovum planted in the soil of the womb of the mother, as it were, develops into the foetus under the influence of the environmental conditions of the womb and the supply of the necessary ingredients for its growth by the psycho-physical conditions of the mother. The human baby, at birth, is the result not only of heredity which consists in the quality of the genes coming from both the parents in the germ cell but also of three quarters of a year of pre-natal environmental life. Growth in the womb is very rapid in the last month. This rate if continued after birth a baby would weigh 160 pounds after 1 year of birth. In the first month of pregnancy the tiny organism increases 10,000 times its initial size. This is by multiplying the cells, but in the last month it increases in volume and size and not in number of cells. In first three months from a simple roundish dot it progresses to an infinitely complicated human form and the total growing takes 267 days and is a marvel of refinement, with incredible accuracy, keeping to the schedule of speed and subtlety which characterise the growth process, the result of which stagers all imagination.

Role of Environment

After birth, the child is subjected to more varied and complex environmental forces in relationship with which his growth continues. This inescapable relationship with the environmental forces which influence the growing and unfolding of rudiments in the germ cell has not been quite realized by some writers, who tend to consider heredity as the chief maker of men. One such enthusiast said, "Nearly all the misery and nearly all the happiness in the world are due not to environment. The differences among men are due to differences in the germ cells with which they are born." The environmentalists (like the Behaviourists) going to the other extreme, challenged the doctrine of heredity and asserted that the subtle socialized types of learning entirely accounted for the development of human beings. Watson (1925) for example, wrote "There is no such thing as an inheritance of capacity, talent, temperament, mental constitution and characteristics". Watson (1928) further said, "The behaviourists believe that there is nothing from within to develop ...You do not need anything else in the way of raw material to make a man, be that man a genius, a cultured gentleman, a rowdy or a thug".

But even Watson (1925, p.77) could not totally deny the inheritance of physical structure as he said, "Yes, there are hereditable differences in form, in structure, but the mere presence of these structures tells us not one thing about function." There is no doubt that habits, emotional reactions and other behaviour patterns are largely the result of training, but insofar as Watson accepted hereditable differences in structures he accepted inheritance, since function being, to a certain extent, a correlative of structure, the potentials of functions become inherited when the structure is inherited.

However, though admitting that there was a distinct difference in the development and function of traits transmitted through the germ-plasm (such as physical resemblance between parents and children) and those individually acquired, Watson as an ardent environmentalist thought that the innate behaviour patterns were nothing but a series of adaptive responses or a chain of "concatenated reflexes". Ogburn (1947), however, said that the order of the unfolding of the separate elements or reflexes is itself a heritable character, as the capacity to learn is inborn.

The Controversy

But the heredity-environment controversy seems futile since if two trees, say a- maple and an elm, standing side by side put out new leaves in spring, neither heredity itself, nor environment alone can explain the difference between the leaves. Without the hereditary factors in the different seeds, there would be no leaves and without the environmental factors of warmth, moisture, etc., there would be no growth and no leaves would come out. Heredity and environment seems to work together in every manifestation of life.

Many experimentalists support this view. Jennings, on the basis of his genetic studies by observation and experiments on the fruit-fly, in particular, concluded that if the environment produced a given effect, it depended upon the genes (since the genes were not fixed or unmodifiable) and if the presence of certain genes produced an effect, it depended on the environment. Growth of an abnormality, for example, depends upon the defective gene and also on the environment: The defective gene growing in the normal environment leads to normal growth. "As described by Jenning (p.13) the growth of an abnormal abdomen, for example, in the fruit-fly would be in the moist environment and the fly would be normal in the dry environment. So the same difference that is produced in some cases by diversity of genes, is produced in others, by alterations of the physical environment and in the case of human beings also by the complex social environment. For this reason, Jennings (p.36) stated that "Temperament, mentality, behaviour, personality—these things depend in manifold ways on the genes", and that the highly complex personal characteristics as laziness, stupidity, slowness, lack of industry, ambition, patience and genius were also determined by the genes. (p.20). But he maintained that these complex personal characteristics were not exclusively determined by genes since environmental conditions had a great effect. Genetic determination did not mean, that personality as a whole was inherited; all that it meant was that no feature of personality was devoid of hereditary influences and that the personal characteristics were altered both by the genes and by the external conditions.

The genes, thus, supply one set of conditions for development, the environment another set. The claims of the behaviourists that heredity has no significance and of many biologists that genes play the preponderating role in determining characteristics are untenable. The heredity and environment dichotomy is really an arbitrary one.

Although the knowledge of the genes of the fertilized ovum may not, at present, be taken as final, it may be said that physique, the endowment of intelligence and temperament are, to a great extent, genetically determined and that they influence the development of personality in that their force is always felt in placing limitations upon the environment.

In the development of any single individual, there is no point in asking whether either heredity or environment is all important, since both are essential. The question is of the relative importance of the two factors. When we compare two persons and try to account for the differences in height, intelligence and in other characteristics, the cause of the difference might lie in heredity or in environment alone, or in both. To discover the effect of differences due to heredity, individuals of different heredity could be exposed to, identical environments, and any differences in the results would be due to heredity. In the same way, to find the influences of environment individuals of identical heredity could be exposed to different environments and the differences thus revealed would be due to environments.

The best evidence for this, at present, is from the studies of identical and fraternal twins brought up together or separated in early childhood, and also from studies on animals. Identical (monozygotic) twins, resulting from the splitting of a single fertilized ovum, serve as the sole instance in human biology of two individuals having exactly the same hereditary constitution, since the gene pattern is exactly similar. Fraternal (dizygotic) twins, developing from separate fertilized egg cells may have a markedly different gene pattern, and hence a different hereditary constitution.

One early study of twins was made by Holzinger (1929) when he compared 50 pairs of identical and 52 pairs of fraternal twins. Identical twins were found to differ much less in height, mental age, educational age, emotionality, etc., than the fraternal twins. The typical correlation (holding age constant) on the average was found to be +90 for identical twins and +60 for fraternal twins, (p.43). Kerr (1936) comparing temperamental differences in the identical and fraternal twins on the Rorschach Test, came to the conclusion that identical were more alike than like-sex fraternals on all comparisons, particularly in temperamental differences. Wilson's studies (1941) in the social competence of twins (ability to care for themselves or to carry on normal social relationships) showed that monozygotic twins were most alike, dizygotic came next and siblings were least similar. Newman, Freeman and Holzinger (1937), in their later study of identical and fraternal twins, support the earlier finding of Holzinger. The average correlation for physical, mental and educational traits for identical was +90, for fraternals about +60, and this was found to be the same for siblings tested at the same or nearly the same age. This indicated that fraternal twins were like siblings but the identical twins were much more similar.

Cross breeding in animals or in plants, as in the case of such hybrids as mules (born as the result of cross fertilization of a mare by a donkey) proves the importance of heredity. Hybridizing or cross-breeding experiments have been tried by geneticists in large numbers and from the days of Gregor Mendel (1866) down to the present day, an amazing body of information has accumulated which should convince any sceptic of the importance of heredity. An individual of normal heredity, when made to develops under abnormal environmental conditions develops peculiar characteristics. As shown by Stockard (1931) fish embryos, for example, just at the eye-forming stage, if placed in water containing magnesium chloride for a few hours, would develop only a single eye, whereas under normal conditions two eyes would develop. Two Japanese doctors Yoshitaka Harada and Hiroyuki Moriyama of Kummoto University have reported that fish caught from sea water polluted by mercury compounds from a chemical factory, when eaten by pregnant women, produced cerebral palsy and mentally disturbed conditions in babies as the mercury from the eaten fish was absorbed by the foetus through the placenta (Hindustan Times, Oct. 30, 1977). This evidence may disabuse our minds of any prejudice against either heredity or environment as important factors in the growth of species. Both of these factors lead to important individual differences in human beings in physique, physical growth, intelligence, temperamental or emotion: qualities, character traits, etc.

Heredity as the Factor

Genetically it is believed that limits of development are set by child's heredity. Heredity refers to the characteristics which are determined by the genes involved in the fertilization of one of the female egg cell by one of the male sperm cell. Since the combination of genes involved in the fertilization varies from individual to individual, they can not be expected to have similar developmental characteristics. Since heredity is set at the time of conception, development tends to follow a basic pattern depending upon the combination of genes involved in the fertilization. Thus, heredity plays a very significant role in determining one's growth and development. That is why it is said that "like begets like". For example, tall parents tend to have tall offsprings, the bright parents tend to have bright children. In fact, heredity is defined as the sum total of tendencies and capacities present in the fertilized cell. The inheritance of the child is not, however, determined solely by his immediate parents. These traits and potentialities inherent in the genes flow like a stream from one generation to another, some of these appearing and some not in the following generation. Mendel an Austrian botanist (1822-1884) stated this in the form of a law as "some characteristics blend while others do not", and also that there is the "segregation of pure gametes". His experiment on crossing the giant peas with dwarf peas for several generations was the basis of drawing this conclusion.The same truth was stated by Francis Galton who wrote *Hereditary Genius* (1825) as "the child is as old as the parent or as old as his ancestors", Weisman, a German biologist (1834-1914) who is known for his "germ-plasm theory" said that the parents are only the custodians of the germ-plasm which they only pass on to the next generation.

Although the basic pattern of growth and development is laid down by child's heredity, significant changes in this basic pattern can be brought about by the manipulation of environmental conditions. This has been described by several authors. Salamander which lives in water was made to learn in water by feeding it thyroid extract (Weiss, 1939). Through the different kind of food served it could be possible to show whether the egg will develop into a queen bee or a worker bee; and foot material could grow as part of the head if during the formation period following conception the material that normally grows into a foot is introduced into the head area (Jordan, 1956). A hen was made to develop secondary male characteristics by environmental manipulation (Crew, 1923). Siamese twins were made to develop in fish through cold, insufficient oxygen or ultra-violet rays (Anastasi, 1937). Two headed monsters in tadpoles and single-eyed minnows could also be produced through artificial environmental conditions (Morgan, 1942), Thus, it would appear that while heredity sets the basic pattern, manipulation of environmental conditions can bring about significant changes in the developmental pattern. The wolf-girl of India learned to live like wild bears; the chimpanzees have been trained as human babies, (Squires, 1927). Sparrows raised in sound proof cages with canaries abandoned their own chirps and learned the cannary call (Conradi, 1905).

The Ultimate Truth

"Intelligent handling of children requires a knowledge of how children grow and how such growth can be influenced favourably", (Breckenridge and Vincent, 1950). To achieve this it is important to realize that neither heredity nor environment alone can direct child's development into desirable channels. It is not possible to change the rate, amount and direction of growth by environmental manipulation except within narrow limits. On the other hand, this is also a fact that hereditary potentialities can never be fully developed in the absence of suitable environment. Every child is born with certain potentials only. He becomes genius, bright or dull depending on the kind of environment he is brought up. Looking from this point of view education becomes important. Education provides the kind of environment which stimulates unfolding and development of basic potentialities. But this also needs .to be noted that very real limitations are imposed on this by heredity. The best and the most realistic view is to provide as good an environment as possible irrespective of whatever the potentialities be.

Maturation and Learning

Normally, a child learns a particular behaviour or skill when he has attained the required level of maturity. A certain degree of maturation is essential before a child can learn certain behaviours. Walking, for example, can not be undertaken before the child has developed a certain bone and muscular structure. If this is so, no amount of special training in advance of the maturation stage should make the child learn the behaviour linked with that maturation level. However, it has been demonstrated that it is possible that at any given age the child is capable of learning, through proper training, more advanced behaviour. For example, the child can be taught to walk, perhaps, as much as six months before he would do otherwise. The question arises, is it worthwhile to speed up child's learning beyond what would come naturally through maturation?

Gesell and Thompson (1929), and McGraw (1935) have experimentally demonstrated that it is possible to speed up the child's learning through special training beyond what would come naturally. One member of a pair of identical twins given special training in certain tasks completely outdistanced the other twin who was allowed to grow at his own rate. But, after the training was discontinued the untrained twin caught up with the trained one in a fairly short time and, then, they both continued to grow at the same rate. This shows that early training is not of much use ultimately, and also that rate of learning is faster when adequate level of maturity is achieved.

Carmichael (1926) demonstrated that the anesthetized tadpoles began to swim soon after removing the anesthetic at the time when the control group of tadpoles began to swim. This shows that certain behaviours are linked with maturation and emerge without any training or experience when that level of maturity is attained. Shepard and Breed (1913) showed that the chicks prevented from pecking by being kept and fed in the dark for the first day began to peck quite efficiently in the daylight immediately after being taken out of the darkness. Dennis (1938) found that children prevented from sitting, reaching, and walking were able to do so as well as those who were allowed the freedom of movement. Spalding (1902) showed that swallows kept till fully fledged in cages flew about as well when released as any other mature swallow. This shows practice in flying was not necessary for performing this behaviour.

Thus, there is evidence to show that special training can lead the child to master certain skills in advance of the maturation level; and also there is the evidence which shows that training is not necessary as when the appropriate level of maturity is reached the relevant behaviour automatically emerges.

The most practical considerations in this regard are:

(1) In case when a particular behaviour is likely to occur normally and more easily at a later stage, special training is uneconomical and wasteful of time and energy.

(2) In case of skills in which muscular strength, speed and precision of movement are crucial factors, maturation is more important a factor and special practice is correspondingly futile. In tasks of greater complexity, however, opportunity and training may play a more essential role.

(3) Special training sometimes may prove harmful also. Forcing the child to the limit of his ability may well result in frustration, discouragement and negative habits and attitudes which may interfere with his subsequent learning. Even the best efforts may be useless if made too early or too fast.

(4) As against the foregoing observations it is also held by many that early training may be of great benefit. It may result into outstanding performance, positive attitudes of self-confidence and higher level of motivation. The crucial point is the manner in which the training is given. It should not expect too much of the child. Expectations should be commensurate with child's basic abilities. Efforts on pushing the child beyond what he is capable of may lead to emotional blocks and negative self-concept.

Developmental Task

The concept of developmental task was popularized by Havighurst (1952). These are defined as developmental problems which must be solved at a particular stage in order to peacefully and successfully march on to the next stage of development. In fact, a developmental task means attaining certain developments corresponding to the respective stage of development. There is an age level by which the child must complete learning of certain tasks. These are the desirable requirements of development at the respective stages, necessary for proper adjustment. Havighurst defines task as one that "—arises at or about a certain period in the life of the individual, successful achievement of which leads to his happiness and to success with later tasks, while failure leads to unhappiness in the individual, disapproved by the society and difficulty with later tasks." By this Havighurst means that in the developmental sequence there are stages at which the child is required to master certain tasks. It is essential because failing at this stage the child will fail to master the tasks of the next higher stage in the developmental sequence. Thus, a developmental task is a sort of adjustment to be made at a particular stage of development.

Cole (1948) for example gives the following list of major developmental tasks of adolescence

1. Self-direction
2. Objective intellectual analysis
3. Integrated philosophy
4. Social acceptance, and
5. Economic adjustment

Havighurst has given a more comprehensive stagewise list of developmental tasks. For the period of adolescence he gives the following list of tasks:

1. Achieving new. and more mature relations with age-mates of both sexes.
2. Achieving a masculine or faminine social role.
3. Accepting one's physique and using the body effectively.
4. Achieving emotional independence of parents and other adults.
5. Achieving assurance of economic independence.

6. Selecting and preparing for an occupation.
7. Preparing for marriage and family life.
8. Developing and achieving socially responsible behaviour.
9. Acquiring a set of values and an ethical system as a guide to behavior.

It is the responsibility of home and the school to help the adolescence and children of other ages to master developmental tasks. Providing right experience at the right time to the child is necessary for mastering these tasks. The school has a special responsibility in this regard.

16

CONFLICT, DEFENCE AND ADJUSTMENT

Life is a long continuous activity of adjustment to the social and physical environment. Every living organism right from its emergence to its disappearance strives to adjust itself to the surrounding conditions. The individual is born in society and lives in society. The society provides him with an environment of a particular type which has its own tempo and own peculiarities. The process of adjustment to this particular type of environment begins at the first moment of his life's emergence. The child strives to adapt to his surroundings. But there are situations in which his needs are thwarted and the adjustment fails. He gets maladjusted and a state of disharmony gets in between the child and the environment.

Nature of Adjustment

Adjustment has been defined as 'the process by which the individual attempts to maintain a level of physiological and psychological equilibrium' (Mouly, 1967). It is also defined as 'the behaviour directed toward tension reduction'. It is also described as an attempt on the part of the individual to strike harmonious relationship between himself and his environment. It is, thus, a form of interaction between the individual and the environment in which he lives.

Promoting adjustment on the part of the child simply means developing child's capacity for adjusting. This implies child's learning to face in an adequate fashion the problems of his life.

Adjustment is directly connected with the concept of needs. In this context it refers to the adequacy of behaviour patterns which the individual adopts for satisfying his needs within the framework of the rules, regulations and mores of the social group in which he finds himself. If he fails to do so, he involves himself in conflict with the social order and lands himself in the midst of many more problems of adjustment.

Adequacy of adjustment depends on the severity of the problem. Severe and continued frustration of needs is likely to lead to maladjustment. Severity of the adjustment problems depends on such factors as (i) the nature of the need being denied, (ii) the extent to which the need is denied, (iii) the possibility of substitute goals and partial satisfaction, and (v) individual's basic security and his degree of awareness of the frustration of his needs. When the problem becomes unusually severe, he is likely to become desperate and deviant behaviour is likely to result.

The process of adjustment is continuous and complex. It depends upon an organization of a number of interacting elements within the individual. It is the total personality which must be considered in the study of adjustment. A well-adjusted person is one "who is happy, free of all complexes and worries and efficient in his surroundings." To make it more complete a "well-adjusted person is one whose needs and satisfaction in life are integrated with a sense of social feeling and an acceptance of social responsibility."

Process of Adjustment

The process of adjustment is very similar to the process of learning. The individual learns behaviours (maladjusted or adjusted; desirable or undesirable) in the same way as he learns academic material. The sequence of steps involved in the process of adjustment is as follows :

1. The individual is motivated by some temporarily unsatisfied need.
2. The individual looks to some goal as a potential satisfier.

3. Progress towards this goal is blocked by a barrier. This barrier may be physical, psychological, societal, personal or cultural or it may be a conflict between incompatible goals.
4. This causes emotional tension. The individual makes attempts on reducing the tension and reaching the goal. He makes varied responses.
5. The individual, then, reaches the goal. This goal may be original or its substitute. But, the equilibrium is reached.
6. The responses and reactions which help in reducing the tension and reaching the equilibrium are learned. Those not effective in this process are dropped.

Thus, the mechanism of adjustment involves a satisfactory and successful interaction between two kinds of forces the subjective and objective, the innate and environmental. The individual is a bundle of drives, impulses, urges, motives, cravings, desires, wants and wishes etc. When any of these is aroused, a particular state of tension is created in the organism of the individual. This state of tension is removed by a particular activity which satisfies the need of the individual. This activity may be called a goal-activity. When this goal-activity is thwarted, the process of adjustment takes a new turn. Normal mental functioning is arrested and there appear mental disorders and diseases and mental disturbances, upsets and abnormalities. At one time or another individual wishes, interests and convictions are bound to collide with those of others around him. There may be clash between his own self and the environment. This may cause a clash within his innermost self. This may result in some kind of disorder of adjustment. The personality becomes mal-adjusted.

Thus, mal-adjustment is caused by two factors, the inability or certain incapacities and inherent defects of the individual and, secondly, the stiff conditions of the environment which are hard to be overcome.

Adjustment and Mal-adjustment

Adjustment differs from maladjustment in degree rather than in kind. Normal adjustment simply means behaviour that is within the range of tolerance. This limit of tolerance may, however, vary from culture to culture, situation to situation.

The adjusted person shows a relatively high degree of integration and consistency in behaviour. He displays behaviour that is essentially effective in attaining his goals. He faces problems realistically, and devotes his energies to the realization of his purposes.

A well-integrated personality is quite well-adjusted to his environmental and social conditions. He is socially well-adjusted. He does not complain or criticise or fall against his fellow beings or social traditions and conventions. He bears with all easily and calmly.

A well-integrated personality develops gradually from the childhood stage in response to proper environment and guidance. The adjusted person is able to find satisfactory solutions for the major problems he faces and has effective ways of releasing tension so that he is relatively free from conflict and tension. Consequently, he also displays emotional and social security.

A mal-adjusted person is one who is caught between a resistant obstacle and a persistent motivation, frustration and tension which cause behavioural disruption and disorganization. His internal conflicts cause him to be at cross purposes with himself which result into his indecision and inability to coordinate his efforts in the attainment of his goals. If this is typical of his behaviour he may be said to be maladjusted.

This must be remembered that there is no clear-cut demarcation between adjustment and maladjustment.

Maladjustment may be revealed through various kinds of symptoms. But these symptoms, in their milder forms, are also the characteristics of the normal adjustment. When they are exaggerated, they characterize maladjustment. Among the more common symptoms are: general restlessness (such as nail-biting and other nervous habits), explosive behaviour, withdrawal (e.g. excessive reading, shyness, avoidance of social situations), preoccupations (e.g., worrying , day- dreaming, absent-mindedness), minor physical dysfunctions, etc. Another set of symptoms which more often are signs of immaturity and may also be indicative of maladjustment are: dependence on others, lack of motivation, crying, temper tantrums, inability to make decisions or assume responsibility, attempts to win sympathy, and selfishness, etc., in exaggerated forms.

Sources of Mal-adjustment

The sources of the individual's conflict or mal-adjustment are his inner drives and needs. There are two important sets of these-the organic and the personal. Air, food, liquid, water, rest and sleep which are necessary for the maintenance of the organism are the organic needs. Affection, belongingness, achievement, independence, social approval, etc., are his personal needs. Besides, there are wants for security, desire for personal worth, "ego-value," want for freedom and sexual urge. All these wants and desires can not be fulfilled. When not fulfilled, frustration, mal-adjustment and disorders appear.

The frustration or the thwarting of needs comes from two directions, internal and external. It remains internal if it is due to some personal defects or limitations or moral ideals. It is external if it is caused by certain environmental conditions such as social restrictions, economic difficulties or political factors.

The intensity of thwarting or mal-adjustment depends upon the (a) type of thwarting, (b) previous experience of the person, (c) person's interpretation of it, (d) the source (personal or impersonal), (e) nature of the need, (f) possibilities of satisfactory solution, and (g) degree of awareness of being thwarted.

In adjusting to life-situations the individual feels the necessity of harmonizing his desires with reality. But very often it is not possible. The individual, therefore, must learn either to accept defeat, to try another or to undertake long and arduous process to reach his goal. The failure to accept certain aspects of reality is a frequent source of continuing conflict for many individuals.

The individual has several desires which are in conflict. Very early in life children learn standards of right and wrong and acquire ideals of conduct which give rise to conflict between natural desires or impulses incompatible with the moral principles of the individual's conduct.

The evidence of mal-adjustment of personality is found in the resulting overt behaviour. These broad types of behaviours result from maladjustment of personality, the aggressive, withdrawing and nervous habits. The aggressive behaviour, again, takes the forms of bullying, stealing, truancy.. disobedience, defiance, insolence, destructiveness and temper-tantrums. Examples of withdrawing behaviour are shyness, fearfulness, daydreaming, unsociability and secretiveness. Nervous habits include nail-biting, fidgeting, and thumb-sucking.

Nature of Conflict

Throughout life the individual has to adjust to the demands of his external environment as well as to those of his physiological and psychological make-up. The adjustments he makes in response to these demands are not always possible, not always desirable, not always undesirable. But, whatever be its kind and quality, adjustment he must try and make. "Only in death does the individual cease to adjust."

Conflict is always a conflict of incompatible motives-motives that impel us to incompatible goals. When there are two strong desires or motives simultaneously impelling the individual to work in two opposite directions, a state of indecision follows. This we call mental conflict. This is the state of mind divided against itself.

Conflict is defined as the tendency to make two or more incompatible responses at the same time. It is possible to desperately want something and desperately fear it at the same time. In such a situation the individual can not get rid of it because he has a strong need for it; nor he just goes ahead and can approach the thing or the goal because of his fear. Conflict, thus, arises and his motivated behaviour is blocked. This gives rise to frustration, anxiety and mental tension. Miller (1944, 1948, 1959) presents a very comprehensive discussion of conflict.

In psycho-analysis, a mental conflict between motives may result into repression of desires and motivational forces. Every individual is a bundle of instinctive urges, many of which can not be allowed to have direct satisfaction as our society has its own code of conduct. None can have direct satisfaction of sex-urge.

None can seize other's things. Everyone can not be rich. Everyone can not have good building. Thus, those who cannot, have to repress their desires which are not fulfilled. Tensions, over assertion, sex, curiosity, acquisition, etc., cause conflicts.

In short, the life of the individual is full of conflict. We can not drink publicly, we can not love other women in the presence of the wife, we can not have riches to our heart's content, we can not all be kings and rulers, we can not all have decent clothes and high posts. As a result of this, constant conflict goes on in the life of the individual. But such conflicts are not very harmful. These are conflicts on the conscious level and many of them are easily resolved. A conflict of motives faced and resolved does not in itself result in mental disorders or any other harm. If the continued conflicting motives are recognised and openly acknowledged they do not produce disorders. Danger of disorder comes when the contending motives work obscurely, unrecognised by rationalization i.e., reasons which we invent to explain and excuse. Danger comes when we repress the conflicting motives. Thus, it is not conflict but rather the repression to which conflict may lead that is the source of mental disorders.

But conflict itself is very painful and wasteful of energy. It may weaken and reduce the human organism and prepare the way for disorders. If the conflict continues sub-consciously it is still more distressing and exhausting to the individual. His energies are consumed. He suffers from the symptoms of lack of energy complicated by an unknown distress. He is restless and distressed, sleeps poorly, can not concentrate his attention, suffers headache and weakness of the cyes and pains about the body.

It is, therefore, very necessary for the educator to avoid situations that cause conflict in the minds of his pupils. He should educate them to consciously recognise certain conflicts such as all can not be rich, or can not be big etc., so that they may not create mental conflicts. The discipline should not be rigid and repressing, as it also creates conflict in the minds of the students.

Types of Conflict

Four types of conflicts have been described as follows :

Approach-Approach Conflict: In this kind of conflict the

individual desires to approach two separate goals. For example, if he approaches one, he loses the other. In other words this is a psychological situation in which the individual is motivated to satisfy two different needs simultaneously which is not possible. For example, a student very much desires to go to U.S.A. for higher studies, but at the same time being very much attached to parents wants very strongly to remain with them also. A classical example is that a woman with two equally attractive suitors, both of whom she wishes to marry, but choosing one essentially results in the loss of the other. To have both is not possible.

Avoidance-Avoidance Conflict: This is a situation in which the individual fears two objects or goals. But, if he avoids one, he can not avoid the other one. For example, an individual does not want to annoy his parents (seeks to avoid displeasure of his parents) and fears the displeasure of the wife who does not like his meeting the parents. Another example may be of a student who dislikes or fears studies and at the same time fears failing in the examination. Avoiding one feared object forces him to face the other. This puts him in a conflicting situation.

The Approach-avoidance Conflict: This kind of conflict occurs when a particular goal is both desired and feared at the same time. For example, a man fears his employment as it is a very humiliating situation for him, but he can not leave it as it is the only means of sustinence for him. Another example may be that of the child of a punitive mother on whom he is totally dependent for love and affection. He can not approach her because of his fear of her and at the same time he can not avoid her because of his dependence on her. Still another example may be of a young girl who very much wants to marry, but at the same time fears it also.

This kind of conflict is more harmful than the first two.

Double Approach-Avoidance Conflict: It is an extension of the approach-avoidance conflict. For example, a woman wants to marry and fears it too; at the same time she must choose one of the two equally attractive and equally feared persons.

Approach-avoidance and double approach avoidance conflicts are more devastating for mental health because they can not be easily resolved. Avoidance-avoidance and approach-approach conflicts can be resolved easily.

Consequences of Conflict

Conflict generates frustration and anxiety. Frustration is painful. If it continues for a long time, it may impair the mental health of the individual. Dollard and Miller (1950) hold that an intense emotional conflict may cause neurosis which is a kind of mental disorder. Phillips (1956) still strongly believes that conflict is the essential basis of psychopathology.

Freud held that a conflict which is resolved does no harm. Nor a continuing conflict which is recognized and openly acknowledged produce mental disorders. It is those conflicts which are disguised and unrecognized and repressed which are dangerous. It is not conflici, but repression of conflict which leads to neurotic disorders.

Mental Conflict

Various theories have been put forward to explain the nature and cause of these conflicts. They are :

Theory of Charcot and Janet : Charcot and Janet developed a theory that severe conflicts such as hysteria are caused by "dissociation" or imperfect integration of personality. A normal personality is a well-integrated personality. When 'Internal divisions' appear and personalities are split, some kind of mental conflict or disorder takes pace. Janet said that neuroses arise from constitutional weaknesses and lack of energy. Fears, obsessions and compulsions all are due to the weakness of the mind. He used the term 'psychasthenia' for this 'weakness of the mind'.

Psycho-analysis

Freud's Theory : Freud said that neuroses have a psychological basis. He held that the unconscious mind, "the greatest segment of the mind" controls the largest fraction of human behaviour. The 'consciousness is just a flickering light given off by the unconscious mind'. This unconscious mind is the reservoir of primitive impulses and strivings and socially disapproved or forbidden desires. These desires always strive to come to the level of consciousness. But the human being (his conscious mind) represses them, as not being desirable, producing, thus, mental conflicts. These conflicts, if serious enough, result in neuroses.

The content of the unconscious, as Freud holds, is generally sexual in nature, This he calls 'Libido', the life-urge.

A conflict according to Freud, thus, is an inconsistency between his primitive animal-like 'Id' and the demands of 'reality'. To resolve these the individual adopts various devices. This he calls 'dynamism'. Such important devices are 'repression' 'sublimation', 'rationalization', 'projection', 'regression'.

The treatment suggested by Freud requires first, to understand the patient's conflicts by "free association" and dream-interpretation and then to free the 'Libido' from its unfortunate fixations and to build up the 'Ego' until the patient can cope with his problems.

Adler's Theory : Adler, a disciple of Freud opposed the distinction between the conscious and unconscious as drawn by Freud. He also disliked the idea of putting emphasis upon sex. He set up a rival school called 'Individual Psychology'.

He said that it is not sex-repression that causes neurotic disorders and mental conflicts, but it is 'thwarted self-assertion'. Adler holds that the basic urge is a striving for superiority. When this urge is thwarted the person feels inferior and an 'inferiority complex results. The individual then tries to compensate by asserting himself in other ways.

Thus according to Adler first 'style of life' or 'the role which the individual adopts in early childhood' should be discovered. The inferiority complex, then, should be talked over and the individual should be made aware of the fact. Then he should be guided towards goals which are more socially acceptable.

Jung's Theory : Another disciple of Freud, Jung set up in Zurich a school of 'Analytical Psychology'. Jung said that it is not only the sex that dominates the life, but there are various other desires, too, which motivate the behaviour. The 'libido' is not only the sex-energy. But it takes many forms. He also said that 'the unconscious is not entirely unmoral'. It also included moral and even religious principles.

To Jung, neuroses are caused partly by complexes built up in childhood and partly by the present difficulties.

Free association and "dream-analysis" are the techniques which he suggested to cure neuroses. His analysis deals with both past and present. He makes a synthesis of both conscious and unconscious trends of personality.

Horney's Theory : Karen Horney, a psycho-analyst of New York says that 'conflicts and neuroses do not arise from instinctual or biological sources', as Freud generally implied. They are produced by the contradictions in our culture. For example, we are taught brotherly love and unselfishness, but competition for success is also stressed in the society. Out of such conflicts come hostilities, fears and other neurotic symptoms.

Defence Mechanism

The terms defense mechanism or adjustment mechanism means the same thing, But, Mouly (1967, p. 434) draws a distinction between the two. Under defense mechanism he classifies those response patterns of the individual by which he attempts to defend himself against feelings of inferiority caused by his failure to attain his goal. This is his attempt on minimizing his failure or attaining success by other means. Adjustment mechanisms, according to him, are behaviour patterns by means of which the individual attempts to satisfy his needs. These are neither disorders nor symptoms of maladjustment. They are simply the adjustments the individual makes when confronted with certain needs on the one hand and certain situational realities, on the other. A few psychologists have used the term "mental mechanism" for the same behaviour patterns which, by others are described as adjustment mechanism or defense mechanism.

Meaning and Nature of Defense Mechanism : "Defence mechanisms are thoughts and behaviours that reduce anxiety through self-deception," They are anxiety-reduction behaviours. They are ways of lying to one self. They are learned habits and behaviours by means of which the individual satisfies his needs, but which are not in the interest of the individual from the standpoint of his long-term welfare. Basically defense mechanism are mental devices aimed at tension reduction. Freud maintained that an individual's own id-impulses that are unacceptable to his ego arouse neurotic anxiety in him. Then these impulses are repressed in the unconscious mind. The psychic energy gets tied up in the unconscious and is less available to the ego for dealing with reality. The individual, then, to get rid of or to reduce the anxiety resorts to various self-deceptive maneuvers. These he calls defense mechanisms.

Freud described a number of defense mechanisms that individuals use to protect themselves from anxiety, i.e., neurotic anxiety which is fear aroused by the individual's own id-impulses that are unacceptable to the ego. When unacceptable impulses, conscious or unconscious, begin to emerge the ego attempts to inhibit their expression and prevent them from entering consciousness, i.e., they are repressed into unconscious. For Freud the most basic defense mechanism was repression in which thoughts are pushed back into the unconscious by the ego. Freud believed that all individuals use most of the defense mechanisms to some extent many of which serve a worth-while adaptive purpose when used in moderate form. But, when self-deception leads to excessive pain that defense mechanism becomes part of neurosis.

Kinds of Defence Mechanism

Defense mechanisms have been classified in different ways by different people. Mouly (1967) classifies them into direct and indirect two categories. In case of direct defense mechanism the individual attempts to overcome the obstacle and reach the original or substitute goal, i.e., he fights the situation. In case of indirect defense mechanism the individual withdraws or gives up trying to reach the goal. A more comprehensive classification system is given by Shaffer and Shobem (1956) in which defense mechanisms are divided into five categories such as :

1. Adjustment by defense
2. Adjustment by withdrawal
3. Adjustment by fears and repression
4. Adjustment by ailment, and
5. Various mal-adjustive reactions.

In all these the individual is attempting, by minimizing his failure or attaining success by others means, to defend himself against feelings of inferiority, pain or anxiety occasioned by his failure to attain his goal.

Compensation: It is an attempt on the part of the individual to overcome feelings of incompetence or inferiority arising out of his failure or personal limitations in a particular area by striving for success in the same or different area. For example, Demosthenes tried to overcome his speech defect by practising speaking with pebbles in his mouth. A student failing in academic courses tries hard to excel in games and sports. Parents having been unable to get education try to go out of the way to have their sons and daughters go to higher education colleges. This is an example of Compensation through others. Compensation is also involved in some cases of attention-getting devices such as boasting, lying, and exhibitionism and also in such behaviours as crusading with unusual zeal against such evils as drinking, smoking, etc. When it is socially desirable compensation is called sublimation; particularly when it applies to the area of sex.

Rationalization: It consists of giving plausible but untrue reasons for one's failure or inadequacy. By objective standards his behaviour is inadequate, silly, irresponsible or unacceptable in some way. But, admitting this is anxiety-provoking. So the individual defends himself against this by resorting to its justification on flimsy grounds. It is an, unconscious mechanism. When false reasons are given consciously, knowingly, it is not rationalization, it is lying.

Rationalization is said to be a "face-saving device". It may take any number of forms such as "sour grapes", "sweet lemons", or blaming of incidental causes, e.g., kicking the stool for its having been in the way.

Projection: Mouly (1967) considers this defense mechanism a form of rationalization mechanism. In this case the individual projects his own thoughts, ideas and feelings which are unacceptable or painful to his ego on to other people, things and objects in his environment. The individual perceives in others the traits or motives in which he feels his own inferiority. For example, a person may accuse another one to be jealous of him while the fact may be that he himself is jealous of the other person.

Projection is best explained by the Hindi poet Goswami Tulsidas.

What one feels within himself, he ascribes the same to others. Most poetic expressions are poet's projections of their feelings and ideas.

These three defense mechanism, rationalization, compensation and projection are grouped by Shaffer and Shoben under the category of adjustment by defense.

Withdrawal Mechanism: In this case the individual instead of fighting the situation or attempting to reach the goal tries to run away from the frustrating situation. For this reason this mechanism is also called an escape mechanism. These escape behaviours are generally undesirable as they do not solve the problem. Yet, the individual resorts to them because they help the individual get some relief from the tension and anxiety that the situation may, otherwise, cause.

A distinction should always be made between simple forms of withdrawal and more serious forms of adjustment such as schizophrenia which is a devastating mental disease. Negativism, general seclusiveness, bashfulness and timidity, etc., are the most common forms of withdrawal mechanism. In these the individual cuts himself of the tension- creating situation. Fantasy, day-dreaming are also well-known forms of withdrawal mechanism. In themselves they are not harmful. But, if they are excessively used interfering with constructive behaviour, they are certainly harmful.

Fear and Repression Mechanism: Sense of guilt engenders fear. The most illustrated example is that of Adam and Eve. They walked with god and conversed with him. Later they hid themselves from him for they disobeyed him by eating the fruit from the forbidden tree. They first developed a feeling of guilt and then, fear. As long as fear and the sense of guilt remain at conscious level, it may not be very harmful. But, when fear and guilt feelings continue and become a source of pain and tension, the individual in order to save himself from that tension represses those feelings into his unconscious mind. The repressed feelings, however, do not die down there. They come up in a disguised form. Repression, thus, serves the purpose of protecting the self of the individual. But, it is considered to be the most dangerous form of mental mechanism, as its underlying dynamics cause many unexplained behaviours such as phobias. In these cases diagnosis of problem behaviour becomes very difficult.

Reaction Formation: It is also accompanied by the repression of guilt feelings. In this an individual goes out of his way to do just the opposite of what he feels within himself. It is a mechanism that protects the individual against strong but unacceptable impulses. In this the individual becomes fanatically committed to a position diametrically opposed to his or her impulses. A person who loves a lady basically at the unconscious level may be showing hatred for her in his apparent overt behaviour. This way of his behaving protects his self from the guilt feeling that he loved the lady. Compulsive disorders marked by rituals that appear silly to the observers only serve as guilt-reducers for the disturbed person. They are attempts on undoing the unnamed wrong. This is also an anxiety reducing self-deception like all other defense mechanisms.

Displacement: It involves the inappropriate transferring of reactions from one object to another. For example, an angry man having been insulted by his boss in his office, comes home and quarrels with his wife and children. He is displacing his anger from the real target since an attack on the boss would be impossible.

Regression: According to McDougall (1933) regression mechanism is indicated when circumstances call for the higher modes of functioning, but the individual is unable to respond with those higher modes and in which there is some actual return to childish or infantile modes of functioning which are no more accessible to the volition of the normal adult. According to Jung's view, regression is a movement away from the adaptations of life back towards that condition of security which the infant experienced in its mother's arm.

The Word regression figures largely in the discussions of psychoanalysis. Freud said that regression plays an important role in the genesis of all neurotic symptoms. As described by McDougall (1933) Freud maintained that the libido of the patient when repressed in the course of conflict, returns to modes of expression which were formed in infancy, ceasing thereupon to find or strive for expression in the modes normal to the adult, the libido flowing backward as it were, opens up again the channels of sexual expression of the polymorphous perverse infant, channels that had been deserted by it, that had run dry and become more or less silted up through disuse, for example, crying or weeping by an adult when faced with some difficult problem.

Mechanisms Involving Ailments: When an individual suffers from some conflict which is difficult to resolve and is painful, he unconsciously resorts to ailments known as psychoneuroses. These ailments have no organic causes. They are only of psychogenic origin. They are of various kinds such as various forms of hysteria, such as localized pains, paralysis, occupational cramps, stammering, stutterings, fatigue, etc. For example, a child failing to cope up with the courses and fearing failure in the examination, on the one hand, and fearing displeasure of the parents to whom he is very much attached falls ill at the time of examination.

Non-adjustive Reactions: When the behaviour used by an individual to reduce tension and anxiety caused by a conflict brings only partial satisfaction, he is compelled to repeat it helplessly to drain off accumulated tension. The tension is only partially reduced; hence he is continuously in need of behaving as he did, and is constantly tension-ridden. This makes him suffer from such problems as digestive upsets, insomnia, anxiety, worry, etc. He can not take positive steps to solve his problems and simply worries without knowing what he is worried about. Among the more common forms of such non-adjustive reactions are neurasthenia, hypochondria.

17

SIGNIFICANCE OF MOTIVATION

Generally, we see in the classroom that some of the students are very much interested in teaching-learning while some are always in a mood of lazyness. There are always some reasons behind these two kinds of behaviour. Here, there is a saying that you can take the horse to a pond but you cannot make him drink. In the same way if the teacher puts his material before the class in a very nice manner even then he may not make his students learn till they are not ready for it. Motivation in education means inculcating and stimulating interest in studies and other such activities in pupils. It involves the understanding and use of natural urges of the child and also assisting him in acquiring new desirable motives. Thomson puts the same views as, "Motivation is the art of stimulating interest in the pupil where there has been no such interest, or where it is yet unfelt by the pupil, and also of cultivating the interest already present on behalf of socially approved conduct."

According to modern psychologists motivation explains the 'Why of human action and behaviour. It answers the question, Why do we love? Why he was angry? Why he stole? Why a worker or farmer works hard? Why does a student read late in the night? Why labourers go on strike? etc. It is clear then that motivation includes all those efforts which are responsible for arousing, sustaining and regulating our behaviours towards the goal. Good supports the same view. The word 'Motivation' is derived from the Latin word 'Motum' which means move, motor, motion. In other words, it is the internal impetus of our behaviour.

Further, education is a life-long process and life is a long continuous activity and every activity has a striving force behind it, which may be called 'Motive-force' of behaviour. No activity goes without motivation. It is in this light that we may define motivation as the force which compels an individual to act or to behave in a particular direction. The direction that such a motivated behaviour takes is the goal. Psychologists have tried to describe this force as the ultimate cause of motivation. It has been variously described as the "will-to-live", "a chain of reflexive acts," "the logic of the situation," "a kind of tropism," "a will", "a desire for pleasure and avoidance of pain", "an emotion," "instinct," "reason," "ideas", "feeling", "the libido," "the sub-conscious mind" and so on. But, pleasure-pain-principle is the most comprehensive explanation. Motivational force may flow out of any one of these.

The Definitions

1. "Motivation is the super-highway to learning."
   .....Charles Skinner
2. "Motivation is the central factor in the efficient management of the process of learning. Some type of motivation must be present in all learning." .... Kelly
3. "Motivation means vitalized effort. It fires the imagination, it arouses and taps hidden and undreamed sources of intellectual energy, it impassions the heart, it releases the flood gates of determination, ambition and purpose, it inspires in the child the will to do, to achieve, to overcome."
   ....Averill
4. "Motivation is the influence of general pattern of activity initiating and directing the behaviour of the organism .
   .... Johnson

Terms Used for Motivation : Most frequently we use the terms as Need, Drive, Incentives and Motives. Below is the explanation of each term.

Need: It is the lack of something which is experienced by the organism. It forces to perform that activity which culminates in the satisfaction of the need. Thus, needs are associated with goals.

Among human beings, needs are relatively permanent tendencies which seek their satisfaction in achieving certain specific goals.

According to Boring, "Need is some sort of deficiency in the body owing to which one feels intense."

Drive: Word drive is usually used when there is a feeling of mental tension or restlessness on account of our bodily needs. A drive is a tendency of shifts in physiological balance, tissue tension, sensitivity to stimuli of a certain class and response in any of variety of ways that are related to the attainment of a certain goal."

According to Dashiell, "Drive is an original source of energy that activates the human organism, or, it is a state of persistent disequilibrium which leads to an increase of general activity."

Incentives: That element in the environment which satisfies the drive is known as incentive. In our schools, children are provided many kinds of rewards for successful performance, such as grade, prize, teacher's approval and the approval of classmates. The children are supposed to work to get these rewards. These rewards are called incentives. It is believed that they will motivate students to work harder and to perform better.

Motive: Motive is a broader term. It includes need, drive and incentive. Some psychologists consider motives as physiological and psychological conditions which are innate. But, all agree that they drive an individual to act in a particular direction. Few psychologists have defined motive in their own ways as :

"A motive may be defined as a tendency to activity initiated by drive and concluded by the adjustment" .....Shaffer

"A motive is a state or set of the individual which disposes him for certain behaviour and for seeking certain goals."
....R.S. Woodworth

"A motive is any condition of the organism which points it towards the practice of a given task and defines the satisfactory completion of that task.". .....Megoarch

The Functions

Below are the main functions of motivation :

1. Motivation is the stirred up stage of human organism. Hence, when it is aroused all the parts of human organism get immediately ready to go into action. Thus, the body

apparatus is put into a state of readyness to act in a particular direction.

2. They are the spring balances of human behaviour. When aroused they cause high performance, raise attention and they make a more vigorous effort to succeed in learning.
3. The behaviour, which results out of motivational stirring are more intensive, effective, suitable and lasting e.g., acts of fighting when a person is enraged.
4. Motives get modified and thus take the form of sentiments, attitudes, interests, purposes, values, etc., which give a quality to human personality.
5. They bring changes in pupil behaviour.
6. Motives energize our behaviour. They release energy and arouse activity. Thus, praise, blame, reward, punishment, etc., are powerful incentives for many of our actions. They make us react in a particular way and are helpful in learning process.
7. They help in character formation.
8. Motives are best selector of our behaviours. They dispose the individual to react to some situations and to ignore others. They determine in considerable amount how one will react to certain situations. When a newspaper is given to different people it is seen that everyone reads that column carefully for which he has a motivation.
9. Motives help in concentrating attention.
10. They direct behaviour. They are not merely selectors but also the directors of behaviour. They direct the behaviour in such a manner that the individual should be made active and motivated to direct his energies towards well defined and attainable goals.

The Classification

Motives are of two types : (1) Natural or innate motives, (2) Acquired motives.

Natural Motives: There are some motives which are universal among all human beings. We experience such motives and drives every day. These, therefore may be described as "natural" motives.

Natural motives mostly consist of simple, elementary drives but, on them are based the more complex and educationally important motives.

Natural motives are due to basic needs such as blood circulation, heart beat, respiration, metabolism, appetites, glandular secretion, etc. Social and emotional needs such as affection, happiness, prestige and comfort also modify behaviour. Drives of avoiding bodily pains, fatigue, exhaustion, disappointment and experience of failure etc., are also important in the modification of child's behaviour.

Acquired Motives : Human beings are capable of acquiring new motives. The interaction of an individual with his environment provides a constant source of modification of his old motives and acquisition of new ones. Acquired motives are also known as learned motives which are nothing but "externalization of drives." They are actually secondary reinforcements. Rats have been experimentally led to learn a completely new maze on the basis of secondary reinforcement.

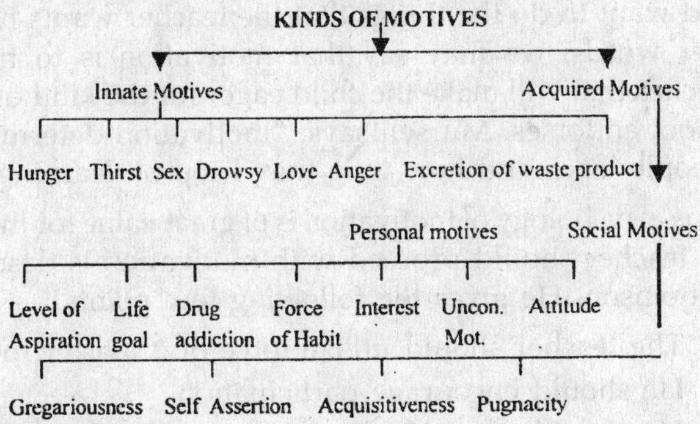

Educational Value

Motivation is very significant in all phases of education and learning. Education is not teaching but enabling the child to learn for himself. It's success depends, therefore, upon appeals, incentives, impression, encouragement and all those forces that set the child ready to learn. In other words, the problem of education is the problem of motivating the child. A well-motivated pupil is highly attentive, he takes to his work wholeheartedly and achieves maximum success in the activity. Problem of discipline is ultimately a problem of rightly motivating the child in the desired channels.

Formation of character and building up a right type of personality depend upon right type of guidance in motivation. If high ideals and virtues of life are substituted as driving forces, lifting up of the personality on to a higher plane becomes a simple job. All methods of teaching go waste without motivating the child. They become effective only when the child is well motivated. Anderson says, "Learning will proceed best if motivated."

In every action of a human being which seeks to realize a goal, motivation plays an important role. In all types of learning there must be a goal and hence, we can say that all learning is motivated. It is therefore important that wherever learning is taking place, it should be ensured that it is properly motivated, because the intensity of the drive, the vividness of perceiving the goal and other similar things make difference in the effectiveness of learning process. It is the task of the teacher to improve the conditions of effective learning. He can do this by influencing motivation. Motivation involves manipulating incentives and goals, creating the proper atmosphere, arousing the emotional interest. The secret of successful teaching is to discover means of making the pupil like and want to do the things that the teacher wants him to do. In other words, we may say that motivation is to find those approaches that will make the child eager for the kind of learning the school endorses. Murseli says, "motivation determines how well people learn and how long they keep on learning."

Thus, psychology of motivation is of great value for the teacher. How a teacher should proceed with motivation is described by M.K. Thomson. He gives the following few points :

1. The teacher should utilize force of a master motive.
2. He should encourage participation.
3. He should appeal to as many motives as possible.
4. He should enlist the whole personality.
5. The teacher should be enthusiastic. Enthusiasm is contagious.
6. He should make special use of the gregarious impulse and the desire for status.
7. He should set the proper example. What you are will speak more eloquently than what you say.
8. Motives have goals. The more clearly the goal is perceived, the more strongly the act is motivated, Every effort to

make the goal more vivid and vital is a step in the direction of effective motivation.

9. He should furnish opportunity for self-expression in as many ways as possible.
10. Individual differences in motivation are due to age, heredity and learning process. Teacher should pay attention to them also.

Various Theories

The main theories of motivation are as under :

1. Instinct Theory of Motivation.
2. Psycho-analytic Theory of Motivation.
3. Behaviouristic Theory of Motivation.
4. Murrary's Need Theory of Motivation.
5. Maslow's Hierarchical Theory of Motivation.
6. Hygiene Theory of Motivation.
7. Pawn Theory.

Instinct Theory of Motivation: The propounder of the Instinct Theory was William McDougall. He gave a very comprehensive definition of the instinct. He called his system as Hormic psychology. Hormic means striving, purposive or non-mechanical. Hormic psychology assumes that human beings are motivated by an 'elan vital' (life force). McDougall called them instinct. According to McDougall, instincts are innate tendencies which have three aspects. The first aspect ensures that the person will see features of environment in a certain way and might be called perceptual, the second aspect consists of an affective response such as, the feeling of fear and might be termed as emotional, the third aspect consists of appropriate action such as trying to run away seeing a car running over him. This might be referred to as conactive aspect. McDougall gave a list of fourteen instincts as Acquisition, Appeal, Sex, Self-assertion, Combat, Constructiveness, Curiosity, Escape, Food seeking. Gregariousness. Hate (Repulsion), Laughter, and Parental Instinct. An emotion is associated with each instinct. So these fourteen instincts and fourteen basic emotions are the primary force of behaviour. Emotion, is the mode of experience that accompanies the working of an instinctive impulse. Emotion is a moved or stirred up state of the individual. When it is aroused, there is a disturbance in muscular and glandular activity of the individual and this motivates him to work in a particular direction.

Because instincts involve sensation, and perception, inherent motivation can be modified through teaming and experiences. These modified instincts and emotions can be described as attitude, value, sentiments, etc. The behaviour of the adult is not motivated directly by instinct but by the learned modifications and combinations of instincts which McDougall calls sentiments and values.

Psycho-analytic Theory of Motivation: Psychoanalysis has been described by one of its proponents as the basic theory of motivational psychology. But the case is not like this. It is a general theory rather than theory of motivation. The propounder of psychoanalytic school is Sigmund Freud.

Freud divided mind into three regions the conscious, the preconscious and the unconscious. The conscious is the region of awareness, the pre-conscious is a region of psychological context which can fairly easily be brought into consciousness, the third or the unconscious is the region of deeply burried psychological context. The context of unconscious according to Freud is 'repressed material'. The material of unconscious is a source of motivation. Unconscious motives make a significant contribution to the explanation of human behaviour. Many of our unconscious motives have their roots in childhood. So, adult actions are motivated by them. Freud believed that all behaviours are motivated behaviours. Motivational forces of behaviour are caused by these two types of factors or conditions i.e., conscious factor and unconscious factor.

Freud found conscious and unconscious motives as useful clinically but they did not correspond with what he was conceiving as functional units of mental life. So, he evolved a second division of personality which correspond to the functioning of mental apparatus. Its three components are Id, Ego and Super-ego. Personality functions at these three levels. In his earlier views, Freud assumed a Hedonistic tendency meaning that behaviour is directed towards maximizing pleasure and minimizing pain. At the time of birth the behaviour of the child is motivated by the forces of 'Id'. 'Id' is also known as pleasure principle. All the activities of the child are motivated by-this principle. He wants to seek pleasure and avoid pain, but later on when he is of two years 'ego' develops in him. He realizes what the reality is? The

to them. He will not forget that, unless a child realizes a need to learn something, the child either will not learn it at all or will learn it only in a functionally useless way.

Murray's Need Theory of Motivation: Murry analysed human behaviour through different tools like. T.A.T., Word Association Test, Sentence Completion and other projective techniques. He was able to analyse human personality in terms of human needs, 24 most important primary needs and in all 32 needs, like-Abasement, Achievement, Acquisition, Affiliation, Aggression, Autonomy, Blame, Counter Action, Cognizance, Construction, Deference, Defendance. Dominance, Exhibition, Exposition,. Harm-avoidance, Intra-avoidance, Nurturance, Order, Play, Rejection, Retention, Sentience, Sex, Superiority, Understanding, etc., refers to an activated need of this kind. There can be one need underlying one behaviour or more than one need. Also, one need can motivate so many behaviours.

Maslow's Hierarchical Theory of Motivation: Maslow's Hierarchical Theory of human motivation is a contemporary organismic theory. Goldstein gave his organismic theory of human motivation and asserted that there is only one fundamental human motive i.e., self actualization from which the other motives arise. Hunger, thirst, desire for knowledge, power, prestige and other primary and social motives are special manifestations of the basic tendency to realize the self. But, Maslow assumed that human motives are arranged along a hierarchy of potency. That need which has the greatest potency at any given time dominates behaviour and demand satisfaction and so on to the top of hierarchy. A schematic representation of the hierarchy of human motives is given in the following figure.

Self Actualisation

↓

Esteem Needs

↓

Love And Belongingness

↓

Safety And Security

↓

Physiological Needs

So, we have physiological needs at the base and then, as the individual comes in contact with the world, social needs take rise. The social needs are, however, quite different from the physiological needs.

Hungry man is dominated by hunger. Its emotions, perceptions, thought process and behaviour in general are pre-occupied solely with getting food and satisfying hunger. As soon as the basic physiological needs are satisfied, the next higher order needs emerge and dominate the individual. He seeks safety or security. Maslow refers to the next higher order of motives as belongingness. These needs emerge if two lower order needs are reasonably well satisfied. The individual seeks friends and strives to find a place in some group. The fourth order needs are the esteem needs. Finally, if all the foregoing needs are satisfied the need for self-actualization impels the individual to make efforts on satisfying it. Maslow has consistently urged that motivational psychology has overstressed the psychological and lower-order needs, which in his opinion are not the chief motivating forces in the normal human adult. He believes that motivational psychology has much to contribute to ethics, philosophy and the good life by turning its attention to the study of needs and self-actualization.

In the words of Maslow, "the self-actualized human being is one in whom all his potentialities are coming to full development, the one whose inner nature expresses itself freely, rather than being wrapped, suppressed or denied." He further maintains that if his inner nature is denied its expression, the person gets sick. In case it happens in our childhood, it leads to 'our secret psychic death' in childhood. It may even lead to neurosis.

Motivating Students : The success of teachers lies in motivating children to learn, because learning has to be motivated. In the beginning learning can be prompted with the help of external motives. In the second stage the child may continue the activity because it gives him pleasure. Lastly, he wants to pursue it because he is motivated to achieve excellence and perfection, Hence, in order to make teaching-learning process effective, a teacher can make use of following motivational techniques

Reward and Punishment: The system of reward and punishment is a very ancient and common device of inducing children to learn. Reward is a positive incentive compared with punishment, which is a negative incentive. Rewards give pleasure and joy which come with success and achievement, give a feeling of security and status, stimulate the individual to compete and excel, to strive to keep up his positions, to exercise initiative and exert utmost. Reward may be symbolic or material. Medals, rolls of honour, front seat in class, etc., are symbolic while prizes, money, books or things of daily use are material rewards, Material rewards sometimes also produce a bad effect on children. They may try to get these by fair or 'foul means. It is the motive behind the reward which is more important than the reward itself. Many progressive schools have banished material rewards or even symbolic distinctions because they see the danger of rewards becoming ends in themselves.

On the other hand, punishment is a deliberate attempt to inflict pain so that the learner gives up wrong responses and adopts the desirable mode of behaviour. Punishment is based on fear caused by loss of status and embarrassment. If reward helps to "stamp in" certain responses, punishment helps to "stamp out" undesirable responses. Punishment is a negative incentive. Frequent and heavy punishments blunt the sensibility of the child and make him react either by totally rejecting or by accepting it and taking it for granted. Such children usually take the punishment as if nothing has happened. This attitude defeats the very purpose of checking undesired habits. Besides, the punished child loses face, status, personality and may develop an inferiority complex. Frequent heavy punishment brutalize the teacher also and vitiate his relations with pupils.

Hence, both rewards and punishment should be so given that they are not frequent. They should be immediate and proportionate. They should in all cases, convince the recipient about their value and utility.

Praise and Blame: Praise and Blame are common motives frequently used in the class room, but their power in motivating students rests on the person giving them. There are people whose praise or blame has no effect, but there are others whose one word of praise elates us and another word of blame fills us with shame. But, like rewards and punishments, if praise and blame are frequently given they lose their effectiveness. The excellent work and desired behaviours are praised by the teacher to increase the probability of such behaviours. Encouragement is also given for good performance, while undesirable behaviours are condemned strongly. On the basis of most studies it is found that praise is more effective than blame, specially in case of girls. A few studies report that blame is effective in case of bright students and should not be used for poor students. Broadly speaking, effectiveness of praise and blame depends upon the teacher, and when and how he uses them with his students, as, for one, just a nod of disapproval or a frown may be enough, while for another even a slap may have no effect.

Success vs Failure: Bernard says that school work should be sufficiently varied so that every student has a chance to succeed at his own level. Further, he says that success develops self-confidence among learners. The success is most effective in case of average student, but it provides motivation to every one.

The failure is opposite to the success technique. Sometimes failure functions as motive. Whenever a learner accepts it as a challenge, he gets force and reinforcement for the work. Its nature is external as well as internal. Too much failures in life lowers down one's level of aspiration. Again, failures can be helpful in motivation only from gifted students' point of view. Hence, it is required that a teacher should help his students to be optimistic and should deal with failures with courage, treating them just as "Rest-Houses" on a very long path to be covered in one's life.

Competition and Co-operation: Competition and cooperation being social motivation are frequently used in classroom teaching. Rivalry between groups stimulates, but needs control. Self-rivalry, or rivalry in the form of competition with one's past record is the most valuable type. However, it must be remembered that too much competition triggers off individualism and egotism. It results in the development of undesirable emotions such as jealousy, resentment, hatred, etc. However, the emotional and social consequences of rivalry must be considered. It is thus suggested that schools should lay more emphasis on group competition and self-rivalry than an individual competition. Psychologically this technique is very significant, as it helps in developing social skills and democratic feelings among students. Finally, this technique as an incentive, therefore should be very carefully used by teachers.

Knowledge of Progress: Self-display (elation) and construction (feeling of creativeness) are the instincts operative here. A child who knows about the progress gets much encouragement and motivation from this knowledge and also satisfies his ego. Generally, in schools the progress report is prepared for every student to provide knowledge of progress. In schools where weekly tests are held pupils work harder than in schools where they are held twice or thrice a year. Experiments conducted by Judd, Thorndike, Stacey and others have shown that knowledge of result is a very powerful incentive leading to improvement in performance and elimination of errors.

The knowledge of progress provides a clear understanding to the learner about his immediate goal. It tells him how far or near he is from his target. If he is prevented from such knowledge he is left with no guide to improve his efforts to reach the goal. In such a case further attempts will prove to be uninteresting and unprofitable.

Novelty: The learner has to adjust to his own environment and novelty satisfies his need. The students get motivation by novelty and take more interest in new assignment. But, it is essential in making use of this technique that new material should be related with the old one or familiar things. Further, novelty is nothing but only the changes and variations which are related to numerous life situations. Hence, in order to encourage the students behaviour the proper use of this technique is essential.

Level of Aspiration: Every individual has certain goals which he aspires to achieve in his life. The standard he expects to achieve in any task is described by psychologists as his 'Level of Aspiration,' or what he hopes or expects to do in future. It indicates his LOA. The LOA of an individual depends on self-esteem, achievement, abilities or his past experiences. If there is a discrepancy between what he is and what he aspires to be, he may either modify his goals or work harder. The person gets success in his life, if he fixes his LOA considering the reality of his life. LOA differs from child to child. Hence, a teacher should help them to have a more realistic approach to their goals. Also, it should involve some frustration, as frustration is necessary for motivation or to spur them on to further struggle.

Interest: The first pre-requisite of effective learning is wholehearted attention and keen interest. Our likes and dislikes, our preferences and rejections express our interests. Once interest is aroused learning is facilitated. Hence, the creation and cultivation of interest is an important educational objective. A clear responsibility of the teacher is to utilize existing interests and cultivate new ones. The simplest way to search about pupils' interests is to ask them which of the several classroom activities they like most. Merely asking them to verbalize their choice may elicit interest. The teacher's own interest and enthusiasm therefore has the most powerful influence in creating and maintaining student's interest.

Other Sources of Motivation: This includes desire for social approval, the urge to mastery or dominance, to excel, to overcome opposition, to acquire the sex and parental approval etc. To repress ruthlessly such urges is to try to denature the individual, but to allow free and unrestrained outlet is equally disastrous. Natural impulses in themselves are neither good nor bad; they become so to the extent that they are directed into desirable or undesirable channels of action. Management may take the form or redirection of sublimation. It is the part of wisdom to provide outlets that are not merely escape values, but positive opportunities for achievement. Pictorial art, music, sculpture, literature etc., are largely expressions of instinctive drives coloured with an emotional tone and given intelligent direction.

Focus Attention on Desired Goals: Many elements of the physical world of the classroom may be manipulated to direct pupil attention towards the objectives. Here is how a eighth-grade general science teacher focussed attention on the unit 'Electric Current' with these words and a demonstration—

I have a large coil which as you can see is insulated wire bound together. I am going to connect the two ends of the coil to this current measuring instrument called a galvanometer. Here is a friend we have already studied, a bar magnet. Watch what happens to the needle of the galvanometer when I push the north pole of the magnet inside the coil of wire (needle moves to the right). Now I am going through the same operations once more, you ask me questions that will help you to decide why the galvanometer reacted the way it did. Similarly, a Geography teacher may attempt to focus attention on a study of 'Bharat'.

These illustrations show that the pupils attention can be focussed through the use of materials and activities that involve a number of sensory perceptions. In the science classroom only seeing and hearing were involved. To focus class attention toward the desired outcome it is essential to appeal to more than one sense, because the usual class always has some pupils who respond better to visual material than they do to spoken words. The teacher takes positive role in order to make certain that the necessary material are arranged and available; in addition, he decides whether or not, once their attention has been generally directed toward a learning outcome, the pupils will be studying from books directly or will engage himself in planning activities.

In some situations it is not necessary to do any more than let the pupils know by oral or written suggestions, what is expected. In certain skill classes a self-activating routine may become quickly established whereby pupils come in even before the bell rings and start to work without the teacher's giving any specific instruction. Further, when projects or activities are started but not finished on one day, the tendency is for the pupils to come back and start immediately where they have left off.

Development of Positive Motives: Human beings are curious about objects and phenomena in the environment. Curiosity is generally expressed towards new and novel objects, ideas and events rather than toward familiar ones. The arousal of curiosity is not dependent on any form of reward or punishment nor it is attached to any specific drive situation, such as, hunger or thirst, Also, when an object, idea, or material is no longer novel it loses its curiosity value. Novel ideas and material can be used purposefully to arouse curiosity.

Interests are also positive motives because the individual purposefully seeks to do things of his interest. One way to find out about student's interests is to ask them which of several classroom activities they prefer most. Even though they might not be highly interested in any, giving them the choice itself may reveal their interest.

A boy should not be excused indefinitely from Maths class simply because he is interested in science not maths. Instead the teacher should utilize this interest in science by helping the boy see the relationship between maths and his existing interest. Interest gathers momentum when the activities are satisfying and rewarding. Getting a student to see the satisfaction in an activity may lead to the formation of a very stable interest.

Use Learning Sets and Advance Organizers: Short instructions should be given to students before starting a task. These instructions may have different purposes, such as prompting the student to recall relevant knowledge, to think of the abilities or skills needed for the new task, to understand the final outcome desired or to compare or contrast ideas in the task. Instruction of this type comprises a learning set, a predisposition to proceed in a certain manner rather than another. Also, advance organizers may be prepared and presented to the students for two main purposes, to provide an organizational framework for the new material so that it will be understood better and to provide transitional material between what is already known and the new material. If knowing how to proceed and what will be learned, produces a desire to learn, these techniques are motivating. The major effect of learning sets and of advance organizers is to produce more efficient learning.

Help Students to Set and Attain Realistic Goals: When a person sets a goal, he tries to attain it. Attaining goals is accompanied with feelings of success. Nothing encourages continued effort and further realistic goal setting more effectively than a backlog of goals successfully attained. Why then do students so infrequently set individual goals in the classroom? There are three main reasons. First, even though individual students vary widely in readiness to learn, they are all given the same material. Second, teachers do not take the time, or have the ability to help each student set and attain realistic goals. Third, instructional materials and activities are often not available to permit the kind of instruction which individual goal-setting requires. Let us consider these and other matters associated with helping each student to set and attain realistic goals.

When a teacher has students representing a wide range of capability for learning new tasks, realistic goal setting by each student, rather than by all students dealing with the same assignment, requires much knowledge and skill. The teacher must-

1. have a fairly accurate estimate of each student's abilities.
2. have a good estimate of the difficulty of the learning activities.
3. encourage varying levels of performance by pupils.
4. Permit students of all abilities to experience many successes and occasional feelings of failure in reaching their goals.

5. realize that goal setting process takes considerably more class time than does giving the same assignments to all students in the class.

Create a Warm, Orderly Atmosphere: Warm, business like, imaginative teacher behaviour is associated with high and consistent pupil achievement and high emotional security. Sentimental and unplanned teacher behaviour is associated with inconsistent student achievement and low achievement for insecure children, Aloof and routine teacher behaviour is associated with low achievement in rebellious student and low emotional security in most children. The association of lower and higher achievement with certain kinds of teacher behaviour involves motivation. Here is an example.

Three pairs of punitive and non-punitive teachers were selected. Children in various classes were asked about pupil misconduct. Those who had the punitive teacher were less concerned about learning and social values than were the children whose teachers were non-punitive. Also, children under punitive teachers manifested more aggression in their misconduct and were more unsettled about misconduct. Personal warmth of the teacher and student interest in science also are highly related.

Creativity also is fostered better in a warm, nurturant environment without teacher domination, than in a non-supportive environment with teacher domination. Formal group instruction in which shame was used as punishment had a relation with creativity. On the other hand, the teacher's manifesting interest in child's ideas and listening to the child was positively correlated with creativity.

Provide Incentives and Punish if Necessary: Punishment may be used to suppress undesirable behaviour. Further, the threat of punishment may be used in order to get the student to perform some task which he would prefer not to do. However, the effects of punishment and threat of punishment are much less predictable than are the effects of positive incentives. Further, the use of punishment tends to put the teacher in an unfavourable light with student and also may cause personal injury to the students.

Concrete and symbolic rewards are sought by adults as well as children and can serve the purpose of getting people to perform even unwanted tasks. If the tasks were pleasant or undertaken to achieve important goals, no rewards would be necessary. Reward used in the schools are of two main types-concrete and symbolic. Concrete reward take form of money, pencil, an excuse from class and the like. Symbolic reward includes letter grades, favourable comments, non-monetary awards and others.

Avoid High Stress and Dis-organization: Trying to achieve a desired goal is always accompanied by some tension. Anxiety and stress may become so high that the student's responses become dis-organized; he does not learn efficiently. This is not likely to occur if the situation permits him to lower his goal. Persons typically set their goals too high and experience frustration by not attaining them, or when they feel that they will lose the approval of peers or other persons whom they admire. Frequently, students who set goals such as making all 'A' grades, experience severe frustration when it become apparent that they will receive 'C' grades or even 'B' grades in one or two courses. The frustration is caused not because they feel they are not learning enough or that the learning in itself is not valuable, but because some reward such as a desired scholarship will be denied or disapproval from parents or teachers will result.

Accounting Factors

There are four factors which account for motivation

(1) Arousal; (2) Expectancy; (3) Incentives; (4) Punishment

"Four concepts — arousal, expectancy, incentives and punishment help us classify the factors which account for motivation." — John P. Deceeco

Arousal: Arousal describes the general state of excitability of an organism, the general level of alertness, responsiveness, wakefulness or vigilance. According to Donald Hebb, "Arousal is an energizer but not a guide, an engine but not a stearing gear." There are various levels of arousal. Sleep is the minimum level of arousal, alertness is the moderate level and anxiety is the highest level of arousal. The optimum level of arousal for our most efficient functioning is an intermediate level.

Human beings have two types of **sources** of arousal :

(a) External source of arousal.

(b) Internal source of arousal.

Internal source of arousal is down flow of thought, symbol and fantasy from the cortex. These internal forces are totally biological and physiological such as chemical changes in the blood. But, the teacher can't control these forces.

External source is the stimulation provided by the environment. In his discussion of play, boredom and the search for excitement Hebb stresses the fact that living things must be active. Ordinarily, environment stimulation and satisfaction of biological needs keeps the brain cell and muscles active. Students may day-dream to keep themselves much less aroused when the classroom fails to provide adequate stimulation. So, activity is called for the required level of arousal, and we try to stay at an intermediate level between boredom and excitement.

Role of the Teacher **:** According to Hebb, Arousal is a general level of behavioural excitability. In education we prefer to define arousal as the student's general level of alertness or attentiveness. The student will perform best when he is neither sleepy nor frantic, but when he is simply alert. In any case an initial responsibility of the teacher is to win and to maintain the attention of the students.

In the daily class-room routine, the teacher must guard against monotony and boredom. He should always provide the students with enough to think about and to do by his talks and activities.

Teaching methods can capitalize on the students' need for new stimulation and on his properties to be curious and to explore. The analogy can be used for the comprehension of the unknown concepts. The discovery and brain storming strategies can be used by the teacher for this purpose. Brunet suggests that when the student is allowed to approach learning as an act of discovery he will keep himself engaged increasingly in learning with the autonomy of self-reward. In Brunet's sense the student provides for his own stimulation and in this way performs his own arousal function.

Expectancy: Vroom (1964) defines, 'Expectancy as a momentary belief that a particular outcome will follow a particular act.' Expectancy is related to arousal state and motivation of human being. We may be aroused when there is a discrepancy between what we perceive and what we expected to perceive; when we neither liked nor expected. A mother becomes angry if the child colours when she expects him to read. Discrepancies between perception and expectancies are sources of arousal. When we become overly familiar with our surroundings. they lose their power to arouse us, when the environment provides us exactly what we expect, we are no longer aroused by it. Hence, when we can sleep in a noisy environment it provides us exactly what we expect: we are no longer aroused by it. Hence, we can sleep in a noisy environment of familiar sounds and suddenly awake at the sound of an unfamiliar footstep.

According to McClelland (1953), the size of the discrepancy determines the feeling we experience. A large discrepancy results in unpleasantness, a small discrepancy results in pleasantness. So, a certain level of discrepancy between happenings and expectancies is necessary. The teacher should not produce discrepancy more than optimum level.

The anticipated satisfaction is called valence. The actual satisfaction is called value. The vigor with which the individual acts is the product of both expectancy and valence. We find students who expect little satisfaction in academic achievement (low valence) even though they have the ability which assures them academic success (high expectancy). We call such students as underachievers.

Expectancies can be a source of arousal, especially when there is a manageable discrepancy between what we see and what we expected to see. Instructional objectives are expectancies that are the teacher's main concern. He must also be concerned with the expectancies and valences of the students. The student must be made to desire instructional outcomes.

Role of the Teacher : The expectancy function requires the teacher concretely to describe to the student what he will be able to do when a particular class, lesson of project is completed. In performing this function the teacher must modify, substitute, or eliminate the student's expectancies in such a way as to increase his efforts to accomplish the new instructional objectives. The teacher should specify the objectives of teaching to the students and make students realize the importance of these objectives. The teacher must relate intermediate expectancies to immediate and remote goals of the students to engage the student's full effort in learning. Sometimes the teacher may change the expectancies of the students and increase the behavioural vigor deliberately and mismatch them, as mismatched expectancies are a source of humour and humour can be a source of motivation. The expectancy function requires the teacher to have sufficient knowledge of the past failure and success of individual students to distinguish among realistic, pessimistic and optimistic expectancies.

Incentives: Incentives are actual goal objects. They can be concrete or symbolic rewards. They incite, arouse and move to action when they are associated with certain stimuli which signal their presence. A rat will run in a maze not only because it is hungry but also because it expects or anticipates food when it reaches the goal box. The larger the incentive the more vigor we find in the rat's responses. The rat runs the maze faster when given several hundred food pellets than when given only a few. So. the vigor of activity is affected by the nature of the incentive.

Positive and negative reinforcers can be viewed as incentives. In Skinner's theory of learning there are two types of reinforcers. A positive reinforcer is a positive reward. A negative reinforcer is a negative reward, a stimulus which gives us relief from an unpleasant state of affairs. Positive incentives are praise, prizes, smiles and money. Negative incentives are the relief from noise which follows closing the window, the anesthesia which reduces dental pain. Both reinforcers strengthen the responses which precede them. The control of behaviour in Skinner's theory is clearly outside the organism.

Albert Bandura (1962) studied the relationship of incentives to learning in children and came to the conclusion that incentives are strong factors which increase the vigor of behaviour. So, incentives are among the factors which increase the vigor of our behaviour.

Role of the Teacher: It is the duty of a teacher that lie should provide incentives for student's activities so that their behaviour may be reinforced for achieving the objectives of learning. Incentives may be feedback of test results, spoken or written praise and encouragement, grades or fruits of successful competition.

Continuous withholding of feedback can have very deleterious effects on student motivation and learning. The teacher should assign grades or marks in evaluating the student's activities. Students ordinarily show keen interest in their test-results. Results which somewhat exceed their expectations give them considerable satisfaction, which becomes a permanent source of motivation for future learning. This type of motivation can be provided by the techniques of praise and blame, encouragement, examination results (grade or divisions) and competition etc. On account of all this the students take interest throughout the teaching-learning process.

Punishment: Solomon (1964) defines punishment as a stimulus the individual' seeks to escape or avoid. Punishment is a negative motive which is based on fear of failure, fear of losing prestige, fear of insult or rejection, fear of failure, and fear of physical pain etc. Experimental evidences has not shown that it is always bad, under certain conditions punishment may be very effective, particularly, when the individual is permitted to make an alternative response which is desirable and incompatible with the punished response.

Actually, punishment is given to check undesirable behaviour. Skinner says that punishment may be necessary to check undesirable behaviour, but, it is not a sound practice because it develops inferiority complex in the child, So, one must use it in rare cases.

Role of the Teacher : The disciplinary function requires the teacher to control deviant behaviour through the use of rewards and punishment. Punishment, not be avoided at all, because, punishment can sometimes produce dramatic, permanent, and desirable changes in behaviour. So, the belief that punishment is not so effective as reward does not indicate that it should be banned. To punish students there can be various ways but (a) this should be used when other methods fail, (b) this should be proportional to the fault committed, (c) this should be determined by the nature of the student. If the student is too much sensitive very harsh punishment should be avoided.

18

Personality Traits

Understanding of human personality has been the focus of attention of all psychologists right from the beginning of civilization. Hence, many psychologists have tried to define personality in their own ways. But, more scientific approaches to define and describe personality were made only around the mid of the 20th century. Allport in 1937 defined personality as "the dynamic organization within the individual of those psychophysical systems that determine his unique adjustments to his environment". This definition has a wider acceptance among the psychologists and is quite comprehensive. Eysenek (1952) said that, "Personality is the more or less stable and enduring organization of a person's character, temperament, intellect and physique that determine his unique adjustments to his environment." To Child (1968) "Personality refers to more on less stable internal factors that make one person's behaviour consistent from one time to another, and different from the behaviour other people would manifest in comparable situations". Allport. after a thoughtful consideration in 1961, replaced the last five words of his definition (i.e., unique adjustment to his environment) by the words. "characteristic behaviour and thought".

Theoretical Approaches

There are various approaches in psychology that have been

used to describe and understand personality. Some of them are as follows :

1. Psychoanalytic approach
2. Neopsychoanalytic approach
3. Constitutional approach
4. Life span approach
5. Trait approach
6. Dimensional approach
7. Phenomenological or humanistic approach
8. Cognitive approach
9. Behaviour and Learning approach
10. Social cognitive approach
11. Type approach
12. Idiographic and Nomothetic approach

In the following sections only (l) type approach or type theory of personality and (2) trait approach or theory of personality have been described in detail.

Type Theory : This is the oldest theory of personality which classified human personality into a few types and, then, described the characteristics of each type. A type is a class of people having similar traits or characteristics but different from those of the class of another type; for example "introvert type" characterized by such traits as shyness, reserveness, unsocial, imaginative etc.

Contributors to Type Theory : Several psychologists have classified people into specific types and have, accordingly, described the characteristics of each type. These are :

Hippocrates: He was, perhaps the first person who attempted classification of people into types 2500 year ago. About 400 B.C., Hippocrates classified people into four types on the basis of bodily fluid or humors. He said that human body had four kinds of humors or fluids - (1) yellow bile. (2) black bile. (3) blood, and (4) phlegm. One of these fluids was said to be dominant in each individual which determined his specific temperamental characteristics making them different from those of the individuals who were dominated by other fluids. Hippocrates, thus, described four types of personalities as follows :

Choleric Type: dominated by yellow bile. People belonging to this type were characterized as being irritable, restless; hot-blooded, angry, passionate and strong with imagination.

Melancholic: dominated by black bile. People belonging to this type were characterized as being depressed, pessimistic, surly; dejected, pensive, deplorable, miserable and selfish.

Sanguine: having more blood in the body. People belonging to this type were characterized as being cheerful, ambitious, optimistic and hopeful, ardent and confident, happy and confident.

Phlegmatic: dominated by colourless and thick phlegm. People belonging, to this type were characterized as being cold, calm, slow, sluggish, indifferent, placid, dull and easily excited.

This approach or theory of personality had been very popular in the olden days.. But, the psychologists of today have completely rejected it. They considered it unscientific and irrational as there could be no relationship between psychological traits and bodily fluids. Yet, the type approach to personality understanding was accepted by modern psychologists also. They, however, adopted two different bases or criteria for describing the types- (i) One, on the basis of bodily characteristics. and another (ii) On the basis of psychological characteristics. Thus, there are two kinds of type theories based on bodily characteristics and psychological characteristics.

Body-based Types: This is also known as constitutional type. In this group contributions of Kretschmer and Sheldon are very popular. These are described as follows:

Kretschmer's Types: Kretschmer described four types along with their temperamental characteristics as follows

(i) *Pyknic Type:* Short limbed with large head, chest and abdomen; plump body roundish and fatty. soft and broad face with broad hands and feet, but slender neck and crooked nose looking like a "devil" as it were.

The psychological' characteristics of this type of people are described to be as being social, enjoying eating and sleeping, cheerful, Kretschmer has named this type of people as cycloid and says that when they contract mental illness, they are likely to exhibit the traits found in the manic-depressive patients.

(ii) *Asthenie Type:* Lean. frail but tall, flat-chest. weak or sick. lacking in strength with debility. usually underweight.

Their psychological characteristics are said to be being irritable, day-dreamers and living with fantasies, prone to be schizophrenic.

(iii) *Athletic Type:* Strongly built with muscular body neither short, nor fatty. Stout and balanced body, wide chest and shoulders.

Psychologically they are said to be well-adjusted, neither depressive nor very active. They enjoy enough social prestige.

(iv) *Dysplastic Type:* They are persons who can not be exclusively classified in any of the foregoing types: rather they have characteristics overlapping with all the other types. They are ill- balanced and under-developed.

This theory was very much criticised by psychologists, particularly by Sheldon who in 1940 propounded his own theory known as somatotype theory of personality. This is described as follows :

Sheldon's Somatotype Theory

Sheldon's theory was based on characteristic features of physique and its structure. On the basis of his observation and analysis of the naked pictures of 4000 college students he divided them into three types or groups and described their temperamental characteristics as follows :

(i) *Endomarph:* Who are short and fatty, flabby with weak bones and muscles, round body very similar to Kretschmer's pyknic type.

The psychological characteristics of this type of people were described to be happy, social, carefree, more interested in eating and restful.

(ii) *Mesomorph:* who have strong muscles and bones but have a slim and balanced body.

The psychological characteristics of such people are described to be aggressive, assertive; risk-taking, dominating and influencive, active, struggling, competitive and achievement-oriented. They are similar to Kretschmer's athletic type. Temperamentally, they are known as Somatotonia people.

(iii) *Ectomorph:* who are tall; weak, frail, skinny, stiff, slender, restrained, afraid and lacking confidence, also known as cerebrotonia.

Psychologically, they are said to be less social, reserved, nervous and of retiring nature suppressing emotions and sorrowful. They, often, suffer from insomnia and are found to be shy and hesitant

Sheldon did not find that these three types were entirely different from one another. Rather he said that although one of the type may be more dominant. Yet some bodily characteristics of the other types may also be present. He rated all the 4000 college students on each of the types on a 7-point scale and described each of them in terms of all the three types. The average type was described to be 4-4-4. In the same way a type described as 1-1-7 means predominant ectomarph having characteristics of other types of very low level. Similarly 7-1-1 type according to Sheldon means predominantly endomorph and 1-7-1 type means predominantly mesomorph.

Types Based on Psychological Characteristics : Some other psychologists such as Lung, Eysenck and Guilford have classified people into groups or types on the basis of psychological characteristics instead of bodily characteristics. Their types are described as follows:

Jung's Types: Jung said that from psychological point of view people can be classified into two types: (i) Extrovert, and (ii) Introvert. The characteristics of each of these types are :

Introvert: These are the people who like to be themselves. They do not very much, like to meet and mix with people. In that sense they are not very social. They have very few friends. They are more self-centered, reserved and thinking type. They are less outgoing. They are conservative and prefer to live alone.

Extroverts: Just opposite to the introverts; the extroverts are more outgoing, social and action-oriented. They take much interest in social activities. They like to meet people, participate in social-functions and group activities. They are more open and enjoy company of people. They are-optimistic, more realistic than idealistic more interested in outside world.

Jung's theory was also criticised by several psychologists saying that no one individual can be put exclusively in the group of introverts or extroverts. To be more realistic every individual is found to have both types of characteristics, although one of these may be more predominant. They said that people are generally, ambivert having characteristics of introverts and extroverts both.

Eysenck's Types: Eysenck (1947) classified people on the basis of psychological characteristics into three types (i) Introversion-Extroversion Type. (ii) Neuroticism-Stability Type, and (iii) Psychotis in -Superego Function Type. Each type according to him was bipolar. Eysenck studied 10,000 normal persons and neurotics and on the basis of statistical analysis of characteristics of his observations he identified these three types. Their characteristics are described as follows :

Introversion-Extraversion Type: This is the type which has both the characteristics of Jung's introversion and extroversion types. Eysenck said that no individual is wholly introvert or extrovert. Everyone is to some extent introvert or extrovert. Hence, introversion and extroversion, should be considered two poles of the same type or scale. It is a different matter that introversion is predominant in a person. There can be no person who is completely devoid of the characteristics of the introvert or the extrovert.

Neuroticism-Stability Type: This is another type of Eysenck. A person who is low on this scale lacks emotional control and suffers from weak will power. He is easily suggestible, slow in thinking and actions, less sociable and repressive of his desires. On the other hand, the individuals who are high on this scale are stable, well-adjusted, self-controlled, active and confident.

Psychotism-Superego Function Type: This dimension was added to his classification by Eysenck later in 1952 as a result of his new research. An individual who is low on this dimension suffers from poor concentration, poor memory, cruelty, insensitivity, low consideration for others, lack of creativity and lack of alertness to impending dangers. On the other hand, one who is high on this scale is dominated by his superego tendencies. He is characterized by high morality and ideals with no psychotic tendencies.

Guilford's Type: Guilford (1959) has only accepted and described the types. *Introversion-extroversion* of Eysenck's classification. He has supported only the views and the theory of Eysenck which were expressed by him in 1947.

Kraeplin's Types: Kraeplin's classification is based on people's mental structure. He classified them into two types (i) cycloids. and (ii) schizoids. This is the same classification as that of Kretschmer's classification into Athletic type and Asthenic type.

Kretschmer used these terms alternatively. The psychological characteristics of Schizoids and Asthenics are described by Kraeplin as follows :

(i) *Cycloid Type:* These are people who are social, good natured, sentimental, emotional but balanced, friendly, helpful.

(ii) *Schizoid Type:* These are people who are self-centered, unsocial hot-tempered, unsympathetic and eccentric but often intelligent and imaginative.

Type Theory

The type theory of personality has certain advantages. One of these is that this theory considers personality as an organized whole. The classification into types and psychological characteristics described under each type both have been the result of scientific observations and analysis. Yet, the theory has been criticised on several grounds as follows :

One weakness of the type approach to personality is that ascribing certain psychological traits exclusively to a certain type can not be considered very valid. It is possible that traits ascribed to one type are found also in the people belonging to another type. Many psychological traits are found overlapping the various types in reality.

Another criticism of type approach to personality is that it is "structure-based" rather than "development-based". It does not describe how the personality develops, i.e., which factors influence its development and how. It describes only the structure of personality, i.e., what it is at a particular time.

The theory is based on the assumption that there is a definite relationship between the body build or constitutional type and psychological traits. This has been criticised by several psychologists. According to Whittakar (1970) the psychological traits are more linked with social and cultural factors than body build and constitutional features. Though Sheldon had reported high correlation (0.78) between his types and their corresponding psychological characteristics, it was not accepted by psychologists as real, particularly by Hall and Lindzey (1957).

In spite of these criticisms many psychologists and researchers do accept this approach.

Trait Approach

Personality, as a whole, cannot be measured or even assessed. In describing or discussing one personality we however use the term traits which themselves are dynamic and not static. The traits are rather qualities or aspects of a total whole and unique in themselves for each personality. Strictly speaking there are no specifically set general traits that characterise the behaviour of the individual in all situations. The fear, for example, expressed by an individual while seeing a snake is not quite the same as the fear expressed by the same individual, when he is called by his boss in his office for coming late. It is a fallacy to assume that a mode of behaviour seen in one situation is really characteristic of the individual in all situations. When we look for various traits we only see in how many situations requiring the particular trait does the individual show the trait as compared with another individual who may show it in only a few or to a less degree.

On that basis we decide that the person is possessing that trait more than the other. So it is really the situations which bring out the trait and there is no generality of the personality traits in the sense that they operate uniformly or universally. If fear as a trait is not the same or of the same potential, intensity or power in all situations, there is no denying the fact that fearfulness as a trait can be given a general name. It is in this sense that we talk of human traits in general, though appearing in different degrees, in different situations, in different individuals. To find out the extent or the degree of the intensity of fearfulness in an individual we put him through various situations arousing fear and determine the degree of the presence of the trait. This degree of the presence of the trait is not final and absolute but it is the degree which we have been able to tap in those situations.

Trait theory defines and describes personality in terms of certain number of traits. "A trait refers to any characteristic that differs from person to person in a relatively permanent and consistent way" (Atkinson-Atkinson and Hilgard, 1983, p. 389). A trait is a behavioural trend, the way the individual behaves in most of the situations in a habitual manner. For example, if an individual is found to be-honest in most situations of life, honesty may be considered a trait of his personality. Thus, a trait is a behavioural characteristic of personality. But every kind of behaviour is not considered a trait. A behaviour, in order to be considered a trait, must exhibit two qualities- (i) it must be consistent. and (ii) stable. If an individual is found to be behaving honestly sometimes and dishonestly other times, he can not be considered to be an honest person and honesty can not be said to be a trait of his personality, as he lacks consistency in his behaviour. Similarly, if he behaves honestly in all situations for few months and after that begins to behave dishonestly, even then he can not be said to have honesty as a trait of his personality as he lacks stability in behaving honestly. Trait theory of personality describes personality as an ensemble of such few important traits as against types of the type theory. According to trait theory the behaviour of the individual is thought to be influenced by some relatively permanent traits of personality not by the types bodily or psychological. Allport and Cattell have made important contributions to trait approach to personality. Their theories are discussed in the following sections :

Allport's Trait Theory : Allport said that the personality of every human being is made of a certain number of psychological traits. He divided these traits into two groups(i) common traits and (ii) Personal traits. He defined these as follows :

Common Traits: Common traits, according to Allport, are those traits which are found in most of the people in a society in different amounts. There may be variations in the degree or amount of the trait among them from the lowest to the highest degree: but it is present in some amount in everyone of them. Hence, the people can be compared among themselves on these common traits.

Personal Traits: These are the traits which are not common to the people of a society. They are unique to the individual himself. They, according to Allport, constitute specific and unique component of an individual's personality. Allport calls them personal dispositions as they are not found in other individuals or all the people of the society. Hence, people can not be compared among themselves on such traits. But, an individual can be compared on this and other traits of his personality. In other words in case of personal traits assessment of inter-individual differences is not possible, while intra-individual differences can be assessed and analyzed. Allport stated that there were as many personal traits as 18,000: He classified these into three kinds of personal dispositions- (a) cardinal disposition, (b) central disposition, and (c) secondary disposition.

He defined *cardinal disposition* as that quality of behaviour and personality which is very obvious and explicit, which is known to everyone and everywhere and which alone can, sometimes, define and describe one's personality. It is personality's peripheral uniqueness which can be easily known. All world famous personalities are known by such traits; For example. 'Ahinsa' and 'peace' were the personal dispositions of Mahatma Gandhi for which he was known all over the world.

Traits falling under *Central disposition* are said to be found in all human beings. Allport identified 5 to 10 such traits which characterize all personalities. For example, sociability, self-confidence, ambition, autonomy, etc. may be examples of cardinal disposition.

Secondary disposition traits are those traits which are less important for the individual and on which. he is found to be less consistent and less stable: for example, a person's eating habits, his style of dressing and living, etc. These traits are less revealing of the individual.

Cattell's Trait Theory : Cattell following Allport classified traits into two groups- (i) Surface traits, and (ii) Source traits. He studied the 18,000 traits which were identified and listed by Allport. Many of these traits as indicated by different words were same or almost similar. Cattell put all such same or similar meaning traits at one place under one name. In this way he reduced 18000 traits to 4,500 only. By taking those traits out of these 4,500 which were in meaning very close to one another and putting them under one title he, again, reduced the number to only 200. After this using factor analysis method of statistics he brought this number of 200 to 35 classified as source traits. He defined these surface and source traits as follows :

Surface Traits: These are the traits which are very frequently and unambiguously expressed by individuals in their behaviours. One can easily identify and label them. They are uniformly well understood by most people. For example, friendliness, sociability, exhibitionism, miserliness, etc. These are clearly and quite frequently manifested in social interactions of people.

Source Traits: These are the traits that pertain to the deeper level of individual's personality and can not be easily and directly known. Their manifestation in individual behaviour is not obvious and apparent. The number of such traits according to Cattell is much less than those of the surface traits. These traits constitute the source of the surface trait. One source trait may generate several surface traits; for example, introversion which is manifested in several surface traits such as reserveness, shyness, self-centeredness, etc. Introversion is a quality which can not be directly observed. It is expressed in surface traits and then only one can know whether a person is introvert or not. Thus, as held by Cattell surface traits are the indicators (trait indicators) of the source traits.

Cattell described 23 source traits which characterise normal personalities along with 12 which are found in abnormal personalities. Out of these 23 source traits Cattell selected 16 traits and developed tests to measure them. Cattell's 16-PF Questionnaire is the Test that measures these 16 traits.

Cattell has classified the source traits into two parts- (i) Constitutional Source Traits which are considered to be more dependent on heredity. and (ii) Environmental mould source traits which are influenced more by the environment.

Cattell has given one more classification of traits- (i) dynamic traits. (ii) ability- traits, and (iii) temperament traits. He defined them as follows :

Dynamic Traits: These are the traits which are goal-directed. Attitudes, needs. values, sentiments are all dynamic traits as each of them is linked with particular goal.

Ability Traits: These are the traits which help in achieving the goal set by the dynamic trait.

Temperament Traits: These are the traits that arise in course of the effort made by an individual on achieving the goal. They pertain to individual's emotional state, energy, etc. For example, emotional controls, tolerance, perseverance, etc., are temperament traits.

Dimensions of Personality

A few researchers have tried to understand and describe personality on the basis of a few broad dimensions. This approach is not different from trait approach: it is the same, but more meaningful. It is just the regrouping or clustering of traits under few dimensions. The researchers who have contributed to this approach are Costa and McCrae (1994), Hogan (1983), McCrae (1994), Noller, Law and Comrey (1987). They all have come to the conclusion that there are Five bipolar dimensions on the basis of which personality can be analysed and understood. Norman (1963) called them the Big Five. These five dimensions are :

(i) ***Openness to Experiences or Culture (O):*** The person high on this dimension is said to be highly sensitive, imaginative, intelligent, and gentle. The persons low- on this dimension lack these qualities or have them in low degree.

(ii) ***Conscientiousness (C):*** The person high on this dimension is characterised by self-discipline, responsibility, being cautious, and prone to reason and thinking. The person low on this is just opposite to him.

(iii) ***Extroversion (E):*** It is the same as Eysenck's extroversion.

(iv) ***Agreeableness (A):*** The person high on this dimension is good-natured, cooperative, friendly, social, talkative sober and one who has faith in others. Those who are low on this dimension are said to be non-cooperative, suspicious of others irritable and unsympathetic.

(v) ***Neuroticism (N):*** The person on this dimension is characterised as emotionally unstable. Sometimes he is emotionally quiet and balanced while another time he is found to be emotionally upset suffering from hypochondrical thoughts, unbalanced and agitated.

19

INTELLIGENCE TESTS

Reasoning, problem-solving and creative ability all belong to the realm of thinking; a highly complex mental operation; a complex form of human behaviour, a mental activity essential for learning. Various forms of thinking such as reflective thinking, productive thinking, divergent thinking, convergent thinking, critical thinking have been described in the literature. They are not the same processes. They have been differentially described by the psychologists. Reasoning, problem-solving and creative thinking are involved in various forms of thinking mentioned above.

Logical Reasoning

Reasoning is more a logical than a psychological term. In psychology it seems to mean the production of ideas, thoughts or solutions which have a reasonable or logical relation to the requirements of the problem. The data at hand are organized into pattern and the production of a solution that fits this pattern takes place with relatively little trial-and-error. According to Guilford the process of reasoning is the same as convergent thinking which is a form of productive thinking (Klausmeier, p. 259). Logical reasoning is concerned with finding out an answer to a question, discovering the solution to some existing problem or establishing the validity of an argument. It is special kind of reasoning which underlies most of the discoveries and scientific knowledge. It is the basis of many of our beliefs, judgements, inferences, generalizations which may or may not be valid. For example, our belief that "all crows are black" is founded on our generalizations based on our observations of a large number of crows, but certainly not based on an observation of all the crows. All knowledge and all the beliefs consist of judgements. Judgements are derived from another judgement or judgements. They are inferences drawn from observed facts, the data. Logical thinking or reasoning is concerned with judging and testing the validity of inferences, validity of arguments. It involves two kinds of reasoning; (i) deductive and (ii) inductive. Production of scientific knowledge makes use of both these kinds of knowledge. Inference is the most important pathway to knowledge. No doubt, there are other avenues of knowledge also, namely, perception and intuition which give us immediate judgements. But, the amount of knowledge that is generated from personal observations and intuition is very limited, not only in quantity but also in quality. The bulk of human knowledge, and especially what is called scientific knowledge is obtained by inference. Scientific knowledge is based on (i) critical discrimination, (ii) generality and system, and (iii) empirical verification, all of which constitute characteristics of logical reasoning.

Kinds of Logical Reasoning : The reasoning by which most of our knowledge is obtained is of two main types depending upon the data or the starting point from which it sets out. It may start from some assertions or statements and seek to unfold their implications. Or it may start from observed facts and try to discover their character and explanation. The former kind of reasoning is described as formal or deductive while the latter is termed as inductive. In a complex argument the two kinds of reasoning may both be used; they frequently are used in conjunction. Sometimes reasoning is mainly concerned with the implications of given assertions or statements. The domain of lawyers furnishes a large class of such cases. Same is the case with state laws and regulations which are interpreted in terms of their implications when applied in a particular situation. It implies formal or deductive reasoning and proving that the inference drawn is valid. Inductive reasoning, on the other hand, aims at discovery of some general truth from which certain observed facts might have been inferred. The following example will clarify the meanings of deductive and inductive reasoning :

(i) Having observed that every man dies - X died, Y died, Z died and so on, if a generalization is made that "all men die", this is an example of inductive reasoning.

(ii) When from a given generalization "All men die", an inference about a person X is drawn that "he will also die some day", this is an example of deductive reasoning,

Both these forms of reasoning are involved in scientific thinking and research.' When a researcher having observed a large number of facts (the data) arrives at a general conclusion, he is actually reasoning inductively. For example, when a researcher having administered an I.Q. test to a large number of 11 year old children and having worked out the mean I.Q. makes a statement based an his data that "11 year old children have an average I.Q. of 110 or so", he is reasoning inductively. Again, when on the basis of this finding he says that an 11 year old child X not included in his earlier study must have an I.Q. of 110 or near about, he is arguing deductively.

In this way, inductive reasoning is arguing on the basis of particular individual observations so as to arrive at a valid general truth. Deductive reasoning, on the other hand, implies drawing a valid inference about a particular individual case from the general truth. Inductive reasoning which is said to be reverse of deductive reasoning moves from particular to general while deductive reasoning goes from general to particular. Both have their own methods of reasoning based on the nature of the data. Methods of logical reasoning are more or less common to all the sciences.

Deductive reasoning is involved in various kinds of inferences which may be drawn legitimately from given propositions. This may include an account of the general nature of propositions, of immediate inference, or the implications of isolated propositions, of immediate inference, or the implications of certain combinations of propositions, and of deductive inference or the application of general propositions to suitable cases or classes of cases. Inductive logic, on the other hand, deals with, chiefly, the problems of inferences drawn from observed facts in order to explain them. It includes reasoning from analogy, from circumstancial evidence, and probable reasoning. Both kinds of reasoning have their own rules and laws violation of which leads to particular kind of fallacy.

The function of logical reasoning is to make intelligible or to explain the general nature of valid inference. This is the purpose of every science, too, to enable people to understand things. The main aim of logical reasoning is not to teach people to reason correctly, but to explain what happens when they do reason correctly and why some reasoning is not correct. Knowledge of principles of logical reasoning may be and should be useful in checking one's conclusions.

Observation and inference involved in inductive reasoning are very complex processes. In this whole process of observation and inference drawing inductive reasoning employs several cognitive processes such as analysis and synthesis, imagination-supposition-idealization, comparison, and perception of analogies. These cognitive functions are regarded as an auxiliary or a preliminary to the inductive methods. Put more appropriately, these are considered constituent processes of inductive reasoning.

Problem Solving

Problem solving is a form of thinking and reasoning which is occasioned by a problem which the individual is required to solve, but the solution is not immediately available to him. It is very much similar in nature to learning and follows the same laws as some forms of learning involving complex relationships.

The Nature of Problem Solving : Psychologists have tried to understand problem solving by analyzing what goes in the mind of the thinker. Analysis of thinker's activities, his thought processes has been used to throw light on what problem solving is, problem solving is a purposeful human thinking. The purpose originates in the problem the individual is faced with.

Johnson (1948) compares problem solving with learning and says that psychology of problem solving and psychology of learning have much in common for both include the acquisition of new response patterns; Dewey (1993) holds a view that "thinking, reasoning and problem solving, used in the technical sense, are essentially synonymous terms."

Steps Involved in Problem Solving : Dewey describes a few steps involved in scientific thinking in his book *How We Think*

(1993). Process of problem solving can be best understood in terms of these. These are as follows

1. Becoming aware of the problem
2. Clarification of the problem
3. Emergence of the hypothesis
4. Evaluation of the hypothesis
5. Testing the hypothesis
6. Generalization

Becoming Aware of the Problem : This is the first step in the process of problem solving. Just emergence of a problem does not initiate the process of problem solving. Only when the individual recognizes the problem, i.e., feels that there is a problem which needs to be solved, but is difficult enough and can not be immediately solved, the process of problem solving begins. Dewey defines it as the "felt need". It must be real and genuine in the sense that for some definite reason it must be solved. The individual must feel motivated to find a solution to the problem. It must be a challenge for him in some way. If, these elements are present, the problem reaches the high level of awareness in the mind of the individual. It is a general rule that when a genuine problem arises attention is focused on the obstacle that interrupts the routine activity, and the individual tries hard to solve the problem. The awareness of the problem creates tension which drives the individual to make efforts to solve the problem. Thus, disturbed equilibrium, tension, motivation and felt difficulty characterize the first step of problem solving process.

Clarification of the Problem : Having felt the need to solve the problem the individual must clarify and understand what exactly the problem is, what issues are involved in it, what kind of information, tools, methods, sources will have to be tapped, whether they are available or can be made available. In order to clarify the problem the individual has to examine and review the information already available. He has to collect data, organize data and relate the same to the problem.

Emergence of the Hypothesis : Having seen the problem in the light of its importance and relationship with other variables at the clarification stage, the individual develops possible or likely solutions. These are in the form of conjectural statements. For example, a school boy preparing for his next day examination at

09.00 p.m. suddenly finds that the light in the house goes off. He is faced with the problem of getting light so as to complete his preparation for the examination. Having realized the importance of the problem he first tries to understand what has happened to light. He develops several hypotheses such as 'the fuse-wire may have burnt', 'there may be a fault in the line', 'there may be roasting by the electricity department', 'the bulb may have fused'. These conjectures help him in identifying what action he has to take in order to solve the problem. They guide him to, gradually, move in the right direction leading to the solution of the problem. His previous knowledge, experience and insight come to his rescue in finding out what alternative solutions (hypotheses) may be possible. If the problem is very complex he may get cues intuitionally also.

Elaboration of Hypotheses : It is not like this that each and every conjecture that strikes his mind is empirically tested. First, the individual evaluates each alternative solution that strikes his mind mentally. For example, he recalls that these are not the roasting hours of the supply of electricity. So he immediately rejects this idea. Similarly, he finds that there is light in other houses around. So he rejects the hypotheses of fault in the line. In this way just by reasoning irrelevant hypotheses are rejected. Elaboration of hypothesis implies objectively evaluating and seeing whether a hypothesis striking his mind is in agreement with known facts. It is a process of identifying and separating the most fruitful and workable hypothesis from the irrelevant and useless ones. It is done at the mental level only through analysis of available information and reasoning. Individual's intellectual capacity, experience, flexibility, originality and critical attitude go a long way in throwing away the half-baked ideas and selecting the worthwhile ones.

Testing the Hypothesis : This is the stage where the individual finds himself left with the most probable solution of the problem that needs to be empirically tested and tried. For example, having rejected the hunch of 'fault in the line', 'roasting of supply', 'fuse wire having been burnt', etc., the person finally decides that the bulb may have fused. He, then, is faced with the problem of testing this hypothesis. He takes out the bulb and checks it. If it is found to have been fused, the problem is solved and he replaces it by the new one. Thus, problem solving involves various degrees of trial and error and insight. Mouly (1967) says that problem solving is not a matter of following in a 1-2-3 fashion the steps listed, but rather a back and forth movement involving all the steps in semi irregular order.

Generalisation : Finding a solution to the problem by testing a pertinent hypothesis is not the end of problem solving. It must also advance knowledge in the field. So the thinker tries to see if the solution obtained can explain other similar phenomena, if it can be of wider application. In other words, he tries to generalize, tries to state the extent to which it can be applicable in other situations also. Of course, this does not happen in case of all kinds and cases of problem solving. But, the process of problem solving underlies all efforts on constructing a coherent pattern or generalization, or principle responsible for advancement of knowledge in any field.

Sub-Processes Involved in Problem Solving : The process of problem solving is activated when an individual is faced with a situation which is difficult for him to overcome as the needed information and tools of thinking are not readily available to him. Overcoming this difficult situation calls for the use of various skills and processes such as analysis and synthesis, reasoning (both convergent and divergent), reflective thinking and critical thinking. A sufficiently high level of intelligence is also needed. Thus, problem solving ability is not a unitary trait or ability; rather, it is a composite of several mental abilities and processes. When the process is activated it involves more or less a sequence of goal setting, evaluation of the problem, locating and defining the problem, mental elaboration of ideas, preparation, analysis, understanding, and identification of relation between the known and the unknown. Though the number of elements in the sequence varies; and this is also not certain that the process continues strictly in the same sequence, it is a fact that problem solving is the highest level of human learning. Gagne (1964), no doubt, puts it at the top of his hierarchy of learning. Looking from Gagne's point of view problem solving ability emerges only after response learning, chaining, verbal reasoning, concept learning and principle learning. Creativity also may be considered a form of problem solving. Harootunian and Tate (1960) correlated problem solving ability with abilities like problem recognition, word fluency, ideational fluency, closure, judgement, I.Q. and reading. It was found that its correlations with reading, judgement, I.Q. and problem recognition were high, while correlations with word fluency, closure, and ideational fluency were positive but low. This also needs to be noted that some authors say that the solution, to a problem is arrived at suddenly while others feel that problems get solved through gradually eliminating errors and putting together correct responses.

Problem Solving and Principle Learning : Gagne (1964), has demonstrated that problem solving, largely, depends on previous learning, previously learned principles which are combined into higher order principles. Problem solving, like learning of concepts and principles, is a way of acquiring substantive knowledge, For example, in finding out the missing number in the series 0.1.8, 27 ..... 64, the individual should know that a zero multiplied by any number yields only zero (principle or rule-1), should know squares and cubes of the numbers (rule-2), should know the meaning of series that the numbers in a series are always in a particular relationship (rule-3). When he, by using this knowledge, finds the answer (solves the problem and says each successive number is its cube) he formulates a higher order principle.

Individual Difference In Problem Solving : Harootunian and Tate (1960) found in his studies that those who are good at problem solving differ from those who are less successful in several ways. More intelligent persons were found to be more successful problem solvers also; although intelligence was not considered to be the only factor of successful problem solving. Wide range of ability to solve problems was found in the individuals having an I.Q. of 140. Sex was found to be related to problem solving as boys emerged to be better than girls on problem solving as revealed by the study made by Duncan (1959). This was supported by Milton's study (1957) in which more masculine minded girls were found to be better in this regard than more feminine girls. Also, it was found that the good problem solvers were not better informed, though they were much better in sorting out the relevant information about the problem from irrelevant information. Those who are successful problem-solvers use more effective approaches and strategies to solve problems, they are more confident and optimistic about their success to solve the problem.

Educational Implications of Problem Solving Learning : Problem solving ability needs to be developed in school children for various reasons. For advancement of knowledge in various fields it has its own importance. In the field of science there are many questions which pose a challenge to man as nobody knows their answers. And if one question or problem is answered, it gives rise to several other problems which need to be answered. In every field of knowledge such problems are posed and their understanding requires more effective tools, techniques and strategies. Problem solving is an effective strategy of discovering solutions to problems. It is a technique, a strategy of learning and understanding higher order rules. There is greater possibility of positive transfer in case of successful problem solving. The principles relevant to the problems are transferred.

Fostering Problem Solving : Following are a few suggestions which may be followed while making efforts on developing problem solving ability in the school children :

1. The children should be gradually taught to depend on themselves rather than on books and teachers. This means that the habit of cramming from books or from teachers without understanding should be discouraged. Situations should be created in which children are made to think for themselves and find solutions to problems at their own.
2. This does not mean that the teacher should do nothing, If something, he is not required to do is spoon-feeding dictating solutions and teaching things without making students understand. He must play a more active and positive role by creating problem situations for the students and motivating them to think.
3. When the students are faced with the problem and are trying to solve that, the teacher should help, guide, provide cues and stimulate. He supplies needed information, clarifies the various aspects of the problem, tells about the source of needed information. He has to act as a resource person.
4. Students must be encouraged to ask why and how rather than what. Questioning may stimulate; and if put in proper sequence may lead the students to reach nearer and nearer the solution. Higher order questions may be more effective. Teachers may do better by asking leading questions rather than supplying answers themselves. They should

discourage pet answers reproduced from the book or from the class notes. They should also avoid, as far as possible, straight jacket lecture. Instead, they should ensure active participation of students for exploring and finding answers to problems created deliberately in the class. The group situation is particularly conducive to encouragement of problem solving.

5. For the class to be effective in promoting problem solving, it is necessary to establish positive socio-emotional climate in the classroom. There should be sufficiently permissive environment, high level of group cohesiveness and group morale.
6. De Cecco and Crawford (1977) present a teaching model for fostering problem solving. The model consists of following five steps: (i) Describing for the students the terminal behaviours or performance which constitutes the solution of the problem, (ii) Assessing the students entering behaviour for the concepts and principles they will need to solve the problem, (iii) Invoking the recall of all relevant concepts and principles (including the use of advance organizers), (iv) Providing verbal directions to the students' thinking short of giving them the solution to the problem, (v) Verifying students' learning by requiring them to give a full demonstration of the problem solution (using other problems of the same class).

Clausmeier and Goodwin also present a model for developing problem-solving abilities which includes following six principles: (i) activate soluble problems, (ii) assist students in stating and delimiting problems, (iii) assist students in finding information, (iv) help students process information, (v) encourage the stating and testing of hypothesis, (vi) encourage independent discovery and evaluation.

The Creativity

The concept of creativity has been understood differently by different workers. It is said to be a congnitive function of the total personality, although it seems that cognition may be the means of expression of creativity while the emotional factors might appear to be the impelling forces. In any case, creativity could be understood as the urge or capacity for producing something new in the realm of ideas, concepts, things or art creations. Many persons have defined it in their own ways. Guilford (1956) for instance, in his article entitled *"The Structure of Intellect"* called it divergent thinking. The primary traits involved in divergent thinking and so in creativity as enumerated by Guilford were the following :

(a) Sensitivity to problems as presented by defects or deficiencies in common implements, objects or social institutions.

(b) Fluency of thinking indicating fertility of ideas.

(c) Flexibility of thinking consisting in ability to produce a variety of ideas as also providing most unusual type of solutions to the problems.

(d) Originality of responses which means new (& not ordinary), clever or unconventional responses bringing out remote associations and relationships.

(e) Redefinition as reflected in improvising or the ability to use familiar objects or their parts in some new ways.

(f) Elaboration or building up something more complex on simple data as, for example, building a new structure on two simple lines.

It is, though, debatable whether creativity is really thinking even of a divergent nature, because thinking seems to concern more with concept, ideas, problem solving, whereas creativity, though using thinking as means of expression, seems to involve other aspects of personality i.e., the whole field of affection or emotional make up of the invididual. E.P. Torrance (1969) thought of creativity as a process of becoming sensitive to problem deficiency, gaps in knowledge, missing elements, searching for solution or making guesses or formulating hypotheses and changing them and communicating the result. Bartlett in his book *Thinking (1958)* thought of creativity as adventurous thinking or as getting away from the main track, breaking out of the mould, being open to experience and permitting one thing to lead to another. In the *Dictionary of Education*, Good and Markel described creativity as associational and ideational fluency, originality, adaptive and spontaneous flexibility and ability to make logical evaluation. Gagne (1970) considers creativity to be a form of problem-solving which involves intuitive leaps or combining of ideas from widely separated fields of knowledge.

Yamamoto in an article *"Creativity" (1965)* wrote that creativity was really like an elephant described by different blind men in their own different ways by touching the trunk, the legs or the body of the elephant which meant that there was no one way of describing creativity, as each individual had his own approach. Otto Rank (1945) much earlier, had described the creative individual as one who is in harmony with himself and who does every task fully and completely in harmony with all his abilities and ideals. Simpson in an article still earlier (1922) thought of creativity as the initiative which one manifests by his power to break away from the usual sequence of thought. The creative mind, according to him was a searching, combining and the synthesising mind. More recently David Ausubel (1963) described creativity as "a rare and unique talent", "a generalised constellation of intellectual abilities, personality variables and problem solving traits". The intellectual abilities are identified as that of fluency, flexibility, originality, elaboration and ability to sense deficiency. Mackinnon (1960) studied creativity in architects, writers, mathematicians and many other creative people such as pictorial artists, musical composers, romantic-creators, like writers, philosophers and mechanical inventor as also the creative people in dealing with other material in art, dramatics, etc. We can see in these attempts to define creativity that the field can be so varied from the realm of concrete things to the realm of ideas and even social behaviour. Another investigator Drevduhl (1956) in his article in the *Journal of Clinical Psychology* thought of creativity as a capacity to produce products, compositions or ideas which were new and even unknown to the producer previously. According to other investigators creativity is the process by which something new is produced. It may be an object in new form or in new arrangement of the old elements or it may be a new idea or it may be a new solution to some old problem. The production of something new is the central element in all the processes of production and creativity is inferred from the new products.

Stages or Phases of Creative Thought : In the creative process there seems to be four factors as given by Wallas (1926) in his book *'The Art of Thought'*.

Preparation: At this stage there is planning, collection of data, changing the material by eliminating the useless stuff just as Darwin, before he propounded his Theory of Evolution, collected so much material consisting of bones, skulls, fossils, etc., and discarded the material irrelevant to his line of thinking.

Incubation: It consists in pondering over the contents and the makeup of the material or bits of ideas and judging, comparing them. It consists in all the processes which are involved in scrutinising and closer study. After this one hits upon the new idea suddenly and this is called illumination.

Illumination: 1t means when new light is seen or a new principle or law is discovered, just as Archimedes called out 'Ureka', 'Ureka' while swimming, as he hit upon the law of Buoyancy which became the underlying law for construction of ships, a law which meant that the weight of the water displaced by the body of the swimmer was equal to the weight of the swimmer.

Verification: The fourth stage of creativity is Verification, when the new idea, the new law discovered by such illumination or sudden dawning of the new idea is tested to find out if the law works and explains the facts or solves the problems. These four factors or stages may not occur systematically or one after the other in any particular creative act. These may all telescope or the cycle may be repeated many times. Every creator, artist, scientist, or a writer has his own creative process gone through.

Origin of Creative Ability : Now the question may arise as to how one person becomes creative when another person is not able to produce anything new. To answer this question, though partially, some theories have been advanced.

First theory is what is called Divine Inspiration Theory supported by thinkers like Plato, Tagore and others. According to this theory, creative powers are gifts from God and gifts are given to some and not to all. It may be that God has been kind to some people in giving them some specific gifts. But for a scientific understanding we have to look elsewhere as in the realm of psychology such resorting to divine power is not a scientific explanation. God who seems to be just to all could not be so partial, as to deprive others of the gifts which are given to some others.

Second point of view of theory is that creativity is like madness as Nietschze thought. Von Gogh the great master as a painter was said to be half mad. Lombraso cited many creative persons who were insane. But there does not seem to be a causal connection. It is one thing that a creative artist looks like a mad man but the madman is not and cannot be a creative person. If it were so, the patients in the mental asylum should all have produced so many pieces of art, inventions, writings or many such new things. For being creative it is not necessary that one has to be mad. The creative person may appear to be mad to the ordinary and the more prosaic people because his ways of behaviour and work are unusual unlike those of ordinary people. He may shut himself in his room, may not talk or communicate, might forget his food while busy in his work, his strange ways may be so surprising or astonishing as he may look a queer oddity, which may be taken as signs of madness.

Creativity is also said to be intuitive genius. It is said to be something native or inborn as a special mental power which cannot be acquired by learning or training. This might mean that some persons are born with certain unusual capacities as the genius with extremely high I.Q. of 150 and about or 200 (as Macaulay was said to have) and as Bacon was said to have 300 I.Q. One may be born with specific structure of the vocal chords to be able to produce many melodious and varied tunes and some person may have the unusually sensitive hearing apparatus so that different notes or sounds of varied wave length could be picked up and reproduced through the extremely sensitive vocal chords as we find in great singers. One may have quick grasp or lightening capacity to see through the phenomenon in any field and hit upon the new idea as Einstein suddenly gave out the theory of relativity and Newton thought of the law of gravitation.

Psycho-analysis like Freud thought that creativity was like emotional purgative. Freud thought that art creation, largely was the expression of repressed desires mostly sexual in nature. Repression of such desires leads to neurosis and many novelists, poets, writers, sculptors, painters and other such art creators produced these artistic new things as the expression of their repressed desires. When a poet like Meera Bai, e.g., sings out so many creative songs (mostly expressing the love for her deity), to the Freudian it was nothing but the expression of her repressed sex desires as she could be in search of a lover, as she had frustration in her marital or sexual life. The painter painting a beautiful figure likewise creates this piece to satisfy his repressed love as his lady love ignored him, jeered at him or deserted him or refused to welcome his advances. The novels of many writers are self-expressions and many such writers' creations are autobiographies in disguised form by giving new names or new environmental settings.

Whether creativity is divine power, madness, intuitive genius or expression of neuroses is difficult to say. Perhaps it has an element of some of these or all of these. It is as difficult to account for one being creative in any field, as it is difficult to exactly account for one possessing high intelligence or even black colour, frail figure or blue eyes. It is, however, a fact that there are so much variations in human beings in various aspects of their personality that it is not always possible to account for these variations which sometimes may be extremely unusual. Creativity is one such extreme variation which is found in some and not in others.

If creativity cannot be understood as something definite as an entity or faculty, it certainly is a function of the total personality of certain gifted people. It is to be understood as the functioning of the whole personality in producing something new in any field such as art creation, painting, sculpture, dance, dramatics, music, scientific or mechanical invention or writing of novels, short stories, poetry, plays, dramas, or in any sch activities requiring histrionic talents.

Creativity is judged from the production in any of these fields. What exactly creativity consists of or is constituted by the various factors or elements, is a matter of study; and just like deciding about the nature of intelligence there were so many factorial studies leading to the generally accepted view that intelligence is composed of general, specific and group factors, so also factorial studies may be conducted in future to throw light on the nature and structure of creativity.

Creativity and Intelligence

A word may be said with regard to the difference between intelligence and creativity, whether the two are independent functions or are interdependent, as some people think of them as cognitive functions. Some studies have been made to throw light on this question. J.P. Guilford, for example, called intelligence as convergent thinking or as the ability known in terms of I.Q. In this function there is the concentration or convergence of the whole mind, as it were, (with of course, the cognitive function) to solve the problem by finding out the one most appropriate idea, movement or the correct response to meet the new situation. Creativity to Guilford, as already pointed out, is divergent thinking which is characterised by fluency, newness or originality, flexibility and foresight and in which there are the possibilities of many responses, and more the responses possible higher could be the level of creativity. For example, one may ask as to in how many ways could a pencil be used? A number of responses about the use of a pencil given by an individual could, in a way, indicate the creative power accompanied by a flight of imagination of the individual.

It is, of course, to be decided whether a highly intelligent person is also highly creative. It may not be true that a very intelligent person is at the same time very creative also. It is to be ascertained by some studies if a very creative person, in some special field, could be of normal or even of less than normal intelligence. It may seem that the path of creativity lies through intelligence and that a large percentage of creative people seem to possess intelligence of a high degree; but we cannot say that an individual is fully functioning intellectually if the ability involved in creative thinking remains undeveloped, unused or paralysed.

To throw light further on the relationship between intelligence and creativity certain co-relational studies have been made with the scores on tests of intelligence and that of creativity. K. Yamamoto, (1965) for example, correlated scores on Torrance's test of creativity with those on some tests of mental ability. He found the coefficient of correlation as +.37 which though low, was found to be significant. It meant that the two functions were interrelated and had some common factors or elements. Perry found the correlation between Torrance's test scores and scores on Otis's test of mental ability to be +.50 which again corroborated Yamamoto's findings.

Some other studies maintained that the two functions were separate modes of thinking. Wallach and Kogan, (1965) for instance, found the inter-correlation between intelligence and creativity scores as +.10, although the inter-correlation between their subtests of creativity were found to be in the order of +.40. This led these investigators to conclude that creativity and intelligence have different dimensions of cognitive function and so are independent. They also made out that creativity consists in the associations which are not only unrelated but are also unique in nature. M.K. Raina (1968) compared the Torrance's tests of creativity with S.S. Jalota tests of Mental Ability and found the correlation as low as .18 which seemed to support the finding of Wallach and Kogan.

However, it seems fallacious to think that intelligence and creativity are two independent variables or that one always develops at the cost of the other. Only future studies will clearly disentangle this question of relationship between intelligence and creativity. Even the low correlation does not bring out the independence of the two. If it were so then a person of low mental ability like a moron could be creative; but in actual experience we do not find a person of low mental level, creating any thing worth the name.

Personality Traits

A question may be raised as to the difference in the personality make-up of the creative and non-creative persons. What traits are generally found in a creative person can be a good pointer to the presence of creative power. According to Torrance (1962) a creative person is independent, self-confident, courageous, intuitive, optimistic, able to take risk and not credulous to accept any idea, views or opinion without proper judgement or scrutiny. He may be a person occupied with his own ideas or things and may be quite selfwilled and rather a difficult person to handle, as compared to the more obedient, studious or a high achiever. In some studies made by comparing the creative and non-creative university students the creative persons were found to be reserved, emotionally stable, assertive with more ego-strength. They were more self-opinionated, self-sufficient, imaginative, experimenting, shrewed, relaxed without caring for others' views or criticism. They are generally careless about themselves and their bodily needs, because they are mostly occupied by something thinking, imagining, or creating. Some of them are happy-go-lucky, out-going, extroverted but there are also other creative people who are of a retiring nature, or introverted or tough-minded. They are often sad and thoughtful about the happenings around them with some degree of helplessness in improving the nature of things roundabout in the world.

Measurement of Creativity : The next question may be as to how creativity could be assessed? Work on this subject is in its infancy. A few tests have been devised, mention of some of which, at least, may be made.

The test devised by M.A. Wallach and M.Kogan is described in the publication *"Modes of thinking in young children, A Study of creativity-intelligence distinction"* (1965). The test consists of 3 verbal tests and two visual or non-verbal tests.

In test Number 1

I. The following items are there:

1. Write down the names of all round things you can think of.
2. Write down names of all things that make noise.
3. Write down names of all things which are squares.
4. Write down all things which move on wheels.

II. In Test Number-2 there are eight items as :

1. Write down all the different ways you could use a newspaper.
2. Write down all the different ways you could use a knife.
3. Write down all the different ways you could use an automobile tyre.
4. Write down all the different ways you could use a cork.
5. Write down all the different ways you could use a shoe.
6. Write down all the different ways you could use a button (as is in clothes).
7. Write down all the different ways you could use the key in a door.
8. Write down all the different ways you could use a chair.

III Test-3 has ten items as under :

1. Write down all the ways a potato and carrot are alike.
2. Write down all the ways a cat and a mouse are alike.
3. Write down all the ways a train and a tractor are alike.
4. Write down all the ways milk and meat are alike.
5. Write down all the ways a grocery store and a restaurant are alike.

6. Write down all the ways a violin and a piano are alike.
7. Write down all the ways a radio and a telephone are alike.
8. Write down all the ways a watch and a typewriter are alike.
9. Write down all the ways a curtain and a rug are alike.
10. Write down all the ways a desk and a table are alike.

Test No. 4 has eight patterns or diagrams and the individual is asked to write down as many things as he can think each pattern may mean. He is free to turn the pattern in any way to the right or left, up or down or in any other position. The 8 patterns or drawings are given as under:

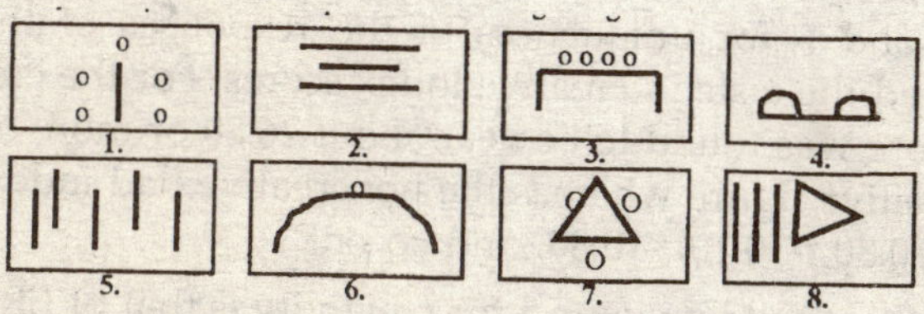

Test No. 5 : This test consists of 9 patterns made by tracing a line in a manner that different patterns and drawings are made. The individual is asked to write down all the different things he can think that each complete line might suggest to him by turning in any way. The nine patterns of the line drawn are given as under:

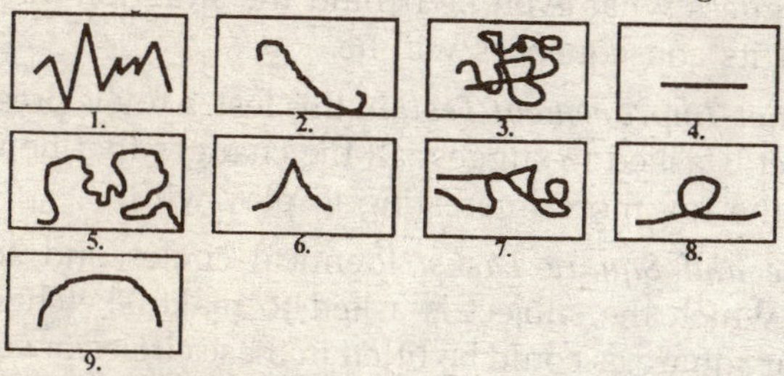

(a) The scores of the individual are in terms of the number of associational responses for each item in these five tests.

(b) All the unique responses which are the responses as given by one individual only in the sample, to which the test is given, are also recorded.

These five tests i.e., three verbal and 2 visual are culture free and could be used for all ages of children through elementary schools, high schools, colleges or university level, as well as, adults outside these institutions.

The reliability of these subtests both with regard to the responses and uniqueness varied from 51 to 93. Discriminative validity was in terms of high inter-correlation among sub-tests and less correlation with I.Q. Predictive validity was found with scores on these tests and the achievement of the testees in different fields. Those who scored high on the test were found to have qualities of leadership and they made contribution in the field of art, writing, science, academic pursuit or other hobbies. This test is untimed. For finding the creativity index scores, scores of each individual as obtained in each of the five subtest for number of responses and for uniqueness were each converted into standard scores separately and the sum of the ten standard scores i.e., 5 for number and 5 for uniqueness of the responses of the subject constituted the testee's creative index scores. For the creative the index score was found to be near about 26.80 or more or less but all in positive figure whereas the noncreative had index score as minus- 10.30, -10.10, -10.80, and so on.

Another well known test for creativity is that of ER Torrance (1962). In this test the items are such as :

Ask and Guess: In this test a picture is presented and the subject is told to ask as many questions as he could about the things that can be answered by looking at the picture. He is then asked to guess what even lie behind the situation in the picture and what its consequences will be.

Product-Improvement Test: In this test, a toy is presented and the subject is asked to suggest all the changes that he would like to make the toy more interesting to play with.

Circle and Square Tasks: Identical circles and squares are given in which the subject is asked to make sketches of things circular or square as could be fitted in these circles or squares. The number of the responses in each case determined the creativity level of the individual.

In the Booklet entitled *"Thinking Creatively with Pictures"* Torrance gives 3 tests.

Picture Construction: A piece of coloured paper cut in a curved shape is given and the testee is asked to think of a picture or an object to be drawn of which this piece of paper is a part. He is then asked to keep adding new ideas to this picture to make it mean as interesting and as exciting a story as he could. He is also asked to give a name or title to this picture depicting the story and it is to be written down at the bottom. The title could be made as clever and unusual as possible.

Picture Completion: There are ten incomplete figures as given below and the testee is asked to sketch some interesting pictures by adding new dimensions, or lines for new ideas for each. He is to write an interesting title for each drawing under it.

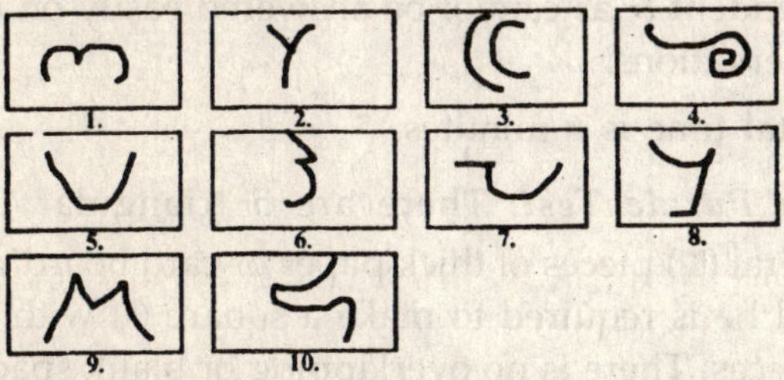

Picture Drawing : There are 10 pairs of straight lines and one is required (in 10 minutes) to make as many objects or pictures by using each pair as is possible. He can draw with pencil or carry on to make different pictures or objects (with each pair) which are as complete and interesting as possible. Names or titles have to be given to the stories depicted by each picture.

Passi, B.K. (1967) constructed the test of creativity consisting of 3 verbal and 3 non-verbal tests as under :

Seeing Problem Test: There are 4 items (a) shoes (b) chair (c) pen and (d) post-card for which the testee is required to write down the defects or problems as he sees concerning these 4 objects. As for example, for the time-piece or table clock the defects & problems can be (i) gets rusty (ii) makes noise (iii) breaks easily (iv) needs winding, etc.

The total time for the 4 items is 8 minutes.

Unusual Uses Tests: There are 2 cells for (a) piece of cloth and (b) bottle in which all the possible unusual uses of these 2 items are to be written down as quickly as possible. As for example, the unusual uses of a match box are (i) for toy making (ii) for using as a container (iii) to learn counting.

The total time for these 2 items is 8 minutes.

Consequences Test: There are 4 statements. (a) If human beings start flying like birds (b) If all houses start flying (c) If all people become mad (d) If all females made male. The testees are required to write down under each statement all the possible consequences they could think of in 8 minutes for all the 4 statements.

Test of Inquisitiveness: There are certain things put covered on the table and the testees are asked to write down all the questions briefly on the answer sheet when the things are uncovered. The questions can be of any type but each question must be different and independent & as cannot be answered easily on the basis of simple observations.

The total time is 6 minutes.

Square Puzzle Test: There are 5 triangular (Δ) and 5 quardrilateral (▯▯) pieces of thick paper or card board given to the subject and he is required to make a square (▯) with the help of these 10 pieces. There is no overlapping or blank space left over.

The time is 3 minutes.

Blocks Test of Creativity: There are 2 boxes, each containing 19 identical cubes and 12 semi-cubes; each surface of the blocks is painted with different colours. The testee is required to make as many different patterns or structures of things as possible by using cubes from one box at a time and arranging them on one cardboard in rotation and each time to show the pattern to the tester. The patterns could be as interesting and new as possible. The patterns for example, can be of a blackboard, an arrow or a maze. The pattern is not to be repeated and the blocks could be placed in anyway liked.

The total time is 10 minutes.

Baquer Mehdi's (1973) Verbal and Non-Verbal Tests of Creative Thinking. This test consists of 4 verbal and 3 non-verbal tests or items as under :

Consequences Test: Consisting of 3 hypothetical situations

(a) What would happen if man could fly like birds

(b) What would happen if our schools have wheels?

(c) What would happen if man does not have any need for food? The testee is required to think as many consequences of these situations as he can and write them.

Time allowed is 12 minutes.

Unusual Uses Tests: In this test 3 common objects (a) a piece of stone (b) a wooden stick & (c) water, are given and the testee is required to write as many novel, interesting and unusual uses of these objects as he may think of.

Time allowed is 15 minutes.

New Relationship Test: This test has 3 pairs of words which are different (a) tree and house (b) chair & ladder (c) air and water and the testee is required to think of as many relationships between these words or objects, as possible.

Total time required is 15 minutes.

Product Improvement Test: In this test the testee is asked to think of a simple toy horse and is asked to think of new additions to it to make it more interesting and to record all those new things, devices. Total time allowed is 6 minutes and for the entire test 48 minutes.

The factors to bring out creativity in this test are Fluency, Flexibility, and Originality and the inter-correlations vary from. 77 to 96. The reliability quotients are 896 to 925. Validity against Teacher ratings for different factors are for Fluency (40) for Flexibility (32) and Originality as (34). Correlation between creativity and intelligence when compared on Ravens Progressive Matrices was found to be 194 and when tested on Mohsin's Verbal group tests of intelligence as 176.

The norms are given in terms of percentiles for the three factors of fluency, etc., and not to be combined unless converted into standard scores for obtaining a composite creativity score. There are 3 non-verbal tests to deal with figural content in a creative manner as under

Picture Construction Activity: Here 2 simple geometrical figures (a) a semicircle and (b) a rhombus are given and the testee is required to construct an elaborate picture using, each figure as an integral part. Pictures made are scored for elaboration and originality. An interesting or unusual title to the picture made is also to be given by the testee. Total time is 10 minutes for each, i.e., 20 minutes for both the figures.

Incomplete Figures Activity: There are 10 incomplete line drawings and the testee is required to make meaningful pictures with each of them and to give a suitable title. Total time is 15 minutes.

Triangles and Ellipses Activity: Here 7 triangles (Δ) and 7 ellipses (⬭) are given and the testee is required to construct different meaningful pictures using these figures by making multiple associations. Scoring is done for elaboration and originality and title if necessary, total time allowed is 10 minutes and for the whole test 45 minutes.

Inter-correlation between Elaboration and Originality was .53 and between verbal and non-verbal tests was 456 for urban and 356 for rural children.

Reliability by test-retest method was 93 for elaboration and 94 for originality. Validity with teacher ratings was 34 for elaboration and 33 for originality. The correlation between creativity and intelligence by using Ravens Progressive Matrices was found. 181 and by using Mohsin's verbal group test of intelligence as 16 only.

Percentile norms are given for elaboration and originality both for urban and rural children.

The raw scores for elaboration and originality are not to be added up to obtain a composite creativity score without converting them into standard scores because of the differences in standard of fluency and originality scores.

20

Mental Hygiene

Mental Hygiene is concerned with preserving good mental health. In other words it is the science of avoiding mental disorders. Its domain is knowing the causes of various mental disorders, locating various situations that can cause mental strains and disorders, suggesting precautions that might enable one to avoid such disorders and finally suggesting treatment for such disorders. If one child is aggressive, aggressiveness being some form of mental disorder, mental hygiene will necessitate to know the causes and full background of circumstances that had led to such behaviour-development. Thus, the science of mental hygiene is a study of maladjustments of personality and deals with the possible ways of avoiding such maladjustments as mal-adjustment is an individual as well as social nuisance'. It studies the influences of poverty, competition, lack of affection, over-indulgence, neglect of children, favouritism etc., upon the development and adjustment of child's personality. It has been found that often these influences lead to the development of neuroses and other severe mental disorders in children.

Mental Hygiene has influenced the school programme also. It is being recognised more and more that adjustment of the pupil to all school situations is very important. Thus, competitions, rewards and punishments, contents of the curriculum, proper adjustment of the teacher, etc., are being studied from this point of view and efforts are being made to bring about the best possible adjustment between these situations and the child's needs. Mental Hygiene has changed the whole attitude towards school discipline. Mental Hygiene asserts that discipline should be positive and self-developed as negative and forced discipline leads to mental conflict and mental disorder.

Mouly (1967) describes three purposes of mental hygiene :

(1) The prevention of mental disorders through an understanding of the principles of adjustment.

(2) The preservation and development of mental health; and

(3) The removal of maladjustment by means of psychotherapy and other measures.

Mental hygiene is a positive programme oriented towards the promotion of adjustment of the child. It is not a body of specialized procedures, but is regarded as part and parcel of parents' and teachers' responsibility to help the child maintain a sound mental health. In the school it is an essential aspect of teaching process (Redl and Wattenberg, 1959). Rivlin (1936) considered mental hygiene "an attitude and a point of view that should influence everything the teacher does professionally". Thus, the aim of education and mental hygiene are one and the same, namely, the promotion of the all round development of the child by fostering the mental health of the child. by promoting personal and social adjustment of the child.

Few Definitions

1. 'Mental Hygiene has implication for all persons in the broad sense, the aim of mental hygiene being to assist every individual in the attainment of a fuller, happier, more harmonious and more effective existence. — Shaffer, L.F:
2. "Mental Hygiene has to do primarily with the development of more wholesome human relationships" — Skinner
3. "Mental Hygiene is concerned with the maintenance of mental health and the prevention of mental disorders. " — Hadfield.
4 "Mental Hygiene means investigation of the laws of mental health and the taking of measures for its preservation. " —Drever
5. "Mental Hygiene is a science of the principles of mental health derived mostly from our understanding of causation and pathology of mental illness. " — Dani, SK

Since mental hygiene is concerned with promotion of mental health, it is necessary to understand nature and dynamics of mental health.

Meaning and Nature

Mental health is a term used to describe how well the individual is adjusted to the demands and opportunities of life. The ideal of mental health is complex and comprehensive. Mental health may be better understood by its comparison with physical health. A person is said to be physically fit when his body is functioning well and he is free from pains and troubles. Similarly, a person is in good mental health when his mind or personality is functioning effectively and he is free from emotional disturbances. In general, he enjoys life and any unhappiness he has can be understandably explained. He is self-confident, hopeful about himself and his opportunities though he may have temporary setbacks and discouragements. He has a few intimate and close friends, maintains cordial relations with a number of people whom he meets and generally gets along with all those with whom he comes in contact in life and work. He is able to meet his problems without much disturbance, and his fears and anxieties are normal. He keeps an equable temper and when aroused expresses his anger in a socially acceptable way. He is concerned about his health but is not hyper-anxious about it. He has emotional maturity, balance and equilibrium. He understands himself, his merits and abilities; he also knows his handicaps and disabilities, but he accepts them and makes the most of what mental and physical capacity he has. Mental health is on a continuum and one can attain optimum mental health by following the golden means; a set of healthy attitudes and realising one's creative potential etc. A mentally healthy person is poised and serene, which points to an inner world of self-assurance and security, and a sense of self-fulfilment.

Mental head stands for a balance that is dynamic. A mentally healthy person is one who is in harmony with his own self and consequently with those around him. The conscious and unconscious aspects of his mind are in tune with each other. In spite of his problems and difficulties he is in consonance with the rhythm of life. He has a wholesome balanced personality, by and large free from schisms and inconsistencies, emotional and nervous tensions, discords and conflicts. Perfect mental health however, is a myth.

On the whole, we can say that the well adjusted individual has integrated his basic needs with the demands of social living and has high frustration-tolerance without being seriously disorganised. His problems pose a challenge to him, they do not weaken his resolve.

According to the modern concept, which is limited, mental health is the capacity to keep oneself integrated in the face of stress and strain through integrative adjustment. There can be a variety of normal adjustments as well as abnormal adjustments. Sometimes severe mal-adjustment in one area leads to severe mal-adjustment in other areas. Mal-adjustments in various areas of life are taken as the evidence of disturbed mental health.

The western approach towards mental health is devoid of a value system and a world-view, without which the picture of mental health remains somewhat incomplete. But, if the two eternal values of love and truth, which can be considered both individual and social endeavours, are included we can attempt a fairly comprehensive definition of a mentally healthy person.

A mentally healthy .person is aesthetic, creative and dynamic, inspired by the 'values of love and truth, with a balance of reason and faith, effort and resignation and self-needs and social needs.

The Definitions

1. "Mental health means the ability to make adequate adjustments to the environment on the plane of reality. "
— Ladell
2. "Mental health is the full and harmonious functioning of the whole personality. " — Hadfield.
3. According to a Dictionary meaning. "Mental health is the ability to cope with one's environment and secure some degree of satisfaction from working and living accompanied by the promise of hope for the future. "
4. H. B., English, (1959), a psychologist says "Mental health is a relatively enduring state wherein the person is well adjusted, has a zest for living, and is attaining self-realisation. It is a positive state and not mere absence of mental disorder. "
5. According to W.W. Boehm, (1955),-a social worker, "Mental health is a condition and level of social functioning which is socially acceptable and personally satisfying."

The Symptoms

A mentally sound person should possess the following characteristics :

1. Tolerance power, 2. Self-confidence, 3. Practical philosophy of life, 4. Emotional stability, 5. Knowledge of environment, 6. Ability to adjust, 7. Ability to decide, 8. Living in real world, 9. Caring for physical health, 10. Sense of self-respect, _ 11. Sense of personal worth, 12. Capacity of self-evaluation, 13. Strong will power, 14. High aspirations.

Teaching-Learning

Education is a social process which aims at fitting the individual in the community or the society. It aims at socialising the individual behaviour. Thus, it makes a distinction between the biological behaviour and the social behaviour and is thus 'dynamic', 'goal-seeking', and 'purposive', in the sense that it is motivated by certain biological drives. But, the individual has to live with others and has to live according to certain rules of conduct which aim at enabling each individual to live happily. The desirability of this makes it imperative for the individual to meet the new situations and adjust accordingly. Thus, he is demanded to override the biological adjustment and to make social adjustment. Social adjustment is a conscious process. This conscious adjustment brought about by efforts as desired by society is the objective of education. But education aims at the adjustment of not this individual or that. It takes into consideration the adjustment of all the individuals.

It not only ensures adjustment, it also treats mal-adjustment. Education is not the gift of the favourite few. It is shared by all. It, therefore should aim at bringing the mal-adjusted individuals back to a state of mental health and desirable adjustment.

The educator, thus encounters a heavy responsibility as the number of such mal-adjusted children is not small in schools and colleges. For proper adjustment of these children and saving from wastage the national man-power and mental energy, he should detect such cases, try to analyse them and treat them.

The knowledge of personality-adjustment and mental conflicts is of great significance for the teacher. It helps him in securing the adjustment of the behaviour of his pupils. It tells him the real causes of mal-adjustment and conflict which arrest the proper growth and development of the child's personality. It helps him in analysing the problem behaviour of his pupils. For example 'moodiness' as the part of an adolescent pupil is a sure sign of conflict within. So are day-dreaming, withdrawing, temper tantrum, negativism, extreme indifference and sadness. All these are great hindrances to educational achievement, social and cultural development and personality growth. The teacher should, therefore know and try, to remove them. In this, he is greatly benefited by the psychology of personality-adjustment and mental conflict.

The adolescent has a tendency to lawlessness. This is due to certain strong emotional conflicts. The powerful sex instinct is greatly responsible for this. Many of his undesirable behaviours are motivated by these conflicts. The education of the adolescents, therefore, is a problem for the teacher. The teacher of the adolescent boys can achieve marvellous success if he works on the principles and knowledge of the psychology of personality adjustment.

Lying is a very common misdemeanour which causes great concern to the educator. Much of the school-boys' and college boys' lying is due to mental conflict. It is a disease of the mind rather than a moral fault. The white lies of the children are due to exuberance of imagination caused by a conflict between the world of fantasy and reality. Morbid lying of adolescents is always due to conflicts caused by repressed complexes. The teachers of the adolescent boys as well as small children should have a thorough knowledge of the adjustment of personality and mental conflicts. Only then they can understand such behaviour problems thoroughly well. Understanding of these is essential for proper educational and personal guidance.

Thefts of school children, not returning borrowed books, defrauding railway authorities, evading income-tax, attitudes of rebellion towards teachers and school authorities and hooliganism can be traced back to certain mental conflicts and repressed desires in the same way. Once the teacher gets at the right cause, he can easily remove it and put the pupil on the right track. This, of course, is a great achievement of the teacher which the psychology of personality-adjustment makes possible for him. There are many instances in which unsocial behaviour can be traced to mal-adjustment. In order that teachers may be of the greatest possible help in preventing the development of untoward traits, it is essential that they may be able to recognize abnormal behaviour and maladjustment in its early stages.

The psychology of personality-adjustment is significant because it emphasizes the role played by the behaviour of the teacher as well as the parents and also the role played by the environmental forces. It implies that the environment should be so organized and the behaviour of the teacher should be such as the least repression is caused and that there are no chances for mental conflict, thwarting and frustration. The methods of teaching and the contents of teaching should be so adjusted as they may not cause mental conflicts. It also emphasizes that the personality of the pupil should be respected at all stages of development. It also asserts that each individual should be studied entirely by the teacher and that the teacher should secure all possible conditions of proper development of the pupils removing all obstacles from their ways.

Thus, knowledge of psychology of personality-adjustment and mental conflicts is of great importance for all the teachers and educators.

Following factors have a direct bearing upon the mental health of the school child. The teacher should help the child face these squarely so as to avoid mental tensions.

1. Emphasis on examinations and competitions creates tension in the minds of some students. Failure and frustration in this regard may bring a setback to some sensitive students. Such tensions should not be allowed to continue for long. The students should be helped to evaluate where he stands or where the group stands objectively. Rationality· should be developed in them through counselling.
2. Discipline is a necessary aspect of growth and as such is. a part and parcel of mental hygiene. Discipline embodies the principles of mental hygiene. As far as possible emphasis should be more on positive discipline. Punitive and psychologically destructive methods should be avoided as far as possible.
3. Socio-emotional climate of the class is the most important consideration in the context of students' mental hygiene. It is relatively synonymous with the concept of mental hygiene. The classroom atmosphere should be of permissive and acceptance type. In such an atmosphere

there are less chances of frustration and tension and the child is free to use his capacities for maximum self realization.

4. The academic work of the classroom should be meaningful to the child in terms of his abilities, purposes and interests.

Related Factors

Some of the factors influencing children's mental health and the measures to be taken in both the home and the school to ensure it are outlined below with special reference to conditions prevailing in India.

Heredity and Environment: As a result of the mechanism of heredity, individuals vary greatly in their capacity to resist possible unfortunate mental effects of environmental hazards. These original differences are further modified by experience and training so that some individuals become hardened and accustomed to misfortunes and disappointments while others are overtaxed and consequently become less able to meet new difficulties. As a result of these forces, the variability in the capacity of different individuals to resist environmental pressures and frustrations affects students 'mental health' differentially.

On logical grounds it is also probable that environmental pressures on individuals vary more or less as a normal curve. Some unfortunate people suffer a series of adversities. Some people in contrast, have a few serious problems to meet; they have good health, economic security, nice friends, congenial family relations, and their time is spent with agreeable activities, occupational or otherwise. Under these conditions, difficulties in mental health do not arise simply from heredity or from environment, but rather from the balance between the two.

Biological Factors: Inadequacy of the biological structure and nervous system very much influences the adjustments of the individual. Children who possess a robust central nervous system are able to handle frustrating situations more effectively than those whose central nervous system is weak. They do not break easily under psychological stress. Physical disabilities may also contribute to mal-adjustment of a child if they prove real barrier in reaching his goals. The physical causes of maladjustment are those personal factors which are present in the physique of the child. A child with defective biological heritage or a physical handicap is liable to develop inferiority complex. Such an adverse development might make him bitter and anti-social. Similarly, a physical disease might become responsible for mal-adjustment. The common physical diseases which usually lead to mal-adjusted behaviour are toxemias, post-encephalitic states and various types of infectious diseases, including severe infections of the central nervous system, various kinds of traumata, etc. However, physical defects in themselves are not the cause of mal-adjustment and mental health problems. It depends on how one perceives his defects and tries to compensate for them.

Psychological Factors: The most important psychological factor in adjustment is self concept. Self concept includes all the perceptions, meanings and attitudes that the child has about himself. It refers to one's perception about his body, appearance, his abilities and social interactions and his attitude towards himself. It represents all those feelings and experiences which help the individual to have an increased awareness of his strengths and attributes. A significant stage in self concept is one's identification with others i.e., the feeling 'What others think of me'? One's perception of what parents, friends, teachers and others 'think I am', is very important for adjustment. If this perception is of liking, approval and acceptance by others, then it helps to develop a feeling of adequacy. On the other hand, if one feels that he is rejected, ignored, and misunderstood by others, he develops the feeling of inadequacy and problems of mental health.

For healthy adjustment the child should have adequate self-acceptance. Self-acceptance leads to self-insight and proper understanding of talents as well as limitations, and to a proper positive attitude towards himself such as, I recognize my limitation, but I will do my best'. Basically, children who over evaluate themselves suffer from a feeling of inferiority but they try to overcome it by proving their superiority. Similarly, children who under-evaluate themselves, suffer from a feeling of incompetence and lack of self confidence. They are overawed by fear of defeat in every thing they intend to do.

Social Factors: A well adjusted and mentally healthy person is one who is happy, free of all complexes and worries and efficient in his surroundings, whose needs and satisfactions in life are integrated with the sense of social feeling and an acceptance of social responsibility. Thus, life is a continuous process of adjustment, with one's physical and social environment, the environment which is constantly acting and reacting upon the organism. Thus, the satisfaction of the child's needs depends on a society. His happiness also depends upon the society. As long as the society satisfies his wants and desires, he is said to be well adjusted; but when the society fails to satisfy his needs and desires. it upsets the mental harmony of the individual and he is unable to adjust and contracts mental illness. Thus, he is said to be a maladjusted individual. It makes the individual unhappy. He feels frustrated; it may give rise to mental disorders and diseases.

Economic Factors: Economic condition of the family has a direct bearing on the problem of adjustment. When a child grows a little older he becomes conscious of socio-economic conditions, and he worries about economic security, his father's job, and his own status among his classmates. The economic strain on the family results in hardening of personality of its members, and development of feeling of insecurity, lack of self-confidence, sense of humiliation and rebellious attitude. It also has an adverse effect on the general health. Adjustment of an individual requires feeling of security which is very much related with the economic security enjoyed by the individual and his family. On the positive side it means to provide the family with comfortable beds, adequate clothing, abundance of food, medical care. recreational opportunities, and leisure for schooling and study.

Factors Relating to Home: The family has a great influence on the adjustment of the child. It provides him the basic feeling of security, acceptance and affection. If the family fails in developing these basic feelings the results is child's poor mental health. The early social environment of the child is made up largely by parents, sisters, brothers and neighbours and relations with them are marked by intimacy and emotional acceptance. Any disturbance in this relation resulting from quarrel with brothers and sisters and rebuke from parents leads to disturbances in behaviour. As the child grows he may become less attractive, physically and socially; there may be the displacement in family affection due to the birth of other children: he may quarrel jealously by being too bright or tall; he may temporarily be rejected by his social environment. Also, both over-protection and rejection of the child by the parents have an adverse effect on his adjustment. Other factors in the family are sibling rivalry, conflicts between parents, faulty parental models, unrealistic expectations of parents from the child, and rigid moral standards of work with too many dont's. Such fluctuations in emotional relationships may cause behaviour disturbances, and unwholesome adjustments.

Factors Relating to School: The school is next only to the home in its influence on the personality and emotional development of the child. Going to school is usually accompanied by moving to a new neighbourhood. A new home means the absence of old and familiar surroundings. The newness or differentness of the new home may lead to general feeling of insecurity. Old friends are no longer around. and new ones are to be cultivated. Little boys frequently have to prove they are "good boys". Little girls must find new playmates. and it is not always as simple for the girl as for the boy to achieve status in the new group. When a child goes to school he is confronted with the complexity and strangeness of a new physical plant, a new teacher replacing parents and class-mates replacing brothers, sisters and neighbours. Quite often this new circle of the school provides for the fulfilment of emotional needs neglected in the home, Often children ill at home, hostile to parents are happy and well adjusted in the school. School experiences give them feeling of security, comfort, strength, self-confidence and stability. They learn to work on co-operative basis and develop habits to overcome their frustrations and failures or atleast to tolerate them or to sublimate their hostile impulses into socially acceptable channels.

But the school may turn out to be a source of constant trouble, worry and anxiety. The child has to learn to bear with new types of pressures such as pressure to pass the examination, to be best with his school work, to form good relations with his peer group and teachers, to secure praise, recognition, status and sense of security for himself in school. When instead of receiving sympathetic attention he receives insults, taunts and rebukes it affects his mental health. It is thus desired that the overall tone of the classroom should be of recognition, acceptance and encouragement, and this is possible if the teacher tries to provide a permissive atmosphere. In and outside the classroom, children need to feel secure, accepted, appreciated and recognised. They need to be encouraged to contribute to the group-life as best as they can and for doing so they need a democratic atmosphere, Further, the democratic atmosphere reduces anxiety and aggression and ensures purposeful participation on the part of the children.

Bibliography

Apter, Michel : *The New Technology of Education*, Macmillan, London, 1968.

Awasthy, G.C. : *Broadcasting in India*, Allied Publishers Private Ltd., Bombay, 1965

Bloom, B.S. : *Taxonomy of Educational Objectives: The Classification of Educational Goals. Handbook 1 Cognitive Domain and Affective Domain*, New York Mackey, 1965.

Bloom, B.S. : *Human Characteristics and School Learning*, Harper, New York, 1976.

Beiggs L.S. : *Instruction Media*, Fitteburgh American Institute for Research, 1966.

Brown, J.W. Lewis, R.B. & Hercleread. A.V. : *Instruction: Materials and Methods*, Mc Graw Hill Book Co., New York, 1964.

Cream, David : *Explaining Teaching Machines and Programmes*, Featon, San Fracisco, 1961.

Chauhan, S.S.A. : *Textbook of Programmed Instruction*, Sterling Publishers, New Delhi.

Chatterjee, R.K. : *Mass Communication*, National Book Trust, India, New Delhi.

Dhinnie, Dinald Mc and Dutt Sunitee : *The Art of Radio*, Faber & Faber, London, 1961.

Dale, Edgare : *Audio Visual Method in Teaching*, Dryden Rinehart and Winston, New York. 1969.

Gagne, R.M. : *The Conditions of Learning*, New York, Holt Binsort and Winston, 1965.

Goodman, Loster. : *Educational Radio*, CET, NCERT, 1977.

Haban, Charles, F. (Jr) : *Movies that Teach*, New York, Dryden Press, 1945.

Hancock, Alan : *Planning for Educational Mass-Media*, Longmans London, 1977.

Kinder, James. S. : *Audio-Visual Materials and Techniques*, American Book Company, New York, 1959.

Kothari, O.S. : *Report of the Indian Education Commission*, New Delhi, 1966.

Kulkarni, S.S. : *Teaching Learning Process: A Systems Analysis*, UNESCO Regional Office for Education in Asia, Bangkok, 1975.

———, *Introduction to Educational Technology*, Oxford Publishing Company, New Delhi.

Kaul, B.N. : *Studies in Distance Education*, Association of Indian Universities, IGNOU, New Delhi, 1988.

Lowman, J. : *Mastering Techniques of Teaching*, Prentice Hall India, New Delhi, 1987.

Mac Iver, R.M. & Page, C.M. : *Society*, Macmillan, London, 1950.

Mackenzie, N. Eraunt, M and Janas, H.C. : *"New Resources for Learning"*. In *Prospects in Education*. Vol-I No. 3, UNESCO., Paris, 1978.

Matheson, Alastair : *The Communication Materials and Methods*. Mc. Graw Hill Book Company, New Delhi, 1964.

Mohanty, J. : *Educational Technology*, Deep & Deep Publications, New Delhi, 1991.

——— *Indian Education in the Emerging Society*, Sterling Publishers, New Delhi, 1982.

——— *Studies in Educational Broadcasting*, Deep & Deep Publications, New Delhi.

——— *Studies in Distance Education*, Deep & Deep Publications, New Delhi.

——— *The Book Through Ages*, J. Mohapatra & Company, Cuttack, 1973.

——— *Educational Guidance, Measurement & Statistics*, Takshashila, 1996.

——— *Dynamics of Higher Education in India*, Deep & Deep Publications, New Delhi.

——— *Current Trends in Higher Education*, Deep & Deep Publications, New Delhi.

——— *Human Rights Education*, Deep & Deep Publications, New Delhi.

Menon, Narayan : *The Communication Revolution*, National Book Trust, India, New Delhi, 1976.

Mc. Whinnie, Donald : *The Art of Radio*, Faber & Faber, London, 1961.

Mukhopadhyay, M. : *Educational Technology Year Book*, 1988, AIAET, New Delhi, 1989.

Munn, Norman L. : *The Fundamentals of Human Adjustment*, Houghter Miffin Co., Boston, 1965.

Ottaway A.K.C. : *Education and Society*, Routldge and Kegan Paul, London, 1962.

Panda, K.C. : *Role of Motivation in School Learning, Current Issues in Education*, RCE, Bhubaneswar, 1978.

Perlberg, Arye "Micro-Teaching : An Innovation Laboratory Procedure." *Prospects in Education*, 1970.

Rahman, S.A. : *Study in Educational Television*, Orissa, 1972.

Rewntreu, Desk : *Educational Technology in Curriculum Development*, Harper and Row Publishers, London.

Sampath, K. : *Introduction to Educational Technology*, Sterling, New Delhi, 1981.

Schramm, Wilbur : *The Process and Effects of Mass Communication*, Uni of Illinois, Urbane.

——— *Big Media, Little Media*, Agency for International Development, 1974.

Schramm, Wilbur : *Programmes Instruction: Today and Tomorrow*, The Funds of Advancement of Education, Newyork, 1962.

——— *New Media: Memo to Educational Planners* UNESCO, 1967.

Sharma, G.D. & Ahmed, S.R. : *Methodologies of Teaching in Colleges*, UNESCO UGC & NIEPA, New Delhi.

Singh, Bakshish : *Correspondence Education in India*, National Council for Correspondence Education, India, 1978.

Vedanayagam, G. : *Teaching Technology for College Teachers*, Sterling Publishers, New Delhi, 1989.

